Country Risk

Norbert Gaillard

Country Risk

The Bane of Foreign Investors

Springer

Norbert Gaillard
NG Consulting
Paris, France

ISBN 978-3-030-45787-7 ISBN 978-3-030-45788-4 (eBook)
https://doi.org/10.1007/978-3-030-45788-4

This Springer imprint is published by the registered company Springer Nature Switzerland AG
The registered company address is: Gewerbestrasse 11, 6330 Cham, Switzerland

To Milena

Acknowledgments

I am grateful to Juan Flores, Andy Hira, Edward Luttwak, and Roger Nye for their comments. I thank Christopher Hajzler, Jonathan Rosborough, Jonathan Powell, Clayton Thyne, and Credendo for sharing their databases.

Abbreviations

AR	Accuracy ratio
BA	Business activity
BERI	Business Environment Risk Intelligence
BIS	Bank for International Settlements
BIT	Bilateral investment treaty
CAP	Cumulative accuracy profile
CFB	Corporation of Foreign Bondholders
Comecon	Council for Mutual Economic Assistance
CR	Country risk
CRA	Credit rating agency
CSP	Center for Systemic Peace
DJIA	Dow Jones Industrial Average
ECR	Euromoney Country Risk
EEC	European Economic Community
EFSF	European Financial Stability Facility
EFW	Economic Freedom of the World
EM-DAT	Emergency Events Database
ERP	European Recovery Program
ESM	European Stability Mechanism
EU	European Union
Exim Bank	Export-Import Bank of the United States
FC	Foreign currency
FCPA	Foreign Corrupt Practices Act
FCSC	Foreign Claims Settlement Commission
FDI	Foreign direct investment
G7	Group of Seven
GATT	General Agreement on Tariffs and Trade
GCI	Global Competitiveness Index
GDP	Gross domestic product
GNP	Gross national product
HIPC	Heavily indebted poor country

IaDB	Inter-American Development Bank
IBRD	International Bank for Reconstruction and Development
ICC	International Chamber of Commerce
ICJ	International Court of Justice
ICRG	International Country Risk Guide
ICSID	International Centre for Settlement of Investment Disputes
ICT	Information and communications technology
IEF	Index of Economic Freedom
IFC	International Finance Corporation
IIA	International investment agreement
IIF	Institute of International Finance
IMF	International Monetary Fund
IPCC	Intergovernmental Panel on Climate Change
ISI	Import substitution industrialization
ITT	International Telephone and Telegraph
LC	Local currency
LDC	Less developed country
MIGA	Multilateral Investment Guarantee Agency
Moody's	Moody's Investors Service
MNC	Multinational corporation
NIC	Newly industrialized country
NTB	Non-tariff barrier
OCC	Office of the Comptroller of the Currency
OECD	Organisation for Economic Co-operation and Development
OPEC	Organization of the Petroleum Exporting Countries
OPIC	Overseas Private Investment Corporation
RTA	Regional trade agreement
S&P	Standard & Poor's
SDR	Special Drawing Right
SEC	Securities and Exchange Commission
TIP	Treaty with investment provisions
TNI	Transnationality Index
UN	United Nations
UNCTAD	United Nations Conference on Trade and Development
USAID	United States Agency for International Development
USSR	Union of Soviet Socialist Republics
WEF	World Economic Forum
WTO	World Trade Organization
WWI	World War I
WWII	World War II

Contents

Chapter 1
Introduction

"Country risk" is a protean term that has long confused scholars. It is easy to grasp but comprehending the concept's multidimensional nature requires proficiency in a wide array of fields—including (among others) economics, finance, and political science.

With any attempt to define *country risk*, one problem that arises is that definitions are contingent on the profiles of country risk experts. For a risk manager in an exporting firm, country risk includes mainly protectionist threats but also political and economic events that could reduce demand for the firm's products and/or services abroad. A foreign creditor is primarily concerned about the likelihood that debtors will pay back the entire amount of cash borrowed, and with the interest due, in a timely manner. A foreign direct investor fears expropriation risk and political, social, economic, and tax shocks that could affect his business operations. In contrast, an *external* analyst (e.g., an economist working for a think tank that is not involved in any form of investment abroad) may adopt a less parochial approach to assessing country risk.

A second problem is related to the *components* of country risk. In particular, they cover many academic fields and present dissimilar features. A component may consist of a shock or a latent threat; may affect a firm in the very short term or in the medium–long term; may result in various types of damages to investors (e.g., from financial losses to reputational damage); and so forth.

A third problem involves country risk *indicators*. These have flourished since the 1980s, placing greater emphasis on particular aspects of country risk (e.g., political risk, sovereign risk) or combining various components. Country risk experts and raters have published their methodologies, reports, and ratings; however, investors have no clear idea about the consistency or accuracy of these indicators.

This book is the first research work to address these three issues and thus to deliver a novel analysis of country risk.[1]

[1] When it is italicized, the term "country risk" designates the concept. Otherwise, it refers to the threats to foreign investments.

N. Gaillard, *Country Risk*, https://doi.org/10.1007/978-3-030-45788-4_1

The rest of the Introduction is organized as follows. Section 1.1 establishes a typology of business activities that underpins a correct understanding of *country risk*. Section 1.2 documents the genealogy of *country risk* and provides several definitions of this concept. Finally, Sect. 1.3 outlines the book's structure.

1.1 Business Activities and Country Risk

Business activities mainly include trade and investment. *Trade* is the "action of buying and selling goods and services,"[2] and *investment* can be defined as "the action or process of investing money for profit."[3] The two basic types of investment are lending and ownership investments.

At the international level, trade consists of importing and exporting goods and/or services. Lending involves a bond purchase or loan agreement with a (public or private) foreign borrower. Ownership investment includes equity and direct investments abroad. It is thus possible to classify business activities into six categories: BA1–BA6. To each type of business activity, there corresponds a set of "country risks" labeled CR1–CR6 (see Table 1.1).

The concept of *risk* refers to "a situation involving exposure to danger."[4] Note that risk differs from uncertainty (see Knight 1921) because the former entails some *measurement* of such exposure (i.e., it involves "risk assessment").

In short: country risk is a set of measurable dangers (CR1–CR6) likely to affect a business (BA1–BA6) abroad.[5] That said, numerous definitions of *country risk* have emerged since the 1960s.

Table 1.1 Investments and risks: Classification and codification

Business activities classification	Business activities codification	Country risk codification	Description of country risk
Export	BA1	CR1	Risks faced by an exporter
Import	BA2	CR2	Risks faced by an importer
Lending to a foreign sovereign borrower	BA3	CR3	Risks faced by a creditor to a foreign government
Lending to a foreign corporate borrower	BA4	CR4	Risks faced by a creditor to a foreign firm
Foreign equity investment	BA5	CR5	Risks faced by a shareholder of a foreign firm
Foreign direct investment	BA6	CR6	Risks faced by a direct investor in a foreign country

Source: Author's classification and codification

[2] See https://www.lexico.com/definition/trade.

[3] See https://www.lexico.com/definition/investment.

[4] See https://www.lexico.com/definition/risk.

[5] The terms "businessman" and "investor" are used interchangeably in the rest of this book.

1.2 Genealogy and Definitions of *Country Risk*

1.2.1 Genealogy of Country Risk

It is difficult to determine exactly when the concept of *country risk* was forged. The expression was used as far back as 1967 by Frederick Dahl—then assistant director of the Division of Examinations at the Board of Governors of the US Federal Reserve System—in a research paper addressing the international operations of American banks. Dahl (1967, p. 116) states that "an appraisal of the so-called country risk inherent in any foreign credit is the major distinction between domestic and international lending. Besides assessing the creditworthiness of the individual borrower, the bank has to exercise a judgment on political, economic, and social conditions in the country of the borrower as they are likely to affect foreign exchange availabilities at the time of repayment of the loan."

It was not until 1975–1977 that the notion of *country risk* began to permeate the economic literature and media. What happened, exactly? Between 1970 and 1975, the external public debt of low- and middle-income countries soared by 144%, while the share of that debt financed by Western banks climbed from 7.5% to 25%.[6] This growing exposure to sovereign debt began to worry the US Office of the Comptroller of the Currency (OCC), which sought to ensure that long-term lending was supported by adequate long-term deposits.[7] By 1977, *country risk* had become a buzzword among bankers and investors. In March of that year, Henry Wallich—a member of the Board of Governors of the Federal Reserve System—used the term in a statement before the Committee on Banking, Finance, and Urban Affairs of the US House of Representatives (Wallich 1977). A few weeks later, in an interview with the *New York Times*, Citibank vice-chairman G. A. Costanzo gave assurances that only a minor part of the loans granted to less developed countries (LDCs) "involved any significant 'country risk'."[8] In its annual report released in June, the Bank for International Settlements (BIS 1977) explained that "country risks [did] add new dimensions to private banking in many ways"; this international institution added that it was "necessary to appraise a country's overall economic and political development and to relate the data on the amount and the structure of its external indebtedness to a number of macro-economic figures, such as current and prospective foreign exchange earnings."

Starting in 1977, however, policy makers and academics offered different definitions of *country risk* (e.g., Friedman 1977; see below). Confusion spread in the following years and remains to this day. The main reason is that country risk experts do not all monitor the same risks; instead, they focus on those risks that impinge on

[6] Author calculations based on World Bank (1975, p. 91; 1983, p. 140).

[7] Charles Stabler, "U.S. Banks' Foreign Activities Will Face More Federal Control, Officials Predict," *Wall Street Journal*, 9 April 1975.

[8] "Banker Sees No Danger of Default by Developing Nations on Loans," *New York Times*, 7 April 1977.

their own respective institutions or clients. In addition, the various focal risks do not systematically match one or more of the six types of country risk (CR1–CR6) identified previously.

1.2.2 *Notable Definitions of* Country Risk

The first definition, in line with Dahl's (1967) approach, includes all the risks that are likely to disrupt *lending* activities abroad—namely, the risks experienced by creditors of foreign sovereign and corporate borrowers (i.e., CR3 and CR4, respectively). For Wallich (1977, p. 5), country risk can be divided into two categories: (1) "balance-of-payments difficulties resulting from external or internal economic causes that can lead to devaluation, foreign exchange controls, or some form of debt rescheduling or even default" and (2) "risks arising from social or political upheavals." In the same vein, the Federal Reserve Bank of New York (1978, p. 2) states that country risk "encompasses the whole spectrum of risks that arise from the economic, social, legal, and political conditions of a foreign country and that may have potential favorable or adverse consequences for loans to borrowers in that country." This definition was adopted by the General Accounting Office (1982, p. i) and Young (1985, p. 32).

A second group of scholars has equated *country risk* with *sovereign risk* (CR3). This proclivity—widespread in the midst of the LDC debt crisis during the 1980s—is evident in Carvounis (1982, p. 17), Shapiro (1985, p. 881), Eaton et al. (1986, p. 482), Cosset and Roy (1991, p. 135), Edwards (1997, p. 99), and Qian and Strahan (2007, p. 2811). From a variant perspective, country risk "comprises the default risk of sovereign external debt (sovereign risk), and of private external debt when the credit risk is due to circumstances unrelated to the solvency or liquidity status of the private debtor" (Iranzo 2008, p. 12); a typical instance is transfer risk, which occurs when there is a lack of foreign currencies in which the external debt is contracted (see Norel et al. 1988, pp. 857–858; Keizer 1993, p. 346).

A third set of researchers and practitioners promotes a broader definition of *country risk*. F. T. Haner—a prominent consultant who worked on political and country risk issues as early as the 1960s (see Sect. 2.3.5.4)—establishes that "the risks confronting business operations in a foreign country fall into four categories: (1) those concerning the host government and its policies, programs, and practices; (2) economic factors, such as real growth, inflation, unemployment levels, and similar criteria; (3) financing and other dealings in the local currency; and (4) administrative and production factors, such as left-wing labor unions, corrupt bureaucracies, and so on" (Haner and Ewing 1985, p. 7). Bouchet et al. (2003, p. 4) provide an extensive definition of *country risk*, arguing that it includes "all the additional risks induced by doing business abroad, as opposed to domestic transactions." Meunier and Sollogoub 2005 (p. 7) view country risk as the myriad risks driven by the vulnerability of business operations inherent to a specific macroeconomic, political, and financial environment.

Two heterodox definitions deserve examination. Irving Friedman (1977, p. 120)—then Senior Vice President and Senior Adviser for International Operations at Citicorp—explains that country risk "comprises the whole spectrum of risk arising from the economic, social and political environments of a given foreign country (including government policies framed in response to trends in these environments) having potential favorable or adverse consequences for the profitability and/or recovery of debt or equity investments made in that country." The risks identified here clearly correspond to those faced abroad by Citicorp as lender and equity investor (i.e., CR3, CR4, and CR5).[9]

From a purely financial perspective, Campbell R. Harvey (1991, p. 111)—then Professor of Finance at Duke University—defines *country risk* as "the conditional sensitivity (or covariance) of the country return to a world stock return." His idiosyncratic approach was followed by other articles (see Erb et al. 1995, 1996).

Export credit agencies developed a particular form of analysis through their country risk assessments, and their methodologies exhibit some dissimilarities. Coface's country risk assessment "measures the way in which company payment behavior is influenced by a country's economic, financial, and political perspectives, as well as by the business climate" (Coface 2004, p. 9; 2018, p. 6). For Atradius (2011, p. 5), "country risk includes political risks and risks related to catastrophes. Political risks include the risks of war, hostilities, civil war, revolution, insurrection and internal disturbances. They also include the risks of a transaction being impeded by government regulations, such as a general debt moratorium, transfer restrictions and blocking of payments. Transfer difficulties and foreign exchange shortages are also included in this category. Catastrophes include epidemics, nuclear disasters and natural disasters such as storms, earthquakes and floods." Euler Hermes examines economic imbalances, the quality of the business climate, the likelihood of political hazards, short-term economic forecasts, and the "macroeconomic indicators that can signal imminent financial crisis as a result of a disruption to financing flows." [10] Instead of studying country risk at large, Credendo focuses specifically on the risks experienced by exporters (political risk and commercial risk) and direct investors (i.e., risks related to political violence, expropriation, inconvertible currencies, and transfer restrictions).[11]

My definition of *country risk* is consistent with those advanced by Haner and Ewing (1985), Bouchet et al. (2003), and Meunier and Sollogoub (2005). I view country risk as including any macroeconomic, microeconomic, financial, social, political, institutional, judiciary, climatic, technological, or sanitary risk that affects (or could affect) an investor in a foreign country. Damages may materialize in several ways: financial losses; threat to the safety of the investing company's employees, clients, or consumers; reputational damage; or loss of a market or supply source (see also Gaillard 2015, p. 165). This definition includes the six types of country risk (CR1–CR6).

[9] See also Friedman (1983, p. 307).

[10] See www.eulerhermes.com/economic-research/about-economic-research/Pages/methodologies.aspx.

[11] See www.credendo.com.

1.3 Outline of the Book

My book is divided into two parts. Part I (Chaps. 2 and 3) offers a historical and analytical study of country risk. Part II (Chaps. 4 and 5) explores sovereign and country risk indicators.

Chapter 2 establishes that impediments to international business preceded any mention of the *country risk* concept. I investigate how country risk has evolved and manifested since the advent of the *Pax Britannica* in 1816. Four distinct periods are examined: the era of *Pax Britannica* (1816–1914), the 1914–1945 period, the Cold War (1945–1991), and the globalization years (1991–2016). For each period, I describe the international political and economic environment and identify the main obstacles to foreign investment.

Chapter 3 documents the numerous forms that country risk may take and provides illustrations of them. Seven broad components of country risk are scrutinized in turn: international political risks; domestic political and institutional risks; jurisdiction risks; macroeconomic risks; microeconomic risks; sanitary, health, industrial, and environmental risks; and natural and climate risks. This taxonomy includes some risks that have materialized since 1945. I also discuss how the different country risk components are factored into the business strategies of the 30 companies on which the Dow Jones Industrial Average (DJIA) index is based.

Chapter 4 focuses on what is known as "type-3 country risk" (CR3)—that is, sovereign risk. This emphasis is motivated by the high likelihood of sovereign risk, which is often equated with country risk, exacerbating all the other risks that affect international investors. I present the sovereign rating methodologies used by Moody's, Standard & Poor's, Institutional Investor, and Euromoney. Next, I measure and compare these four raters' performance (i.e., their ability to forecast sovereign defaults). Finally, I identify the strengths and weaknesses of these methodologies and make recommendations.

Chapter 5 studies the various indicators used to assess type-1, type-2, type-4, type-5, and type-6 country risks (i.e., CR1, CR2, CR4, CR5, and CR6)—in other words, the risks likely to affect (respectively) exporters, importers, foreign creditors of corporate entities, foreign shareholders, and foreign direct investors. In doing so, I present the country risk rating methodologies used by six major raters: International Country Risk Guide, Credendo, the Organisation for Economic Co-operation and Development, the Fraser Institute, the Heritage Foundation, and the World Economic Forum. In parallel, I discuss eight types of shocks that reflect the main components of country risk analyzed in Chap. 3. Each type of shock has occurred a number of times since the early 1980s, resulting in country risk crises. Next, I measure the track records of Euromoney and the six raters in terms of anticipating these crises.[12] Finally, I deliver a critical view of these indicators.

In Chap. 6, I summarize the findings and explain why globalization is now at a crossroads.

[12] Euromoney ratings were initially *sovereign* risk ratings, but methodological amendments transformed them into *country* risk ratings (see Sect. 4.1.3).

References

Atradius (2011). *Export credit insurance on behalf of the Dutch Government*, Amsterdam.

Bank for International Settlements (1977). *Annual Report*, Basle.

Bouchet, M. H., Clark, E., & Groslambert, B. (2003). *Country risk assessment—A guide to global investment strategy*. Chichester: Wiley.

Carvounis, C. C. (1982). The LDC Debt problem: Trends in country risk analysis and rescheduling exercises. *Columbia Journal of World Business, 17*(1).

Coface (2004). *Guide Risque Pays 2004, Le Moci*. Paris: Coface et Dunod.

Coface (2018). *Coface handbook—Country & sector risks 2018*.

Cosset, J.-C., & Roy, J. (1991). The determinants of country risk ratings. *Journal of International Business Studies, 22*(1).

Dahl, F. R. (1967). International operations of U.S. banks: Growth and public policy implication. *Law and Contemporary Problems, 32*(1).

Eaton, J., Gersovitz, M., & Stiglitz, J. (1986). The pure theory of country risk. *European Economic Review, 30*(3).

Edwards, S. (1997). Latin America's underperformance. *Foreign Affairs, 76*(2).

Erb, C. B., Harvey, C. R., & Viskanta, T. E. (1995). Country risk and global equity selection. *Journal of Portfolio Management, 21*(2).

Erb, C. B., Harvey, C. R., & Viskanta, T. E. (1996). Political risk, economic risk, and financial risk. *Financial Analysts Journal, 52*(6).

Federal Reserve Bank of New York (1978). A new supervisory approach to foreign lending. *FRBNY Quarterly Review, 3*(1).

Friedman, I. S. (1977). Evaluation of risk in international lending: A lender's perspective. *Key Issues in International Banking, Conference Series No. 18, Federal Reserve Bank of Boston*.

Friedman, I. S. (1983). *The World Debt Dilemma: Managing country risk*. Philadelphia: Council for International Banking Studies, Robert Morris Associates.

Gaillard, N. (2015). Le concept de risque pays. *Politique Etrangère, 80*(2).

General Accounting Office (1982). *Bank examination for country risk and international lending*, GAO/ID-82-52, 2 September, Washington, DC.

Haner, F. T., & Ewing, J. S. (1985). *Country risk assessment: Theory and worldwide practice*. New York: Praeger.

Harvey, C. R. (1991). The world price of covariance risk. *Journal of Finance, 46*(1).

Iranzo, S. (2008). *Delving into country risk. Banco de España: Documentos Ocasionales*. No. 0802.

Keizer, B. (1993). La gestion des risques dans les banques. *Revue d'économie financière*, No. 27.

Knight, F. H. (1921). *Risk, uncertainty and profit*. Boston and New York: Houghton Mifflin Company.

Meunier, N., & Sollogoub, T. (2005). *Economie du risque pays, collection Repères*. Paris: La Découverte.

Norel, P., Quenan, C., & Sarry, M.-C. (1988). Stratégies bancaires et risque-pays. *Economie Appliquée, XLI*(4).

Qian, J., & Strahan, P. E. (2007). How laws and institutions shape financial contracts: The case of bank loans. *Journal of Finance, 62*(6).

Shapiro, A. C. (1985). Currency risk and country risk in international banking. *Journal of Finance, 40*(3).

Wallich, H. C. (1977). Statement Before the Subcommittee on Financial Institutions Supervision, Regulation and Insurance of the Committee on Banking, Finance and Urban Affairs of the U.S. House of Representatives, 23 March, Washington, DC.

World Bank (1975). *Annual report*. Washington, DC.

World Bank (1983). *Annual report*. Washington, DC.

Young, J. E. (1985). Supervision of bank foreign lending. *Economic Review, Federal Reserve Bank of Kansas City, 70*(5).

Part I
Understanding Country Risk

Chapter 2
Two Centuries of Country Risk, 1816–2016

This chapter investigates the international business environment as well as the most salient threats to foreign investment since 1816. I examine four distinct periods: the era of *Pax Britannica* (1816–1914) in Sect. 2.1; the years 1914–1945 in Sect. 2.2; the Cold War (1945–1991) in Sect. 2.3; and the globalization years (since 1991) in Sect. 2.4. A greater emphasis is placed on the postwar decades.

2.1 Foreign Investment During the *Pax Britannica*

The Napoleonic regime's collapse opened an era of relative political stability and economic growth that lasted until World War I (WWI). Between 1820 and 1913, world GDP growth increased by 1.5% annually—five times the rate during 1500–1820.[1]

This period of economic growth was inextricably connected to the emergence of a new geopolitical paradigm under which European and North American powers elaborated strategies to strengthen their status, in the eyes of the world, as major international investors (Lipson 1985, pp. 9–12). As Miles (2013, p. 23) states, these strategies included "the securing of 'friendship, commerce and navigation' treaties, [and] the acquiring of concessions, diplomatic pressure, capitulation treaties, extraterritorial jurisdiction, military intervention, and colonial annexation of territory. Significantly, this process of Western commercial and political expansionism was facilitated by international law."

Although Western business interests were generally promoted and protected by their respective governments, business people faced various challenges when investing abroad. I start by examining the challenges that affected all types of investors; then I turn to the risks that specifically affected merchants, direct and equity investors, and lenders.

[1] Author calculations based on Angus Maddison's historical statistics, available at www.ggdc.net/maddison/historical_statistics/horizontal-file_02-2010.xls.

N. Gaillard, *Country Risk*, https://doi.org/10.1007/978-3-030-45788-4_2

2.1.1 Overall Risks

Contrary to common belief, the *Pax Britannica* era was punctuated by many interstate wars.[2] Several of them disturbed the activities of foreign enterprises. An instructive case is that of the Ottoman Empire during the second half of the nineteenth century. The Crimean War (1853–1856) dramatically increased the Empire's borrowing needs; the response of Sultan Abdülmecid I was to initiate the printing and circulating of paper money, which aggravated inflation (Pamuk 2004, p. 25). After two wars against Montenegro during 1858–1862, Ottoman finances continued to deteriorate. Several loans were arranged in London but in 1875 the Turkish government had to declare a moratorium on its outstanding debt (Pamuk 1984, p. 113). The decade that followed was, in terms of financial viability, a lost cause for the Ottoman Empire as well as for all types of foreign investors there.

During 1879–1887, Ottoman imports declined 0.8% yearly, as compared with the 5.5% annual *growth* in the decade preceding the Crimean War (Pamuk 1984, p. 109). Moreover, the annual flows of net foreign direct investment (FDI) to the Ottoman Empire tumbled during 1876–1887, accounting for only a third of the annual inflows recorded during the two previous decades (Pamuk 1984, p. 113). Following the Muharrem Decree of December 1881, European creditors "accepted" a 45% haircut on the Ottoman bonds issued between 1858 and 1874.[3]

Civil wars were the second type of impediment to all types of businesses abroad. Consider, for instance, the period of civil unrest that hit Venezuela during 1898–1899 (Dixon and Sarkees 2015, pp. 187–188). Caracas stopped repaying its foreign debt as early as 1898 (Corporation of Foreign Bondholders 1903, p. 419) and subsequently expropriated the properties of several American and European investors (Maurer 2013, pp. 80–85; Miles 2013, p. 67).[4] In addition, Venezuelan imports fell by 19% in 1898 and by 16% in 1899 and 1900.[5]

Third, economic backwardness also hindered international business. In the nineteenth century, Spain suffered from both a structural fiscal deficit (Carreras and Tafunell 2005, p. 951) and a lack of industrialization (Simpson 1997). These two persistent weaknesses resulted in massive defaults on its sovereign debt (Suter 1989, p. 27) and led the country to expropriate holdings of the few foreign investors that had ventured there (Keefer 1996, pp. 171–173). After gold convertibility was suspended in 1883, the Spanish economy became even more isolated (Martín-Aceña et al. 2012, p. 146).

Economic and financial contagion was yet another overall threat to foreign investments. Two aspects of contagion in particular are noteworthy. The first is the

[2] A total of 74 interstate conflicts can be identified based on Goldstein (1992). The period under consideration is 1816–1913.

[3] Author calculations based on Agoston and Masters (2009, p. 182).

[4] The terms expropriation, nationalization, takeover, and forced divestment are used interchangeably in the rest of this book.

[5] Author calculations based on Department of Commerce and Labor (1905, p. 625).

spread of risk aversion from one *asset class* to another. Starting in 1889, when Argentina proved unable to exploit its accumulated capital inflows, British banks stopped lending to Buenos Aires. Finding itself short of foreign currencies, the Argentinean government defaulted in 1890; GDP then fell dramatically and imports plummeted by 53% within a year.[6] By 1891, the crisis also affected direct investments to Argentina (Ford 1956). The second aspect of contagion is its *geographical* dimension. Argentina's turmoil drove up the bond yields of other Latin American economies (Mitchener and Weidenmier 2008) and was the catalyst for Uruguay's debt restructuring in 1891 (Corporation of Foreign Bondholders 1903, p. 395).

2.1.2 International Business Environment for Exporters

During the period 1820–1830, Great Britain was by far the world's leading industrial economy (Bairoch 1982). As a result, the British Empire needed to stimulate international trade in order to export its manufactured goods and consolidate its hegemony. Such "stimulation" took various forms that ranged from diplomatic discussions to military threats (O'Brien and Pigman 1992). One of the most commonly used coercive tools for converting foreign countries to free trade was the signing of "unequal treaties," which prevented peripheral states (e.g., China, the Ottoman Empire, Siam, and countries in Latin America) from adopting high tariffs (Bairoch 1999, pp. 64–65). Other European powers followed suit, leading to the "first era of trade globalization" by the turn of the twentieth century (Estevadeordal et al. 2003).

However, exporters still had to overcome high tariffs in some other parts of the world. For instance, the United States retained protectionist trade policies throughout the nineteenth century, and both Japan and Russia significantly increased their tariffs in the decades preceding WWI (Bairoch 1999, pp. 44, 63). The most protectionist policies were implemented in Latin America: during 1865–1913, the absolute gap between Latin American and world average tariffs was about 25 percentage points (Coatsworth and Williamson 2004, p. 211).[7]

The other major hurdles in importing countries were nationalism (Wilkins 1970, pp. 101–103), subsidization of domestic industries, and foreign exchange risk (Kirchner 1981, pp. 273–274).[8]

---

[6] Here the values compared are those for 1891 and 1890; author calculations based on Ford (1956, p. 149).

[7] A fundamental reason is that customs duties were relatively easy to levy in countries where tax collection was inefficient and that were waging interstate and/or civil wars (Coatsworth and Williamson 2004, p. 216).

[8] Foreign exchange risk was a serious threat to investors engaged in trade with peripheral economies. Bear in mind that, during 1880–1913, peripheral countries were either intermittent in their adherence to the gold standard or opted for floating–exchange rate regimes. In contrast, core economies never wavered from the gold standard (Flandreau and Zumer 2004, p. 129).

2.1.3 *International Business Environment for Foreign Direct and Equity Investors*

There were many drivers of foreign direct and equity investment. The most basic ones involved firms (e.g., mining and plantation companies) seeking to exploit resources that were unavailable in their home country. Other drivers were the needs to circumvent high tariffs, to avoid damage when shipping perishable products, to counter nationalistic biases, to lower production costs, to obtain better access to local markets, and to learn more about competitors (Phelps 1936, pp. 43–89; Wilkins 1970, pp. 52–79; Godley 1999).

Foreign-owned property enjoyed a high level of protection during the *Pax Britannica*. Such safety was consistent with the imperialistic strategies followed by European powers. Thus, as these powers took possession of various countries and territories and transformed them into colonies or protectorates, it remained abundantly clear that no violation of the property rights of their nationals abroad would be tolerated.

International investment law was shaped by capital-exporting nations, especially Great Britain, for the express purpose of promoting the interests of their respective domestic businesses (Lipson 1985, pp. 37–40). This legal structure relied on two key principles: the "extraterritoriality" rule for foreign investors (Miles 2013, p. 27),[9] and the obligation of governments to pay prompt, adequate, and effective compensation after expropriating an alien's property (Herz 1941). If the host country failed to do so, European powers were likely to employ coercion or "gunboat diplomacy" (Lipson 1985, pp. 14–15).

Until 1914, this framework of international law helped limit the number of confiscations. Most expropriating governments were either Latin American (e.g., Brazil, Paraguay, and Venezuela) or peripheral European states (e.g., Greece, Portugal, and Spain). In some cases, foreign investors managed to obtain compensation promptly or through international arbitration. In other cases, they convinced their respective government to deploy military force (Macchione Saes 2013, p. 248; Miles 2013, pp. 52–69). However, the main sources of concern among foreign direct and equity investors during the nineteenth century were actually the lack of information about the host country as well as political instability and inadequate commercial law (Phelps 1936, pp. 90–126).

---

[9] Under "extraterritoriality," foreign property rights were guaranteed by the extraterritorial application of European and US laws.

2.1.4 International Business Environment for Foreign Creditors

The main reason why investors lent to foreign entities was that they expected higher returns than were available in their home country. Even the latter part of the financial globalization era witnessed significant return spreads between peripheral and core countries. An examination of sovereign risk premia reveals that the average spread between Argentina, Brazil, Greece, Portugal, and Spain, on the one hand, and Belgium, France, Germany, the Netherlands, and the United Kingdom, on the other hand, reached 226, 594, and 106 basis points in (respectively) 1883, 1898, and 1913.[10]

Consider, as another example, the investment strategy of a famous British fund of that time: the Foreign and Colonial Investment Trust (FCIT). In their study of the period 1880–1912, Chambers and Esteves (2014) find that the FCIT delivered average real returns in excess of 5% (vs. 2.2% offered by the risk-free British consols). This profitability mainly reflected the Trust's extensive purchases of North and South American railroad bonds, thus demonstrating the attractiveness of certain foreign corporate securities.

Contrary to other types of investments, foreign lending was often discouraged by the governments of capital-exporting nations because such lending tended to increase domestic interest rates while underwriting foreign competitors at the expense of domestic industries (Hobson 1914, pp. xiii–xix). That is one reason why, in the event of default, the holders of foreign bonds could expect little help from their own government. In this respect, Lord Palmerston's circular published in 1848 is telling. Though it asserted the right to use force when seeking to recover foreign government debts, Great Britain was more inclined to adopt a policy of nonintervention because (i) lenders were aware that the chance to earn higher returns required that they assume more risk and (ii) British authorities preferred to avoid disputes with foreign states regarding matters on which they had not been consulted (Cairncross 1935, pp. 67–68).

Such reluctance was justified also in light of the frequency and magnitude of nineteenth-century debt crises. During the 1830s and in the second half of the 1870s, no fewer than 15 sovereign borrowers were in default (Suter 1989, p. 26).[11] Some countries (e.g., Argentina, Ecuador, El Salvador, Greece, Guatemala, Honduras, Liberia, Peru, and Spain) remained insolvent for several consecutive decades, while others (e.g., Brazil, Colombia, Costa Rica, the Dominican Republic, Mexico, Nicaragua, Portugal, and Venezuela) can fairly be described as "serial defaulters."[12]

The riskiness of foreign government debt led to the creation of bondholders' associations in creditor countries—for instance, the 1868 establishment in London

---

[10]Author calculations based on Flandreau and Zumer (2004, p. 125). These results are consistent with Lehfeldt's (1913) analysis.

[11]The defaults could take various forms; for details, see Gaillard (2014b, pp. 3–12).

[12]Author classifications based on Suter (1990, p. 283).

of the Corporation of Foreign Bondholders (CFB). These institutions were designed to inform private bondholders and to coordinate their actions in cases of default (Winkler 1933, pp. 153–157).

2.2 Deglobalization and Threats to Foreign Investment: 1914–1945

Factors that had ensured the prosperity of foreign investors during the *Pax Britannica*—namely, international investment law, unequal trade treaties, gunboat diplomacy, and the relative cooperation among Great Powers on international monetary and financial issues—faded with the outbreak of World War I.

2.2.1 *The World War I Shocks*

2.2.1.1 The Legal Shock

So that they could strike at their enemies (and, to a lesser extent, wage war), European belligerent countries broke the long-standing tradition of respect for foreign investors' rights that they had defended so ferociously during the previous century.

In the first weeks of WWI, Austria-Hungary, France, Germany, Great Britain, and Russia enacted legislation that not only prohibited trade with the enemy but also confiscated—and, in some cases, liquidated—the businesses owned by enemy aliens located on their territory (Caglioti 2014).[13] In doing so, combatant nations violated the principle of "immunity of private enemy property" established by the Hague Conventions of 1899 and 1907. Retaliatory measures also affected the holders of some bonds. In December 1914, Austria-Hungary announced that its 4.5% Treasury notes would be redeemable only when accompanied by an affidavit stating that they were not the property of an alien whose country was at war with Vienna and Budapest (Moody's Investors Service 1918, p. 909).

The violation of foreign investors' rights by capital-exporting powers was a landmark in the history of international business because it led to the establishment of a legal basis for debt repudiation and expropriation. With regard to the former, Alexander Sack (1927) forged the doctrine of "odious debt" whereby a government could repudiate its public debt under certain conditions. With regard to the latter, Article 297 of the Treaty of Versailles (1919)[14] paved the way for the large-scale

[13] In the United States, the so-called Alien Property Custodian confiscated German and Austrian properties during 1917–1918 (Potterf 1927, pp. 460–469).

[14] Article 297 stipulates that "the Allied and Associated Powers reserve the right to retain and liquidate all property, rights and interests belonging at the date of the coming into force of the present Treaty to German nationals, or companies controlled by them, within their territories, colonies, possessions and protectorates, including territories ceded to them by the present Treaty."

expropriations that occurred during the following decades (for a discussion, see Sects. 2.2.4 and 2.3.5 as well as Borchard 1946b).

2.2.1.2 The Economic Shock

The economic consequences of World War I were unprecedented. First, waging war obliged the belligerent countries to siphon domestic savings through war loans and tax increases and also to abandon gold convertibility.[15] This development ushered in the breakdown of the gold standard, a monetary system that until then had eased capital flows worldwide. The depreciation of major currencies (e.g., the French franc and the German mark), when combined with the inflationary pressures due mainly to the circulation of paper money, prevented restoration of the gold standard at the end of hostilities.

Second, international trade declined dramatically—although this contraction primarily affected the Continent. Between 1913 and 1918, European exports declined by 69% even as non-European exports increased by 27%.[16] With its share of world exports falling from 56% in 1913 to 24% in 1918,[17] Europe lost its previously unassailable leadership in trade.

Finally, the massive public debts accumulated by European economies weakened their credit position.[18] One group of combatants, including France and the United Kingdom, remained solvent but endured skyrocketing ratios of public debt to GDP.[19] Another group, which included Austria-Hungary and Germany, managed to repay their debt but experienced episodes of high inflation (if not hyperinflation) after 1918. A third set of nations consists of those that defaulted during the war; among these were Bulgaria, the Ottoman Empire, and Russia (Suter 1990, p. 283). The foreign holders of bonds issued by governments in this last category suffered major losses. The ruin of French savers who had purchased Russian bonds is a notorious illustration (Oosterlinck 2016).

---

[15] The United Kingdom was an exception; it was formally committed to the gold standard until March 1919 (Bordo 2005, p. 211).

[16] Author calculations based on Federico and Tena-Junguito's (2016) database, available at https://e-archivo.uc3m.es/bitstream/handle/10016/22230/wp1601_data.xlsx. Export values are in 1913 constant prices.

[17] Idem.

[18] Moody's Investors Service, "The Credit of Foreign Governments," *Moody's Investment Letter*, 3 April 1919.

[19] See Reinhart and Rogoff 's (2011) database (available at www.carmenreinhart.com/data/browse-by-topic/topics/9).

2.2.2 *Nationalism, Isolationism, and Lack of International Cooperation*

The business climate's deterioration during the interwar years was driven mainly by the lack of cooperation among major capitalist nations, especially the victors in WWI. By failing to build an enduring international monetary and financial architecture, these countries—France, the United Kingdom, and the United States (the new leader in exporting capital)—impeded the activities of investors abroad.

2.2.2.1 A Short-Lived Monetary System

The Genoa Conference of 1922 resulted in a partial return to the gold standard. Governments willing to adopt this monetary system could achieve that end in one of two ways: by implementing a deflationary policy and setting a high exchange rate; or by devaluating and then stabilizing their currency. In order to maintain London's role as a major international financial center, Great Britain imposed austerity measures and passed the Gold Standard Act in 1925.[20] In contrast, France struggled against speculation until 1926 and was then forced to devaluate its currency (Einzig 1935).

Notwithstanding these governmental efforts, lenders considered the new gold standard system to be less credible than its pre-1914 predecessor; hence lenders, when assessing a government's credit position, were mainly concerned with its terms of trade and public debt (Obstfeld and Taylor 2003).[21] As the Genoa system's sustainability came into question, threats soon materialized. Once the French franc was officially stabilized in 1928, the Bank of France reduced its reserves of British pounds and accumulated gold (Accominotti 2009, p. 354). The US Federal Reserve followed suit until mid-1931 (Board of Governors of the Federal Reserve System 1943, p. 537). These gold-hoarding policies increased the pound's vulnerability, and its overvaluation became obvious. In September 1931, the MacDonald government bowed to the inevitable and left the gold standard. The Genoa system's disintegration accelerated in the following years. President Roosevelt abandoned convertibility of the US dollar in 1933 and refused to coordinate with other governments (Einzig 1935); these actions dealt the death blow to international monetary cooperation. Thereafter, the world was fragmented into monetary zones and blocks (Feiertag and Plessis 2000).

[20] This decision favored British bankers, as well as direct and equity investors abroad, at the expense of exporters.

[21] The criteria for such risk assessment contrasted with those that prevailed before 1914, when adherence to the gold standard was viewed as a signal of financial robustness (Bordo and Rockoff 1996).

2.2.2.2 The Rise and Fall of the League of Nations

The League of Nations fared no better than the Genoa monetary system. As established by Part I of the Treaty of Versailles (1919), the League's primary mission was to maintain world peace. Yet it also aimed, through its Economic and Financial Organization (EFO), to promote economic cooperation (Clavin 2013, pp. 11–46). The EFO enabled the recovery of many countries—especially in Central and Eastern Europe—and helped them access capital markets. During 1923–1928, for example, the organization arranged international loans for Austria, Bulgaria, Danzig, Estonia, Greece, and Hungary (Flores Zendejas and Decorzant 2016). These loans, which were typically secured by domestic taxes and duties, contributed to restoring the credit position of economies in financial distress during the early 1920s.

Following the outbreak of another world crisis in 1930, investors tended to grant the League loans a de facto senior status—most likely because they hoped the organization would act as the "lender of last resort" in cases of default.[22] Yet because the League was not backed by major capital-exporting nations, it was in no position to bail out distressed economies. This loss of the EFO's credibility foreshadowed the League's failure to preserve peace in the second half of the 1930s.

The collapse of both the Genoa monetary system and the League of Nations in the 1930s were natural outcomes of increased nationalism and isolationism. This fraught landscape was anything but conducive to international business. Furthermore, there were other factors that handicapped foreign investors during the interwar period.

2.2.3 *The Slide Toward Protectionism*

In 1918, world trade (imports plus exports) amounted to only 68% of its 1913 level.[23] In order to stimulate their exports, some governments took unprecedented measures. For example, Great Britain passed the Overseas Trade (Credits and Insurance) Act and the Trade Facilities Act in 1920 and 1921, respectively. The purpose of this legislation was to authorize the undertaking of insurance and the granting of credits to domestic exporters; another aim was to guarantee foreign loans whose proceeds would be used to purchase British goods (James 1926).

Such interference in the economic life of corporations, which disadvantaged non-British exporting firms, was emulated in other countries and led to the creation of export credit agencies (Hanna 1931; Dietrich 1935; Bonin 2002) and export–import banks (see Patterson 1943 on establishment of the US Exim Bank).

[22] For a given sovereign bond issuer, this preferred creditor status was mirrored in the lower yields observed for its League loans as compared with other bonds (Flores Zendejas 2017).

[23] Author calculations based on Federico and Tena-Junguito's (2016) database, available at https://e-archivo.uc3m.es/bitstream/handle/10016/22230/wp1601_data.xlsx.

The emergence of these novel institutions was indicative of the difficulties experienced by exporting companies at the time.

Trade barriers were actually erected as early as the 1920s, when Central and Eastern European countries increased tariffs and implemented import quotas and export licensing requirements (Liepmann 1938). Soviet Russia shifted to an autarkic economic model (Hough 1986, p. 495). More importantly, the Fordney–McCumber tariff of 1922—enacted in response to the 1919–1920 American farming crisis—increased duties on foreign agricultural products and commodities (Berglund 1923).

The Smoot–Hawley Act of 1930 triggered an ultimately fatal vicious cycle: protectionism fed the abandonment of the gold standard, competitive devaluations, and exchange controls, which in turn prompted even higher tariffs (Eichengreen and Irwin 1995). Great Britain passed its Import Duties Act in 1932; this legislation introduced a general tariff of 10% on most imports, albeit with some exemptions for products from members of the British Empire. Under these isolationist conditions, where trade blocs constantly vied with one another, exporters were forced either to skirt or to comply with a host of antibusiness policies: import quotas, a greater number of regulations and formalities, and the need to bargain bilaterally on matters of compensation, clearing, and payments agreements (for an exhaustive analysis, see Condliffe 1940, pp. 178–294).

2.2.4 *The Increasing Vulnerability of Foreign-Owned Property*

The development of trade barriers convinced multinational corporations (MNCs) to open even more subsidiaries abroad (Jones 2005, p. 84). This largely explains why FDI increased 81% during 1914–1938 while world trade was increasing by only 39%.[24] The establishment and acquisition of plants in foreign countries had far-reaching consequences for manufacturers, enabling them to boost their market shares (e.g., General Motors in Europe; see Foreman-Peck 1982), diversify their production in a context of capital controls (e.g., Unilever in Germany; see Wilson 1954), imitate local firms (Wilkins 1974), and export from their foreign units (e.g., GM's Opel subsidiary in Germany; see General Motors Corporation 1937, p. 17). However, these nascent strengths were offset by three major risks: adverse economic conditions, political instability, and large-scale expropriations.

The Great Depression was certainly the most serious macroeconomic impediment to international business during the interwar years. The GDP growth of the top 15 recipient countries of US direct investment in 1929 fell

[24] Author calculations based on Jones (2005, p. 82) and on Federico and Tena-Junguito's (2016) database, available at https://e-archivo.uc3m.es/bitstream/handle/10016/22230/wp1601_data.xlsx.

by 15% (on average) during 1929–1932,[25] reflecting the collapse of consumption. Price volatility was another challenge: after inflationary pressures in the early 1920s, most host countries struggled with deflation in the first half of the 1930s and with inflation shortly before World War II.

Political risk also shaped the interwar period. Among the 15-country sample, only Australia, Canada, France, and the United Kingdom managed to avoid being hit by a coup, a revolution, or an interstate war or being run by a dictator during 1919–1938.[26] Businessmen who followed the financial and economic press during 1936–1937 could reasonably predict that the increased nationalism and expenditures for rearmament would eventually plunge Europe into another major conflict.[27]

A more diffuse aspect of political risk stemmed from the sentiment among local population and politicians that foreign firms perpetuated colonialism and extracted undue profits (Coudert and Lans 1946). Such frustration was likely to engender xenophobic regulations and legislation—as observed in the early 1930s regulation of Argentina's meatpacking industry (Phelps 1936, pp. 166–193)—or, more radically, large-scale expropriations.

The most striking nationalization episode followed the Soviet Revolution of 1917, when the communists seized all property belonging not only to foreigners (mainly British, French, and German firms) but also to its own citizens and businesses (Root 1968, p. 70). Other significant expropriations occurred in Bolivia and Mexico in 1937 and 1938, respectively. These latter nationalizations affected American and British oil companies: Jersey Standard, Consolidated Oil Corporation, and Royal Dutch Shell.[28]

It is worth noting that the Bolivian and Mexican expropriations did not trigger military intervention or even strong diplomatic pressures. The passivity of British authorities reflected that country's political and economic decline, while the "good neighbor" diplomacy embraced by President Roosevelt was used to justify the non-interventionist US posture (Gellman 1979, pp. 49–53).

This geopolitical retreat contributed to a deteriorating international business climate at a time when the legal position of foreign direct investors (and especially American ones) was weakening. Perhaps the best illustration of this trend is the Convention on the Rights and Duties of States, which was signed at Montevideo in 1933 and consecrated the "equality of treatment" rule at the expense of the "extraterritoriality" rule (for a discussion, see Borchard 1940).[29]

---

[25] Author calculations based on Zettler and Cutler (1952, p. 8) and on Angus Maddison's historical statistics, available at www.ggdc.net/maddison/historical_statistics/horizontal-file_02-2010.xls. This 15-country sample consists of Argentina, Australia, Brazil, Canada, Chile, China, Colombia, Cuba, France, Germany, Italy, Mexico, Peru, the United Kingdom, and Venezuela.

[26] Author classification based on www.proquest.com.

[27] See "Economic Consequences of Rearmament," *Barron's*, 25 May 1936; Standard Statistics, "Foreign Trade Outlook Despite War Dangers," *Standard Trade and Securities*, 1 January 1937.

[28] For an exhaustive analysis, see Maurer (2013, pp. 260–278).

[29] Article 9 of the Convention states that "nationals and foreigners are under the same protection of the law and the national authorities and the foreigners may not claim rights other or more extensive than those of the nationals."

2.2.5 *Foreign Creditors in Turmoil*

The countries involved in WWI saw their public debt increase dramatically. Two of them went bankrupt, imposing heavy losses on their foreign creditors. The Ottoman Empire, dismantled by the Treaty of Sèvres (1920) and the Treaty of Lausanne (1923), did not resume payment on its external debt until 1928 (Wynne 1951, pp. 485–510). Soviet Russia repudiated its debt in 1918 and remained insolvent until the end of the twentieth century (Oosterlinck 2016). Despite these setbacks, three factors contributed to *reduce* sovereign risk in the 1920s: the international recovery, the positive role played by the League of Nations (see Sect. 2.2.2.2), and a new debt cycle that enabled local and central governments to borrow abroad—especially on the New York Stock Exchange.

During 1915–1917, J. P. Morgan had lent extensively to support British and French governments (Moody's Investors Service 1918, pp. 924, 981; 1920, pp. 1241–1242, 1312–1313). Once the war ended, American bankers continued to profit from the enhanced creditor position of the United States and from the US dollar's strength. From 1919 to 1929, the average annual amount of foreign government bonds and foreign corporate bonds issued in the United States reached (respectively) $700 million and $300 million, compared with $37 million and $8 million in 1914.[30]

However, American creditors failed to perceive the deterioration in the quality of these foreign bonds, especially sovereign bonds (Mintz 1951, pp. 29–43). In the second half of the 1920s, smaller and less prestigious banks began to underwrite foreign government securities whose ratings were increasingly low (Flandreau et al. 2009). The US economic downturn and the Smoot–Hawley Act of 1930 depressed commodities prices, which shook Latin American economies. Most of them defaulted during 1931–1933 (Gaillard 2011, pp. 191–192).

The spread of protectionism and the establishment of capital controls worldwide exacerbated the international debt crisis. The fraction of foreign government bonds that Moody's rated as "speculative" soared from 21% in 1931 to 64% in 1938 (Gaillard 2011, pp. 40–41). On the eve of World War II, one-fourth of all countries were in default on their external debt—a proportion that rose to one-third in 1942 (Gaillard 2011, p. 7).

The losses incurred by American foreign bondholders in the 1930s and 1940s turned out to be abnormally high. Several reasons can be identified. First, American investors—unlike their British counterparts, who could rely on the CFB—were not well organized. And even after the US Foreign Bondholders Protective Council was created in 1933, it was too intransigent to reach any debt restructurings with defaulting governments (Adamson 2002). Second, some Latin American debtors anticipated that they would not face sanctions; hence they shunned debt negotiations and launched buyback programs at discounted prices (Jorgensen and Sachs 1989, pp. 65–68). Third, the outbreak of WWII further postponed resumption of

[30]Author calculations based on Young (1930, pp. 12–13).

debt payments, especially in Central and Eastern Europe (Suter 1990, p. 283). The confluence of these factors led to realized internal rates of return being persistently lower than the contractual rates for all foreign government bonds, excepting French ones, denominated in US dollars (Eichengreen and Portes 1989, pp. 32–34).

2.2.6 *World War II*

World War II was the inevitable outcome of a decade of nationalism and isolationism. On narrow economic grounds, the costs of trade destruction during WWI and WWII were comparable (Glick and Taylor 2010), but the collapse of GDP and consumption was much more pronounced during the latter conflict (Barro and Ursúa 2008, pp. 271–274).[31] When GDP growth finally rose (e.g., in Great Britain and the United States), it did so mainly because of the boom in military expenditures. At the same time, the widespread confiscation of enemy private property further undermined the sanctity of foreign private property (Borchard 1946b). Moreover, the Soviet Union's ascension to "great power" status jeopardized the future of liberalism and capitalism.

2.3 International Business in a Bipolar World: 1945–1991

2.3.1 *Reconstructing the World Economy*

Reconstruction of the world economy took several years and was largely shaped by the United States. Four steps can be identified: establishing a durable peace, laying the foundation of a new monetary system, stimulating international trade, and accelerating the economic recovery of Western Europe.

2.3.1.1 The United Nations

In the spring of 1945, representatives of 50 countries met in San Francisco at the United Nations Conference on International Organization to draw up the United Nations (UN) Charter. The UN officially came into existence in October 1945 upon ratification of its Charter by China, France, the Soviet Union, the United Kingdom, the United States, and other signatories.

The UN's purposes, as presented in Article 1 of the Charter, are: (i) "to maintain international peace and security," especially through "collective measures for the

[31] The exceptions were Latin American economies, which actually prospered during WWII.

prevention and removal of threats to the peace, and for the suppression of acts of aggression or other breaches of the peace"; (ii) "to develop friendly relations among nations based on respect for the principle of equal rights and self-determination of peoples"; (iii) "to achieve international co-operation in solving international problems of an economic, social, cultural, or humanitarian character, and in promoting and encouraging respect for human rights and for fundamental freedoms for all"; and (iv) "to be a centre for harmonizing the actions of nations in the attainment of these common ends."[32]

Under Article 24 of the Charter, the Security Council—which consisted of ten nonpermanent and five permanent members (China, France, the Soviet Union, the United Kingdom, and the United States)—has primary responsibility for maintaining international peace and security. In effect, the preservation of peace devolved to the two superpowers (i.e., the Soviet Union and the United States) and depended on their averting a war between each other.

2.3.1.2 The Bretton Woods Monetary System

Following the Bretton Woods Conference of July 1944, the United States and its allies established the International Bank for Reconstruction and Development (IBRD) and the International Monetary Fund (IMF). These two institutions began their operations in 1946 (see IBRD 1946; IMF 1946).[33]

The IBRD's mission was to assist in reconstructing and developing the territories of its members and to promote international investment by guaranteeing or participating in loans and acquisitions made by private investors (IBRD 1946, pp. 4–5). The IMF was responsible for maintaining the new international monetary system (IMF 1946, pp. 9–16). The guiding philosophy of this system involved fixing a foreign par value for a currency by using gold—or a currency tied to gold—and then keeping the exchange rate within 1% of its par value. Toward that end, exchange rates remained adjustable in the medium term (with IMF assistance, as need be) and the Fund facilitated loans to countries experiencing temporary balance-of-payments deficits (for an overview, see McKinnon 1993, pp. 11–15).

2.3.1.3 The General Agreement on Tariffs and Trade

The Havana Charter of March 1948 established a multilateral trade agreement known as the General Agreement on Tariffs and Trade (GATT).[34] This agreement's objective was to fight protectionism by promoting "most favored nation" treatment, dismantling trade barriers and discriminatory practices, limiting export subsidies,

[32] www.un.org/en/sections/un-charter/chapter-i/index.html.

[33] The IBRD is commonly referred to as the World Bank.

[34] https://www.wto.org/english/docs_e/legal_e/havana_e.pdf.

and allowing countries to levy duties to counteract dumping. The GATT did include some exceptions to free-trade principles, however. For instance, quantitative restrictions were authorized for addressing balance-of-payments issues and for other specific purposes. Note that the GATT's signatories were required to cooperate with the IMF (for an exhaustive analysis of this agreement, see Hexner 1950–1951).

2.3.1.4 The European Recovery Program of 1948

The Cold War and the perceived risk that communist parties might come to power in France and Italy induced the United States to provide massive economic assistance to European nations. This goal was formalized in April 1948 by the European Recovery Program (ERP), more widely known as the "Marshall Plan" after its chief proponent, George C. Marshall.[35]

The objectives of the ERP were (i) to promote "industrial and agricultural production in the participating countries," (ii) to further "the restoration or maintenance of the soundness of European currencies, budgets, and finances," and (iii) to facilitate and stimulate "the growth of international trade of participating countries with one another and with other countries by appropriate measures including reduction of barriers which may hamper such trade" (Title I, Sec. 102(b)).

The 16 Marshall Plan countries were Austria, Belgium, Denmark, France, Great Britain, Greece, Iceland, Ireland, Italy, Luxembourg, the Netherlands, Norway, Portugal, Sweden, Switzerland, and Turkey. A total of $27 billion was authorized for the four-year period 1948–1952. The aid consisted of grants and loans, and the US Exim Bank served as the official lending agency.[36] Thanks in no small part to this assistance, Western European economies were in a position to thrive again by the early 1950s.

2.3.2 *The Geopolitical Context*

During the Cold War, several geopolitical factors affected the development of international investments. I focus here on four major factors: the Soviet bloc, the US financial assistance policy aimed at containing communism, the decolonization process, and the new role played by oil-exporting countries.

---

[35] https://www.cia.gov/library/readingroom/docs/1948-04-03b.pdf.

[36] https://www.marshallfoundation.org/marshall/the-marshall-plan/foreign-assistance-act-1948/the-european-recovery-program.

2.3.2.1 The Communist Bloc

In 1949, the communist bloc led by the Soviet Union (and including Albania, Bulgaria, Czechoslovakia, East Germany, Hungary, Mongolia, the People's Republic of China, Poland, Romania, and Yugoslavia) comprised more than 800 million inhabitants, accounting for a third of the world's population.[37] Some Western experts doubted that planned economies would adopt multilateral free trade and free-enterprise principles or would become significant business partners (Condliffe 1947, pp. 33–42). The bloc's 1949 creation of the Council for Mutual Economic Assistance (Comecon), a response to the Marshall Plan, seemed to support this view.[38]

Yet those doubts proved not to be well founded. In the 1960s, annual growth in exports of the developed economies to Comecon members exceeded that of intra-Comecon trade (Familton 1970, p. 31). An explanation for this trend was that commercial exchanges between the two spheres evidenced a certain complementarity: the West exported manufactured products while importing fuels, raw materials, and food. Furthermore, the 1970s context of "peaceful coexistence" led to the West's increased participation in—and financing of—Russian and Eastern European industrial projects (Zwass 1976, p. 5). As might be expected, credit risk materialized shortly thereafter: in 1981, both Poland and Romania defaulted on their foreign currency (FC) bank loans.[39] The *perestroika* reforms implemented by Russian President Mikhail Gorbachev in the second half of the 1980s allowed for the development of Western direct investment in Czechoslovakia, Hungary, and Poland through the creation of joint ventures (Michalak 1993). This shift presaged the collapse of planned economies and their conversion to capitalism.

In sum, it was reasonable in 1950 for Western investors to view communist countries as lost markets. Yet through succeeding decades, European and American businesses became increasingly involved in Comecon economies and coped with much the same risks as those present in free-market economies.[40]

---

[37] Author calculations based on Angus Maddison's historical statistics, available at www.ggdc.net/maddison/historical_statistics/horizontal-file_02-2010.xls.

[38] The founding members of the Comecon were Bulgaria, Czechoslovakia, Hungary, Poland, Romania, and the Soviet Union. In the following months, Albania and East Germany joined the organization.

[39] See Beers and de Leon-Manlagnit's (2019) database.

[40] Even so, the Coordinating Committee for Multilateral Export Controls (CoCom)—established shortly after WWII by the United States and its allies—*restricted* technological transfers to the East. See Mastanduno (1992) for an exhaustive study of the CoCom.

2.3.2.2 Foreign Loans and Grants as the Continuation of Politics by Other Means

One of the chief objectives of US diplomacy was to contain both communism and the variety of threats to international investments around the world. Three years after passage of the Marshall Plan, the Mutual Security Act of 1951 extended US assistance abroad—especially toward developing countries. The US foreign aid program was reorganized by the Foreign Assistance Act of 1961; this legislation set up the United States Agency for International Development (USAID), which is still active today.[41]

Not surprisingly, the economic assistance provided by the United States during 1946–1991 was directed mainly to allies and strategic countries. Consider the top ten recipient nations, which received 52% of all funds.[42] Two of them (South Korea and the Philippines) had each signed a mutual defense treaty with Washington in the early 1950s. Three others (Germany, Turkey, and the United Kingdom) were members of the North Atlantic Treaty Organization, and one (Pakistan) was part of other US-led collective defense treaties. The US financial support of the four remaining states (Egypt, India, Israel, and Vietnam) was driven by their geopolitical significance (for a concise analysis of the Egyptian-Israeli Peace Treaty's economic implications, see Korn 1979; for the US administration's role in helping India become self-sufficient with respect to food production, see Goldsmith 1988).[43]

The US Exim Bank's policy was consistent with USAID programs in the sense that loans were granted to friendly or strategic nations (Feinberg 1982, pp. 59–68). In September 1978, ten countries account for 58% of the Bank's exposure: Algeria, Brazil, Iran, Japan, Mexico, the Philippines, South Korea, Spain, Taiwan, and Yugoslavia (Exim Bank 1979, pp. 12–15). However, the pro-Western alignment of the Exim Bank's debtors hardly guaranteed that they were risk free. During 1980–1984, five nations (Brazil, Iran, Mexico, the Philippines, and Yugoslavia) defaulted on their FC sovereign debt.[44] In addition, Iran and Mexico expropriated assets of foreign investors (Kobrin 1984, p. 346; Minor 1994, p. 181). The Exim Bank was itself severely affected by the economic crisis that hit these LDCs (General Accounting Office 1982b).

In total, US overseas economic assistance during 1946–1991 exceeded $250 billion.[45] The Exim Bank lent some $76 billion, and the amounts covered by its guarantee and insurance operations reached $137 billion.[46] Although these capital

---

[41] See https://www.usaid.gov/who-we-are/usaid-history for more information.

[42] Author calculations based on USAID data (available at www.nber.org).

[43] The bulk of the US assistance to Vietnam was remitted before the country's pro-American regime's fall in 1975. Egypt and Israel obtained 95% of their funds after 1970. Author calculations based on USAID data (available at www.nber.org).

[44] See Beers and de Leon-Manlagnit's (2019) database.

[45] Author's calculations based on USAID data, available at www.nber.org.

[46] Author's calculations based on Becker and McClenahan Jr. (2003, pp. 306–314).

flows fell short of their objectives in some cases (most spectacularly, Iran and Vietnam), they stimulated world demand and foreign investment.

2.3.2.3 The Decolonization Process

Former British dependencies were decolonized over a period of five decades. In contrast, France and Belgium lost most of their colonies during (respectively) 1945–1962 and 1960–1962. Portugal did not grant independence to Angola, Cape Verde, Guinea Bissau, Mozambique, or São Tomé and Príncipe until 1974–1975.[47] By the mid-1970s, more than half of the UN's members were countries that had gained their independence in the preceding 35 years.[48]

This new international landscape engendered diverging analyses. An illustrative case is that of African nations in the early 1960s.[49] On the one hand, US diplomat Kenneth T. Young Jr. (1961) believed that those countries were driven by nationalistic forces and would remain aloof from the West and the East alike. And according to journalist Walter Kolarz (1962), African nationalism had "entered into a working agreement with Marxism" that would inevitably scare off foreign investors. On the other hand, in a propitious report on investment laws and regulations, the UN Economic Commission for Africa (1963) documented that two thirds of African countries had an integrated law or code on investments, and it pointed out that several of them (e.g., Ghana, Guinea, Libya, Nigeria, and Sudan) had passed laws protecting foreign private property and guaranteeing fair compensation in case of expropriation. Thus the UN report suggested that business opportunities did, in fact, exist in Africa.

A brief look at the investment policy (i.e., with regard to loans and equity) that was followed by the International Finance Corporation (IFC)[50] clarifies the business climate in countries that gained independence after 1939. Those countries accounted for 25–39% of IFC commitments in 1964, 1969, 1974, 1979, and 1984.[51] More importantly, the return on assets posted by the IFC ranged from 1.7% to 2.4%—which compares favorably with the 0.4–0.6% range earned by Wells Fargo, a San Francisco–based bank whose activities were based essentially within the United States.[52] Although it is impossible to assess the precise contribution made to IFC income by investments in young nations, the high level of observed profitability strongly suggests that those countries offered fruitful business opportunities.

---

[47] www.un.org

[48] Author calculations based on www.un.org.

[49] In the history of decolonization, 1960 was a milestone because 17 African nations became independent in that year (www.un.org).

[50] The IFC is a member of the World Bank Group.

[51] Author calculations based on IFC (various reports).

[52] Author calculations based on IFC (various reports) and on Wells Fargo & Company (various reports).

2.3.2.4 The New Role of Oil-Exporting Countries

The Organization of the Petroleum Exporting Countries (OPEC) was established in 1960 by Iran, Iraq, Kuwait, Saudi Arabia, and Venezuela. Its objective was to "co-ordinate and unify petroleum policies among Member Countries, in order to secure fair and stable prices for petroleum producers."[53] The baseline price of crude oil was maintained below $3 (US) per barrel until the 1973 Arab–Israeli War. In October of that year, OPEC unilaterally raised the per-barrel price of crude oil from $3 to $5.10; a second increase, to $11.65/barrel, was announced in December 1973.

This near quadrupling of the oil price within three months had wide-ranging and drastic effects. In the short term, it led to a recession and double-digit inflation in most Western industrialized economies and to a contraction of world trade volume in 1975 (IMF 1977). In the medium–long term, the consequences were far more complex.

The total current account surplus earned by oil exporters during 1974–1981 exceeded $400 billion.[54] A large portion of these "petrodollars" was invested through major Western commercial banks, which lent funds to oil-importing LDCs (for a banker's perspective on this phenomenon, see Safer 1978). Yet the loans neither enabled those countries to offset their growing current account deficits, which came to more than $420 billion during 1974–1981,[55] nor prevented their terms of trade from deteriorating. Instead, the credit position of Third World countries weakened, especially after oil prices shot upward and the Federal Reserve decided to raise its federal funds rate in 1979. It is therefore not surprising that most developing countries defaulted on their external debt in the first half of the 1980s (see Sect. 2.3.6).

It is important to highlight the paradoxical and pernicious scope of OPEC's policy. The oil price increases during October–December 1973 occurred amid a growing debate about the "new international economic order" (for an overview, see White 1975). The UN resolution adopted on this matter in May 1974 insisted, inter alia, on the "right of every country to adopt the economic and social system that it deems the most appropriate for its own development" and on the "full permanent sovereignty of every State over its natural resources and all economic activities" (United Nations General Assembly 1974). In 1973, LDCs could certainly argue that the OPEC's pricing move opened the way to "full permanent sovereignty" and that they had no choice but to follow suit. As it turned out, those expectations faded and these countries broadened their economic and financial dependence.

The two oil shocks also eroded the competitiveness of many manufacturing firms in most Western capitalist economies as well as in the planned economies of Eastern Europe. Protectionist measures, subsidies, and bailouts all failed to curb the deindustrialization process that accelerated unemployment. In the West, welfare capital-

---

[53] See https://www.opec.org/opec_web/en/about_us/24.htm. During 1961–1991, OPEC expanded to include Algeria, Ecuador, Gabon, Indonesia, Libya, Nigeria, Qatar, and the United Arab Emirates.

[54] Author calculations based on IMF (1978, p. 18; 1984, p. 23).

[55] Idem.

ism's crisis in the late 1970s and early 1980s prompted a shift from the Keynesian to the "neoliberal" paradigm (for an archetypal criticism of Keynesian policies, see Buchanan and Wagner 1977). In the East, planning inefficiencies led the Soviet bloc to collapse.

2.3.3 A Precarious International Monetary System Based on the US Dollar

The Bretton Woods system relied fundamentally on the US dollar. Yet even after this monetary system collapsed in 1973, the US currency continued to play a key role in international economic and financial relations.

2.3.3.1 1946–1959: The Dollar "as Good as Gold"

In the late 1940s, the US dollar was the only major currency offering gold convertibility. The currencies of most countries could not be converted into gold, into dollars, or even into other currencies. As a result, non-US economies had to obtain US dollars in order to pay for their imports. Doing so required that they obtain financial assistance from Washington and/or increasing their volume of exports.

In 1949, the currency devaluation of several major European countries—including France, (West) Germany, and Great Britain—boosted their exports, brought back US dollars, and provided some basis for progress toward the goal of convertibility (IMF 1950, p. 28). After a prolonged series of efforts—which included import restrictions, disinflationary policies, and even additional devaluations (especially in France)—14 Western European countries established convertibility for their currencies in January 1959 (IMF 1959, p. 125).[56] This decisive step made possible a revival of capital movements among industrial economies, although imbalances in payments appeared soon thereafter.

2.3.3.2 1959–1967: An Unstable System

The frailty of the Bretton Woods system was presciently described by Robert Triffin as early as 1959 (see Triffin 1978). He forecast that the United States would eventually face an unresolvable dilemma. On the one hand, if Washington managed to balance its payments then the US dollar would continue to be the world's preferred reserve currency but would be *not* be able to support the expansion of international

---

[56] The parties to this agreement were Austria, Belgium, Denmark, Finland, France, (West) Germany, Ireland, Italy, Luxembourg, the Netherlands, Norway, Portugal, Sweden, and the United Kingdom.

trade and financial flows. On the other hand, increasing balance-of-payments deficits would keep the world economy liquid but would undermine the dollar's credibility and thus end its gold convertibility.

Deterioration in the US balance-of-payments deficit was accelerated mainly by three factors. First, exports from Japan and the European Economic Community[57] grew more rapidly than did US exports during the 1960s (IMF 1971, p. 51).

Second, the Vietnam War (see Dudley and Passell 1968) and the increase in US direct investments abroad substantially increased capital outflows. The latter point merits closer examination. Cutler (1971) estimates that US direct investment outflows between 1950 and 1966 rose by a factor of 7. He also finds that more than half of the flows for 1966 went to foreign affiliates established or acquired during 1963–1966, which suggests that direct investments were not only expanding but also intensifying. The implication of this pattern was that the US balance-of-payments deficit was likely to increase even more significantly in the following years.

Third, policies implemented by President Kennedy and President Johnson, which aimed to preserve the US monetary position, were counterproductive. For instance, the interest equalization tax, established in 1963 to discourage long-term US lending to foreign entities, resulted in non-US borrowers raising funds in Europe and *not* in the United States (IMF 1964, pp. 94–95). Also, the mandatory direct investment program of 1968, which imposed a partial moratorium on US direct investment and the repatriation of some earnings and financial assets held abroad (IMF 1968, p. 58), ended up convincing US businesses to give their foreign subsidiaries *more* responsibilities.

In fact, these capital control measures encouraged offshore markets to use eurodollars,[58] which attracted both bankers and multinational firms. The former could obtain higher returns than in the United States, while the latter could circumvent restraints on international capital movements. At the macroeconomic level, the growth of euromarkets increased the US balance-of-payments deficit.

2.3.3.3 1967–1973: The Agony of Bretton Woods

Both the US payments imbalances and the November 1967 devaluation of the British pound were accompanied by a strong demand for gold. In March 1968, the governors of the central banks of Belgium, Germany, Italy, the Netherlands, Switzerland, the United Kingdom, and the United States announced that gold would henceforth be used only to effect transfers among monetary authorities (IMF 1968,

---

[57] The European Economic Community (EEC) was established in 1957 and included Belgium, France, (West) Germany, Italy, Luxembourg, and the Netherlands. In the 1970s and 1980s, the EEC expanded to include Denmark, Greece, Ireland, Portugal, Spain, and the United Kingdom.

[58] The Bank for International Settlements (BIS 1964, p. 127) defines a *eurodollar* as "a dollar that has been acquired by a bank outside the United States and used directly or after conversion into another currency for lending to a non-bank customer." Eurodollars are traded on offshore markets (initially in London) known as euromarkets.

p. 87). The IMF's creation of Special Drawing Rights (SDRs) was intended to provide a supplementary international reserve asset.[59]

The 1969 devaluation of the French franc and revaluation of the German mark, combined with the increasing mobility and volatility of capital flows and the sharp deterioration in the US balance of payments, were clear indicators that the monetary system could no longer be sustained (see IMF 1970, 1971). When the dollar's gold convertibility ended and the dollar was devalued in 1971, the collapse of the Bretton Woods system was complete.[60] Hence one can view "the floating–exchange rate era" as beginning in February 1973, when the US dollar was devalued with *no* margins for fluctuation (IMF 1973, pp. 5–6).

2.3.3.4 1973–1991: The Era of Floating Exchange Rates

The Jamaica Accords of January 1976 sanctioned the shift to a regime of flexible exchange rates. At this time, the IMF's Articles of Agreement were amended as follows. First, members agreed to collaborate with the Fund and with other members in order to assure exchange arrangements and to promote a stable system of exchange rates. Second, gold's function as the SDR's unit of value was eliminated—as was its role as the common denominator of currency par values. Third, the SDR replaced gold as a means of payment by the Fund. Fourth, the Fund's financial operations and transactions were simplified and expanded (IMF 1976, pp. 43–46).

This new era was characterized by large swings in exchange rates. The extensive use of eurodollars, which accounted for more than 25% of official foreign exchange reserves between 1974 and 1977,[61] and the increasing US trade deficit resulted in the dollar depreciating against the currency of major exporters: the US dollar declined 32% and 16.5% against the German mark and the Japanese yen, respectively, between 1973 and 1980.[62] This trend reversed at the turn of the 1980s, when demand for US dollars was boosted by a surge in US interest rates in 1979 and the Third World debt crisis starting in 1982. Between 1980 and 1985, the US currency appreciated by 62% against the German mark and by more than 100% against the French franc and the Italian lira.[63] Following the Plaza Accord of 1985, the dollar depreciated again until 1987. During 1987–1991, exchange rates among the currencies of major industrialized countries generally stabilized (IMF 1986, 1991).

---

[59] The SDR was initially defined as the equivalent of 0.888671 g of fine gold. Following the Bretton Woods system's collapse, the SDR was redefined as a basket of currencies (see https://www.imf.org/en/About/Factsheets/Sheets/2016/08/01/14/51/Special-Drawing-Right-SDR).

[60] After stabilizing at more than $20 billion in the 1950s, US gold reserves declined from $19.5 billion in 1959 to less than $11 billion in March 1971 (IMF 1960, p. 60; 1971, p. 28).

[61] Author calculations based on IMF (1979, p. 59).

[62] Author calculations based on the Pacific Exchange Rate Service (available at http://fx.sauder.ubc.ca).

[63] Idem.

The volatility of exchange rates within the EEC declined notably over this period. In 1979, the countries of Belgium, Denmark, France, (West) Germany, Ireland, Italy, Luxembourg, and the Netherlands established the European Monetary System (EMS). These countries then maintained maximum margins of 2.25% (6% for the Italian lira) on exchange rates for transactions involving their currencies. Their central banks cooperated closely in order to ensure the EMS's stability, and they organized devaluations and revaluations when a significant inflation gap and/or current account imbalance became evident.[64]

The collapse of the Bretton Woods system complicated international business. Consider the case of US investors conducting business with a country whose currency was floating. Exporters could take advantage of the dollar's relative weakness until 1979–1980, but they were adversely affected when the dollar subsequently appreciated.[65] Investors eager to acquire assets abroad were in the opposite position. Lenders faced a dilemma. Although they needed a strong dollar to preserve the long-term credibility of their activities, the credit position of their foreign debtors was undermined by excessive appreciation of the US currency.[66]

Relatively high risks were encountered also by US investors exporting goods, services, or capital to any country that "pegged" its currency's exchange value at a fixed rate. The main reason is that some currency pegs were not sustainable. When such economies experienced a balance-of-payments deficit, they were prone to speculative attacks that could force devaluation (for a seminal theoretical analysis, see Krugman 1979).[67] Irrespective of such external threats, a government might be tempted to devalue simply to increase the competitiveness of its exporting firms. In their study of exchange rate pegs in 17 Latin American economies during the post–Bretton Woods era, Klein and Marion (1994) found that devaluation was more likely following appreciation in the real exchange rate, increased trade concentration, and/or reduced openness of trade.

This unstable international monetary system spurred academic research on foreign exchange risk and the tools to manage it (Shapiro and Rutenberg 1976; Giddy 1977; Soenen 1979). In particular, meticulous investigations of hedging techniques reflected the growing importance of accounting and financial strategies among multinational companies.

[64] In the 1980s, the currencies of France, Italy, and Ireland were frequently devalued and those of Germany and the Netherlands were often revalued (IMF, various years).

[65] Between June 1975 and June 1980, the US dollar depreciated against two-fifths of the currencies that were floating at the start of this period. Between June 1980 and June 1985, however, the US dollar appreciated substantially against almost all floating currencies. Author calculations based on IMF (1975, pp. 68–70; 1980, pp. 106–109; 1985, pp. 92–95).

[66] This risk was concomitant with the sovereign debt crisis of 1982; see Sect. 2.3.6.

[67] See Kaminsky et al. (1997) for a review of the literature on currency crises.

2.3.4 Growth of International Trade and New Export Risks

2.3.4.1 The Role of the GATT and Its Limits

During 1947–1991, world exports increased (on average) by more than 6% annually.[68] This expansion of international trade was spurred by the GATT and was achieved through a series of multilateral negotiations known as "trade rounds." Until the early 1960s, these GATT rounds concentrated mainly on reducing tariffs. The so-called Kennedy Round (1964–1967) led to an average tariff cut of 35% on industrial products and included an antidumping code (Miles 1968). The Tokyo Round (1973–1979) brought the average tariff on industrial products down to 4.7%. Several agreements and arrangements were reached to fight non-tariff barriers (NTBs), but not all GATT members subscribed to these agreements.[69] The Uruguay Round (1986–1994) covered even more aspects of international trade—including, among others, services and intellectual property—and tackled most of the impediments to such trade (e.g., domestic subsidies, safeguard measures, etc.).[70]

Although the GATT managed to reduce tariffs dramatically in the postwar decades, it was unable to curb the rise of NTBs. Hiscox and Kastner (2002, pp. 33–35) use "gravity" model–based estimates of trade policy orientations, including all forms of trade restrictions, to show that all developed nations (excepting Portugal, Spain, and Switzerland) were more protectionist in 1990 than in 1960. By the same token, more than half (58%) of the top three economies in each of four areas—Africa, East Asia, Latin America, and the Middle East—had a less liberal trade policy in 1990.[71]

It is not surprising that the resurgence of protectionism in the 1970s led to more trade disputes. For example, the number of disputes settled within the GATT system rose from 28 during 1948–1969 to 72 during 1970–1991.[72] The fierce criticisms lodged against this system in the latter period (for discussions, see Hudec 1980; Davey 1987) mirrored the frustration and persistent difficulties experienced by exporters.

The financial support of export–import banks and the insurance contracts provided by export credit agencies against an increasing array of risks[73]—from basic

---

[68] Author calculations based on IMF (various reports).

[69] https://www.wto.org/english/thewto_e/whatis_e/tif_e/fact4_e.htm

[70] The number of countries participating in GATT rounds increased from 23 for the first round (in 1947) to 123 for the Uruguay Round (https://www.wto.org/english/thewto_e/whatis_e/tif_e/fact4_e.htm).

[71] Author classification based on Hiscox and Kastner (2002) and on Angus Maddison's historical statistics, available at www.ggdc.net/maddison/historical_statistics/horizontal-file_02-2010.xls. The selection criterion for these estimates is GDP in 1960. The 12 countries included in the sample are Egypt, Nigeria, and South Africa; China, India, and Indonesia; Argentina, Brazil, and Mexico; and Iran, Iraq, and Turkey.

[72] Author calculations based on https://www.wto.org/english/tratop_e/dispu_e/gt47ds_e.htm.

[73] See Sect. 2.3.5.2 for analysis of the enhanced role of export credit agencies since the 1960s.

commercial risk in the 1950s to political risk in the 1960s and exchange rate risk in the 1970s (Greene 1965; Archives de l'Etat en Belgique 2008)—were helpful in this challenging trade environment. However, they were not enough to render it generally profitable.

2.3.4.2 New Export Risks in LDCs

In the postwar years, several influential ideologies drove some LDCs to follow protectionist policies. These policies had the effect of impeding export activities.

The autarkic policy followed by Maoist China left very few opportunities for Western businesses until economic reforms were instituted in 1978. Until then, only exporters from Australia, Canada, Japan, New Zealand, and communist countries had trade relationships with Beijing (Perkins 1971–1972). After stagnating in the 1960s and growing considerably in the 1970s, the volume of Chinese trade increased by a factor of 6 during 1978–1990 (Park 1993, p. 52).[74] Yet despite the open-door policy promoted by Deng Xiaoping, China remained among the most closed economies in the world in 1990 (Hiscox and Kastner 2002, p. 33).

One of the most pervasive risks faced by exporters was the implementation of "import substitution industrialization" (ISI) policies,[75] which were widespread among Latin American economies (Baer 1972). A striking illustration is the automobile industry's development in the 1960s (Munk 1969). European, Japanese, and US automakers had difficulties exporting to Latin America, yet setting up branches there would enable them to take advantage of the subsidies and tax rebates offered by host governments. However, the shift to direct investment created several problems. On the one hand, it induced additional risks—for example, the possibility of expropriation. On the other hand, it undermined profitability because the cost of producing cars locally turned out to be higher than simply exporting them (Munk 1969, pp. 91–94).

However, ISI could succeed provided it involved the production of nondurable consumer goods and was complemented by export-promotion policies, such as those adopted in Hong Kong, Singapore, South Korea, and Taiwan (Balassa 1971, 1978).[76] These countries managed to reduce their dependence on imports and to stimulate the development of a domestic industry through "backward integration." Their firms reached economies of scale and expanded production capacity to enable the export of manufactured goods with increasing value added. This economic

---

[74] The integration of China into world trade and business is analyzed in Sect. 2.4.3.

[75] The advocates of ISI strategies assumed that the income elasticity of demand for imports of LDCs' nonindustrial products by developed countries was *lower* than the income elasticity of demand for imports of industrial products. If so, then ISI could probably correct the disparity in income elasticities (Prebisch 1959)—an outcome that supported the establishment of tariffs and quotas as well as the subsidizing of domestic producers or foreign direct investors. The ISI policies were also intended to preserve foreign exchange.

[76] These economies were commonly referred to as *newly industrialized countries* (NICs).

model posed two threats to Western exporters: In the short term, it reduced the demand for some of their goods, and in the longer term, it led to the emergence of new competitors (e.g., the Korean *chaebols*).

Another manifestation of country risk in LDCs stemmed, somewhat paradoxically, from the growing importance of export credit schemes. In this respect, the US Exim Bank played a leading role until the 1970s. The huge amounts lent to foreign entities for the purpose of buying US products distorted competition and handicapped non-US exporters. In particular, it was difficult for European manufacturers to sell their airplanes and tractors in the countries where Boeing and Caterpillar—two firms that benefited mightily from US Exim Bank credits—exported under the aegis of that Washington-based institution.

2.3.4.3 New Export Risks in Developed Countries

Starting in the 1970s, the growing competition of Japan's and NICs' exporters combined with the oil shock to slow down economic growth in North America and Western Europe. A typical response of old capitalist countries would be to implement new norms and regulations—in addition to traditional NTBs—with the aim of discriminating against foreign firms. These measures, broadly referred to as "regulatory protectionism" (Sykes 1999), include technical barriers, sanitary barriers, and national preference policies.[77]

Technical barriers—such as regulations covering electrical equipment, electronic devices, motor vehicles, and so forth—became a major protectionist tool of policy makers in the United States, in the EEC, and even in Japan (Drifte 1983; Schoenbaum 1984). These measures reflected the efforts of US and European authorities to protect uncompetitive industrial firms as well as the "mercantilist" policy followed by Tokyo.

Discriminatory sanitary norms resulted from countries resolving to preserve domestic agriculture. A memorable example dates to the mid-1980s, when the EEC prohibited beef imports from nations that permitted the injection of growth hormones into cattle destined for human consumption. Because this policy penalized US farmers, President Reagan ordered retaliatory tariffs against some European exporters (Sykes 1999, pp. 1–3).[78]

National preference measures include imposition of "local content" requirements and the prohibition of foreign companies from bidding on government contracts in some sectors. An illustration of national preference in a highly sensitive area was the Bayh–Dole Act of 1980, which reformed the US patent and trademark system. Section 204 of this legislation stipulates that no entity that patents any

[77] See Messerlin (1981, 1982) for analysis of the political economy of protectionism.

[78] The US retaliation proceeded under Section 301 of the Trade Act of 1974, which authorized the president to take all appropriate steps to disallow any foreign government's policy that restricted US commerce. The thrust of this section illustrated Washington's awareness of the need for a prompt response to protectionist policies adopted by trade partners.

invention with federal assistance can "grant to any person the exclusive right to use or sell any subject invention in the United States unless such person agrees that any products embodying the subject invention or produced through the use of the subject invention will be manufactured substantially in the United States" (for an analysis, see Coriat 2002, p. 182).

These aspects of "regulatory protectionism" were so inconvenient that they were addressed during GATT's Uruguay Round. Several formal agreements were reached: one dealing with technical barriers to trade, a second on the application of sanitary and phytosanitary measures, and a third on trade-related aspects of intellectual property rights.[79]

2.3.5 *Foreign Direct Investment at Risk*

No type of investment was ever more hazardous than foreign direct investment in the decades following World War II. Various political and economic factors combined to disturb international business. Despite these impediments, US direct investment abroad soared from $7.2 billion in 1946 to $467.8 billion in 1991—an annual growth rate that exceeded 9.5%.[80] This paradox can be explained by the myriad business opportunities worldwide and by the array of tools that capital-exporting nations and foreign investors deployed to reduce country risk, especially expropriation risk.[81]

2.3.5.1 Hostile Business Environment of the Postwar Decades

The treatment of enemy property in the aftermath of WWII was tough and foreshadowed the fragility of foreign direct and portfolio investments during the Cold War, especially in LDCs. The Potsdam Declaration of 1945 regarding German reparations and the peace treaties concluded in 1947 with Bulgaria, Hungary, Italy, and Romania provided that the Allies had the right to seize and liquidate all properties within their territory and belonging to the enemy State or its nationals (for discussions, see Borchard 1946a; Martin 1948).

---

[79] See https://www.wto.org/english/thewto_e/whatis_e/tif_e/agrm4_e.htm and https://www.wto.org/english/thewto_e/whatis_e/tif_e/agrm7_e.htm.

[80] Author calculations based on Pizer and Cutler (1956, p. 15) and https://www.bea.gov/international/di1usdbal.

[81] There are three reasons why this section focuses on nationalization risk. First, starting in the 1950s, that threat became a major concern among MNCs operating in LDCs. Second, other risks (e.g., subsidies to local producers, exchange controls, other macroeconomic risks) were addressed in Sects. 2.3.3 and 2.3.4. Third, and as described in what follows, expropriation risk turned out to be a driver of political and country risk analysis.

In the meantime, the Bulgarian, Czechoslovakian, Hungarian, Polish, Romanian, and Yugoslavian governments—already within the Soviet zone of influence—enacted nationalization laws inspired by socialist and communist doctrines. It is interesting that compensation policies differed considerably across countries, with the Hungarian regime being much more favorable to foreign investors than the Bulgarian (Doman 1948, pp. 1152–1158).

In subsequent years, other newly communist powers undertook expropriation acts. The most striking cases were observed in mainland China (1949–1950), Cuba (1959–1960) and Ethiopia (1975) as well as in Angola and Mozambique during the second half of the 1970s (see US House of Representatives 1963, p. 16; Johnson 1965; Kobrin 1984; Maurer 2013, pp. 347–348). These large-scale nationalizations affected most economic sectors.

A second driver of the expropriation of foreign ownership was the extensive interpretation of every State's right to dispose of its wealth. This principle—promoted by UN General Assembly Resolution 626 (VII) of 21 December 1952 on the right to exploit freely natural wealth and resources and Resolution 1803 (XVII) of 8 December 1962 on permanent sovereignty over natural resources—convinced several countries (including those that had just gained independence) to nationalize their own petroleum and mining sectors.

Major takeovers of foreign oil companies' properties occurred in Iran (during 1951), Iraq (1961), Ceylon (1962), Argentina (1963), Algeria (1967), Peru (1968), Bolivia (1969), Libya (1970), Nigeria (1971), Arab oil-exporting countries (1972),[82] and Venezuela (1975) (US Department of State 1972; Genova 2010, pp. 120–121; Maurer 2013, pp. 304–305, 358–361, 382–384).[83] Mining companies that operated abroad were also vulnerable to expropriation risk. For example, Bolivia nationalized the tin and zinc sectors in 1952 and 1971, respectively. The Democratic Republic of the Congo, Zambia, and Chile followed a similar strategy with copper in (respectively) 1966, 1969, and 1971 (US Department of State 1972; Maurer 2013, pp. 297–301).[84] It is noteworthy that the agrarian reforms implemented in many LDCs led to significant forced divestments of foreign landowners (US Department of State 1972; Kobrin 1980; Bandyopadhyay 1996).

Nationalizations were sometimes driven by more idiosyncratic political motives. Thus, the 1951 takeover of the Anglo-Iranian Oil Company by Iran's Prime Minister Mossadegh, and that in 1956 of the Suez Canal by Egypt's President Nasser, reflected the eagerness of these two leaders to enhance the geopolitical status of their respective countries and to counter Western influence. The expropriation of foreign firms operating in Indonesia during 1960–1965 was part of a massive attack against US interests that was likely to spill over into Southeast Asia (Van der Kroef 1965). Furthermore, the MNCs despoiled by the new Iranian regime in 1979–1980

[82] The Arab oil-exporting countries referenced here are Kuwait, Saudi Arabia, and the United Arab Emirates.

[83] Only the starting year of the nationalization process is indicated.

[84] For information on other minerals that were nationalized, see US Department of State (1972) and Rood (1976).

paid the price of a complex revolution that mixed religious fundamentalism, state intervention, and anti-US sentiments (Halliday 1982).

During 1960–1979, a total of 79 LDCs engaged in 559 expropriation acts against 1,705 foreign firms (Kobrin 1984). International investors had several options for protecting their ownership and preserving their interests. They could act preventively by using guarantees or insurance contracts; and once nationalization occurred, they could mobilize political, arbitrational, and judicial means to secure adequate compensation. At the same time, these investors could improve their decision-making by enhancing their knowledge about the investment climate abroad.

2.3.5.2 Foreign Investment Guarantees

The Investment Guaranty Program, which originated with the European Recovery Program of 1948, was a milestone in the history of capital export because it offered guarantees—against convertibility risk—to new US direct, equity, and loan investments in ERP countries. The coverage was expanded in 1950 and 1956 to include (respectively) expropriation risk and war damage risk. The Mutual Security Act of 1959 shifted the set of recipient countries from Western Europe to underdeveloped nations exclusively (von Neumann Whitman 1959, pp. 36–37). Following the Cuban deprivations of US-owned wealth, the Foreign Assistance Act of 1961 revised the guaranty program in order to include risks of insurrection, revolution, and accompanying civil unrest and to provide arbitration procedures for settling investor claims. Guaranty schemes were reorganized and reinvigorated with the establishment of the Overseas Private Investment Corporation (OPIC) in 1971. As a self-sustaining US government agency, OPIC had considerable autonomy. For instance, it could insure joint ventures and grant loans (Lipson 1978, pp. 361–366).[85] During 1971–1991, OPIC's insurance claims settlements totaled $509 million, 77% of which involved expropriation claims.[86]

European countries—primarily through their export credit agencies—started offering political risk guarantees to their investors in the late 1950s. Germany moved forward as early as 1959; Switzerland, Belgium, France, and the United Kingdom followed suit in 1970–1972 (Laviec 1985, pp. 215–217; Ducroire 2006). Private insurance companies (e.g., Lloyds and AIG) did not play a significant role in this field until the 1980s (Williams 1993, pp. 96–97).

It is noteworthy that, after a quarter century of laborious efforts (see Broches 1962), the Multilateral Investment Guarantee Agency (MIGA) was ultimately established in 1988. The seminal objectives of this World Bank agency were to issue guarantees against political risks and to stimulate the flow of capital to developing countries (MIGA 1989, pp. 1–6).

---

[85] See also https://www.opic.gov/who-we-are/opic-history.

[86] Author calculations based on O'Sullivan (2005, pp. 51–64).

2.3.5.3 Compensation from Expropriating States

The Western doctrine stating that the nationalization of foreign properties must be balanced by "prompt, adequate, and effective" compensation (Hyde 1939) was not a "general rule of law applicable in all circumstances" (Schachter 1984). In light of the diverging interpretations of what "prompt, adequate, and effective" (or *just*) compensation should be, the prospects for foreign investors receiving at least *satisfactory* indemnification depended on their ability to (i) negotiate directly with host governments, (ii) settle disputes by means of arbitrational or judicial recourses, and/or (iii) prevail upon their home government to exert diplomatic or economic pressure.[87]

In some expropriation acts, direct and prompt negotiations enabled aggrieved foreign investors to settle agreements with host countries. Such agreements were underpinned by different motives. In 1969, the US copper mining company Anaconda accepted the Chilean government's acquisition of 51% of its properties because political pressure for *complete* expropriation was high (Central Intelligence Agency, 1969, pp. 4–5). The following year, Roan Selection Trust (another copper mining company) settled with Zambia. Although the compensation amount for the takeover of majority ownership was underestimated, the firm was satisfied with the agreement's other provisions, such as sales and management contracts and the absence of tax increase for a ten-year period (US Department of State 1972, p. 110). In 1975, Venezuela anticipated the expiration of oil concessions—scheduled in 1983—and announced a nationalization program. This decision relieved US oil companies, facilitated negotiations, and led to relatively just compensations (Maurer 2013, pp. 382–383).

A second set of remedies included recourse to judicial, quasi-judicial, and arbitration tribunals. International investors might seek redress in the host country's courts—but with little chance of success because litigation before those courts was constrained by state doctrine and the principle of sovereign immunity. Even the trend toward a restrictive approach to immunity, especially after the European Convention on State Immunity of 1972 and the US Foreign Sovereign Immunities Act of 1976, did not ensure the processing and adjudication of claims (for a discussion on the US legal landscape, see Leigh 1990). The International Court of Justice (ICJ) was a potential forum provided that the investors' claims were supported by their home government (Snyder 1963, p. 1099).[88] Ad hoc tribunals might also be formed.

In fact, three ways of recourse were effective in resolving disputes: the Court of Arbitration of the International Chamber of Commerce (ICC); the International

[87] These avenues of redress are designed to resolve a large set of investment disputes and not exclusively those arising out of expropriation acts. However, it is their capacity to deal with nationalization problems that is studied here.

[88] For instance, in the 1977 dispute between Texaco and the Libyan government, the ICJ arbitrator delivered an award on the merits in favor of the company (see Von Mehren 1978).

Centre for Settlement of Investment Disputes (ICSID); and, in the case of US investors, the Foreign Claims Settlement Commission (FCSC).

Established in 1923,[89] the Court of Arbitration of the ICC is entitled to settle commercial disputes in cases where the parties had included ICC arbitration clauses in their contract (for a thorough analysis, see Craig et al. 2000).[90] Created in 1954 as a quasi-judicial, independent agency within the US Department of Justice, the FCSC administered the War Claims Act of 1948 and the International Claims Settlement Act of 1949. The Commission adjudicated claims of US nationals against Maoist China, Communist Eastern Europe, and other expropriating countries (Re 1962; FCSC 2018). The ICSID was established in 1966 under the auspices of the World Bank. Its objective is to depoliticize investment disputes between states and private investors by providing facilities for conciliation and arbitration;[91] however, the parties must have previously consented to submitting the dispute to the Centre (see Broches 1965; Shihata 1992).

A third set of recourse for foreign investors was to request the support of their home government to foster settlements providing for just compensation. What follows is a brief recounting of the initiatives carried out by the administrative apparatus of the United States.

First, MNCs were likely to resort to traditional diplomatic channels to advance their claims as International Telephone & Telegraph (ITT) did in Brazil in 1962–1963 (US House of Representatives 1963). Diplomatic pressure could be stronger. Following the expropriation of US tin companies in Bolivia in October 1952, the incoming Eisenhower administration committed to endorsing its businesses and reminded Bolivia that its tin had to be smelted in Texas. An agreement was reached in June 1953 (Maurer 2013, pp. 298–300).

In some cases, Washington exerted more coercive measures to protect its MNCs. In 1962, the increasing hostile investment climate in Latin America convinced Congress to modify the Foreign Assistance Act via the Hickenlooper Amendment, which provided for the suspension of assistance to countries that took over US-owned properties without making prompt, adequate, and effective compensation. This amendment was first applied to Ceylon in 1963; in response to the resulting capital flight, Ceylon's economy suffered dramatically. However, a new government in 1965 enabled the parties involved to secure a satisfactory agreement (Maurer 2013, pp. 332–336). In fact, US presidents frequently *threatened* to suspend aid—sometimes by recalling the Hickenlooper Amendment provisions—rather than cut it off immediately. This strategy proved successful during 1971–1976 in the cases of Benin, the People's Republic of the Congo, and Guyana

[89] https://iccwbo.org/about-us/who-we-are/history

[90] Although the ICC Court of Arbitration's work is confidential, some information is available regarding the disputes stemming from expropriation; see, for example, the ICC award made in Case no. 2139 in 1974: https://www.trans-lex.org/202139/_/icc-award-no-2139-yca-1978-at-220-et-seq-

[91] For an early ICSID award in connection with an expropriation case, see *AGIP S.p.A. v. People's Republic of the Congo* (ICSID Case no. ARB/77/1); for additional details, see Baker (1999, p. 76).

(Akinsanya 1981, p. 782; Maurer 2013, p. 356, n. 7).[92] The combination of suspending US aid and reducing bilateral and multilateral lending was tried out against Bolivia and Peru in 1968–1971. Although the efficiency of this policy is debatable, it seems to have prevented significant losses to Gulf Oil and the International Petroleum Company (Olson 1975; Maurer 2013, pp. 363–379).

The most radical measures in favor of US firms took the form of covert actions. Chile is a tragic example of such efforts. Once elected in 1970, President Allende expropriated US copper mining companies and industrial firms but did not offer adequate compensation. Fearing the spread of hard leftist policies in Latin America and encouraged by ITT, the Nixon administration and the Central Intelligence Agency approved a covert operation. President Allende was overthrown in September 1973. His successor, General Pinochet, reached agreements on compensation with the copper companies as early as 1974 (US Senate 1975; Sigmund 1977, p. 261).

However, these attempts to constrain expropriating governments to settle agreements with aggrieved investors did not systematically guarantee *just* indemnification. In many cases, compensation was not "prompt, adequate, and effective" because negotiations took excessive time,[93] settlements required reinvestment in the host country, payouts consisted of annual installments or long-term bonds, and/or enforcement was poor.

Another option to reduce expropriation risk abroad involved collecting information and using country risk indicators.

2.3.5.4 Investment Climate and Country Risk Analyses

In the decade that followed WWII, news on the investment climate was the main resource at the disposal of MNCs seeking to assess country risk. Such news included data, notes, and reports published by international institutions (e.g., the United Nations, the IMF, the World Bank); the Bureau of Foreign Commerce of the U.S. Department of Commerce (viz., *Foreign Commerce Weekly*) and its counterparts in capital-exporting nations; trade and industry associations; chambers of commerce; leading international banks; trade commissioners; and commercial attachés.[94]

A few firms specialized in providing information and advice to international investors; these included the Economist Intelligence Unit (EIU), S. J. Rundt &

[92] The United States passed additional laws that provided for retaliation against expropriating countries. Examples include the González Amendment of 1972 (https://history.house.gov) and Section 502(b) of the Trade Act of 1974.

[93] Some formal claims agreements were settled several decades after the expropriation occurred; see FCSC (2018).

[94] See, for instance, National Industrial Conference Board (1951) and United States Council of the International Chamber of Commerce (1953).

Associates, and Business International.[95] It is worth mentioning also that Norman M. Littell, who served as Assistant Attorney General of the United States during 1939–1944, published three prominent articles in the *Virginia Law Review* that summarized the legal climate for investment abroad (Littell 1950, 1952, 1954).

The risks experienced by MNCs were not addressed by the academic community until the creation in the late 1950s of several journals dealing with international business: *Business Horizons*, *California Management Review*, *The International Executive* (continued as *Thunderbird International Business Review*), and *Management International* (continued as *Management International Review*).[96] Political scientists added their contribution by undertaking cross-national comparisons (see Deutsch 1960; Banks and Textor 1963). In one noteworthy article, Feierabend and Feierabend (1966) used 30 variables to establish an index of political stability for 84 countries.

Starting in the late 1960s, three complementary strands of research grew and enabled international businesses to monitor the investment climate much more accurately.

A first set of academic works focused on the assessment of political risk. This discipline was concerned with the systematic identification, analysis, and management of political and socioeconomic restraints on foreign investments (see e.g. Stobaugh 1969; Nehrt 1970; Robock 1971; Zink 1973; Kobrin 1977, 1982; Overholt 1982; Simon 1982).

A second group of articles conducted in-depth studies on specific threats. For example, investigations of expropriation risk proliferated (e.g., Root 1968; Truitt 1970; Knudsen 1974; Williams 1975; Hawkins et al. 1976; Rood 1976; Kobrin 1980, 1984).

A third group of studies implemented methodologies designed to evaluate political and economic risk and to rate countries.[97] Some models were established by academics (e.g., Coplin and O'Leary 1972; Hibbs 1973; Green 1974; Haendel et al. 1975) and others by Business Environment Risk Intelligence (BERI) and Business International, two influential consulting firms.[98] Although the accuracy of such ratings was questioned—especially after the Iranian revolution in 1979 (see Kennedy Jr.

[95] These three entities were established in 1946, 1952, and 1954, respectively; see EIU (2006, p. 3), Howell (2001, p. 185), and E. McDowell, "Spotlight; Orville Freeman, Businessman," *New York Times*, 14 September 1980.

[96] Two important reviews emerged a few years later: the *Columbia Journal of World Business* in 1965 (continued as *Journal of World Business*) and the *Journal of International Business Studies* in 1970.

[97] The increasing threat of nationalization in LDCs may explain the development of these ratings. Yet one could advance another reason—namely, the growing share of manufacturing in total US investments abroad. Because industrialists generally had more options (than did mining and oil companies) when selecting a host country, they needed some tools to discriminate among potential recipients.

[98] F. T. Haner founded BERI in 1966 after working several years for US companies; www.beri.com/Dr.-F.T.-Haner.aspx. For a thorough analysis of BERI methodologies, see Haner and Ewing (1985).

1984)—their use spread and new raters emerged in the 1980s, such as Nord Sud Export and the International Country Risk Guide.[99]

Between the 1950s and the 1980s, the number of available means for reducing country risk mushroomed. Guarantee and insurance schemes as well as judicial and arbitrational recourse contributed to limit financial losses, while political and business risk ratings helped investors anticipate (to some extent) political and economic shocks. At the onset of financial globalization, MNCs were undoubtedly better prepared than ever to run their businesses abroad.

2.3.6 *A Long Debt Cycle That Leads to a Major Financial Crisis*

Sovereign lending went through dramatic changes during 1945–1991. Contrary to what occurred in the 1920s, foreign government bond markets did not rebound after WWII and bondholders failed to reach debt restructurings with several defaulting countries. Also, the nature of sovereign lending evolved substantially. Suppliers' credits and bilateral and multilateral loans accounted for the bulk of the capital flows to LDCs until commercial banks became major creditors in the 1970s. The debt crisis that erupted in 1982 led the IMF to steer the most important debt negotiations in history. It is noteworthy that the high debt levels of the late 1970s and the financial turmoil of the 1980s stimulated sovereign risk analysis. By 1991, creditors had many indicators that could be used to anticipate debt crises.

2.3.6.1 Unfortunate Foreign Bondholders and Dormant Sovereign Bond Markets

There was little activity on sovereign bond markets during the Cold War. Several reasons can be advanced: creditor countries enacting capital controls, which are intended to direct domestic savings into *domestic* investments and to avert payments imbalances; the importance of bilateral and multilateral loans; and the stigma of the painful bond restructuring processes conducted since the 1930s.

At the end of 1945, 52% of outstanding foreign government bonds remained in default. Seven years later, this percentage had declined slightly to 42% (IBRD 1955, p. 2). The most recalcitrant debtors (whose defaulting bonds exceeded $200 million in December 1952)[100] were the Soviet Union, Romania, Yugoslavia, Greece, China, and Hungary. These six distressed countries were still in default in 1960 (Corporation of Foreign Bondholders 1961).

---

[99] See Bouchet et al. (2003, pp. 82–83) and Howell (2001, p. 19).

[100] Author calculations based on IBRD (1953b, 1955).

In the 1950s–1960s, most of the sovereign borrowers that tapped capital markets were industrialized countries, not LDCs. In 1963–1965, publicly issued bonds accounted for less than 2% of the total debt incurred by LDCs (World Bank 1967, p. 34). The profile of issuers was not fundamentally changed either by the development of offshore markets in the 1970s or by the foreign bond market's revival in the United States following expiration (in 1974) of the interest equalization tax. Venezuela was the sole LDC that managed to offer both medium-term notes and long-term bonds.[101]

2.3.6.2 A Long Indebtedness Cycle Fed by Various Types of Creditors

During 1946–1950, capital flows to the underdeveloped world reached $6.4 billion; of this amount, 57% took the form of grants and 43% were loans. About 83% (resp., 17%) of the loans came from governments and international organizations (resp., from private entities).[102]

The LDCs' indebtedness cycle—driven by urgent infrastructure needs and weak export volumes—began in the 1950s and lasted nearly three decades. During 1955–1981, the external public debt of a set of 34 LDCs[103] increased (on average) by more than 18% annually; during 1962–1981, that of 22 newly independent African countries[104] increased by more than 25% annually. Several types of institutions lent to LDCs.

The 1950s featured a predominance of bilateral and multilateral loans. In this respect, two institutions played leading roles: the US Exim Bank and the World Bank. During 1950–1959, the former lent $3.7 billion and the latter $2.5 billion to LDCs' central and local governments, their agencies, and private firms with a public guarantee.[105] A third important source of fresh capital was officially guaranteed private export credits (mainly from France, Germany, Italy, and the United Kingdom), which totaled $1.3 billion for the period 1956–1959 (United Nations 1966, p. 65).

---

[101] See *Moody's Bond Survey*, 31 January 1977 and 27 April 1981.

[102] Author calculations based on IBRD (1953a, pp. 26–27).

[103] Author calculations based on Avramovic et al. (1964, pp. 104–105) and World Bank (1985). The 34 countries in the sample are: Argentina, Bolivia, Brazil, Chile, Colombia, Costa Rica, Ecuador, Egypt (formerly United Arab Republic), El Salvador, Ethiopia, Greece, Guatemala, Honduras, India, Israel, Jordan, Lebanon, Liberia, Mexico, Myanmar (formerly Burma), Nicaragua, Pakistan, Panama, Paraguay, Peru, the Philippines, Portugal, Sri Lanka (formerly Ceylon), Syria, Thailand, Turkey, Uruguay, Venezuela, and Yugoslavia.

[104] Author calculations based on Avramovic et al. (1964, pp. 104–105) and World Bank (1985). The 22 countries in the sample are: Benin (formerly Dahomey), Burkina Faso (formerly Upper Volta), Burundi, Cameroon, the Central African Republic, the Democratic Republic of Congo (formerly Zaire), Gabon, Ghana, Guinea, Ivory Coast, Mauritania, Morocco, Niger, Nigeria, the Republic of Congo, Rwanda, Senegal, Sierra Leone, Somalia, Sudan, Togo, and Tunisia.

[105] Author calculations based on Exim Bank and World Bank annual reports for fiscal years 1950–1960. A small part of the credits authorized by the Exim Bank went to LDCs' private firms but with no public guarantee.

Commercial banks in the United States developed their sovereign lending activities step by step. After underwriting part of the World Bank's obligations in 1950 (World Bank 1950, p. 40), they began participating in the loans granted by that international institution in 1954 (World Bank 1954, p. 2). The commercial banks' policy consisted of taking up the loans with shorter maturities but without the Bank's guarantee (World Bank 1955, p. 14). In the meantime, some banks lent directly to sovereign governments. For example, the Chase National Bank of New York granted a $5 million loan to Peru; this loan complemented a US Treasury stabilization credit line and an IMF standby arrangement (IMF 1954, p. 107). Between 1955 and the early 1980s, US commercial banks increased the number of their foreign branches by a factor of 8 and expanded the volume of their foreign assets from $1.1 billion to $242.8 billion (OCC 1956, 1981).

These developments resulted in a dramatic change in the contribution of different creditors to financing of the Third World. Between 1967 and 1981, the share of official bilateral lending and non-bank credits (including suppliers' credits) in total LDCs' external public debt outstanding fell, respectively, from 54% to 29% and from 23% to 9%. In contrast, the percentage of official multilateral[106] and commercial banks' loans increased (respectively) from 17% to 23% and from 6% to 39%.[107]

The indebtedness cycle of 1955–1981 was characterized by several multilateral debt relief episodes. The associated debt negotiation meetings were organized under the auspices of the "Paris Club," an informal group established in 1956 and composed of representatives from major Western creditor countries. During 1956–1973, nine countries reached debt rescheduling or refinancing agreements: Argentina, Brazil, Chile, Ghana, India, Indonesia, Pakistan, Peru, and Turkey (Klein 1973, pp. 17–20). The type of external debt most frequently subject to consolidation involved suppliers' credits—primarily because their shorter maturities and higher interest rates burdened debt service payments. These first debt restructuring deals established the senior creditor status of international financial institutions, especially the World Bank (see IBRD 1969, pp. 35–38).

In the context of an oil crisis, a global economic slowdown, and the external imbalances of 1974–1981, Paris Club creditor countries conducted debt relief operations with 14 debtor countries: the Central African Republic, Chile, the Democratic Republic of Congo, Liberia, Madagascar, Pakistan, Peru, Poland, Senegal, Sierra Leone, Sudan, Togo, Turkey, and Uganda.[108]

Yet the most distinguishing aspect of this period was the restoration, by commercial banks, of its distressed debtors' creditworthiness. One example is the treatment of the Democratic Republic of Congo (formerly Zaire) in 1975–1976. Commercial banks accepted the Mobutu regime's refinancing proposals provided it reached an agreement with the IMF. The latter would end up arranging a standby

---

[106] Multilateral loans were driven by the activities not only of the World Bank but also of, among others, the Inter-American Development Bank and the Asian Development Bank (established in 1959 and 1966, respectively).

[107] Author calculations based on World Bank (1975, p. 91; 1983, p. 141).

[108] See www.clubdeparis.org.

credit line in return for strict control over the country's fiscal policy (Beim 1977, pp. 726–727).[109]

Commercial banks relied on the IMF to impose harsh conditions on sovereign borrowers, conditions that would presumably enhance their capacity to repay debts. This strategy was clearly expressed by Irving Friedman (Senior Vice President and Senior Adviser for International Operations at Citicorp, and former top officer at the IMF and the World Bank) in testimony to the US Senate in October 1977 (US Senate 1978, pp. 147–148). In fact, all the countries for which a bank debt restructuring or refinancing scheme was approved during 1978–1981 had already signed such an agreement with the IMF (see Dillon et al. 1985, p. 6; IMF various years).

Coordination between the IMF and private creditors strengthened as both increased their exposure to LDCs.[110] On the one hand, the banks' claims in non-oil-developing countries—though they were already a source of concern in 1977—grew by more than 20% annually during 1978–1981 (Brau et al. 1983, p. 5; see also Wallich 1981). On the other hand, the IMF liberalized existing loan facilities, and also established new ones, to support structural reforms and to compensate countries for the increase in oil prices and the volatility of food prices (Boughton 2001, pp. 705–733).

For example, the IMF supplementary financing facility of 1977 (a.k.a. the "Witteveen facility") was praised by some famous economists—for example, Fishlow (US Senate 1978, p. 61) and Von Neumann Whitman (1978)—who considered it a necessary "bailout of the international financial system." Yet when the sovereign debt crisis erupted in 1982, other experts (e.g., Vaubel 1983) blamed the IMF lending policy and regarded it as a source of moral hazard. However, the tight relationships between the Washington-based institution and private banks turned out to be essential when LDC debts had to be restructured.

2.3.6.3 The Debt Crisis of the 1980s and Its Resolution

The catalyst for the sovereign debt crisis was the August 1982 announcement by Mexican authorities of a moratorium on the repayment of its bank debt due in 1983. With an exposure to Mexico amounting to $25 billion—the highest among LDCs (Federal Financial Institutions Examination Council 1982)—US banks had reason to worry.

The IMF's Managing Director, Jacques de Larosière, affirmed in November 1982 that the Fund would commit to arranging a $1.2 billion facility for Mexico and that official creditors could lend $2 billion –provided the private sector would come up with complementary financing of $5 billion and consent to a debt restructuring

[109] See also Charles N. Stabler, "Zaire's Lenders Hope Accord to Restore Creditworthiness Will Be Model to Others," *Wall Street Journal*, 9 November 1976. The private creditors affected by the default organized themselves into an informal group called the London Club.

[110] Extensive meetings and exchanges of information between the IMF and commercial banks were also an important aspect of their cooperation (see Sgard 2016).

package. Despite some initial reluctance, US commercial banks accepted this "offer" after domestic regulators assured them that the fresh loans would be deemed "performing" (Mendelsohn 1983; Sgard 2016).

In fact, President Ronald Reagan and US regulators viewed the interests of Wall Street as converging with those of Washington (see Cohen 1986). More importantly, the US administration reckoned that a well-endowed IMF was a convenient option for supporting its banks (Cohen 1985); this reasoning paved the way to an IMF quota increase in 1983.

One should bear in mind that the Mexican crisis was resolved through a novel burden-sharing agreement based on informal rules, whereby each party (bilateral and multilateral official creditors, private financial institutions, and debtor countries) had an implicit veto right. This "ad hoc machinery" shaped many subsequent debt restructuring and refinancing packages (Dillon et al. 1985; Alvarez and Flores 2014; Sgard 2016). During 1983–1989, no fewer than 55 countries reached a debt restructuring deal with their foreign private creditors and/or the Paris Club.[111] An examination of just the bank debt restructurings reveals that $390 billion was involved. The total weighted average haircut exceeded 15%, accounting for nearly $60 billion. More than 90% of the total haircut was concentrated in ten countries: Mexico, Brazil, Argentina, Poland, Nigeria, Venezuela, the Philippines, Chile, South Africa, and Yugoslavia.[112]

However, collective action incentives started to wane in the mid-1980s. Confronted with an intrusive IMF conditionality—especially in the realm of fiscal policy (see Polak 1991, pp. 39–40)—and a severe recession in 1982–1983, several Latin American countries established the Cartagena Group in 1984. This debtors' cartel sought to coordinate negotiating positions and to reduce debt burden, but creditors viewed it as a threat (Central Intelligence Agency 1986). Hence, US commercial banks reacted by increasing their loan-loss reserves and securitizing part of their claims (Monteagudo 1994, pp. 62–73).[113] This "exit strategy" reflected that the percentage of debt restructuring agreements including previously restructured debt jumped from 0% in 1983 to 42% in 1985 and then to 58% in 1987.[114] The consensual approach set up during the Mexican debacle loosened in 1989 when the IMF gave up on its "no lending into arrears" doctrine (i.e., the IMF accepted lending to countries that were still in default to private creditors; Sgard 2016).

---

[111] Author calculation based on Cruces and Trebesch's (2013) database and www.clubdeparis.org.

[112] Author calculation based on Cruces and Trebesch's (2013) database.

[113] Securitization paved the way for implementation of the Brady deals in the 1990s (see Sect. 2.4.4.2).

[114] Author calculation based on Cruces and Trebesch's (2013) database.

2.3.6.4 Development of Sovereign Risk Assessment

This section begins by examining the sovereign risk analyses performed by major creditors: the World Bank, the US Exim Bank, and some commercial banks. It then focuses on related external indicators and academic research.

The World Bank

Following WWII, one of the first tasks of creditors was to gather data for the purpose of estimating the external debt of LDCs. As a result, the World Bank established the Debtor Reporting System (DRS) in 1951. Although it excluded short-term debt and remained dependent on the capacity and willingness of developing countries to report their debt data accurately, the DRS was instrumental in setting up the World Debt Tables.[115]

The World Bank played a pioneering role also in terms of credit risk assessment. This multilateral lender identified and assessed criteria believed to reflect the borrowing country's creditworthiness: its foreign exchange earnings (driven mainly by its exporting capacity), annual debt service, inflation rate, level of exchange reserves, and attitude toward creditors in the event of debt restructuring (IBRD 1960, pp. 4–7). World Bank economists also attended to the factors affecting a country's balance of payments and its capacity to service debt in the short and medium term; however, they did not point to a single indicator capable of predicting a sovereign default or restructuring (Avramovic et al. 1964, pp. 13–37, 85–94).

Because the proceeds of its loans were used for specific purposes, the World Bank was also required to implement project appraisals (IBRD 1960, pp. 12–22). The fundamental issue was that of assessing the "economic rate of return" on every project—that is, comparing "the measurable costs and benefits of the project to the economy as a whole" (King 1967, p. 6). The goals of such assessment were to limit substantial time delays and cost overruns. These project performance audits were conducted on a regular basis by the bank and enhanced economic returns (World Bank 1975, pp. 3–13; 1982, pp. 174–178). In fact, the institution's "senior status" convinced its own experts to place even greater emphasis on microeconomic risk analysis.[116]

[115] See https://datahelpdesk.worldbank.org/knowledgebase/articles/381934-what-is-the-external-debt-reporting-system-drs and World Bank (1985, p. ix).

[116] The defaulted debt owed to the World Bank was negligible until the mid-1980s. Thereafter, it increased but remained significantly lower than that owed to the IMF; see Beers and de Leon-Manlagnit's (2019) database.

The US Exim Bank

The US Exim Bank's lending policy was contingent on three criteria. First, the bank evaluated the borrower's status and its capacity to obtain preferential treatment—such as a state guarantee, a complementary state loan, subsidies, and/or tax concessions. Second, "self-liquidating" projects (i.e., those generating adequate foreign exchange) were prioritized. Third, the bank rated countries on a 4-notch scale.[117] The key determinants of the sovereign rating methodology were the global level of indebtedness, the risk of balance-of-payments problems, and the repayment performance of previous loans, especially Exim Bank loans (Feinberg 1982, pp. 69–82).

Nonetheless, the Exim Bank's risk assessment policy was extremely lax. In several annual reports, the bank stated that "because of the unpredictable nature of future economic and political conditions throughout the world, the risk of loss on Exim Bank's loans, guarantees, and insurance [was] not susceptible to accurate measurement" (Exim Bank 1969, p. 21). It is therefore not surprising that the share of outstanding loans classified as delinquent or rescheduled increased inexorably in the 1970s and exceeded 10% in 1981 (General Accounting Office 1982b, p. 6). The 1982 debt crisis undermined the Exim Bank's credibility and expedited its decline.

Commercial Banks

Starting in the mid-1970s, the increasing commitment of commercial banks to LDCs was mirrored in the more extensive use of the term "country risk" (see Sect. 1.2). A study investigating the country evaluation systems developed by 37 US banks exposed the rudimentary nature of those systems (Exim Bank 1976). For example, most of the surveyed banks did not back-test their country risk methodologies and used them primarily to set maximum exposure limits for each country. Smaller banks' foreign lending policies relied on analyses conducted by the World Bank, the IMF, the OECD, the Exim Bank, the US State Department, or such prominent institutions as Morgan Guaranty and Bank of America.[118]

During 1977–1979, top officers at Citicorp, First National Bank of Boston, Bank of Montreal, and Bank of America disclosed their country risk methodologies (see, respectively, Friedman 1977; Thornblade 1978; Nagy 1978; Wilson 1979). Their rating systems were unexpectedly dissimilar. The systems used by Citicorp and First National Bank of Boston relied on checklists, whereas those of the two other establishments were more sophisticated. Bank of Montreal estimated the likelihood of debt not being serviced as well as the loss that would be incurred; Bank of

---

[117] The rating system was discontinued in 1977 but resumed ten years later (Feinberg 1982, p. 46; "Ratings by Ex-Im Bank," *New York Times*, 9 March 1987).

[118] David R. Francis, "Banks Tighten Credit Ratings to Identify Overseas Risks," *New York Times*, 15 May 1977.

America used "analytical" ratings based on an economic stability index and an external debt servicing capacity index.[119]

In 1978, the three Federal bank regulatory agencies (the Office of the Comptroller of the Currency, the Federal Reserve Board, and the Federal Deposit Insurance Corporation) adopted a uniform examination procedure for evaluating country risk factors involved in international lending by US banks. In addition, this procedure limited the concentration of exposure to any individual country (Federal Reserve Bank of New York 1978). The system consisted of "identifying countries with actual or potential debt-servicing problems, calling loans to these countries to the attention of bank management in examination reports, and evaluating bank internal country exposure management systems" (General Accounting Office 1982a, p. i). Despite this new regulatory framework, banks' country risk methodologies failed to anticipate the sovereign debt crisis of 1982–1985.

External Indicators

Mounting concerns about the ability of major commercial banks to assess sovereign risk convinced two business magazines, *Institutional Investor* and *Euromoney*, to publish their own risk analyses and ratings in (respectively) September and October 1979. The paradox is that these supposedly external country risk ratings reflected bankers' own opinions and lending strategies.

The *Institutional Investor* ratings were based on a survey of 50 leading international banks and interviews with 40 bank executives. Bankers were asked to grade countries on a scale that ranged from 0 to 10, with 0 representing the least creditworthy countries.[120] *Euromoney* ratings were a function of the weighted average spread between the interest rate charged to a particular country and the London Interbank Borrowing Rate (LIBOR). Next, *Euromoney* divided borrowers into seven categories: the countries with the lowest weighted average spreads were awarded seven stars; those with the highest spreads, just one.[121] The *Institutional Investor* and *Euromoney* rating methodologies have been amended regularly and have gained influence since the 1980s (see Sects. 4.1.2 and 4.1.3).

Academic Research

The most significant progress in terms of sovereign risk analysis was driven by academic research. A vast set of studies were published in the 1970s. Their purpose was to measure the debt-servicing capacity of LDCs and then to identify the variables that could have enabled the anticipation of past debt restructurings. The statis-

---

[119] For complementary analyses, see Basagni (1981, pp. 81–94) and Heffernan (1986, pp. 66–72).

[120] *Institutional Investor*, September 1979, p. 243.

[121] *Euromoney*, October 1979, p. 130.

tical procedures used, which were much more sophisticated than those employed by major banks, included discriminant analysis (e.g., Frank and Cline 1971; Sargen 1977), principal components analysis (Dhonte 1975), logit models (Feder and Just 1977; Feder et al. 1981), and probit models (Kharas 1981). The ratio of debt service payments to exports was a key determinant of debt restructurings, yet also other indicators turned out to be significant: the GDP per capita, the inflation rate, and the ratios of external debt to exports and of reserves to imports.[122]

Some economists have offered alternative approaches to these empirical studies. For example, Aliber (1980) stresses the need to distinguish between liquidity and solvency risks. The persistent appreciation of a country's currency in real terms may signal liquidity problems, whereas a recession and a contraction of exports may lead to a solvency crisis in the medium term. Gasser and Roberts (1982) emphasize the "vulnerability indicator," which was based on imports of goods and services *plus* bank claims maturing within one year *less* international reserves, the result then weighted by exports of goods and services. Although this indicator was not intended to measure the probability of default or of debt restructuring, it did reflect sensitivity to unexpected shocks.

Research dealing with sovereign risk assessment evolved substantially after the Mexican debt crisis of 1982. The failure of private lenders to discriminate between good and bad borrowers naturally induced some practitioners and academics to compare sovereign risk analyses (see Haner and Ewing 1985; Heffernan 1986).

A second strand of literature proposed a rethinking of sovereign risk methodologies. Bird (1986) and Norel et al. (1988) argue that more attention should be given to structural economic features (e.g., terms of trade, productivity of capital, evolution of real exchange rates). In a different vein, Citron and Nickelsburg (1987) and Simon (1992) state that political risk does affect a country's creditworthiness.

A third set of articles investigated the determinants of *Euromoney* and *Institutional Investor* ratings. Feder and Uy (1985) show that the key explanatory variables are GNP per capita, average GDP, average rate of export growth, and the ratios of debt to GNP and of international reserves to imports. In a subsequent paper, Cosset and Roy (1991) conclude that there are three fundamental determinants of country risk ratings: GNP per capita, the propensity to invest, and the ratio of foreign debt to exports. Brewer and Rivoli (1990) find that the frequency of governmental regime change affects country creditworthiness more significantly than does armed conflict or political legitimacy indicators. These studies laid the groundwork for an extensive sovereign ratings literature, which flourished in the following decades (for an overview, see Gaillard 2011, p. 40).

[122] See McDonald (1982) and Heffernan (1986) for a complementary review of the literature. Kosmidou et al. (2008) present a more recent quantitative analysis of the methodologies designed to develop country risk assessment models.

2.4 The Globalization Years, 1991–2016

The collapse of the Soviet Union in 1991 marked the utter failure of planned economies. The spread of capitalism around the world boosted international trade and cross-border capital flows, enabling MNCs to thrive as never before. Yet fierce economic competition between nations, China's emergence, and the greater instability of financial markets have engendered new risks that jeopardize globalization.[123]

2.4.1 *A New Paradigm: Free-Market Capitalism*

The process of financial and trade globalization that shaped the 1991–2016 period was largely based on the free-market capitalist principles established by the Washington Consensus.[124] Implementation of those principles was facilitated by an extensive use of risk indicators.

2.4.1.1 The Washington Consensus

The term "Washington Consensus" was coined by economist John Williamson in 1989 and popularized the following year. Williamson (1990) identifies ten policy instruments designed to ensure macroeconomic stabilization and restore growth.[125] These ten points, which are akin to policy recommendations, are fiscal discipline, new public expenditure priorities, reform of the tax system, liberalization of interest rates, achievement of a competitive exchange rate, free trade, liberalization of "inward" FDI, privatization, deregulation, and enforcement of property rights.[126]

Fiscal discipline is considered necessary for countries that ran chronic fiscal deficits and defaulted on their external debt during 1982–1985. Public infrastructure, education, and health must be prioritized over the use of indiscriminate subsidies. An efficient tax system should combine a broad tax base with moderate marginal tax rates. Interest rates should be not only determined by market forces but also significantly higher than the inflation rate. The real exchange rate must be suffi-

[123] This section is deliberately abbreviated because many of the issues addressed here are developed in Chaps. 3, 4, and 5.

[124] *Globalization* refers to "the growing interdependence of the world's economies, cultures, and populations, brought about by cross-border trade in goods and services, technology, and flows of investment, people, and information" (see https://www.piie.com/microsites/globalization/what-is-globalization).

[125] The term "Washington" refers to the US Congress, the Federal Reserve Board, US economic agencies, and Washington-based international financial institutions and think tanks that agreed with Williamson's proposals.

[126] The Washington Consensus was not a "neoliberal" agenda because it did not advocate cutbacks in social welfare programs, deregulation of the financial sector, massive tax cuts, and so forth.

ciently competitive in order to boost exports, while trade policy should eliminate barriers to imports. Promoting inward FDI is indispensable for increasing capital, skills, and know-how. Privatization programs are based on the belief that private firms are managed more efficiently than state-owned enterprises. Deregulation aims to stimulate competition, and the enforcement of property rights is crucial to reassure foreign businesses.

The Washington Consensus was influenced by experiences of the IMF and the World Bank as well as by Balassa's works (e.g., Balassa et al. 1986). It draws from the lessons of different policies conducted by developing countries during the three previous decades, and it pronounces the export promotion model to be "superior."

Since the 1990s, the ability of emerging and developing economies to attract FDI and raise capital has depended, in large part, on their proficiency at implementing Williamson's recommendations. That proficiency has been tracked by an increasing number of indicators.

2.4.1.2 From Country Risk to Attractiveness Indicators

The globalization years featured the sophistication and refinement of existing country risk ratings and, more importantly, the creation of new indicators aimed at measuring a country's "attractiveness."

Since 1991, export credit agencies have expanded their activities beyond their home countries and offered a wider array of services. Thus they now collect extensive microeconomic data, recover unpaid receivables, offer policies to insure against many types of risks, and provide training, advisory services, and other tailored solutions.[127] In addition, these agencies have enhanced their country risk rating methodologies. For example, Credendo has established distinct rating systems to evaluate the risks affecting exporters and those affecting direct investors.[128] Coface assigns *country risk* ratings and *business environment* ratings; the former assesses "the average credit risk on a country's businesses" and the latter "the quality of a country's private sector governance."[129]

However, the preglobalization indicators that gained tremendous power in the 1990s are the credit ratings issued by Moody's and Standard & Poor's (S&P). The incorporation of ratings into financial regulatory rules transformed credit rating agencies (CRAs) into gatekeepers of capital markets (Sinclair 2005, pp. 42–46; Gaillard and Waibel 2018, pp. 1081–1094) and required that debt issuers always request a credit rating. For the 124 sovereign debt issuers that obtained their first

[127] According to group.atradius.com, www.coface.com, www.credendo.com, www.eulerhermes.com, www.ksure.or.kr, and www.sacesimest.it.

[128] www.credendo.com.

[129] www.coface.com.

rating from either these CRAs during 1991–2016,[130] fiscal discipline became the keystone of their economic policy (see Sect. 2.4.4).

It is noteworthy that the 1990s and 2000s saw the advent of two types of indicators to measure economic freedom and competitiveness. Both are the outcomes of the globalization process: They discard the concept of *country risk* and postulate that countries are now motivated to improve their *attractiveness* to investors.

Economic freedom indices were launched in 1994–1996 by two neoliberal think tanks, the Heritage Foundation and the Fraser Institute. Those organizations view economic freedom as a prerequisite for achieving growth and prosperity, and their indices are published on a yearly basis (see Sects. 5.1.4 and 5.1.5 for more details). Leading business newspapers (e.g., the *Wall Street Journal*) and several academic reviews (especially *Public Choice* and *The Independent Review*) played a major role in disseminating their ideas.[131]

Competitiveness indicators—which rate countries based on macroeconomic, microeconomic, social, and regulatory data—flourished in the 1990s and 2000s, aiming to support business executives and entrepreneurs in their international investment decisions. The most prominent studies on competitiveness are the World Economic Forum's *Global Competitiveness Report* and the World Bank's *Doing Business* report.

These two publications differ in both their methodologies and their objectives. The *Global Competitiveness Report* documents a country's ability to implement sound macroeconomic policies and to promote a stable, transparent, and innovative business environment (see Sect. 5.1.6). *Doing Business* takes a more corporate-oriented approach and discusses regulations that encourage (or constrain) business activity.

Such indicators are consistent with the Washington Consensus in the sense that they promote free-market capitalism, contribute to "discipline" emerging economies, and support the idea that all countries are involved in a global economic race and so can be presumed (if they are not, in fact, obliged) to be "pro-business." These "mechanisms of governance without government" (Sinclair 1994) are studied thoroughly in Chaps. 4 and 5.

2.4.2 *Financial Globalization: Opportunities and Dangers*

Financial globalization—defined as the increasing interconnectedness between growing cross-border capital flows—is a complex phenomenon. As pointed out by Prasad et al. (2003), it is contingent on "pull" and "push" factors. *Pull factors* include capital account liberalization, privatization programs, and policies designed to enhance a country's attractiveness; *push factors* include the macroeconomic envi-

[130] Author calculations based on Moody's and S&P's databases.

[131] Author analysis based on search.proquest.com and www.jstor.org.

ronment in top capital-exporting nations and the factors that may lead foreign firms to invest in (or disinvest from) a host country.

This section focuses on three drivers of financial globalization: financial liberalization (a pull factor), financial innovation (a push factor), and the Federal Reserve's accommodative monetary policy (another push factor). With financial liberalization, even a minor change in any pull or push factor will likely affect the quantity, source, and/or destination of cross-border capital flows. The volatility of those flows is exacerbated by contagion effects and, paradoxically, by certain financial techniques designed to protect against risk. Such instability is magnified by the abundant liquidity resulting from the Federal Reserve's policy.

2.4.2.1 Financial Liberalization, Capital Flows, and Crises

Financial liberalization was the dominant pattern of the 1990s. A brief look at Chinn and Ito's (2006) updated database shows that the top three economies in Latin America (i.e., Brazil, Mexico, and Argentina) and sub-Saharan Africa (i.e., South Africa, Nigeria, and Sudan) significantly increased their financial openness between 1990 and 2000.[132] In Europe and Asia, the top three economies underwent the same evolution (France, Italy, and China) or witnessed a stabilization of their openness (Germany, Japan, and India).

The dismantling of capital controls enabled emerging countries to absorb growing FDI and foreign portfolio equity and bond investments. However, the latter type of capital flows appears to have amplified procyclicality. During boom periods, they helped create asset "bubbles" (e.g., in housing and stock markets), fueled credit growth, and led to overvalued exchange rates. Any sign of overheating or of doubt concerning the short-term GDP growth could spark a confidence crisis, result in a sudden reversal in capital flows, trigger a banking and/or currency crisis, and depress economic activity (Kaminsky et al. 2003; Reinhart and Rogoff 2009). The greatest crises caused by massive capital flight affected Mexico in 1994–1995, Southeast Asia in 1997, Russia in 1998, Argentina in 2000–2001, Iceland in 2008, and Eastern Europe (especially Hungary, Latvia, and Lithuania) during 2008–2009.[133]

A central feature of financial liberalization was that it accelerated the propagation of crises. In addition to existing "monsoonal" effects and spillovers,[134] the phenomenon of financial liberalization gave rise to the threat of "pure contagion." Under this threat, a surge in risk aversion—one that is disconnected from macroeconomic fundamentals—may be self-fulfilling and trigger a crisis (Masson 1998).

---

[132] Economic size is based on 1990 gross domestic product.

[133] Most frequently, the magnitude of these crises obliged the IMF to intervene as lender of last resort (see Sect. 2.4.4.3).

[134] *Monsoonal* effects are caused by exogenous common shocks that affect several economies, whereas *spillovers* involve a shock—often in an emerging country—whose effects spread to interconnected and neighboring countries.

Volatility, pro-cyclicality, and contagion risks convinced economists and international investors to develop early warning systems that would facilitate the prediction of currency, banking, and financial crises (Kaminsky et al. 1997; Sollogoub 2001; Bussière and Fratzscher 2006; Frankel and Saravelos 2010). Empirical analyses conclude that an excessive appreciation of the real exchange rate and a low level of reserves are the most relevant indicators. The use of early warning systems reflects not only the need to anticipate sudden capital flow reversals but also the "short-termism" of some portfolio investors.

2.4.2.2 New Financial Instruments

The deep-rooted causes of financial innovation are traditionally located in tax systems and financial regulatory frameworks. The efforts deployed by businessmen to avoid or circumvent supposedly high taxes and detrimental regulatory rules have often incentivized some experts, such as financiers and lawyers, to devise new financial techniques (Miller 1986).[135]

However, the magnitude and pervasiveness of the financial innovation that started in the 1980s suggest that this process was much more than a set of ploys designed to exploit imperfections in the financial system. Instead, *during the first years of globalization*, financial innovation enabled the business community to expand its operations in a world economy crippled by major macroeconomic imbalances (see Sect. 2.3.3.4).

The inability of the Group of Seven (i.e., Canada, France, Germany, Italy, Japan, the United Kingdom, and the United States) and leading central banks to stabilize exchange rates, combined with the limited resources of export credit agencies to insure foreign ventures, paved the way for development of derivatives markets (forwards, swaps, and options). Thus, it became easier to hedge currency and interest rate exposures, which fostered international capital flows. Next, in the adverse context of the 1980s—characterized by the debt crisis of LDCs, the debacle of the savings and loan institutions, and the banking sector's excess capacity—securitization techniques helped US banks increase the marketability and liquidity of their assets. In sum, derivatives and securitized products helped free up banks' balance sheets, diversify revenue sources, and restore profitability.

Yet after more than 30 years of financial globalization, one must admit that the extraordinary variety of financial techniques failed to ensure efficient allocation of capital, reliable information transmission, and adequate risk management. Several abuses and dangers can be identified.

Financial instruments were frequently used for speculative purposes. For example, the development of "naked" credit default swaps (i.e., a swap in which the buyer does not own the underlying debt) worsened the 2008 financial debacle and

[135] The study of financial innovation is beyond the scope of this book, but the factors that drove the creation of new financial instruments—and led to their extensive use by international investors—certainly merit further examination.

the European sovereign debt crisis in 2009–2011 (see, respectively, Murdock 2013; Gaillard 2011, pp. 173–183, 2014a, pp. 220–223). Securitization fed opaque off–balance sheet activities and enabled risky firms to issue high-rated securities, thus misleading investors about their true credit position (Hill 1996; Gaillard and Harrington 2016). Note also that the widespread application of new computer technology to financial transactions since the 2000s (e.g., algorithmic trading) has magnified stratification in markets at the expense of smaller investors; it has also increased information asymmetry and encouraged short-termism (Mattli 2019).

The incommensurate size of the US financial sector (see Rethel and Sinclair 2012; Greenwood and Scharfstein 2013) transformed *liberal* capitalism into *finance* capitalism in the United States.[136] This shift concentrated risks on financial intermediaries and magnified cross-border contagion effects. A dramatic illustration was the US subprime crisis, which triggered a spectacular reversal of portfolio equity flows to low- and middle-income countries: from +$134 billion in 2007 to −$61 billion in 2008.[137] This episode evidenced the world economy's dependence on the US domestic business cycle. That dependence increased in response to the Federal Reserve's monetary policy.

2.4.2.3 An Accommodative US Monetary Policy

The financial globalization process intensified as a result of the policies implemented by major central banks, especially the Federal Reserve.

Under Alan Greenspan's tenure (1987–2006), the US central bank opted for persistently low Fed Funds rates in order to reduce business cycle volatility and to compensate for insufficient GDP growth. This "great moderation" was perpetuated and amplified by successor chairs Ben Bernanke and Janet Yellen who (respectively) launched and maintained quantitative easing[138] measures to counter the 2007–2009 recession and preserve the ongoing economic recovery.

The accommodative monetary policy resulted in US real interest rates being lower than the GDP growth rate during 1991–2016; they were even negative about half the time (see Fig. 2.1). This development encouraged excessive borrowing and leverage among US investors, which fed asset bubbles in the United States (Mian and Sufi 2014) as well as in emerging economies (Bhattarai et al. 2018).

The US federal government itself borrowed huge amounts: its total debt increased fivefold during 1991–2016. However, this increase was considered to be a balancing factor for the international financial system because it allowed Washington to con-

---

[136] In "finance" capitalism, the role and influence of financial institutions are so disproportionate that they tend to affect the interests of other economic sectors and taxpayers.

[137] These figures are based on the World Bank's World Development Indicators.

[138] *Quantitative easing* consists of purchasing government securities (and possibly other securities) in order to increase the money supply and to stimulate lending.

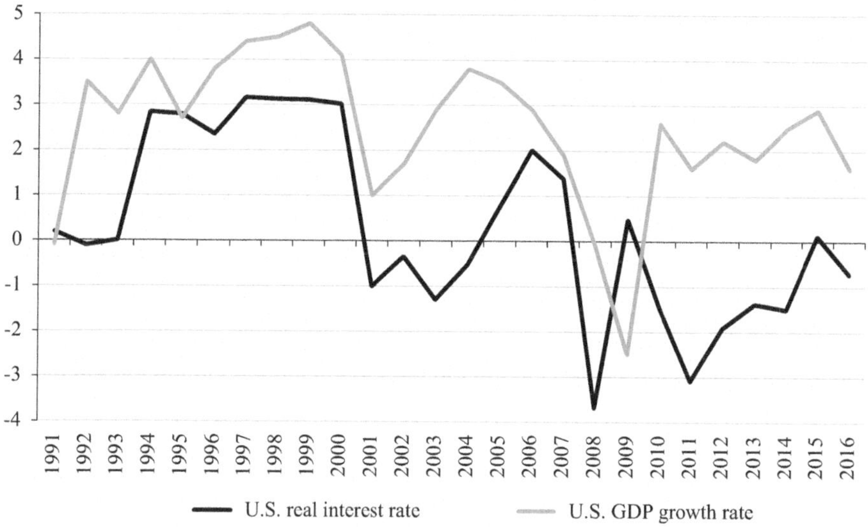

Fig. 2.1 US GDP growth rate and US real interest rate, 1991–2016. *Note*: The US real interest rate is calculated as the effective Federal Funds rate *minus* the growth rate of the consumer price index. *Source*: https://fred.stlouisfed.org

tinue ensuring the world economy's liquidity without jeopardizing the US dollar's status as primary reserve currency. This capacity to overcome the Triffin dilemma (see Sect. 2.3.3) was made possible because major exporters such as China and Japan sought to avert any appreciation in their national currency. Toward that end, these countries accumulated US assets—especially risk-free Treasury bonds. In return, the United States dramatically increased its volume of imports.[139]

The Federal Reserve's lax monetary policy was essential for the intensification of cross-border financial flows and the expansion of international trade,[140] but it bears some responsibility for the increasing speculation and financial instability since observed worldwide.[141]

[139] In 1991, Washington balanced its current account. Twenty-five years later, it posted a $452 billion deficit while Tokyo and Beijing reported an aggregated $383 billion surplus (World Bank's World Development Indicators).

[140] China adopted an accommodative monetary policy *following* the East Asian crisis but did not significantly raise its benchmark interest rate thereafter (Bell and Feng 2013, pp. 178–208). This new pattern's effects on financial globalization were limited owing to the Chinese economy's relatively small extent of financial openness.

[141] Crotty (2009) and Gaillard and Michalek (2019) show how the Federal Reserve and other US financial regulatory bodies failed to reduce risk taking and leverage among US investors.

2.4.3 *The Boom of the Chinese Economy*

The rise of China was certainly the biggest "game changer" of the globalization years. The reforms launched by Deng Xiaoping, embodied in the 1979 promulgation of the Joint Venture Law and in the establishment that same year of the China International Trust Investment Corporation (see, respectively, Richdale and Liu 1991, pp. 125–128; Collier 2017, pp. 74–77), led to four decades of sustained GDP growth—nearly 10% during 1979–2016—and propelled China to its position as the world's second-largest economy.

Beijing learned from the success of newly industrialized countries yet followed its own path. It attracted FDI, managed to obtain technology transfers, and moved up in the manufacturing value chain. In addition, Chinese authorities opted for financial repression measures in order to channel growing savings toward domestic firms and to facilitate the undervaluation of its currency. These policies yielded spectacular results: between 1991 and 2016, the share of China in world trade, inward FDI stock, and outward FDI stock rose by a factor of 9, 5, and 23, respectively (see Fig. 2.2).[142] The country is now a major capital exporter, and, for the first time ever, its outward FDI stock exceeded its inward FDI stock in 2016.

This emergence of "the Middle Kingdom" reshaped the world economy as well. Several structural trends can be observed. Chinese demand led to a boom in commodity markets during the 2000s (e.g., crude oil, aluminum, copper, iron ore, soybeans), which supported economic growth in emerging countries as well as in

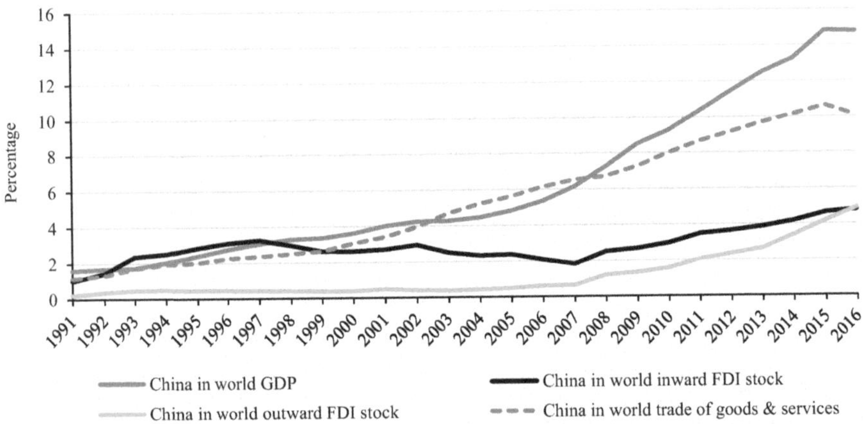

Fig. 2.2 China in the world, 1991–2016. *Source*: Author calculations based on https://unctad.org and the World Bank's World Development Indicators

[142]Author calculations based on https://unctad.org and the World Bank's World Development Indicators.

Australia and Canada (World Bank 2009, pp. 51–73; Roberts et al. 2016).[143] Moreover, China's capacity to produce and export a massive quantity of low-priced manufacturing goods had deflationary effects on the rest of the world; this dynamic has depressed the profitability of its foreign competitors and in some cases has led to their bankruptcy (Qiu and Zhan 2016, pp. 49–51).

The combination of these trends entails that emerging economies risk losing part of their industrial capabilities and also risk being confined to the production of agricultural and mining products. These downsides are a major challenge for countries seeking to diversify their economy (see Costa et al. 2016, who examine the case of Brazil).

Another aspect of China's success was the rapid ascent of its firms in the global value chain: some of them managed to upgrade their status from subcontractor (to Japanese, US, or European MNCs) to international leader in certain sectors. Lenovo and BYD are two examples. Lenovo was Hewlett-Packard's distributor in China in the 1990s before acquiring IBM's personal computer segment in 2005.[144] Established in 1995, BYD started out manufacturing rechargeable batteries but expanded its activities to become the world's third leading seller of plug-in electric vehicles in 2016—trailing only Tesla and Renault-Nissan.[145]

The Chinese growth model provided an alternative to *liberal* capitalism and thus restored the status of *state* capitalism in the eyes of some foreign policy makers. Beijing promoted this model and developed training programs for Asian and African officials (Kurlantzick 2016, pp. 108–114). However, such initiatives were limited by the failure of state capitalism in most countries (especially in Algeria, Argentina, Iran, and Venezuela).

2.4.4 A New Sovereign Debt Landscape

Three prominent changes affected international lending during the globalization era: the increasing debt accumulated by *developed* economies, the resumption of emerging sovereign bond markets, and the greater capacity of *private* creditors to cope with sovereign risk.

[143] See https://www.indexmundi.com/commodities.

[144] See "Legend in the Making," *The Economist*, 13 September 2001, and Sumner Lemon, "Lenovo Completes Purchase of IBM's PC Unit," *PC World*, 2 May 2005.

[145] See M. Gunther, "Warren Buffett Takes Charge," *CNN Money*, 13 April 2009 (available at https://money.cnn.com/2009/04/13/technology/gunther_electric.fortune), and J. Cobb, "China's BYD Becomes World's Third-Largest Plug-in Car Maker," *Hybrid Cars*, 7 November 2016 (available at https://www.hybridcars.com/chinas-byd-becomes-worlds-third-largest-plug-in-car-maker).

2.4.4.1 Growing Concerns About High-Income Countries' Public Debt

The general government debt of the Group of Seven rose by 6% annually during 1991–2016.[146] This debt burden became a source of concern among business circles and was reflected in sovereign ratings. In January 1991, the seven economies were assigned the top rating (Aaa) by Moody's. Twenty-six years later, four of them (France, Italy, Japan, and the United Kingdom) had a lower credit rating. In the case of Italy, the magnitude of the downgrade reached 8 notches.

The vulnerability of some high-income countries became evident during the 2008 financial crisis and the European sovereign debt crisis. The financial and economic difficulties experienced in Cyprus, Greece, Iceland, Ireland, Portugal, and Spain necessitated intervention by the IMF and the creation of ad hoc mechanisms in the European Union (viz., the European Financial Stabilisation Mechanism, the European Financial Stability Facility, and the European Stability Mechanism)[147] to support and bail out these governments or their respective banking systems.

Economic history teaches that even some high-income countries have defaulted on their sovereign debt. However, such episodes were usually driven by political upheaval and not, as during the European debt crisis, by economic disruption (Gaillard 2014d).

Several factors can be posited to explain the weakened credit position of some high-income countries. First, the accommodative monetary policies of many OECD economies fed asset bubbles and kept "zombie" firms alive, thus misallocating capital and hampering economic performance (Banerjee and Hofmann 2018). Second, financial and banking crises obliged most governments to guarantee or bail out failing firms and banks to avert a systemic crisis. Such interventions crippled public authorities with contingent liabilities (Gaillard 2017). Third, southern European governments proved unable to reform their costly and inefficient welfare states (Hemerijck 2013). Fourth, eurozone membership depressed economic activity in countries that had traditionally relied on currency depreciation to boost their exports and preserve their domestic industry; examples include Greece, Italy, Portugal, Spain, and (to a lesser extent) France.[148]

Now more than ever, creditors must pay attention to the sustainability of public debt in rich countries and scrutinize their debt ratios. The decision by the Institute of International Finance (IIF) to launch its *Quarterly Global Debt Monitor* in 2015—in response to growing demand from IIF members—reflected the increased riskiness of public debt in both emerging and developed economies.[149]

---

[146] Author calculations based on https://www.imf.org/external/datamapper/datasets.

[147] For an exhaustive analysis of the EU's financial mechanisms, see Bianco (2015).

[148] Greece is a dramatic illustration. Prior to its joining the eurozone in 2001, the drachma had depreciated by some 14% annually against the Deutsche mark during 1973–1994 (author computation based on Frieden 2015, p. 154).

[149] Established in 1983, the IIF is one of the financial industry's leading associations. "Its mission is to support the financial industry in the prudent management of risks; to develop sound industry practices; and to advocate for regulatory, financial and economic policies that are in the broad

2.4.4.2 Resumption of Markets for Sovereign Bonds of Emerging Economies

A remarkable feature of the globalization era was the enhanced credit position of many emerging economies. This development is perhaps best captured by the modest growth of external debt. During 1991–2016, the public and public-guaranteed external debt of 34 major emerging countries increased (on average) by 4% annually.[150] This rate was much lower than that observed during the 1960s and 1970s (see Sect. 2.3.6).

This positive evolution was driven by the relative efficiency of the macroeconomic policies implemented in these economies. Measures designed to increase domestic savings, attract FDI, boost exports, and curb inflation enabled reductions in payments imbalances and mitigated the problem of "international original sin" (Eichengreen et al. 2005).[151]

Figure 2.3 plots the composition of public and public-guaranteed external debt. After accounting for almost a third of lending to emerging economies in the 1990s, bilateral loans saw their share decline dramatically during the subsequent two decades. In the meantime, the percentage of multilateral loans stabilized. Yet the most prominent development was the resumption of sovereign bond markets. During 1991–2016, the volume of bonds issued by major low- and middle-income governments increased by a factor of 11 and their share in total public external debt quadrupled.[152]

The boom in sovereign bond markets can trace its roots to the financial disintermediation of the 1980s, but it was catalyzed by the Brady Plan. This initiative—which was launched in 1989 and amounted to transforming commercial bank loans into bonds (see Vásquez 1996)—resolved the public debt crisis and encouraged an increasing number of emerging countries to tap capital markets. The growth of foreign government bond markets was accompanied by development of a new "business ecosystem" (Buckley 1997, 2006).

The most prominent feature of this trend was the inordinate power of credit rating agencies. Ever since credit ratings were incorporated into regulatory rules and

---

interests of its members and foster global financial stability and sustainable economic growth" (https://www.iif.com/about-us).

[150] Author calculation based on the World Bank's World Development Indicators. The countries under consideration are the low- and middle-income economies whose total public and public-guaranteed external debt exceeded $10 billion (US) in 2016. Six countries are excluded because of insufficient data for 1991. The 34 countries included in this data set are: Angola, Bangladesh, Brazil, Bulgaria, China, Colombia, Costa Rica, the Dominican Republic, Ecuador, Egypt, Ethiopia, Ghana, India, Indonesia, Jordan, Kenya, Lebanon, Mexico, Morocco, Myanmar, Nigeria, Pakistan, Peru, the Philippines, Romania, Russia, Sri Lanka, Sudan, Tanzania, Thailand, Tunisia, Turkey, Venezuela, and Vietnam.

[151] For example, the so-called BRIC countries (Brazil, Russia, India, and China) were especially successful in cutting the share of their public debt denominated in foreign currency or indexed to a foreign currency.

[152] Author calculations based on the World Bank's World Development Indicators.

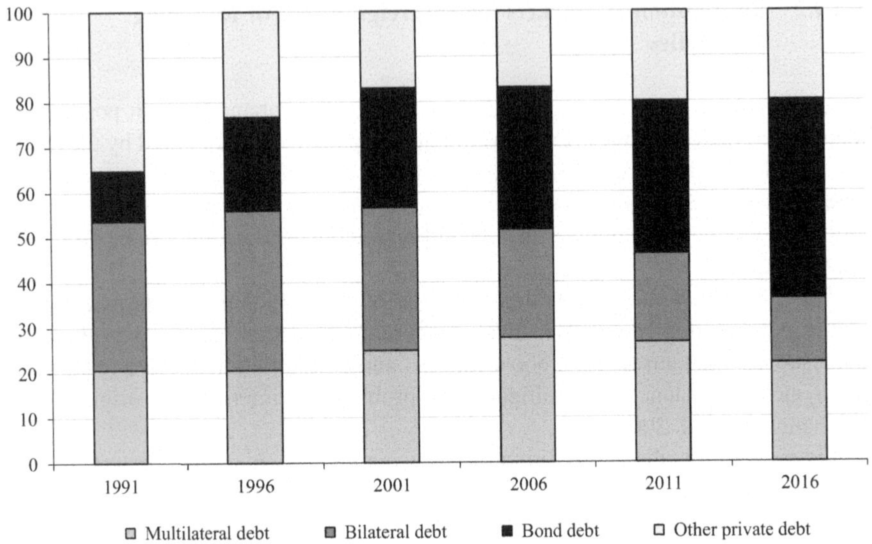

Fig. 2.3 Composition of public and public-guaranteed external debt, 1991–2016. *Notes*: The data set's 40 countries have low- and middle-income economies whose total public and public-guaranteed external debt exceeded $10 billion (US) in 2016. Those countries are Angola, Azerbaijan, Bangladesh, Belarus, Brazil, Bulgaria, China, Colombia, Costa Rica, the Dominican Republic, Ecuador, Egypt, Ethiopia, Ghana, India, Indonesia, Jordan, Kazakhstan, Kenya, Lebanon, Mexico, Morocco, Myanmar, Nigeria, Pakistan, Peru, the Philippines, Romania, Russia, Serbia, South Africa, Sri Lanka, Sudan, Tanzania, Thailand, Tunisia, Turkey, Ukraine, Venezuela, and Vietnam. The data set for 1991 *excludes* Azerbaijan, Belarus, Kazakhstan, Serbia, South Africa, and Ukraine because of insufficient data. *Source*: Author calculations based on World Bank's World Development Indicators.

investors' prudential guidelines, bond issuers have been obliged to obtain a rating—and the higher, the better. Higher ratings corresponded to greater investor confidence and lower borrowing costs. Credit ratings are lagging indicators, not leading indicators (Gaillard 2011, pp. 175–183; 2014b; Nye 2014, pp. 39–40). Yet a downgrade, a review for possible downgrade, or a negative outlook is likely to exacerbate risk aversion and trigger sell-offs.[153]

It is noteworthy that S&P and Moody's methodologies compel borrowers to remain solvent on their bond debt: Any missed payment or (even minor) debt restructuring is considered a sovereign default and results in a downgrade to the bottom of the rating scale. In addition, CRAs frequently use the FC sovereign rating as the ceiling for FC ratings of other debt issuers domiciled within that country;

[153] The pro-cyclical effects of rating downgrades were obvious in November–December 1997 during the East Asian crisis (Ferri et al. 1999) and between December 2009 and April 2010 during the Greek debt crisis (Gaillard 2011, pp. 173–185). Sinclair (2005, pp. 160–167) analyzes how the East Asian crisis undermined the CRAs' legitimacy.

hence, a reduction in the former rating leads to downgrading the latter.[154] This policy—which aims to account for the risk of a government restricting access to foreign exchange—highlights the importance of sovereign ratings for *all* borrowers.

Major financial institutions took advantage of this propitious environment to expand their operations in emerging financial markets. An illustrative example is that of JP Morgan. In 1991, the New York–based bank created a special "emerging markets" group to provide an array of services to these economies (JP Morgan 1992). Later, it launched a series of indices that track foreign currency–denominated bonds—the Emerging Markets Bond Index (EMBI), the EMBI+, and the EMBI Global—as well as local currency–denominated debt instruments (JP Morgan 1995, 1996, 1999). More importantly, JP Morgan was the most active underwriter of emerging government bond issues during 1993–2007 (Flandreau et al. 2009).

Another group of organizations gained ground during the globalization: bondholders' associations.[155] In addition to the IIF and the International Securities Market Association (ISMA, established in 1969), new organizations—such as the Emerging Markets Traders Association (EMTA) and the Emerging Markets Creditors Association (EMCA)—were set up to monitor sovereign bond market activity and to promote creditors' rights (see EMTA 2015). The IIF is certainly the most influential among these associations; its members include investment and commercial banks, insurance companies, sovereign wealth funds, asset management firms, hedge funds, and central banks.

2.4.4.3 Coping with Sovereign Risk

Both the number and the percentage of countries in default reached record highs during the globalization years. In 1994, 114 sovereign debtors—accounting for 54% of all countries in the world—had failed to repay debt to their public or private creditors. This figure fell 10 percentage points by 2016, but it remained higher than any year during 1960–1981.[156] Yet unlike what occurred in the 1930s and 1980s, no massive wave of sovereign bond or bank defaults was observed during 1991–2016. The explanation for this paradox involves (a) official creditors and China agreeing to restructure more sovereign debts and (b) private creditors managing to cut their losses by exploiting the new international financial architecture and a more secure legal environment.

---

[154] Increased financial globalization prompted Moody's and S&P to relax their policy on this matter in the 2000s. In 2011, however, very few debt issuers were assigned a FC rating higher than that of their government (see S&P 2011).

[155] The Council of the Corporation of Foreign Bondholders (arguably the most important association of bondholders in history) was liquidated in 1988, a few months prior to the resumption of sovereign bond markets.

[156] See Beers and de Leon-Manlagnit's (2019) database.

How Official Creditors and China Absorbed Losses

In 1996, the international financial community launched the Heavily Indebted Poor Country (HIPC) Initiative in order to reduce the external debt of low-income economies. The Paris Club—as well as multilateral, non–Paris Club official bilateral, and private commercial creditors—all participated in this program. The initiative's eligibility criteria required that candidate countries have an unsustainable debt burden (even after obtaining traditional debt relief); a track record of sound policies through IMF- and World Bank–supported programs; cleared any arrears with the IMF, the World Bank, and the African Development Bank (AfDB); and prepared a credible "poverty reduction strategy" (see IMF 2019, pp. 7–8).

In 2005, the Multilateral Debt Relief Initiative (MDRI) complemented the HIPC Initiative.[157] Under the MDRI, several agencies—including the IMF, the International Development Association (IDA),[158] the African Development Fund (AfDF), and later the Inter-American Development Bank (IaDB)—committed to alleviating the debt burden of low-income economies. By the end of 2017, the total costs of debt relief to creditors under the HIPC Initiative and the MDRI were estimated at $76 billion and $43 billion, respectively (IMF 2019, pp. 12–14).

In addition to these specific programs, the Paris Club continued to reschedule and cancel the external debt of low- and middle-income economies. For all types of treatments, the Paris Club signed 248 agreements involving 79 countries during 1991–2016.[159]

The high proportion of defaulting sovereign debt issuers in the 1991–2016 period was driven also by the many debt restructurings and write-offs negotiated by China and its state-owned banks, especially since 2000 (Horn et al. 2019, pp. 30–32). This pattern reflects both the weak credit rating system used by Beijing and the poor credit position of its debtors (Gaillard 2016)—an interpretation supported by the massive defaults in 2016 of Angola, Cuba, and Venezuela on their debt to China.[160]

How Private Creditors Limited Losses

Several of the sovereign debt crises that arose during 1991–2016 involved major, "systemic" economies. In the context of financial globalization, these shocks threatened not only private creditors but also the international financial community as a whole. In order to prevent a systemic crisis, policy makers instigated a new international financial architecture that proved to be a boon for private creditors.

[157] See https://www.imf.org/external/np/exr/facts/mdri.htm.

[158] A member of the World Bank Group, the IDA lends money on concessional terms to the world's poorest countries.

[159] See www.clubdeparis.org.

[160] See Beers and de Leon-Manlagnit's (2019) database.

This new architecture was shaped around the IMF. It became manifest in 1994 when that Washington-based institution—supported by the US Treasury, the World Bank, and the IaDB—intervened to stop capital outflows from Mexico, thereby preventing a default and, quite possibly, a serious international financial crisis (Camdessus 1995).[161] These same players were at work in 1997 to resolve the East Asian crisis.[162] The total last-resort lending for these two rescue packages reached $117 billion (Kindleberger and Aliber 2005, p. 271). In the following years, other bailouts were secured for major emerging countries (e.g., Brazil, Colombia, and Turkey) so that they could remain solvent.

These last-resort loan interventions reduced the number of governments in default on their bond debt[163] and cut the percentage of distressed debt owed to private creditors (i.e., among the total sovereign debt in default) from 65% in 1992 to 22% in 2011.[164] Nonetheless, IMF economists admitted that such bailouts were likely to encourage both debtor and creditor moral hazard. *Debtor* moral hazard was identified in the loans to Argentina in 2000–2001 (Jeanne and Zettelmeyer 2005, pp. 79–80), and *creditor* moral hazard seems to account for the massive private capital inflows to Russia before its bankruptcy in 1998 (Mussa 1999, pp. 228–229).

The IMF conditionality required that distressed countries accept restrictions minimizing the problems associated with debtor moral hazard. However, a side effect of both financial globalization and the new international financial architecture is that creditor moral hazard remains a fundamental challenge for policy makers.

Another factor that strengthened creditors' position was the enhanced legal and contractual protection of their rights. Thus, for example, the Foreign Sovereign Immunities Act of 1976 and the US Supreme Court's statement that the issuance of debt was a commercial act (see *Republic of Argentina v. Weltover*, 1992) virtually consecrated the restrictive theory of sovereign immunity. This new paradigm spurred the insertion of clauses favorable to creditors in sovereign bond contracts. So starting in the 1990s, contracts were more likely to include a waiver of the sovereign's immunity from suit and execution. Other clauses (e.g., "consent to jurisdiction" and governing law clauses) were inserted to facilitate the enforcement of sovereign debt contracts (Choi et al. 2012; Weidemaier 2014).

Such enforcement became uncertain when creditors doubted their status or disagreed over how best to cope with a distressed sovereign debtor. The fear of legal subordination in favor of another creditor led to a proliferation of *pari passu* clauses (see Buchheit and Pam 2004; Cohen 2011). By the same token, the need to expedite

---

[161] Michel Camdessus (2014, p. 309), then Managing Director of the IMF, reports that Stanley Fischer (then First Deputy Managing Director) feared the Mexican crisis endangered Western civilization.

[162] The Asian Development Bank replaced the IaDB in resolving the East Asian crisis.

[163] Only 29 countries lapsed into default on their FC bond debt during 1991–2016; some of them defaulted several times (author calculations based on the database of Beers and de Leon-Manlagnit 2019).

[164] Author calculations based on Beers and de Leon-Manlagnit's (2019) database.

debt restructuring deals favored the insertion of so-called collective action clauses (e.g., collective modification provisions and collective acceleration provisions).

Despite these protections, bondholders have suffered some setbacks in the recent years. For instance, they were forced to accept haircuts exceeding 50% after the debt restructurings of Argentina and Greece in 2005 and 2012, respectively (Gaillard 2014c, pp. x, 11). Bondholders have also encountered some coordination problems. The successful strategies followed by certain holdout creditors (e.g., the lawsuits brought by Elliott Management against Argentina) suggest that a creditor's most dangerous opponent might well be another creditor.[165]

2.4.5 *The New World Economy: Between Interdependence and Competition*

Globalization contributed to blur the lines between exporters and foreign direct investors as well as between capital-exporting and capital-importing nations. At the same time, it accelerated the transformation of capitalism and generated a new set of risks.

2.4.5.1 The New Dynamics of Free Trade and FDI

International trade went through unexpected and paradoxical changes during the globalization era. Multilateralism waned, but the process of trade liberalization continued. For instance, the average tariff rate for the Group of Twenty (G20) fell from 13% during 1991–1994 to 5% during 2013–2016.[166] How can this evolution be explained?

After the General Agreement on Tariffs and Trade was superseded by the World Trade Organization (WTO) in 1995, several challenges arose that rendered multilateral trade talks increasingly complex and lengthy (Baldwin 2016a; Jean 2019). First, under the WTO regime, tariff rates and market-opening commitments are binding, which deters members from further liberalizing their trade policy. Second, the WTO's admission of China in 2001 stirred mistrust among other WTO members, whatever their income level. Third, as industrialized countries had reduced their tariffs substantially during the previous GATT rounds, they had little maneu-

[165] It is worth mentioning that *commercial* creditors also sued sovereign debtors, including HIPCs (see IMF 2019, p. 51). For a study of litigation against defaulting sovereigns, see Schumacher et al. (2015).

[166] Author calculations based on the World Bank's World Development Indicators. The G20 comprises Argentina, Australia, Brazil, Canada, China, the European Union, France, Germany, India, Indonesia, Italy, Japan, Mexico, Russia, Saudi Arabia, South Africa, South Korea, Turkey, the United Kingdom, and the United States. It accounted for more than 80% of merchandise trade in 2016 (author calculation based on https://data.wto.org).

vering room left to obtain trade liberalization in emerging countries—with regard to financial services, for example. Fourth, the sustained growth of international trade in the 1990s and 2000s called into question the relevance of new multilateral talks.

In this context, it is not surprising that the Doha Round, launched in 2001, failed to achieve any trade liberalization agreements (see Cohn 2007). However, some minor progress was observed with the Nairobi Package of 2015, which removed subsidies for farm exports.[167] In fact, other means were employed to effect trade liberalization during 1991–2016: unilateral actions, regional trade agreements (RTAs), and international investment agreements (IIAs).

Unilateral tariff cuts by several emerging countries (e.g., China, India, and Indonesia) were part of offshoring-led development strategies designed to attract foreign investments. These countries' final objectives were to integrate themselves into global value chains, absorb knowledge and technologies, and export an even wider range of products and services.

The signing of RTAs was another feature of globalization. The number of RTAs in force rose by a factor of 5 within 25 years.[168] However, the nature of those agreements changed significantly during that time span. Contrary to what was observed at the dawn of globalization, the bulk of RTAs signed in the 2010s were "deep" agreements. Thus, they transcend traditional tariff cuts to cover multiple policy areas: competition policy, antidumping measures, environmental laws, labor market regulations, and so forth (see Mattoo et al. 2017).

The boom in IIAs was certainly the most salient feature of the past three decades. These agreements, which include treaties with investment provisions (TIPs) and bilateral investment treaties (BITs), have contributed to reshaping international business relations and increasing the levels of protection enjoyed by foreign investors. A typical IIA's main provisions include protection against expropriation risk, convertibility risk, and arbitrary or discriminatory measures; they may also ensure "protection and security", and/or "most favored nation" treatment.[169]

These new trends in international investment rule-making merit comment. First, they reflect the outright triumph of globalization. Second, they enabled developing countries to gain credibility. Vashchilko (2011) shows that risky economies that signed BITs managed thereby to reassure international investors, which stimulated FDI inflows. Third, the growing proportion of BITs involving exclusively low- and middle-income countries evidenced the ongoing enlargement of the group of capital-exporting nations.[170] Such evolution went hand in hand with the mutation of capitalism.

---

[167] See https://www.wto.org/english/news_e/news15_e/mc10_19dec15_e.htm.

[168] See https://www.worldbank.org/en/topic/regional-integration/brief/regional-trade-agreements.

[169] The "protection and security" provisions require that host countries take measures to prevent the destruction of an investor's property.

[170] About 33% of the BITs that entered into force during 2016 did not involve a high-income economy, compared with less than 12% in 1991 (see https://investmentpolicy.unctad.org/international-investment-agreements/advanced-search).

2.4.5.2 Untrammeled Capitalism

The transformation of international, liberal capitalism into what I call "untrammeled capitalism" was a complex and incremental process. This transformation was driven by five sets of factors.

1. The first group includes all the factors that contributed to enhance the capacity of countries, especially emerging and developing ones, to host FDI. Once communism collapsed, governments worldwide had little choice but to integrate themselves into the world economy. Beyond the Washington Consensus, which offered some macroeconomic guidelines (see Sect. 2.4.1.1), it was necessary for low- and middle-income nations to identify and explore their competitive advantages (Porter 1990). Doing so would increase their attractiveness to investors.
2. Adequate specialization and enhanced attractiveness, combined with the information and communication technology (ICT) revolution of the 1990s, catalyzed what Baldwin (2016b) refers to as the "second unbundling".[171] This phenomenon consists of offshoring some production stages to economies that offer decisive advantages to foreign investors. These advantages include a low-cost workforce, proficient engineers, experience in business process outsourcing, government support for the ICT sector, and favorable tax and regulation systems. Offshoring enabled many emerging countries to boost their FDI inflows,[172] and it led to a new international division of labor (UNCTAD 2004, pp. xxiv–xxv).

   This new international division of labor mirrored much more than a world economy in which developed countries produce goods and services with higher value added while developing countries specialize in labor-intensive activities. In particular, the division was also the result of value chains being extensively reorganized by multinational firms.
3. The reorganization of value chains, which Gerlach (1992) and Dunning (1995) label "alliance capitalism," casts transborder activities as being "increasingly affected by the collaborative production and transactional arrangements between firms" (Dunning 1995, p. 462). Cooperative strategies may take various forms, from wholly owned foreign affiliates and joint ventures to licensing, franchising, and contractual alliances (Dunning and Lundan 2008, pp. 260–262). The major goals of such strategies are to cut costs, incorporate new technologies, upgrade manufacturing methods, and improve R&D performance.

   Japanese MNCs pioneered these types of interfirm alliances and networks (see Gerlach 1992). Mitsubishi Corporation is an illustration. Its 1991 annual report listed its foreign partners in different sectors; its 2015 annual report went further and included statements by some of its key partners (Mitsubishi Corporation 1991, pp. 14–21; 2015, pp. 51–75).

---

[171] The "first unbundling" was the separation of production and consumption locations that occurred in the nineteenth century.

[172] *A. T. Kearney Global Services Location* indices show that India, China, and Malaysia were the top three beneficiaries of offshoring strategies during 2004–2016 (A. T. Kearney 2004, 2016).

The spread of this alliance capitalism pattern made value chains global, which amplified the interdependence not only of participating firms but also of their contractors and subcontractors. In addition, it helped expand the international presence of MNCs. For example, the average Transnationality Index (TNI) for the world's top 100 nonfinancial MNCs rose from 55% in 1996 to 66% in 2016.[173]

4. The participation in global value chains and the increasing internationalization of MNCs were not limited to firms located in traditional capital-exporting countries. Starting in the 1990s, emerging economies globalized their businesses as well—with a remarkable surge in MNCs. The number of emerging countries hosting the world's top 100 nonfinancial MNCs increased from two in 1996 to ten in 2016. The average TNI of these ten mega-firms (CK Hutchison Holdings Ltd., Hon Hai Precision Industries, CNOOC, Teva Pharmaceutical Industries Ltd., Samsung Electronics, Broadcom Ltd., Petronas, China COSCO Shipping Corp. Ltd., Vale SA, and América Móvil) was comparable to that of other leading MNCs.[174]
5. The fifth feature of untrammeled capitalism is the trend of multinational firms registering outside their home country—usually in a tax haven (e.g., the Cayman Islands) or a territory offering a favorable tax regime (e.g., Luxembourg). These strategies were designed to enhance profitability, and they convinced some countries (e.g., Ireland) to engage in "tax-dumping" policies (Hira et al. 2019).

The advent and development of untrammeled capitalism revealed that MNCs were able to offshore most of their business segments and support functions.

2.4.5.3 Country Risk During to the Globalization Era

Three categories of risks are examined here: the "traditional" but "manageable" risks; the "traditional" but growing risks, especially creeping protectionism; and a new type of threat inherent to untrammeled capitalism.

1. International investors managed to cope with some traditional risks simply because such risks materialized much less frequently than during the Cold War. Expropriation and convertibility risks are two examples. The collapse of the Soviet Union considerably reduced the likelihood that a government might shift to a socialist economic policy and expropriate foreign holdings. The few countries that followed this path (e.g., Bolivia, Ecuador, and Venezuela) accounted for most of the expropriation cases (see Sect. 3.3.1). By the same token, emerging countries were much more reluctant to implement capital controls. The imposi-

[173] This ranking is based on the total value of foreign assets. The TNI is calculated as the average of the following three ratios: foreign assets to total assets, foreign sales to total sales, and foreign employment to total employment; author calculations based on UNCTAD (1998, pp. 36–38) and https://unctad.org.

[174] Author calculations based on UNCTAD (1998, pp. 36–38) and https://unctad.org.

tion of nonconvertibility was most often a desperate measure driven by an economic or political crisis, as observed in Argentina, Iceland, and Cyprus in 2001, 2008, and 2012, respectively (see Sects. 3.4.1.1 and 5.2.7).

Next, some traditional risks were controlled by the increased ability of investors to insure against them. Political risk was mitigated through the guarantees or insurance contracts provided by an increasing number of institutions (see MIGA 2014): export credit agencies, insurance companies, MIGA, and OPIC. During 1992–2016, 62% of OPIC's insurance claim settlements arose from damages caused by episodes of political violence (OPIC 2017). The countries involved were Afghanistan, Chad, the Central African Republic, Colombia, the Dominican Republic, the Democratic Republic of Congo, Ethiopia, Haiti, Liberia, Mali, Rwanda, Sierra Leone, South Sudan, Yemen, the former Yugoslavia, and Zambia. Note also that derivative financial instruments enabled international investors to hedge risks stemming from foreign currencies, interest rates, and commodity prices.

Foreign currency and interest rate risks were a major concern among all MNCs. For example, the Indian rupee, the Brazilian real, and the Russian ruble fell by (respectively) 47%, 69%, and 91% against the US dollar between January 1997 and December 2016.[175] Because these depreciations were concentrated in specific periods (1997–1998, 2008, and 2012–2013 for India; 1998–1999, 2001–2002, 2008, and 2014–2015 for Brazil; 1998–1999 and 2014–2015 for Russia), they required that domestic central banks hastily tighten their monetary policy; this dynamic made financing abroad even more difficult.

Meanwhile, the extensively fluctuating exchange rates of *major* currencies remained a serious impediment to international business, as it was in the 1970s and 1980s (for an analysis of the global monetary disorder, see Cohen 2013). Hence hedging became indispensable for most MNCs (for an illustration of the extensive use of hedging techniques in the commercial airplane industry, see Airbus 2017, p. 16; Boeing 2017, p. 98).

Commodity price volatility was especially challenging for oil and mining companies and manufacturing firms. Chevron (1999, p. 27) and Glencore (2017, p. 182) indicate that they hedged against commodity price risk when, respectively, the price of crude oil reached record lows in 1998–1999 and the price of copper and nickel plunged between 2014 and 2016. Manufacturing firms behaved likewise when seeking to offset the commodity price boom of the 2000s (see e.g. Reliance 2007, p. 160; Ford Motor Company 2008, p. 50).

2. A growing risk for exporters and foreign direct investors was the development of "creeping protectionism." This trend, already underway in the 1980s, has accelerated since then.

---

[175] Author calculations based on the Pacific Exchange Rate Service; available at http://fx.sauder.ubc.ca.

During 2009–2016, more than 56% of the new protectionist measures took the form of nontariff barriers.[176] Such NTBs include subsidies (e.g., financial grants, state loans, bailouts, loan guarantees, production subsidies, and tax or social insurance relief), import controls (e.g., quotas and licensing requirements), export controls (e.g., export subsidies and trade finance), public procurement policies, localization measures, capital controls, and currency depreciation. Nontariff barriers were rife in the United States, India, and Russia; the sectors most affected were electric energy, domestic appliances, and products of iron or steel (Bertelsmann Stiftung 2017).

By discriminating against foreigners, NTBs distort competition and unravel what the WTO, BITs, and TIPs had previously accomplished. The surge in NTBs nurtured trade defense measures and more than doubled the number of disputes brought to the WTO from 239 cases during 1970–1994 (under the GATT system) to 518 during 1995–2016. Moreover, the number of investment disputes settled by the ICSID increased dramatically—from 26 during 1967–1991 to 584 during 1992–2016.[177]

In this neo-mercantilist environment, MNCs need the support of their home country as well as a top-flight legal department to counter the anti-business practices implemented by importing and host countries. However, such safeguards may not be effective for investors in the world's two largest economies: the United States and China.

In China, both the low-interest loans granted to strategic MNCs and the transformation of state companies into "weapons of trade policy" are extremely detrimental to the interest of foreign firms (Kurlantzick 2016, pp. 89–91, 203–204). And the negative real interest rates prevailing in the United States unfairly advantage US companies, especially the largest ones. Furthermore, US courts play a relatively active economic role. For instance, prosecutors generally compromise with domestic firms, which pay far smaller fines (on average) than do their foreign competitors (Garrett 2014, pp. 218–249).

The protectionist policies followed by the two economic superpowers extend beyond NTB measures and include such heterodox macroeconomic measures as financial repression. This tendency suggests that free-market capitalism might be waning. Instead, the world economy may reach the apex of what Luttwak (1990, p. 19) calls *geo-economics*, or "the admixture of the logic of conflict with the methods of commerce."

3. The third category of threats includes all the risks inherent to untrammeled capitalism. Most of them are microeconomic risks characteristic of global value chains, but some are political in nature.

   The first set of risks is related to the host country's business and regulatory environment. These risks are analyzed in the World Bank's *Doing Business* reports, which present data—for nearly all of the world's economies—on eleven

[176] Author calculations based on https://www.globaltradealert.org.

[177] Author calculations based on https://icsid.worldbank.org/en/Pages/cases/AdvancedSearch.aspx.

areas of business regulation: starting a business, dealing with construction permits, obtaining electricity, registering property, securing credit, protecting minority investors, paying taxes, trading across borders, enforcing contracts, resolving insolvency, and regulating the labor market (World Bank 2016, p. 20). The risks identified in *Doing Business* reports consist mostly of the *extra* time, cost, and procedures required in these eleven areas.[178]

Another set of risks reflects the need for MNCs to monitor their partners, suppliers, and contractors by checking their respective credit positions, ownership, and reputations as well as the quality and ethics of their managers and employees. Firms that specialize in business data and information (e.g., Dun & Bradstreet) help MNCs perform these duties by offering services designed to make global value chains safer and to avoid supply disruptions.[179]

The third set of risks stems from (a) the potential delinquent behavior of MNCs and of their partners, suppliers, and/or contractors and (b) the negative externalities generated during the production process. Fraud, violating laws and regulations, allowing poor labor conditions, and polluting are likely to tarnish the MNC's reputation and could lead to significant financial losses. So in order to preserve their interests and improve their social, environmental, and ethical performance, MNCs have developed *corporate social responsibility* standards. Such standards, which serve as "international private business self-regulation" (Sheehy 2015), are increasingly scrutinized by the media and the public.

The last group of threats associated with untrammeled capitalism involves not microeconomic but rather political risks. The globalization process described here has troubled Western societies in the sense of rising inequality (Piketty 2013) and increased deindustrialization (Nickell et al. 2008). These destabilizing trends have exacerbated frustration among European and American citizens while nurturing populism and isolationism—especially since the Great Recession.[180] Populism is a complex challenge for international investors because it renders economic policies less certain and may well undermine the rule of law (as in Viktor Orban's Hungary).

It is interesting that globalization's negative effects on developed economies were clearly identified, more than two decades ago, by Rodrik (1997) and Luttwak (1999). However, their warnings were largely ignored by policy makers.

---

[178] These issues are partly addressed by the World Economic Forum's *Global Competitiveness Report* and A. T. Kearney's *Foreign Direct Investment Confidence Index*.

[179] See https://www.dnb.com.

[180] The Brexit vote and the election of Donald Trump in 2016 are two illustrations.

References

Accominotti, O. (2009). The sterling trap: Foreign reserves management at the Bank of France, 1928–1936. *European Review of Economic History, 13*(3), Foreign Exchange Reserves and the International Monetary System.

Adamson, M. R. (2002). The failure of the Foreign Bondholders Protective Council experiment, 1934–1940. *Business History Review, 76*(3).

Agoston, G. & Masters, B. (2009). *Encyclopedia of the Ottoman empire*. New York: Facts on File.

Airbus (2017). *Financial statements 2016*.

Akinsanya, A. (1981). Host governments' responses to foreign economic control: The experiences of selected African countries. *International and Comparative Law Quarterly, 30*(4).

Aliber, R. Z. (1980). A conceptual approach to the analysis of external debt of the developing countries. *World Bank Staff Working Paper No. 421*.

Alvarez, S., & Flores, J. H. (2014). Trade finance and Latin America's lost decade: The forgotten link. *Investigaciones de Historia Económica/Economic History Research, 10*(2).

Archives de l'Etat en Belgique (2008). *Inventaire des archives de l'Office national du Ducroire, 1924–2006/M. Jacquemin*, BE-A0510_004796_005495_FRE, Archives générales du Royaume de Belgique.

A. T. Kearney (2004). *A.T. Kearney's 2004 offshore location attractiveness index*.

A. T. Kearney (2016). *2016 A. T. Kearney global services location index*.

Avramovic, D., et al. (1964). *Economic growth and external debt*. Baltimore: Johns Hopkins Press.

Baer, W. (1972). Import substitution and industrialization in Latin America: Experiences and interpretations. *Latin American Research Review, 7*(1).

Bairoch, P. (1982). International industrialization levels from 1750 to 1980. *Journal of European Economic History, 11*(2).

Bairoch, P. (1999). *Mythes et paradoxes de l'histoire économique*. Paris: La Découverte/Poche.

Baker, J. C. (1999). *Foreign direct investment in less developed countries: The role of ICSID and MIGA*. Westport (CT) and London: Quorum.

Balassa, B. (1971). Industrial policies in Taiwan and Korea. *Weltwirtschaftliches Archiv*, Bd. 106.

Balassa, B. (1978). Export incentives and export performance in developing countries: A comparative analysis. *Weltwirtschaftliches Archiv*, Bd. 114, H. 1.

Balassa, B., Bueno, G. M., Kuczynski, P.-P., & Simonsen, M. H. (1986). *Toward renewed economic growth in Latin America*. El Colégio de Mexico, Fundação Getúlio Vargas, Institute for International Economics, Mexico City, Rio de Janeiro, and Washington.

Baldwin, R. (2016a). The World Trade Organization and the future of multilateralism. *Journal of Economic Perspectives, 30*(1).

Baldwin, R. (2016b). *The great convergence: Information technology and the new globalization*. Cambridge: Harvard University Press.

Bandyopadhyay, R. (1996). Global review of land reform: A critical perspective. *Economic and Political Weekly, 31*(11).

Banerjee, R., & Hofmann, B. (2018, September). The rise of zombie firms: Causes and consequences, *BIS Quarterly Review*.

Bank for International Settlements (1964). *Annual report*, Basle.

Banks, A. S., & Textor, R. S. (1963). *A cross-polity survey*. Cambridge: MIT Press.

Barro, R. J., Ursúa, J. F. (2008, Spring) Macroeconomic crises since 1870. *Brookings papers on economic activity*, Vol. 2008.

Basagni, F. (1981). Recent developments in international lending practices. In B. J. Cohen & F. Basagni (Eds.), *Banks and the balance of payments—Private lending in the international adjustment process*. London: Rowman and Allanheld.

Becker, W. H., & McClenahan, W. M., Jr. (2003). *The market, the state, and the Export-Import Bank of the United States, 1934–2000*. Cambridge: Cambridge University Press.

Beers, D., & de Leon-Manlagnit, P. (2019). The BoC-BoE sovereign default database: What's new in 2019? *Bank of Canada Staff Working Paper 2019-39*.

Beim, D. O. (1977). Rescuing the LDCs. *Foreign Affairs, 55* (4).
Bell, S., & Feng, H. (2013). *The rise of the People's Bank of China: The politics of institutional change*. Cambridge and London: Harvard University Press.
Berglund, A. (1923). The tariff act of 1922. *American Economic Review, 13*(1).
Bertelsmann Stiftung (2017). *Hidden protectionism: Non-tariff barriers and implications for international trade*, GED Study.
Bhattarai, S., Chatterjee, A., & Park, W. Y. (2018). Effects of US quantitative easing on emerging market economies. *Asian Development Bank Institute, ADBI Working Paper No. 803.*
Bianco, G. (2015). EU financial stability mechanisms: Few certainties, many lingering doubts. *European Business Law Review, 26*(3).
Bird, G. (1986, October). New approaches to country risk. *Lloyds Bank Review*, No. 162.
Board of Governors of the Federal Reserve System (1943). *Banking and monetary statistics, 1914–1941*. Washington, DC: Federal Reserve.
Boeing (2017). *Annual Report Pursuant to Section 13 or 15(d) of the Securities Exchange Act of 1934 for the fiscal year ended December 31, 2016*, Form 10–K.
Bonin, H. (2002). Aux origines de l'assurance-crédit en France (1927–1939): la création et l'essor de la SFAC et le repli de ses concurrentes. *Histoire, Économie et Société, 21*(3).
Borchard, E. M. (1940). The "Minimum Standard" of the treatment of aliens. *Michigan Law Review, 38*(4).
Borchard, E. M. (1946a). The effect of war on law. *American Journal of International Law, 40*(3).
Borchard, E. M. (1946b). Protection of foreign investments. *Law and Contemporary Problems, 11*(4).
Bordo, M. D. (2005). *The gold standard and related regimes: Collected essays*. Cambridge: Cambridge University Press.
Bordo, M. D., & Rockoff, H. (1996). The gold standard as a good housekeeping seal of approval. *Journal of Economic History, 56*(2). Papers Presented at the Fifty-Fifth Annual Meeting of the Economic History Association.
Bouchet, M. H., Clark, E., & Groslambert, B. (2003). *Country risk assessment—A guide to global investment strategy*. Chichester: Wiley.
Boughton, J. M. (2001). *Silent revolution—The International Monetary Fund, 1979–1989*. Washington, DC: International Monetary Fund.
Brau, E., Williams, R. C., Keller, P. M., and Nowak, M. (1983). Recent multilateral debt restructurings with official and bank creditors. *IMF Occasional Paper No. 25.*
Brewer, T. L., & Rivoli, P. (1990). Politics and perceived country creditworthiness in international banking. *Journal of Money, Credit and Banking, 22*(3).
Broches, A. (1962). International investment guaranties: Possibilities and problems. *Proceedings of the American Society of International Law at its fifty-sixth annual meeting held at Washington, D. C., April 26-28, 1962.*
Broches, A. (1965). The convention on the settlement of investment disputes. *Section of International and Comparative Law Bulletin, 9*(3).
Buchanan, J. M., & Wagner, R. E. (1977). *Democracy in deficit: The political legacy of Lord Keynes*. New York: Academic Press.
Buchheit, L. C., & Pam, J. S. (2004). The *Pari Passu* clause in sovereign debt instruments. *Emory Law Journal*, 53, Special Edition.
Buckley, R. P. (1997). The facilitation of the Brady plan: Emerging markets debt trading from 1989 to 1993. *Fordham International Law Journal, 21*(5).
Buckley, R. P. (2006). A force for globalization: Emerging markets debt trading from 1994 to 1999. *Fordham International Law Journal, 30*(2).
Bussière, M., & Fratzscher, M. (2006). Towards a new early warning system of financial crises. *Journal of International Money and Finance, 25*(6).
Caglioti, D. L. (2014). Property rights and economic nationalism. In U. Daniel, P. Gatrell, O. Janz, H. Jones, J. Keene, A. Kramer, & B. Nasson (Eds.), *1914–1918 Online International Encyclopedia of the First World War*. Berlin: Freie Universität Berlin.

Cairncross, A. K. (1935). Did foreign investment pay?. *Review of Economic Studies, 3*(1).
Camdessus, M. (1995). The IMF and the challenges of globalization—The Fund's evolving approach to its constant mission: The case of Mexico. *Address at the Zurich Economics Society*, Zurich, 14 November.
Camdessus, M. (2014). *La scène de ce drame est le monde—Treize ans à la tête du FMI*. Paris: Editions des Arènes.
Carreras, A., & Tafunell, X. (2005). *Estadísticas históricas de España: siglos XIX-XX*. Bilbao: Fundación BBVA.
Central Intelligence Agency (1969). *Chile: US copper investments under fire*. Intelligence Report, 14 July.
Central Intelligence Agency (1986). *The Cartagena Group: Politicizing the Debt in Latin America*, Intelligence Assessment.
Chambers, D., & Esteves, R. (2014). The first global emerging markets investor: Foreign & Colonial Investment Trust 1880–1913. *Explorations in Economic History, 52*.
Chevron (1999). *1998 Annual report*.
Chinn, M. D., & Ito, H. (2006). What matters for financial development? Capital controls, institutions, and interactions. *Journal of Development Economics, 81*(1).
Choi, S. J., Gulati, M., & Posner, E. A. (2012). The evolution of contractual terms in sovereign bonds. *Journal of Legal Analysis, 4*(1).
Citron, J.-T., & Nickelsburg, G. (1987). Country risk and political instability. *Journal of Development Economics, 25*(2).
Clavin, P. (2013). *Securing the world economy. The reinvention of the League of Nations, 1920–1946*. Oxford: Oxford University Press.
Coatsworth, J. H., & Williamson, J. G. (2004). Always protectionist? Latin American tariffs from independence to Great Depression. *Journal of Latin American Studies, 36*(2).
Cohen, B. J. (1985). International debt and linkage strategies: Some foreign-policy implications for the United States. *International Organization, 39*(4).
Cohen, B. J. (1986). *In whose interest? International banking and American foreign policy*. New Haven and London: Yale University Press.
Cohen, B. J. (2013). The coming global monetary (dis)order. In D. Held & C. Roger (Eds.), *Global governance at risk*. Cambridge: Polity.
Cohen, R. A. (2011). Sometimes a Cigar is just a Cigar: The simple story of *Pari Passu*. *Hofstra Law Review, 40*(1).
Cohn, T. H. (2007). The Doha round: Problems, challenges, and prospects. In I. Studer & C. Wise (Eds.), *Requiem or revival?—The Promise of North American integration*. Washington, DC: Brookings Institution Press.
Collier, A. (2017). *Shadow banking and the rise of capitalism in China*. London: Palgrave Macmillan.
Condliffe, J. B. (1940). *The reconstruction of world trade*. New York: W.W. Norton.
Condliffe, J. B. (1947). *Obstacles to multilateral trade. Planning Pamphlets No. 59*. Washington, DC: National Planning Association.
Coplin, W. D., & O'Leary, M. K. (1972). *Everyman's prince: A guide to understanding your political problems*. North Scituate, MA: Duxbury Press.
Coriat, B. (2002). Du 'super 301' aux trips : la 'vocation impériale' du nouveau droit américain de la propriété intellectuelle, *Revue d'économie industrielle*, 99, 2nd trim. Les droits de propriété intellectuelle : nouveaux domaines, nouveaux enjeux.
Corporation of Foreign Bondholders (1903). *Annual report*, London.
Corporation of Foreign Bondholders (1961). *Annual report*, London.
Cosset, J.-C., & Roy, J. (1991). The determinants of country risk ratings. *Journal of International Business Studies, 22*(1).
Costa, F., Garred, J., & Pessoa, J. P. (2016). Winners and losers from a commodities-for-manufactures trade boom. *Journal of International Economics, 102*.

Coudert, A., & Lans, A. (1946). Direct foreign investment in undeveloped countries: Some practical problems. *Law and Contemporary Problems, 11*(4). International Trade Barriers.

Craig, W. L., Park, W. W., & Paulsson, J. (2000). *International Chamber of Commerce arbitration*. New York: Oceana Publications/Dobbs Ferry.

Crotty, J. (2009). Structural causes of the global financial crisis: A critical assessment of the 'New Financial Architecture'. *Cambridge Journal of Economics, 33*(4). Special Issue: The Global Financial Crisis.

Cruces, J. J., & Trebesch, C. (2013). Sovereign defaults: The price of haircuts. *American Economic Journal: Macroeconomics, 5*(3).

Cutler, F. (1971, August). Benchmark Survey of U.S. Direct Investment Abroad, 1966. *Survey of Current Business, U.S. Department of Commerce, 51*(8).

Davey, W. J. (1987). Dispute settlement in Gatt. *Fordham International Law Journal, 11*(1).

Department of Commerce and Labor (1905). *Statistical abstract of the United States—1904*, Washington.

Deutsch, K. W. (1960). Toward an inventory of basic trends and patterns in comparative and international politics. *American Political Science Review, 54*(1).

Dhonte, P. (1975). Describing external debt situations: A roll-over approach. *IMF Staff Papers, 22*(1).

Dietrich, E. B. (1935). British Export Credit Insurance. *American Economic Review, 25*(2).

Dillon, K. B., Watson, C. M., Kincaid, G. R., & Puckahtikom, C. (1985). Recent developments in external debt restructuring. *IMF Occasional Paper No. 40*.

Dixon, J., & Sarkees, M. (2015). *A guide to intra-state wars—An examination of civil, regional, and intercommunal wars, 1816–2014*. Los Angeles: Sage.

Doman, N. R. (1948). Postwar nationalization of foreign property in Europe. *Columbia Law Review, 48*(8).

Drifte, R. (1983, Summer). The European Community and Japan: Beyond the economic dimension. *Journal of International Affairs, 37*(1). Japan's New World Role.

Ducroire, S. A. (2006). *Rapport annuel 2005*, Brussels.

Dudley, L., & Passell, P. (1968). The war in Vietnam and the United States balance of payments. *Review of Economics and Statistics, 50*(4).

Dunning, J. H. (1995). Reappraising the eclectic paradigm in an age of alliance capitalism. *Journal of International Business Studies, 26*(3).

Dunning, J. H., & Lundan, S. M. (2008). *Multinational enterprises and the global economy*. Cheltenham (UK) and Northampton (USA): Edward Elgar.

Economist Intelligence Unit (2006). *Celebrating 60 years… With a glimpse of the future*.

Eichengreen, B., & Irwin, D. A. (1995). Trade blocs, currency blocs and the reorientation of world trade in the 1930s. *Journal of International Economics, 38*(1–2).

Eichengreen, B., & Portes, R. (1989). After the deluge: Default, negotiation, and readjustment during the interwar years. In B. Eichengreen & P. H. Lindert (Eds.), *The international debt crisis in historical perspective*. Cambridge: MIT Press.

Eichengreen, B., Hausmann, R., & Panizza, U. (2005). The mystery of original sin. In B. Eichengreen & R. Hausmann (Eds.), *Other people's money*. Chicago: Chicago University Press.

Einzig, P. (1935). *World finance since 1914*. London: Kegan Paul, Trench, Trubner.

Emerging Markets Traders Association (2015). *EMTA @ 25 (1990–2015)*.

Estevadeordal, A., Frantz, B., & Taylor, A. M. (2003). The rise and fall of world trade, 1870–1939. *Quarterly Journal of Economics, 118*(2).

Export-Import Bank of the United States (various years). *Annual report*, Washington, DC.

Export-Import Bank of the United States (1976). *A survey of country evaluation systems in use*, 22 December, Washington, DC.

Familton, R. J. (1970). East-West trade and payments relations. *IMF Staff Papers, 17*(1).

Feder, G., and Just, R. (1977). A study of debt servicing capacity applying logit analysis. *Journal of Development Economics*, *4*(1).

Feder, G., & Uy, L. V. (1985). The determinants of international creditworthiness and their policy implications. *Journal of Policy Modeling*, *7*(1).

Feder, G., Just, R., & Ross, K. (1981). Projecting debt servicing capacity of developing countries. *Journal of Financial and Quantitative Analysis*, *16*(5).

Federal Financial Institutions Examination Council (1982). *E.16 Country Exposure Lending Survey*, 6 December.

Federal Reserve Bank of New York (1978). *Uniform procedure for examination of 'Country Risk' in international lending*. 17 November, Mimeo.

Federico, G., & Tena-Junguito, A. (2016). World trade, 1800–1938: A new data-set. *EHES Working Papers in Economic History*, No. 93.

Feierabend, I. K., & Feierabend, R. L. (1966). Aggressive behaviors within polities, 1948–1962: A cross-national study. *Journal of Conflict Resolution*, *10*(3).

Feiertag, O., & Plessis, A. (2000). Conjoncture et structures monétaires internationales en Europe à la fin des années trente: Dislocation et convergences. *Revue économique*, *51*(2). De l'Europe d'avant-guerre à l'Europe d'aujourd'hui: Regards sur l'Europe de 1939.

Feinberg, R. E. (1982). *Subsidizing success—The Export-Import Bank in the U.S. Economy*. Cambridge: Cambridge University Press.

Ferri, G., Liu, L.-G., & Stiglitz, J. (1999). The procyclical role of rating agencies: Evidence from the East Asian crisis. *Economic Notes, Banca Monte dei Paschi di Siena SpA*, *28*(3).

Flandreau, M., & Zumer, F. (2004). *The making of global finance—1880–1913*. OECD, Paris: Development Centre Studies.

Flandreau, M., Flores, J. H., Gaillard, N., & Nieto-Parra, S. (2009). The end of gatekeeping: Underwriters and the quality of sovereign bond markets, 1815–2007. *NBER Working Paper No.15128*.

Flores Zendejas, J. H. (2017). Averting defaults in turbulent times: Controversies over the League of Nations preferred creditor status. *Working Papers of the Paul Bairoch Institute of Economic History, 5/2017*.

Flores Zendejas, J. H., & Decorzant, Y. (2016). Going multilateral? Financial markets' access and the League of Nations loans, 1923–8. *Economic History Review*, *69*(2).

Ford, A. G. (1956). Argentina and the Baring crisis of 1890. *Oxford Economic Papers*, *8*(2).

Ford Motor Company (2008). *2007 Annual report*.

Foreign Claims Settlement Commission of the United States (2018). *2017 Annual report*. Washington, DC: US Department of Justice.

Foreman-Peck, J. (1982). The American challenge of the twenties: Multinationals and the European motor industry. *Journal of Economic History*, *42*(4).

Frank, Jr., C. R., & Cline, W. R. (1971). Measurement of debt servicing capacity: An application of discriminant analysis. *Journal of International Economics*, *1*(3).

Frankel, J., & Saravelos, G. (2010). Are leading indicators of financial crises useful for assessing country vulnerability? Evidence from the 2008–09 global crisis. *NBER Working Paper No. 16047*.

Frieden, J. A. (2015). *Currency politics—The political economy of exchange rate policy*. Princeton and Oxford: Princeton University Press.

Friedman, I. S. (1977). Evaluation of risk in international lending: A lender's perspective. *Key Issues in International Banking, Conference Series No. 18, Federal Reserve Bank of Boston*.

Gaillard, N. (2011). *A century of sovereign ratings*. New York: Springer.

Gaillard, N. (2014a). What is the value of sovereign ratings? *German Economic Review*, *15*(1).

Gaillard, N. (2014b). How and why credit rating agencies missed the Eurozone debt crisis. *Capital Markets Law Journal*, *9*(2).

Gaillard, N. (2014c). *When sovereigns go bankrupt—A study on sovereign risk*. Cham: Springer.

Gaillard, N. (2014d). Assessing sovereign risk: The case of rich countries. *Journal of Financial Economic Policy* *6*(3).

Gaillard, N. (2016). What credit rating system for the 'Belt and Road' initiative? Speech delivered to the *2016 China (Ningxia) Forum on Credit System along the 'Belt and Road'*, Yinchuan, 27 September.

Gaillard, N. (2017). Credible sovereign ratings: Beyond statistics and regulations. *European Business Law Review*, *28*(1).

Gaillard, N., & Harrington, W. J. (2016). Efficient, commonsense actions to foster accurate credit ratings. *Capital Markets Law Journal*, *11*(1).

Gaillard, N., & Michalek, R. J. (2019). How and why moral hazard has distorted financial regulation. In A. Hira, N. Gaillard, & T. H. Cohn (Eds.), *The failure of financial regulation—Why a major crisis could happen again*. Cham: International Political Economy Series, Palgrave Macmillan.

Gaillard, N., & Waibel, M. (2018). The Icarus syndrome: How credit rating agencies lost their quasi immunity. *Southern Methodist University Law Review*, *71*(4).

Garrett, B. L. (2014). *Too big to jail: How prosecutors compromise with corporations*. Cambridge, MA: Belknap Press of Harvard University Press.

Gasser, W. J., & Roberts, D. L. (1982, Autumn). Bank lending to developing countries—Problems and prospects. *Federal Reserve Bank of New York Quarterly Review*.

Gellman, I. F. (1979). *Good neighbor diplomacy: United States policies in Latin America, 1933–1945*. Baltimore and London: Johns Hopkins University Press.

General Accounting Office (1982a). *Bank Examination for Country Risk and International Lending*, GAO/ID-82-52, 2 September, Washington, DC.

General Accounting Office (1982b). *Examination of the Export-Import Bank's fiscal year 1981 financial operations and related issues*, Report to the Congress by the Comptroller General of the United States, 18 November, Washington, DC.

General Motors Corporation (1937). *Twenty-eighth annual report—Year ended. December 31, 1936*.

Genova, A. (2010). Nigeria's nationalization of British petroleum. *International Journal of African Historical Studies*, *43*(1).

Gerlach, M. L. (1992). *Alliance capitalism. The social organization of Japanese business*. Oxford: Oxford University Press.

Giddy, I. H. (1977). Exchange risk: Whose view? *Financial Management*, *6*(2).

Glencore (2017). *Annual report 2016*.

Glick, R., & Taylor, A. M. (2010). Collateral damage: Trade disruption and the economic impact of war. *Review of Economics and Statistics*, *92*(1).

Godley, A. C. (1999). Pioneering foreign direct investment in British manufacturing. *Business History Review*, *73*(3).

Goldsmith, A. A. (1988). Policy dialogue, conditionality, and agricultural development: Implications of India's green revolution. *Journal of Developing Areas*, *22*(2).

Goldstein, E. (1992). *Wars and peace treaties, 1816–1991*. London and New York: Routledge.

Green, R. T. (1974). Political structures as a predictor of radical political change. *Columbia Journal of World Business*, *9*(1).

Greene, M. R. (1965). Export credit insurance—Its role in expanding world trade. *Journal of Risk and Insurance*, *32*(2).

Greenwood, R., & Scharfstein, D. (2013). The growth of finance. *Journal of Economic Perspectives*, *27*(2).

Haendel, D., West, G. T., & Meadow, R. G. (1975). *Overseas investment and political risk*. Philadelphia: Foreign Policy Research Institute.

Halliday, F. (1982, Fall/Winter). The Iranian revolution: Uneven development and religious populism. *Journal of International Affairs*, *36*(2). Religion and Politics.

Haner, F. T., & Ewing, J. S. (1985). *Country risk assessment: Theory and worldwide practice*. New York: Praeger.

Hanna, J. (1931). Credit insurance. *University of Pennsylvania Law Review and American Law Register*, *79*(5).

Hawkins, R. G., Mintz, N., & Provissiero, M. (1976). Government takeovers of U.S. foreign affiliates. *Journal of International Business Studies*, *7*(1).
Heffernan, S. A. (1986). *Sovereign risk analysis*. London: Allen & Unwin.
Hemerijck, A. (2013). *Changing welfare states*. Oxford: Oxford University Press.
Herz, J. H. (1941). Expropriation of foreign property. *American Journal of International Law*, *35*(2).
Hexner, E. (1950–1951). The general agreement on tariffs and trade and the monetary fund. *IMF Staff Papers*, 1.
Hibbs, D. A., Jr. (1973). *Mass political violence: A cross-national causal analysis*. New York: Wiley.
Hill, C. (1996). Securitization: A low-cost sweetener for lemons. *Washington University Law Quarterly*, *74*(4).
Hira, A., Murata, B., & Monson, S. (2019). Regulatory mayhem in offshore finance: What the Panama papers reveal. In A. Hira, N. Gaillard, & T. H. Cohn (Eds.), *The failure of financial regulation—Why a major crisis could happen again*. Cham: International Political Economy Series, Palgrave Macmillan.
Hiscox, M. J., & Kastner, S. L. (2002). *A general measure of trade policy orientations: Gravity-model-based estimates for 82 nations, 1960 to 1992*. Retrieved from http://www.tinyurl.com/khsjudg
Hobson, C. K. (1914). *The export of capital*. London: Constable and Company.
Horn, S., Reinhart, C., & Trebesch, C. (2019, June). China's overseas lending. *Kiel Working Paper No. 2132*.
Hough, J. F. (1986). Attack on protectionism in the Soviet Union? A comment. *International Organization*, *40*(2).
Howell, L. D. (2001). *The handbook of country and political risk analysis*. East Syracuse, NY: The PRS Group.
Hudec, R. E. (1980). GATT dispute settlement after the Tokyo round: An unfinished business. *Cornell International Law Journal*, *13*(2).
Hyde, C. C. (1939). Compensation for expropriations. *American Journal of International Law*, *33*(1).
International Bank for Reconstruction and Development (1946). *First annual report by the executive directors*, Washington, DC.
International Bank for Reconstruction and Development (1953a). *International movements of public long-term capital and grants, 1946–1950*, 21 September, Washington, DC.
International Bank for Reconstruction and Development (1953b). *Survey of publicly-held foreign bonds—Part I: Bonds issued in the United States*, 15 December, Washington, DC.
International Bank for Reconstruction and Development (1955). *Survey of publicly-held foreign government bonds*, 28 January, Washington, DC.
International Bank for Reconstruction and Development (1960, September). *Some techniques of development lending*. Washington, DC.
International Bank for Reconstruction and Development (1969). *Multilateral debt renegotiations: 1956–1968*, 11 April, Washington, DC.
International Finance Corporation (various years). *Annual report*, Washington, DC.
International Monetary Fund (1946). *Annual report of the executive directors*, Washington, DC.
International Monetary Fund (various years). *Annual report*, Washington, DC.
International Monetary Fund (2019, August). *Heavily indebted poor countries (HIPC) initiative and multilateral debt relief initiative (MDRI)—Statistical update*. Washington, DC: IMF Policy Paper.
James, F. C. (1926). Government assistance in financing foreign trade. *Annals of the American Academy of Political and Social Science*, *127*, Markets of the United States.
Jean, S. (2019). Désaccords commerciaux internationaux: au-delà de Trump. *Politique Etrangère*, *84*(1).

Jeanne, O., & Zettelmeyer, J. (2005). The Mussa theorem (and other results on IMF-induced moral hazard). *IMF Staff Papers*, 52, IMF Conference in Honor of Michael Mussa.
Johnson, L. L. (1965). U.S. business interests in Cuba and the rise of Castro. *World Politics*, *17*(3).
Jones, G. (2005). Multinationals from the 1930s to the 1980s. In A. D. Chandler & B. Mazlish (Eds.), *Leviathans—Multinational corporations and the new global history*. Cambridge: Cambridge University Press.
Jorgensen, E., & Sachs, J. (1989). Default and renegotiation of Latin American foreign bonds in the interwar period. In B. Eichengreen & P. H. Lindert (Eds.), *The international debt crisis in historical perspective*. Cambridge: MIT Press.
J. P. Morgan (1992). *1991 Annual report*. New York.
J. P. Morgan (1995). *Introducing the emerging markets bond index plus (EMBI+)*. 12 July, New York.
J. P. Morgan (1996). *Introducing the emerging local markets index (ELMI)*. 24 June, New York.
J. P. Morgan (1999). *Introducing the J. P. Morgan emerging markets bond index global (EMBI Global)*. 3 August, New York.
Kaminsky, G., Lizondo, S., & Reinhart, C. (1997). Leading indicators of currency crises. *IMF Working Paper WP/97/79*.
Kaminsky, G., Reinhart, C., & Vegh, C. (2003). The unholy trinity of financial contagion. *Journal of Economic Perspectives*, *17*(4).
Keefer, P. (1996). Protection against a capricious state: French investment and Spanish railroads, 1845–1875. *Journal of Economic History*, *56*(1).
Kennedy, Jr., C. R. (1984). Multinational corporations and political risk in the Persian Gulf. *International Journal of Middle East Studies*, *16*(3).
Kharas, H. (1981). *The analysis of long-run creditworthiness: Theory and practice. Domestic Finance Study No. 73*. Washington, DC: World Bank.
Kindleberger, C. P., & Aliber, R. Z. (2005). *Manias, panics, and crashes: A history of financial crises*. Hoboken: John Wiley & Sons.
King, J. A., Jr. (1967). *Economic development projects and their appraisal—Cases and principles from the experience of the World Bank*. Baltimore: Johns Hopkins Press.
Kirchner, W. (1981). Russian tariffs and foreign industries before 1914: The German entrepreneur's perspective. *Journal of Economic History*, *41*(2).
Klein, M. W., & Marion, N. P. (1994). Explaining the duration of exchange rate pegs. *NBER Working Paper No. 4651*.
Klein, T. M. (1973). Economic aid through debt relief. *Finance and Development*, *10*(3).
Knudsen, H. (1974). Explaining the national propensity to expropriate: An ecological approach. *Journal of International Business Studies*, *5*(1).
Kobrin, S. J. (1977, January). The conditions under which political disruption results in increased political risk. *M.I.T., Alfred P. Sloan School of Management, Working Paper 900-77*.
Kobrin, S. J. (1980). Foreign enterprise and forced divestment in LDCs. *International Organization*, *34*(1).
Kobrin, S. J. (1982). *Managing political risk assessment: Strategic response to environmental change*. Berkeley: University of California Press.
Kobrin, S. J. (1984). Expropriation as an attempt to control foreign firms in LDCs: Trends from 1960 to 1979. *International Studies Quarterly*, *28*(3).
Kolarz, W. (1962). The impact of communism on West Africa. *International Affairs*, *38*(2).
Korn, M. (1979, April–May). Paying for peace in the Mideast. *Harvard International Review*, *1*(3).
Kosmidou, K., Doumpos, M., & Zopounidis, C. (2008). *Country risk evaluation—Methods and applications*. New York: Springer.
Krugman, P. (1979). A model of balance-of-payments crisis. *Journal of Money, Credit and Banking*, *11*(3).
Kurlantzick, J. (2016). *State capitalism—How the return of statism is transforming the world*. Oxford and New York: Oxford University Press.

Laviec, J.-P. (1985). *Protection et promotion des investissements—Etude de droit international économique*. Geneva: Publications de l'Institut Universitaire de Hautes Etudes Internationales.
Lehfeldt, R. A. (1913). The rate of interest on British and foreign investments. *Journal of the Royal Statistical Society, 76*(2).
Leigh, M. (1990). Sabbatino's Silver Anniversary and the restatement: No cause for celebration. *The International Lawyer, 24*(1).
Liepmann, H. (1938). *Tariff levels and the economic unity of Europe*. London: Allen & Unwin.
Lipson, C. (1978). The development of expropriation insurance: The role of corporate preferences and state initiatives. *International Organization, 32*(2).
Lipson, C. (1985). *Standing guard—Protecting foreign capital in the nineteen and twentieth centuries*. Berkeley and Los Angeles: University of California Press.
Littell, N. M. (1950). Obstructions to private investment abroad. *Virginia Law Review, 36*(7).
Littell, N. M. (1952). Improvements in legal climate for investments abroad. *Virginia Law Review, 38*(6).
Littell, N. M. (1954). The international investment of private capital. Opportunities and problems: Legal incentives for private investments abroad. *Virginia Law Review, 40*(8).
Luttwak, E. N. (1990). From geopolitics to geo-economics: Logic of conflict, grammar of commerce. *The National Interest*, No. 20, Summer.
Luttwak, E. N. (1999). *Le turbo-capitalisme*. Paris: Editions Odile Jacob.
Macchione Saes, A. (2013). Modernizing electric utilities in Brazil: National vs. foreign capital, 1889–1930. *Business History Review, 87*(2).
Martin, A. (1948). The treatment of enemy property under the peace treaties of 1947. *Transactions of the Grotius Society, 34*, Problems of Public and Private International Law, Transactions for the Year 1948.
Martín-Aceña, P., Martínez-Ruiz, E., & Nogues-Marco, P. (2012). Floating against the tide: Spanish monetary policy, 1870–1931. In A. Ögren & L. F. Øksendal (Eds.), *The gold standard peripheries: Monetary policy, adjustment and flexibility in a global setting*. Basingstoke: Palgrave Macmillan.
Masson, P. (1998). Contagion: Monsoonal effects, spillovers, and jumps between multiple equilibria. *IMF Working Paper WP/98/142*.
Mastanduno, M. (1992). *Economic containment: CoCom and the politics of East-West trade*. Ithaca: Cornell University Press.
Mattli, W. (2019). *Darkness by design: The hidden power in global capital markets*. Princeton and Oxford: Princeton University Press.
Mattoo, A., Mulabdic, A., & Ruta, M. (2017). Trade creation and trade diversion in deep agreements. *World Bank Policy Research, Working Paper 8206*.
Maurer, N. (2013). *The empire trap—The rise and fall of U.S. intervention to protect American property overseas, 1893–2013*. Princeton and Oxford: Princeton University Press.
McDonald, D. C. (1982). Debt capacity and developing country borrowing: A survey of the literature. *IMF Staff Papers, 29*(4).
McKinnon, R. I. (1993). The rules of the game: International money in historical perspective. *Journal of Economic Literature, 31*(1).
Mendelsohn, M. S. (1983). *Commercial banks and the restructuring of cross-border debt*. New York: Group of Thirty.
Messerlin, P. (1981). The political economy of protectionism: The bureaucratic case. *Weltwirtschaftliches Archiv*, Bd. 117, H. 3.
Messerlin, P. (1982). Les déterminants de la demande de protection: le cas français. *Revue économique, 33*(6). Le protectionnisme.
Mian, A., & Sufi, A. (2014). *House of Debt: How they (and you) caused the great recession, and how we can prevent it from happening again*. Chicago: University of Chicago Press.
Michalak, W. Z. (1993). Foreign direct investment and joint ventures in East Central Europe: A geographical perspective. *Environment and Planning A, 25*(11).

Miles, C. M. (1968). After the Kennedy round. *International Affairs (Royal Institute of International Affairs). 44*(1).
Miles, K. (2013). *The origins of international investment law—Empire, environment and the safeguarding of capital.* Cambridge: Cambridge University Press.
Miller, M. H. (1986). Financial innovation: The last twenty years and the next. *Journal of Financial and Quantitative Analysis, 21*(4).
Minor, M. S. (1994). The demise of expropriation as an instrument of LDC policy, 1980–1992. *Journal of International Business Studies, 25*(1).
Mintz, I. (1951). *Deterioration in the quality of foreign bonds issued in the United States 1920–1930.* Cambridge: National Bureau of Economic Research.
Mitchener, K. J., & Weidenmier, M. D. (2008). The Baring crisis and the great Latin American meltdown of the 1890s. *Journal of Economic History, 68*(2).
Mitsubishi Corporation (1991). *Annual report 1991*, Tokyo.
Mitsubishi Corporation (2015). *Integrated report 2015*, Tokyo.
Monteagudo, M. (1994). The debt problem: The Baker plan and the Brady initiative: A Latin American perspective. *The International Lawyer, 28*(1).
Moody's Investors Service (1918). *Moody's manual of investments—American and foreign government securities*, New York.
Moody's Investors Service (1920). *Moody's manual of investments—American and foreign government securities*, New York.
Multilateral Investment Guarantee Agency (1989). *Annual report 1989*, Washington, DC.
Multilateral Investment Guarantee Agency (2014). *World investment and political risk 2013*, Washington, DC.
Munk, B. (1969). The welfare costs of content protection: The automotive industry in Latin America. *Journal of Political Economy, 77*(1).
Murdock, C. W. (2013). Credit default swaps: Dubious instruments. *Harvard Business Law Review Online, 3*, March 30, 2013.
Mussa, M. (1999). Reforming the international financial architecture: Limiting moral hazard and containing real hazard. In D. Gruen & L. Gower (Eds.), *Capital flows and the international financial system.* Sydney: Reserve Bank of Australia.
Nagy, P. (1978). Quantifying country risk: A system developed by economists at the Bank of Montreal. *Columbia Journal of World Business, 13*(3).
National Industrial Conference Board (1951). *Obstacles to direct foreign investment*, Report prepared for the President's Committee for Financing Foreign Trade, New York.
Nehrt, L. C. (1970). *The political environment for foreign investment.* New York: Praeger.
Nickell, S., Redding, S., & Swaffield, J. (2008). The uneven pace of deindustrialisation in the OECD. *The World Economy, 31*(9).
Norel, P., Quenan, C., & Sarry, M.-C. (1988). Stratégies bancaires et risque-pays. *Economie Appliquée, XLI*(4).
Nye, R. P. (2014). *Understanding and managing the credit rating agencies.* London: Euromoney Books.
O'Brien, P. K., & Pigman, G. A. (1992). Free trade, British hegemony and the international economic order in the nineteenth century. *Review of International Studies, 18*(2).
O'Sullivan, R. C. (2005). Learning from OPIC's experience with claims and arbitration. In T. H. Moran & G. T. West (Eds.), *International political risk management—Looking to the future.* Washington, DC: The World Bank.
Obstfeld, M., & Taylor, A. M. (2003). Sovereign risk, credibility and the gold standard: 1870–1913 versus 1925–31. *Economic Journal, 113*(487).
Office of the Comptroller of the Currency (1956). *Annual report*, Washington, DC.
Office of the Comptroller of the Currency (1981). *Annual report*, Washington, DC.
Olson, R. S. (1975). Economic coercion in international disputes: The United States and Peru in the IPC expropriation dispute of 1968–1971. *Journal of Developing Areas, 9*(3).

Oosterlinck, K. (2016). *Hope springs eternal: French bondholders and the repudiation of Russian sovereign debt*. New Haven and London: Yale University Press.
Overholt, W. H. (1982). *Political risk*. London: Euromoney Publications.
Overseas Private Investment Corporation (2017). *Insurance claims experience to date: OPIC and its predecessor agency*, 30 September.
Pamuk, S. (1984). The Ottoman Empire in the great depression of 1873–1896. *Journal of Economic History*, *44*(1).
Pamuk, S. (2004). The evolution of financial institutions in the Ottoman Empire, 1600–1914. *Financial History Review*, *11*(1).
Park, J. H. (1993). Impact of China's open-door policy on Pacific Rim trade and investment. *Business Economics*, *28*(4).
Patterson, G. (1943). The Export-Import Bank. *Quarterly Journal of Economics*, *58*(1).
Perkins, D. H. (1971–1972, Winter). Is there a China market? *Foreign Policy*, No. 5.
Phelps, D. M. (1936). *Migration of industry to South America*. New York and London: McGraw-Hill Book Company.
Piketty, T. (2013). *Le capital au XXIème siècle*. Paris: Editions du Seuil.
Pizer, S., & Cutler, F. (1956, August). Growth of foreign investments in the United States and abroad. *Survey of Current Business, U. S. Department of Commerce*, *36*(8).
Polak, J. J. (1991). The changing nature of IMF conditionality. *Essay in International Finance No. 184, Department of Economics, Princeton University*.
Porter, M. (1990, March–April). The competitive advantage of nations. *Harvard Business Review*.
Potterf, R. M. (1927). Treatment of alien enemy property in war time and after by the United States. *Indiana Law Journal*, *2*(6).
Prasad, E., Rogoff, K., Wei, S.-J., & Kose, M. A. (2003). Effects of financial globalization on developing countries: Some empirical evidence. 17 March, *International Monetary Fund*.
Prebisch, R. (1959). Commercial policy in the underdeveloped countries. *American Economic Review*, *49*(2).
Qiu, L. D., & Zhan, C. (2016). China's global influence: A survey through the lens of international trade. *Pacific Economic Review*, *21*(1).
Re, E. D. (1962). The Foreign Claims Settlement Commission: Its functions and jurisdiction. *Michigan Law Review*, *60*(8).
Reinhart, C., & Rogoff, K. (2009). *This time is different: Eight centuries of financial folly*. Princeton: Princeton University Press.
Reinhart, C., & Rogoff, K. (2011). From financial crash to debt crisis. *American Economic Review*, *101*(5).
Reliance (2007). *Annual report 2006–07*.
Rethel, L., & Sinclair, T. J. (2012). *The problem with banks*. London: Zed Books.
Richdale, K. G., & Liu, W. H. (1991). The politics of 'Glasnost' in China, 1978–1990. *Journal of East Asian Affairs*, *5*(1).
Roberts, I., Saunders, T., Spence, G., & Cassidy, N. (2016). China's evolving demand for commodities. In I. Day & J. Simon (Eds.), *Structural change in China: Implications for Australia and the world*. Sydney: Reserve Bank of Australia.
Robock, S. H. (1971). Political risk: Identification and assessment. *Columbia Journal of World Business*, *6*(4).
Rodrik, D. (1997). *Has globalization gone too far?* Washington, DC: Institute for International Economics.
Rood, L. L. (1976). Nationalisation and indigenisation in Africa. *Journal of Modern African Studies*, *14*(3).
Root, F. R. (1968). The expropriation experience of American companies. *Business Horizons*, *11*(2).
Sack, A. N. (1927). *Les effets des transformations des Etats sur leurs dettes publiques et autres obligations financières*. Paris: Sirey.
Safer, A. E. (1978). Oil and the international economy. *Business Economics*, *13*(1).

Sargen, N. (1977, Fall). Economic indicators and country risk appraisal. *Federal Reserve Bank of San Francisco Economic Review*.
Schachter, O. (1984). Compensation for expropriation. *American Journal of International Law, 78*(1).
Schoenbaum, T. J. (1984). Trade friction with Japan and the American policy response. *Michigan Law Review, 82*(5/6).
Schumacher, J., Trebesch, C., & Enderlein, H. (2015). What explains sovereign debt litigation? *Journal of Law and Economics, 58*(3).
Sgard, J. (2016). How the IMF did it—sovereign debt restructuring between 1970 and 1989. *Capital Markets Law Journal, 11*(1).
Shapiro, A. C., & Rutenberg, D. P. (1976). Managing exchange risks in a floating world. *Financial Management, 5*(2).
Sheehy, B. (2015). Defining CSR: Problems and solutions. *Journal of Business Ethics, 131*(3).
Shihata, I. F. I. (1992). *Towards a greater depoliticization of investment disputes: The roles of ICSID and MIGA*. Washington, DC: World Bank.
Sigmund, P. E. (1977). *The overthrow of Allende and the politics of Chile, 1964–1976*. Pittsburgh: University of Pittsburgh Press.
Simon, J. D. (1982). Political risk assessment: Past trends and future prospects. *Columbia Journal of World Business, 17*(3).
Simon, J. D. (1992). Political-risk analysis for international banks and multinational enterprises. In R. L. Solberg (Ed.), *Country-risk analysis—A handbook*. London and New York: Routledge.
Simpson, J. (1997). Economic development in Spain, 1850–1936. *Economic History Review, 50*(2).
Sinclair, T. J. (1994). Passing judgement: Credit rating processes as regulatory mechanisms of governance in the emerging world order. *Review of International Political Economy, 1*(1).
Sinclair, T. J. (2005). *The new masters of capital: American bond rating agencies and the politics of creditworthiness*. Ithaca and London: Cornell University Press.
Snyder, E. (1963). Foreign investment protection: A reasoned approach. *Michigan Law Review, 61*(6).
Soenen, L. A. (1979). Foreign exchange exposure management. *Management International Review, 19*(2).
Sollogoub, T. (2001). Les outils du risque pays appliqués aux pays en transition—Analyse méthodologique. *Direction des Etudes Economiques et Financières, Etudes des Risques Pays, Crédit Lyonnais*.
Standard & Poor's (2011). *Corporate and government ratings that exceed the sovereign rating*. 3 June.
Stobaugh, Jr., R. B. (1969, September–October). How to analyze foreign investment climates. *Harvard Business Review*.
Suter, C. (1989). Long waves in the international financial system: Debt-default cycles of sovereign borrowers. *Review (Fernand Braudel Center). 12*(1).
Suter, C. (1990). *Schuldenzyklen in der Dritten Welt—Kreditaufnahme, Zahlungskrisen und Schuldenregelungen peripherer Länder im Weltsystem von 1820 bis 1986*. Frankfort-on the-Main: Anton Hain.
Sykes, A. O. (1999). Regulatory protectionism and the law of international trade. *University of Chicago Law Review, 66*(1).
Thornblade, J. B. (1978). A checklist system: The first step in country evaluation. In S. H. Goodman (Ed.), *Financing and risk in developing countries*. New York: Praeger Publishers.
Triffin, R. (1978). The international role and fate of the dollar. *Foreign Affairs, 57*(2).
Truitt, J. F. (1970, Autumn). Expropriation of foreign investment: Summary of the post World War II experience of American and British investors in the less developed countries. *Journal of International Business Studies, 1*(2).
United Nations (1966). *The financing of economic development. World Economic Survey 1965—Part I*. New York, Department of Economic and Social Affairs.

United Nations Conference on Trade and Development (1998). *World investment report 1998: Trends and determinants.* United Nations, New York and Geneva.

United Nations Conference on Trade and Development (2004). *World investment report 2004: The shift towards services*, United Nations, New York and Geneva.

United Nations Economic Commission for Africa (1963). *Investment laws and regulations in Africa*, U.N., E/CN.14/INR/28.

United Nations General Assembly (1974). *Resolution adopted by the General Assembly—3201 (S-VI). Declaration on the Establishment of a New International Economic Order*, U.N., A/RES/S-6/3201, New York.

United States Council of the International Chamber of Commerce (1953). *Doing business abroad.* Report of the Committee on Foreign Establishments.

United States Department of State (1972). Report on nationalization, expropriation, and other takings of U.S., & certain foreign property since 1960. *International Legal Materials, 11*(1).

United States House of Representatives (1963). *Expropriation of American-owned property by foreign governments in the twentieth century*, Report Prepared by the Legislative Reference Service (Library of Congress) at the request of the Committee on Foreign Affairs, Washington, DC.

United States Senate (1975). *Covert Action in Chile: 1963–1973.* Staff Report of the Select Committee to Study Governmental Operations with Respect to Intelligence Activities, Washington, DC.

United States Senate (1978). The Witteveen facility and the OPEC financial surpluses. *Hearings before the subcommittee on foreign economic policy of the committee on foreign relations—September 21, 23, October 6, 7, and 10, 1977*, Washington, DC.

Van der Kroef, J. M. (1965). Indonesian communism's expansionist role in Southeast Asia. *International Journal, 20*(2).

Vashchilko, T. (2011). *Three essays on foreign direct investment and bilateral investment treaties*, Dissertation in Political Science, Pennsylvania State University, Graduate School, College of the Liberal Arts.

Vásquez, I. (1996). The Brady plan and market-based solutions to debt crises. *Cato Journal, 16*(2).

Vaubel, R. (1983). The moral hazard of IMF lending. *World Economy, 6*(3).

Von Mehren, R. B. (1978). International Arbitral Tribunal: Award on the merits in dispute between Texaco Overseas Petroleum Company/California Asiatic Oil Company and the Government of the Libyan Arab Republic (Compensation for Nationalized Property). *International Legal Materials, 17*(1).

Von Neumann Whitman, M. (1959). The United States investment guaranty program and private foreign investment. *Princeton Studies in International Finance No. 9.*

Von Neumann Whitman, M. (1978, Spring). Bridging the gap. *Foreign Policy, No. 30.*

Wallich, H. C. (1981, September/October). LDC Debt... to worry or not to worry. *Challenge, 24*(4).

Weidemaier, W. M. C. (2014). Sovereign immunity and sovereign debt. *University of Illinois Law Review, 2014*(1).

Wells Fargo & Company (various years). *Annual report.*

White, R. C. A. (1975). A new international economic order. *International and Comparative Law Quarterly, 24*(3).

Wilkins, M. (1970). *The Emergence of Multinational Enterprise: American Business Abroad from the Colonial Era to 1914.* Cambridge: Harvard University Press.

Wilkins, M. (1974). *The Maturing of Multinational Enterprise.* Cambridge: Harvard University Press.

Williams, M. L. (1975). The extent and significance of the nationalization of foreign-owned assets in developing countries, 1956–1972. *Oxford Economic Papers, New Series, 27*(2).

Williams, S. L. (1993). Political and other risk insurance: OPIC, MIGA, EXIMBANK and other providers. *Pace International Law Review, 5*(1).

Williamson, J. (1990). What Washington means by policy reform. In J. Williamson (Ed.), *Latin American adjustment: How much has happened?* Washington DC: Peterson Institute for International Economics.
Wilson, C. (1954). *The history of Unilever, 2*. London: Cassell & Co..
Wilson, J. O. (1979). Measuring country risk in a global context. *Business Economics, 14*(1).
Winkler, M. (1933). *Foreign bonds—An autopsy*. Philadelphia: Roland Swain.
World Bank (various years). *Annual report*, Washington, DC.
World Bank (1985). *World debt tables—External debt of developing countries, 1984–85 Edition*, Washington, DC.
World Bank (2009). *Global economic prospects: Commodities at the crossroads*, Washington, DC.
World Bank (2016). *Doing business 2016*, Washington, DC.
Wynne, W. H. (1951). *State insolvency and foreign bondholders* (Vol. II). New Haven: Yale University Press.
Young, R. A. (1930). *Handbook on American underwriting of foreign securities*. Washington, DC: U.S. Department of Commerce.
Young, Jr., K. T. (1961). New politics in new states. *Foreign Affairs, 39*(3).
Zettler, J. A., & Cutler, F. (1952, December). United States direct investments in foreign countries. *Survey of Current Business, U. S. Department of Commerce, 32*(12).
Zink, D. W. (1973). *The political risks for multinational enterprise in developing countries*. New York: Praeger.
Zwass, V. (1976). East-West trade today—An evaluation and a perspective. *Soviet and Eastern European Foreign Trade, 12*(2/3), East-West Trade Today—An Evaluation and a Perspective.

Chapter 3
Taxonomy of Country Risk

This chapter investigates the numerous forms that country risk may take and also provides illustrations of them. Seven broad components of country risk are scrutinized in turn: international political risks; domestic political and institutional risks; jurisdiction risks; macroeconomic risks; microeconomic risks; sanitary, health, industrial, and environmental risks; and natural and climate risks. Each of these risks consists of various "subrisks" that have specific features. Their effects may be direct or indirect (or both) and may become manifest in the short, medium, or long term. These "subrisks" may be latent or constitute a shock that affects all or only some investors. For instance, environmental risks are much more likely to affect foreign bondholders of corporate debt, shareholders, and especially direct investors—corresponding to type-4, type-5, and type-6 country risks (CR4, CR5, and CR6)—than to affect exporters, importers, and foreign bondholders of sovereign debt, which correspond to type-1, type-2, and type-3 country risks (CR1, CR2, and CR3).

My analysis focuses on the postwar years, with a greater emphasis on the globalization era (i.e., since the 1990s). Various sources are used: academic works, professional publications, press articles, and corporate annual reports. I also discuss how the 30 companies included in the Dow Jones Industrial Average (DJIA) index[1] factored the different country risk components into their 2016–2017 business strategies.[2]

[1] As of 1 April 2017, the 30 companies listed on the DJIA were 3M Company (3M), American Express Company (American Express), Apple Inc. (Apple), The Boeing Company (Boeing), Caterpillar Inc. (Caterpillar), Chevron Corporation (Chevron), Cisco Systems, Inc. (Cisco), The Coca-Cola Company (Coca-Cola), The Walt Disney Company (Disney), E. I. du Pont de Nemours and Company (DuPont), Exxon Mobil Corporation (Exxon Mobil), General Electric Company (General Electric), The Goldman Sachs Group, Inc. (Goldman Sachs), The Home Depot, Inc. (Home Depot), International Business Machines Corporation (IBM), Intel Corporation (Intel), Johnson & Johnson (Johnson & Johnson), JPMorgan Chase & Co. (JPMorgan Chase), McDonald's Corporation (McDonald's), Merck & Co., Inc. (Merck), Microsoft Corporation (Microsoft), Nike, Inc. (Nike), Pfizer Inc. (Pfizer), The Procter & Gamble Company (Procter & Gamble), The Travelers Companies, Inc. (Travelers), United Technologies Corporation (United Technologies), UnitedHealth Group Incorporated (UnitedHealth), Verizon Communications Inc. (Verizon), Visa Inc. (Visa), and Wal-Mart Stores, Inc. (Walmart).

[2] I examine "Item 1A. Risk Factors" of the US Securities and Exchange Commission (SEC) Form 10-K as filed by the 30 DJIA companies for the fiscal year ended between April 2016 and March 2017.

N. Gaillard, *Country Risk*, https://doi.org/10.1007/978-3-030-45788-4_3

3.1 International Political Risks

This section explores three aspects of international political risk: the bilateral relations between the host country and the investor's country (Sect. 3.1.1), international sanctions and embargoes (Sect. 3.1.2), and international tensions and warfare (Sect. 3.1.3).

3.1.1 Bilateral Relations Between the Host Country and the Investor's Country

Bad or deteriorating diplomatic relations between the host country and a business's home country is alarming. This is a crucial issue for firms headquartered in a nation whose foreign policy is regarded as excessively proactive or interventionist.

After his coup in January 1959, Fidel Castro gave up the pro-American diplomacy of his predecessor Fulgencio Batista.[3] Castro's "anti-imperialistic" stance foreshadowed the expropriation measures announced in the following months (Johnson 1965). The Cuban episode shows that diplomatic rows between the United States and various Latin American countries may result in the expropriation of US direct investors there. Two examples are illustrative: the 1970 election of Salvador Allende in Chile and the 1998 election of Hugo Chavez in Venezuela. In both cases, the newly elected president criticized US foreign policy[4] and promoted a Marxist agenda that ended up with industries being nationalized. The first US firms affected were Bethlehem Steel[5] in Chile and Williams (a company operating in the oil and gas industry) in Venezuela.[6]

Firms with a subsidiary in a territory that gained independence from their home nation may also suffer from the bad relations between the former colonial power and the former colony. For example, after years of mistrust with Belgium, the Congo's government announced in 1966–1967 that it intended to "Congolize" Belgian companies.[7] By the same token, Algeria seized 51% of the oil fields of French firms in 1971 (Grimaud 1972).

[3] R. H. Phillips, "Castro Rules Out Any Foreign Hand in Cuban Affairs," *New York Times*, 4 July 1959.

[4] J. Novitski, "Chile Restores Formal Ties with Cuba; End of Alignment with U.S. Policy Seen," *New York Times*, 13 November 1970; "'Back Off' Says Venezuela in Light of Bad Economy," *Orlando Sentinel*, 6 February 2000.

[5] See J. de Onis, "Chile to Buy Bethlehem Mines in First Major Take-Over Pact," *New York Times*, 27 March 1971.

[6] See The Williams Companies, Inc. (2003, pp. 23–24; 2004, p. 22) and Hajzler and Rosborough's (2016) database.

[7] C. H. Farnsworth, "Belgium and the Congo," *New York Times*, 7 January 1967.

With the number of such expropriation acts declining since the 1980s (see Sect. 3.3.1), bad diplomatic relations between a host country and the United States have been reduced to a minor concern among US firms. In 2016–2017, American Express was the only DJIA company that referred explicitly to this risk (see Appendix 1). This multinational financial services corporation fears that "a negative perception of the United States arising from its political or other positions" could harm the perception of the company and its brand (American Express 2017, p. 22). This reputational concern partly echoes that of Wyndham Worldwide Corporation—one of the world's largest hospitality companies—which has repeatedly worried about the "potential adverse changes in the diplomatic relations of foreign countries with the United States" (Wyndham Worldwide Corporation 2008, p. 33; 2012, p. 33; 2016, p. 26).

It is noteworthy that bad relations between two countries will likely affect creditors as well. In 1960, Cuba suspended the interest payments on its 4.5% external US dollar bond.[8] It is safe to assume that the sole objective of this default was to steal from American bondholders.[9] A more recent illustration involves Russia's seizure of the Crimean Peninsula from Ukraine in 2014; that action led Kiev not only to withhold payment on $3 billion worth of bonds owed to Moscow but also to declare, in 2015, a moratorium on any repayment of that debt (Moody's 2015b; Ukraine 2016).

3.1.2 International Sanctions and Embargoes

I examine here the international sanctions and embargoes that hit foreign investors in countries where they could, *until then*, do business on a regular basis.[10]

South Africa is an instructive case. Adopted unanimously in November 1977, United Nations Security Council Resolution 418 imposed a mandatory arms embargo against the apartheid regime.[11] Resolution 418 caused the last-minute cancellation of certain contracts signed with the South African authorities. Thus, the sale of two A69 avisos built by the French shipyard Dubigeon-Normandie was suspended, which obliged the French parties to compensate Pretoria (Sada 1990, p. 291).

In October 1986, the US Congress passed the Comprehensive Anti-Apartheid Act; this legislation prohibited US firms from either granting loans to or investing in South Africa.[12] Some of them (e.g., Emhart and PepsiCo) divested from South

[8] P. Heffernan, "Bonds: Prices of Prime Securities Tend to Decline," *New York Times*, 4 April 1961; see also Suter (1990, p. 283).

[9] The trading range of this bond plummeted from 102–106 in 1958 to 23–37 in 1962 and then to 18–27 in 1969 (Moody's 1963, p. a4; 1970, p. a3).

[10] The two embargoes imposed by the United States on Cuba in October 1960 and February 1962 are not studied because they were announced *after* the wave of expropriations. For the chronology of events, see Peterson Institute for International Economics (2011).

[11] See https://www.sipri.org/sites/default/files/2016-03/418.pdf.

[12] See https://www.gpo.gov/fdsys/pkg/STATUTE-100/pdf/STATUTE-100-Pg1086.pdf.

Africa,[13] and Rank Xerox South Africa Pty. Ltd. was sold to a local company (Xerox Corporation 1988, p. 7). However, other US firms (e.g., Citibank and Mobil) remained in the country.[14] In 1989, Colgate-Palmolive Company (1990, p. 17) still had a subsidiary there.

During 1993–1996, 35 countries were subject to US unilateral economic sanctions. The promotion of human rights and democratization was the most frequently cited purpose, followed by "anti-terrorism" (National Association of Manufacturers 1997). As of March 10, 2017, more than 30 nations were affected by a variety of US restrictions and sanctions. Most of them were subject to restrictions regarding defense articles and services (Thompson Coburn LLP 2017). Of these, 17 countries were—to a greater or lesser degree—"blacklisted" by the United States both during 1993–1996 and in March 2017: Afghanistan, Burundi, China, Cuba, the Democratic Republic of the Congo (formerly Zaire), Haiti, Iran, Iraq, Libya, Myanmar, North Korea, Qatar, Russia, Saudi Arabia, Sudan, Syria, and the United Arab Emirates.[15]

Losman (1998, p. 40) investigates the cost of international economic sanctions. Direct costs may include loss of current earnings, sale of properties at distressed prices, and loss of a major supplier or customer. Indirect costs may entail additional expenses for marketing, administration, and compliance. For instance, Section 219 of the Iran Threat Reduction and Syria Human Rights Act of 2012 added new Section 13(r) to the Securities Exchange Act of 1934, which imposed new reporting requirements on US companies (see American Express 2017, p. 15; Boeing 2017, p. 47).[16] Another indirect cost is the possible "imposition of retaliatory sanctions against U.S. multinational corporations by countries that are or may become subject to U.S. trade sanctions" (Coca-Cola 2017, p. 16).

In a different connection, the willful violation of US economic sanctions can be much more disastrous. In 2015, BNP Paribas was sentenced for conspiring to violate the Trading with the Enemy Act and the International Emergency Economic Powers Act by processing billions of dollars of transactions through the US financial system on behalf of Sudanese, Iranian, and Cuban entities subject to US

[13] D. Kneale, "Sullivan Urges Firms to Quit South Africa—Principles' Author Calls for Broader Sanctions," *Wall Street Journal*, 4 June 1987.

[14] Ibid.

[15] It is worth remarking that the countries included in this list considerably outnumber those that can be viewed as "rogue states." For a thorough analysis of this latter concept and the countries it includes, see Saunders (2006).

[16] The main objective of the Iran Threat Reduction and Syria Human Rights Act was to strengthen Iran sanctions laws for the purpose of compelling that country to abandon its pursuit of nuclear weapons and other threatening activities. See https://www.congress.gov/112/plaws/publ158/PLAW-112publ158.pdf.

economic sanctions.[17] The French financial institution was ordered to forfeit $8.8 billion to the United States and to pay a $140 million fine.[18]

3.1.3 International Tensions and Warfare

Interstate wars can be the most disastrous events for any investor. Section 2.2.1 documented how World War I not only depressed international trade and destroyed the global integration of capital markets but also led *capitalist* powers to break their long-standing tradition of respect for foreign individual property.

However, this section does not review the interstate conflicts that occurred in recent decades (but for a remarkable work on this topic, see Goldstein 1992). Neither does it classify interstate wars nor discusses the relevance of "low-intensity," "mid-intensity," and "high-intensity" conflicts; these two issues have been addressed by, respectively, Vasquez and Valeriano (2010) and Bellamy (1998). Instead, I focus on the period 1975–2015 and analyze how foreign investors suffered from this type of international political risk.

Figure 3.1 presents the major episodes of international political violence (e.g., interstate wars, occupations of disputed territories, and invasions) as assessed by the Center for Systemic Peace. The number of international conflicts has significantly declined since 1975. At the beginning of the period, East Asia, Middle East, and North Africa were the riskiest areas. The most recent war episodes involved Iraq and the United States.

The interstate conflicts that occurred during 1975–2015 seem to have had relatively limited consequences for major foreign direct investors. Several reasons can be advanced for this surprising result.

First, three major military powers—Russia, the United Kingdom, and the United States—were involved in wars outside their own borders.[19] As a result, these interventions did not affect the foreign firms that had commercial or financial interests in these three countries. Second, some governments were embroiled in interstate conflicts after years of civil war; examples include Zimbabwe (formerly Rhodesia) during 1975–1979, Cambodia and Vietnam during 1975–1989, and Rwanda during 1996–2002. Thus, the business climate in these areas was already gloomy when

[17] The Trading with the Enemy Act of 1917 restricts trade with countries hostile to the United States. The International Emergency Economic Powers Act of 1977 authorizes the President to regulate commerce after declaring a national emergency in response to any unusual and extraordinary threat to the United States that has a foreign source. See https://definitions.uslegal.com/t/trading-with-the-enemy-act-twea and https://definitions.uslegal.com/i/international-emergency-economic-powers-act.

[18] Department of Justice, "BNP Paribas Sentenced for Conspiring to Violate the International Emergency Economic Powers Act and the Trading with the Enemy Act," *Office of Public Affairs, Press Release No. 15-549*, 1 May 2015.

[19] The three governments fought against (respectively) Afghanistan and Georgia; Argentina; and Afghanistan, Iraq, and Panama.

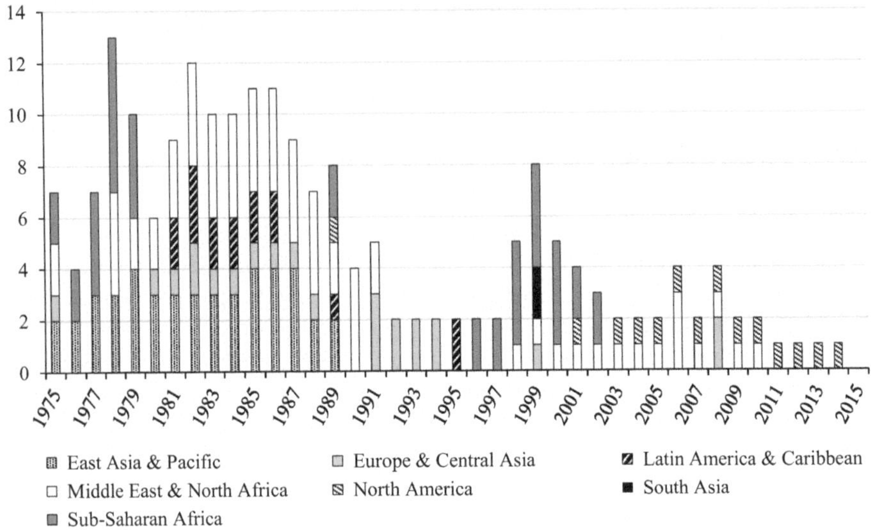

Fig. 3.1 Major episodes of international political violence, 1975–2015. *Sources:* Author's calculations based on international major episodes of political violence (MEPV) listed by the Center for Systemic Peace; database available at http://www.systemicpeace.org/inscr/MEPV2015.xls

international hostilities began. Third, in a few cases, international political risk was dwarfed by business opportunities. For example, Ethiopia's border war with Eritrea in the late 1990s did not prevent the former from launching a large-scale privatization process to attract foreign firms.[20] In the meantime, the International Finance Corporation (IFC 1999, p. 73) announced its first investment in the country since 1967.

The Iraqi invasion of Kuwait in 1990 has idiosyncratic features. Most American companies with operations in the small emirate were caught off guard. They had to set up 24-h hotlines to inform relatives of the Americans in Kuwait, organize the evacuation of their employees, save hostages, and so forth.[21] Texaco held a concession representing a 50% undivided interest in the onshore portion of the Partitioned Neutral Zone, an area located between Saudi Arabia and Kuwait. Because of the invasion, its wells and related facilities were severely damaged, and all operations were suspended (Texaco Inc. 1991, p. 67; 1992, p. 4). However, the short-term financial consequences were quite different: The firm reported a 35% jump in its fourth quarter earnings for 1990 at $388 million, reflecting the surge in crude oil prices.[22]

[20] "Ethiopia Set to Privatize 120 State-Owned Enterprises in Next Three Years," *BBC Monitoring Africa—Economic*, 24 April 1999.

[21] C. Johnson, "Many Americans Trapped in Kuwait Escape Detection," *Wall Street Journal*, 22 August 1990; D. Medina and C. Phillips, "Companies with Hostages in Persian Gulf Struggle to Help Stateside Families Cope," *Wall Street Journal*, 26 September 1990.

[22] J. P. Hicks, "Earnings Jump 35% at Texaco," *New York Times*, 24 January 1991.

Chevron and Exxon posted even bigger profits over the same period.[23] The first Gulf War shows that, paradoxically, adverse political events may have positive effects for some types of investors.

The fate of the bankers and bondholders who had lent to belligerent governments merits some more specific comments. Only five countries (accounting for 10% of all observations)[24] defaulted in the same year or the year after they entered an international war: Iran in 1980, Lebanon and Argentina in 1982, Kuwait in 1990, and Croatia in 1992.[25] Moreover, it is not certain whether becoming embroiled in war is *causally* related to debt default (except in the case of Kuwait). In fact, the economic difficulties experienced by the four other countries are certainly the main driver for their inability to honor their financial obligations.

The international wars that occurred during 1975–2015 were not a major threat to foreign investors because most were low-intensity conflicts that hit already unstable political regimes. That said, any war of even medium intensity in Eastern Europe, the Middle East, or East Asia could spiral out of control and have immeasurably negative consequences.

3.2 Domestic Political and Institutional Risks

This section tackles two aspects of domestic political risk: the risks stemming from institutional organization and access to power (Sect. 3.2.1) and the various forms of political tensions that may lead to civil unrest or war (Sect. 3.2.2). Section 3.2.3 discusses the two paradoxes of political risk.

3.2.1 Institutional and Political Instability

Any regime change or shift in a country's executive or legislative power is a potential threat to foreign investors. Such adverse changes may occur after an independence proclamation, a democratic election, a nondemocratic power succession, a coup, or a revolution.

---

[23] "Earnings/Energy—Exxon, Chevron Profits Surge; Gulf Crisis Cited," *Los Angeles Times*, 25 January 1991.

[24] Author's calculations based on the Center for Systemic Peace database. An observation is an episode of international violence for a given country. For example, a country involved in a sustained ten-year international conflict will yield one observation.

[25] About 45% of the countries were already in default when the conflict began; 45% remained solvent in the short to medium term.

3.2.1.1 Independence Proclamation

Between 1945 and 2002, more than 80 territories gained independence from a colonial power.[26] The leaders of these newly independent states were frequently considered nationalists or, at least, politicians willing to unify their nation (Young Jr. 1961). Many of them embraced economic policies that were not especially friendly to foreign exporters (e.g., import–substitution industrialization and protectionist measures) or that overtly discriminated against foreign direct investment (e.g., expropriation; see Sect. 3.3.1). Such options were rife in the 1950s–1970s and involved countries that had just emancipated themselves from France (e.g., Guinea in 1958), Belgium (e.g., the Republic of the Congo—now Democratic Republic of the Congo—in 1960), the United Kingdom (e.g., Ghana in 1960), and Portugal (e.g., Mozambique in 1975). This pattern is observed also with regard to the territories that became sovereign in the aftermath of the Soviet Union's dissolution in 1991.

3.2.1.2 Democratic Election

Democratic elections enabled politicians who were poorly perceived by investors to come to power (e.g., Salvador Allende in Chile in 1970, François Mitterrand in France in 1981, Hugo Chavez in Venezuela in 1998, Evo Morales in Bolivia in 2005, and Rafael Correa in Ecuador in 2006). Take, for example, the case of Evo Morales. During the 2005 presidential election campaign, this leader of the Movement for Socialism announced that he would void all contracts allowing mining, gas, and oil exploration by foreign companies.[27] Anticipating Morales's election, the head of Repsol's Bolivian operations initiated discussions with the public authorities at La Paz.[28] These fears materialized quickly: As early as 2006, the Spanish oil company was among the first foreign firms to be expropriated by the Bolivian government.[29]

Political risk may also arise when the executive and legislative powers are at odds (typically in a presidential regime) or when no party is able to secure a majority at the parliament. The latter scenario is likely when the electoral system is based on proportional representation and/or the political landscape is fragmented. Such scenarios are observed in both developing and developed countries. For instance, it took 18 months during 2010–2011 for the Belgian government to be sworn in.[30] In 2015–2016, Spain had to organize two general elections before a government could be formed—and a third general election was averted only because the party that came in second did not vote against the leading party, allowing government formation to proceed (Lancaster 2017).

---

[26] Author's estimations based on http://www.un.org.

[27] D. Rieff, "Che's Second Coming?," *New York Times*, 20 November 2005.

[28] J. de Cordoba, "Bolivia Election Portends Foreign-Investor Clash; Outright Presidential Win Gives Morales Clout to Push for Gas Nationalization," *Wall Street Journal*, 20 December 2005.

[29] See Hajzler and Rosborough's (2016) database.

[30] S. Castle, "18 Months after Vote, Belgium Has Government," *New York Times*, 2 December 2011.

An additional challenge to democratic societies is the influence of "anti-system" parties, which traditionally undermines government stability (Taylor and Herman 1971; Hartleb 2015). The recent electoral success of the League and the Five Star Movement in Italy suggests that "anti-system" parties *can* come to power.[31]

3.2.1.3 Nondemocratic Power Succession

Nondemocratic power successions can trigger an adverse change in the policies implemented by the outgoing administration or government. More dramatically, they may exacerbate political rivalries and increase instability. Following the death of Marshal Tito in 1980, a rotating system of succession was put into operation among the leaders of the different Yugoslavian provinces.[32] This system failed to maintain the country's cohesion. In 1981, protests broke out in Kosovo and opened a period of repression, which spread throughout the country and led to civil war and the dismantling of Yugoslavia in the early 1990s. Today, succession in Arab monarchies remains a source of concern among foreign direct and equity investors (Billingsley 2010).

3.2.1.4 Coup

A coup is certainly the most unexpected catalyst for institutional and political shocks. For Luttwak (1969, p. 12), "a coup consists of the infiltration of a small but critical segment of the state apparatus, which is then used to displace the government from its control of the remainder."

Figure 3.2 presents all instances of coup attempts that occurred during 1975–2015. Their frequency has significantly declined over the past four decades. During 1975–1984, there were (on average) ten coup attempts per year, when compared to three annually during 2006–2015. Sub-Saharan Africa has been especially afflicted by such events; this region accounts for 55% of all coups (followed by Latin America, with 21% of the total).

A coup is likely to have various consequences on MNCs and foreign lenders.

A few successful coups triggered bloody civil wars that eliminated most forms of business (e.g., Afghanistan in 1978; El Salvador in 1979). However, many coups occurred *amid* an episode of civil violence or civil war: Chad (seven coups during 1975–2006), Lebanon (1976), Angola (1977), Ethiopia (1977 and 1989), Mauritania (1978), Turkey (1980), Guatemala (four coups during 1982–1989), Nigeria (four coups during 1983–1993), Sudan (1985, 1989, and 2012), Uganda (1985), the Philippines (four coups during 1986–1990), Iraq (1991, 1992, and 1995), Liberia

31 "Demagogues Win as Europe's Populist Tide Sweeps Italy," *New York Times*, 6 March 2018.

32 "Tito Dies at 87; Last of Wartime Leaders," *New York Times*, 5 May 1980.

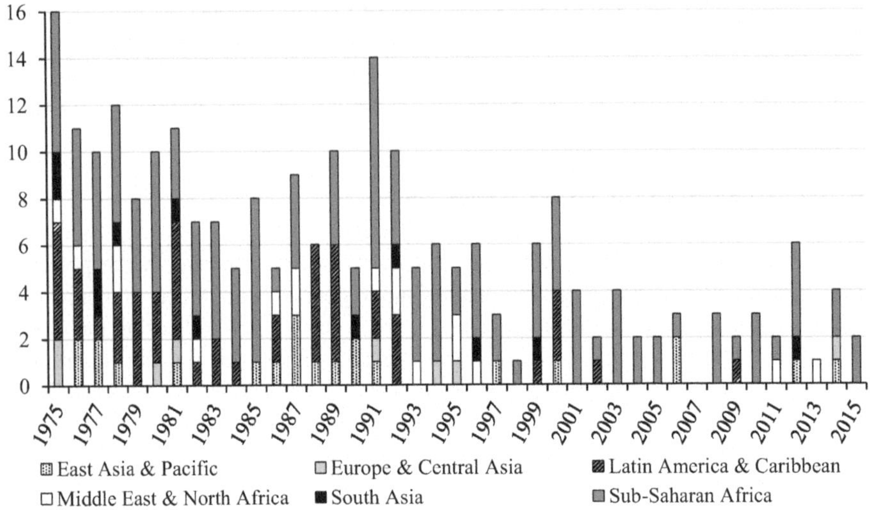

Fig. 3.2 Coup attempts, 1975–2015. *Notes:* Both successful and unsuccessful coups are included. There was no coup attempt in North America during 1975–2015. *Sources:* Author's calculations based on Powell and Thyne's (2011) updated database.

and Rwanda (each in 1994), and Zaire (2004).[33] Foreign investors were either already leaving the host country when the coup occurred (e.g., Lebanon in 1975–1976)[34] or had contemplated doing so (e.g., the Philippines in 1989).[35] The case of sub-Saharan Africa in the late 1970s and early 1980s was even more dramatic, as US firms became increasingly reluctant to invest there (Seymour Whitaker 1983).[36]

In at least two instances, a successful coup seems to have *directly* caused the default of the debtor country. In 1980, after a military coup, the Bolivian government ceased making amortization payments to foreign banks. Those banks accepted a rescheduling of that debt while the IMF maintained a standby agreement signed with the previous government.[37] In 1999, Ivory Coast's President Konan Bédié was overthrown by General Guéï. A few weeks later, the new head of state announced that the country would default on its foreign currency bonds (Moody's 2015a, p. 22).

[33] Author's classification based on Powell and Thyne's (2011) updated database and the Center for Systemic Peace's database; see www.systemicpeace.org.

[34] J. M. Markham, "Foreign Businesses Are Casualties of Lebanon's Strife," *New York Times*, 17 October 1975.

[35] D. E. Sanger, "In Manila Coup Effort, Economy Is Big Victim," *New York Times*, 20 December 1989.

[36] Although Seymour Whitaker was not speaking quantitatively, her analysis is corroborated by the decline—for Sub-Saharan Africa—in the ratio of foreign direct investment inflows to GDP: from 1% in 1975 to 0.5% in 1983. This ratio exceeded 2.5% in 2015 (World Development Indicators).

[37] "10 U.S. Banks Agree to New Terms on $172 Million Bolivia Debt," *New York Times*, 13 September 1980.

In some cases, foreign investors refrained from divesting from the country that had faced a coup. Despite the coup that shocked Fiji in 2000, the Asian Development Bank (2001, pp. 108–109; 2002, pp. 65–66) disbursed some $9 million in 2000–2001 to that Pacific state while claiming the situation there was being closely monitored. Similarly, Attijariwafa Bank maintained its activities in Mali after the March 2012 coup there. By 2013, its subsidiary—the Banque Internationale pour le Mali—had expanded its network and increased its total amount of loans by 16% over 2011 (Attijariwafa Bank 2012, p. 57; 2014, p. 59). It is noteworthy that neither the multilateral bank nor the Moroccan financial institution mentioned the word "coup" in their annual reports. Instead, they used (respectively) the terms "widespread civil unrest" and "crisis" (Asian Development Bank 2001, p. 108; Attijariwafa Bank 2013, p. 62).

These results are intriguing. Therefore, I further investigate the relation between the occurrence of coups d'état and investment decisions. I focus on the investment strategy followed by the IFC because this financial institution has been a global investor with a wide range of activities (including equity investment, lending operations, technical assistance, and advisory services) for a long time. In 1976, its cumulative gross commitments amounted to $1.5 billion and ranged across 61 countries (IFC 1976, p. 32). Forty years later, they reached $245 billion in 155 countries (IFC 2016, pp. 112–115). Studying the annual reports published during 1976–2006, I find that the IFC invested in 47 countries in which a coup occurred during the previous year.[38] Much like the Asian Development Bank and Attijariwafa Bank, the IFC reports do not refer directly to the coups and instead mention only "political uncertainties" and "political instability."

The tendency of foreign investors to downplay these political shocks reached an extreme in the case of Thailand. There were 12 coups in Bangkok during 1950–2016. The last two (in 2006 and 2014) were perceived in positive terms by some international bankers, which viewed them as potentially enabling the restoration of political stability in the medium term.[39]

The impact of a coup d'état on MNCs and foreign creditors varies across sectors, countries, and periods. However, investors must bear in mind that coups led to major expropriations (e.g., Cuba in 1959–1960), horrific civil wars (e.g., Nigeria in 1966–1970, El Salvador in 1979–1992), and transformed a regime into a "rogue state" (e.g., Sudan in 1989).

[38] The reference period is the IFC fiscal year (i.e., July 1–June 30), so I checked whether a recipient country faced a coup the previous fiscal year. Author's calculations are based on IFC (various reports) and Powell and Thyne's (2011) updated database.

[39] "Coup? What Coup? Thailand's Bond Market Is Unruffled," *Euroweek*, 29 September 2006; J. Maxwell Watts, "Thailand Investors Shrug Off Coup," *Wall Street Journal*, 24 May 2014.

3.2.1.5 Revolution

As defined by Huntington (1968, p. 264), a revolution is "a rapid, fundamental, and violent domestic change in the dominant values and myths of a society, in its political institutions, social structure, leadership, and government activity and policies."[40] Postwar history shows that revolutions are likely to have very different consequences on foreign businesses. Here, I examine how the Iranian and Egyptian revolutions, which took place in (respectively) 1978–1979 and 2011–2013, affected the hotel industry.

After months of protestations, strikes, and civil resistance that paralyzed Iran, the Shah exiled himself from that country in January 1979. This triumph of the revolutionary groups enabled establishment of the Islamic Republic of Iran. The new regime's fierce opposition to Western powers obliged the Carter administration to impose sanctions and an embargo on trade with Iran in 1979–1980.[41] In the meantime, American firms had to leave the country. Several hotel and leisure companies (e.g., Hilton, Hyatt, Sheraton, and Starwood) operated properties there when the Islamic Revolution broke out.[42] In fact, Hilton Hotels (1964, p. 14) had opened the tallest building in the capital, the Royal Tehran Hilton, in 1963. In 2016, these firms had still not returned to Iran.[43]

Like its precursor, the Egyptian revolution started with protestations and strikes, and a military junta overthrew President Hosni Mubarak in February 2011. After a series of popular elections, the Muslim Brotherhood took power and Islamist Mohamed Morsi became head of state in June 2012. A second coup, organized by General Abdel Fattah El-Sisi, ousted Mohamed Morsi in July 2013 (Tabaar 2013). During this period, major hotel companies admitted that their operations in Egypt were depressed but did not terminate them (e.g., Marriott International Inc. 2014, p. 10; Melia Hotels International 2014, p. 106).

The respective creditors of the two countries experienced diverging fates, too. Iran stopped repaying its debt shortly after the beginning of the Islamic Revolution. The US Exim Bank (1981, p. 19) and Wells Fargo & Company (1980, p. 3) announced that their loans to Iranian entities were in default. Iran proved unable and/or unwilling to respect its financial obligations for two decades. In contrast, Egypt remained solvent during the period 2011–2013 and beyond (see the database of Beers and de Leon-Manlagnit 2019).

The political upheavals that shook Tehran and Cairo suggest that foreign investors can survive a revolution provided it does not lead to antibusiness measures, international disputes, or major episodes of host-country violence.

---

[40] This definition is debatable because some revolutionary processes did *not* entail violence—for example, the "Velvet Revolution" in Czechoslovakia during 1989.

[41] See http://iranprimer.usip.org/resource/us-sanctions.

[42] "Marriott Is First US Hotel Group to Eye Iran," *Press TV*, Tehran, 7 December 2016.

[43] Ibid.

3.2.2 *Domestic Violence and Warfare*

Episodes of political violence have two basic dimensions: their intensity and their length. It is with reference to these dimensions that I categorize such episodes into two groups, as described next.

3.2.2.1 Riots and Terrorist Attacks

Sporadic riots and violent demonstrations are unlikely to affect equity and direct investors unless they target the firms from a specific country or business sector. In May 2014, many riots erupted in Vietnam. Hundreds of stores and factories owned by Chinese and Taiwanese merchants were looted and torched. Foreign workers died, and some companies suspended their operations in Vietnam indefinitely. A *Wall Street Journal* investigation showed that anti-Chinese and anti-Taiwanese sentiment was the main motive for these riots.[44]

Protesters may also target specific businesses. In the 1990s–2000s, the operations of foreign mining companies in Indonesia were frequently disturbed by human rights defenders, environmentalists, and illegal miners. In March 2006, five Indonesian security officers working for PT Freeport Indonesia—a subsidiary of Freeport-McMoRan—were killed by protesters in the West Papuan capital of Jayapura.[45]

Political violence may affect a single firm, as the next two examples illustrate. In 1969, on the occasion of Nelson Rockefeller's visit to Buenos Aires as a special envoy of President Nixon, several supermarkets located in Argentinean cities were bombed because they were controlled by the Rockefeller family (Robock 1971, p. 9). More recently, Centerra Gold Inc. (2015, p. 85) complains that protesters and other groups have regularly attempted to access its Kyrgyz site. The Toronto-based gold mining company warns that a trespass could "cause harm to employees or property, or result in business interruption."

Terrorist attacks constitute an even more serious risk for a foreign direct investor, especially when their purpose is to disrupt operations or eliminate a key market or supply source. A striking illustration is the tragedy that shocked the nuclear company Areva in Niger. In May 2013, suicide bombers attacked the Somaïr uranium mine owned by that French firm. One employee was killed, and 14 staff members were wounded (Areva 2014, p. 24). If the company lost this mine, then it would be forced to rely on scarce alternative supply sources (in Kazakhstan and Canada).[46]

---

[44] E. Dou, J. W. Hsu, and T. K. Vu, "World News: Vietnam Unrest Shakes Foreign Firms," *Wall Street Journal*, 17 May 2014; E. Dou and R. Paddock, "Firms Learn Business Risks in Vietnam," *Wall Street Journal*, 19 June 2014.

[45] "The Fun of Being a Multinational," *The Economist*, 20 July 1996; "Indonesia: Mining Looks Good, Despite Violent Protests," *Oxford Analytica Daily Brief*, 4 April 2006.

[46] V. Le Billon, "Areva en terrain miné au Niger," *Les Echos*, 13 June 2013.

3.2.2.2 Political Unrest and Civil War

Political unrest and civil war are certainly the most dangerous plagues for any businessman because damages accumulate over an extended period. These damages manifest as threats to the safety of the investing company's employees, clients, and consumers as well as loss of a market or supply source and massive financial losses.

Figure 3.3 presents all major episodes of *domestic* political violence for the period 1975–2015. They include civil and ethnic violence and warfare. Sub-Saharan Africa—the most violent region—accounts for one-third of all observations.[47] Political violence reached a peak in 1992 and declined until 2010. Since then, there has been a resurgence of ethnic and civil war (mainly because of the so-called Arab Spring). The countries of Egypt, Libya, Syria, and Yemen have been especially hard-hit.[48]

Close examination of these events reveals that ethnic conflicts were the main component of domestic political violence, accounting for more than half of all observations. Furthermore, the most violent episodes (as classified by the Center for Systemic Peace) were driven by interethnic tensions: the wars in Ethiopia in the late 1970s, Iraq in the 1980s, and India in the early 1990s and the Rwandan genocide of 1994.

In the early 1990s, attacks conducted by Separatists of the Jammu and Kashmir Liberation Front, insurgencies (in Jharkhand, Chhattisgarh, and Andhra Pradesh) by the Maoist People's War Group, and Hindu–Muslim tensions throughout the country caused thousands of deaths and undermined political stability in India. Such violence scared some financiers but did not discourage industrialists with long-term projects.[49] Long-lasting civil wars in small territories are more likely to hamper foreign investments. In Burundi, ethnic violence during 1993–2005 compelled mining companies involved in nickel and gold exploration to declare *force majeure*, which allowed them to suspend or terminate the performance of their obligations (African Mining 2002a, 2002b, 2002c).[50] In some cases, anarchy and political unrest led to the destruction of foreign factories and stores. For example, French small- and medium-sized enterprises were severely affected by the civil war that destabilized Ivory Coast in 2004. Losses were estimated at €60 million, and 55% of French citizens living in the country were evacuated over a nine-day period (Assemblée Nationale 2007, pp. 9, 27).

---

[47] Here, an observation is an episode of violence for a given country a given year. For example, a country in which a civil war lasts for ten years will yield ten observations.

[48] For more information, see https://www.amnesty.org/en/latest/campaigns/2016/01/arab-spring-five-years-on.

[49] M. V. Brauchli, "India's Violence Fuels Doubt about Course of Economic Reform," *Wall Street Journal*, 15 December 1992.

[50] See K. Damsell, "Argosy Stops Work on Burundi Nickel Mine: Force Majeure Declared," *National Post*, 5 May 2000; see also https://minerals.usgs.gov/minerals/pubs/country/africa.html.

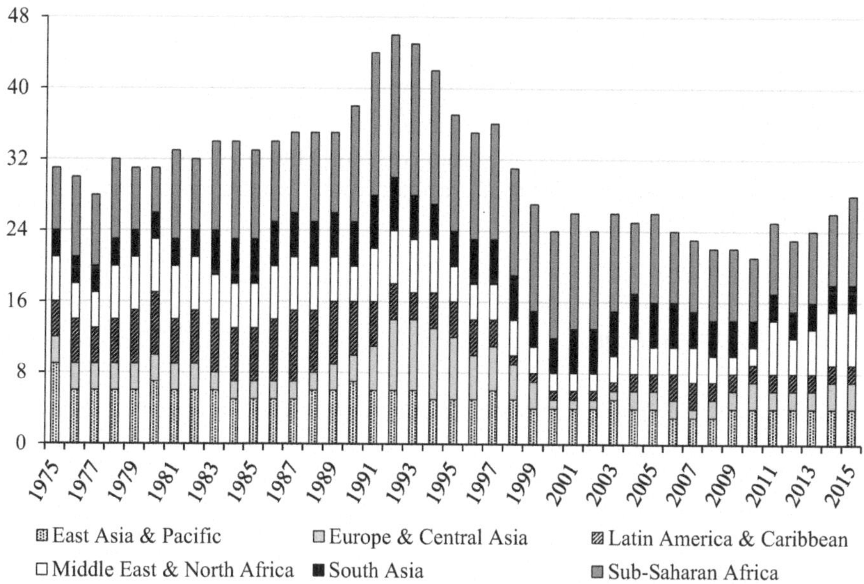

Fig. 3.3 Major episodes of domestic political violence, 1975–2015. *Note:* There was no episode of domestic political violence in North America during 1975–2015. *Sources:* Author's calculations based on domestic MEPV listed by the Center for Systemic Peace; database available at http://www.systemicpeace.org/inscr/MEPV2015.xls

3.2.3 The Two Paradoxes of Political Risk

Political risk is a paradoxical concept: It remains a key component of country risk, but it is mentioned only briefly—and in general terms—in the annual reports published by MNCs (e.g., the DJIA firms; see Appendix 2). It may be that multinationals fear local authorities will view any extensive political analysis as interference. Nonetheless, some major companies have developed idiosyncratic strategies to reduce this type of risk.

In 1997, Cabinda Gulf Oil (a subsidiary of Chevron) convinced the Angolan government to hire an American surveillance and security firm to provide protection against guerrilla attacks from the Front for the Liberation of the Enclave of Cabinda (O'Brien 2000, p. 57). It is often the case that a MNC's interconnectedness with state structures is a crucial factor in the development of business operations as with the ties between Shell and Nigeria (Frynas 1998).[51] In some cases, investors have compromised with a dictator in order to preserve their own interests. Bucheli and Kim (2012) analyze how United Fruit Company thrived in Central America—until the 1954 Guatemalan coup and subsequent institutional changes in the region tarnished the company's reputation and reduced its profitability. This process, called "obsolescing legitimacy" by Bucheli and Kim (2012), supports the view that one result of any "solution" to political risk will be yet another challenge.

[51] Frynas (1998) argues that political instability may be conducive to business precisely when a foreign firm has developed privileged ties with top politicians and civil servants.

3.3 Jurisdiction Risks

I investigate how foreign investors may be affected by adverse, inefficient, unstable, and arbitrary laws, regulatory rules, judicial proceedings, and business practices. Sect. 3.3.1 analyzes the most brutal and adverse form of jurisdiction risk: expropriation. Section 3.3.2 studies other legal, regulatory, and judicial risks. Section 3.3.3 focuses on corrupt practices.

3.3.1 Expropriation

According to Kobrin (1984, p. 330), expropriation is "the involuntary forced divestment of foreign direct investment." This broad definition includes any seizure of foreign property by a government, whether or not any compensation is paid.

Figure 3.4 plots the expropriation acts that occurred during the 1960s and 1970s. Their number increased from 136 acts in the 1960s to 423 in the 1970s. Analysis of these two decades combined reveals that sub-Saharan Africa was the riskiest region (accounting for 43.5% of all takeovers), followed by Latin America (27%). Ten host countries—Algeria, Angola, Chile, Ethiopia, Indonesia, Mozambique, Peru, Tanzania, Uganda, and Zambia—accounted for 41% of the total (Kobrin 1984, p. 331). The manufacturing and petroleum sectors were the most affected: They represented, respectively, 27% and 19% of all takeovers observed during 1960–1979.[52]

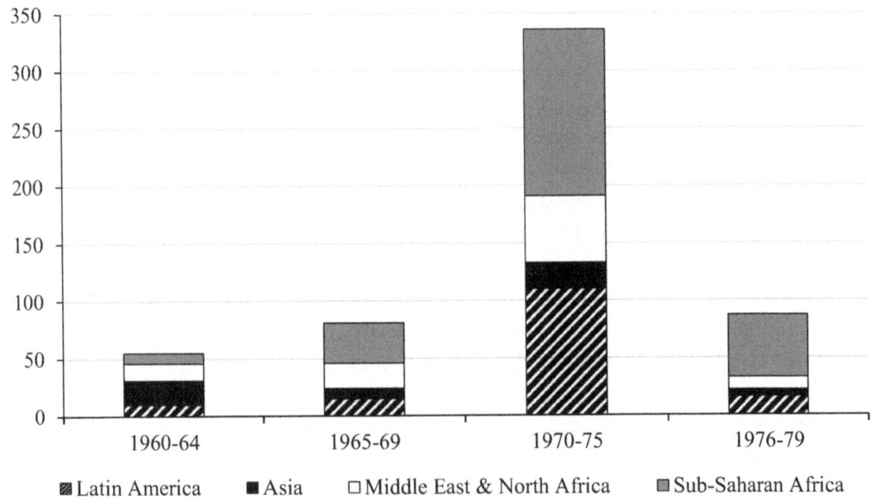

Fig. 3.4 Expropriation acts by region, 1960–1979. *Sources:* Author's calculations based on Kobrin (1984)

[52]Author's calculations based on Kobrin (1984).

At least three reasons may be advanced to explain why forced divestments were widespread during those two decades. First, the practice can be viewed as political revenge by former colonies. It is interesting that, of the 17 states that undertook more than ten expropriation acts, 13 had gained independence after WWII.[53] Second, expropriation was part of socialist economic policies, which were still considered possible paths for development—either on behalf of independence and sovereignty (Rood 1976) or owing to perceived limits of capitalism, especially in light of the economic crisis that erupted in 1973 (Weeks 1977). Third, there were some cases of new regimes seeking to exercise state powers in the *economic* rather than the *military* realm (Nye 1974).

A large number of firms were affected by the seizure of their business properties abroad. The nationalization of MNC subsidiaries sometimes hit the headlines; examples include International Petroleum Company (a subsidiary of the Standard Oil Company) in Peru in 1969 and British Petroleum's interests in Nigeria in 1979.[54] However, small firms were also the targets of expropriation (Truitt 1970, p. 30; Rood 1976, pp. 432–434). In many instances, compensation was low or not even offered (Root 1968, p. 74; Williams 1975, pp. 267–272).

The evolution of forced divestments since 1980 presents a very different picture (see Fig. 3.5). In particular, the frequency of expropriations declined dramatically in the 1980s. Minor (1994, pp. 180–182) argues that this trend was driven by two fundamental factors. First, the 1979 oil shock and the resulting economic crisis induced many developing countries to revise their policies and take advantage of FDI. Second, some governments realized that it could be more efficient to regulate than to nationalize foreign businesses.

I offer two additional explanations. First, the debt crisis of the 1980s *obliged* most developing and emerging countries to adopt market-friendly policies—including legal security for property rights, privatization of state-owned enterprises, and the liberalization of trade and finance. Second, the shift to this new paradigm led to myriad bilateral investment treaties in the 1980s and 1990s (Vashchilko 2011).

The resurgence of expropriation acts since 1998 reflects policy shifts in some countries. For example, more than 17% of forced divestments involved former Soviet republics that became independent in the 1990s. This finding is in line with observations following WWII and suggests that young nations may be tempted by nationalist economic measures. Bolivia, Ecuador, and Venezuela—which together accounted for 46% of the nationalizations during 1998–2014—opted for "Bolivarian" policies, in which state interventionism is high.[55]

---

[53] Ibid.

[54] See (respectively) P. L. Montgomery, "Peru Seizing All International Petroleum Assets," *New York Times*, 7 February 1969; and "Nigerians Move to Take Over All of BP's Interests," *Wall Street Journal*, 1 August 1979.

[55] For an overview of the different strategies followed by Latin American economies since the 1990s, see Hira and Gaillard (2011).

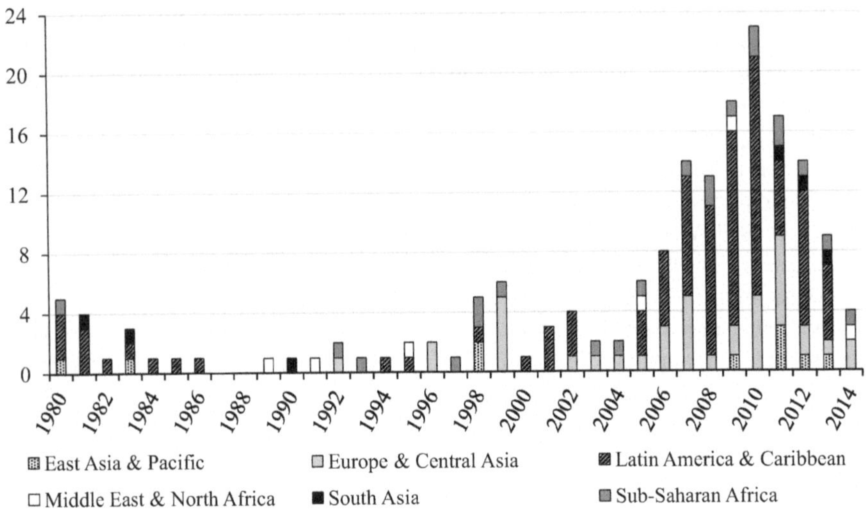

Fig. 3.5 Expropriation acts by region, 1980–2014. *Notes:* For the period 1980–1988, data are from Minor (1994); for the period 1989–2014, data are from Hajzler and Rosborough's (2016) database. *Sources:* Author's calculations based on Minor (1994) and Hajzler and Rosborough's (2016) database

Mining companies were the most affected businesses (24% of all takeovers), followed by the manufacturing and petroleum sectors (14% each).[56] As during the 1960s and 1970s, it was difficult for the expropriated firms to secure fair compensation (see Hajzler and Rosborough's 2016 database).

Investors reacted very differently to such expropriation. In 2010, after Hugo Chavez's regime seized 11 rigs and associated real and personal property owned by a subsidiary of Helmerich & Payne, the company announced it was leaving Venezuela (Helmerich & Payne, Inc. 2010, p. 80).[57] The following year, the drilling company filed a lawsuit in the United States for indemnity (Helmerich & Payne, Inc. 2016, p. 29). Yet during the same period and in the same country, Casino Group (2011, pp. 4–5) presented the takeover of 80.1% of its subsidiary by the Venezuelan government as a "strategic partnership"; the French retailer was to receive $622.5 million for this "transaction."

The expropriation of Glencore in Bolivia provides another case. The constitution that came into effect in 2009 mandates that mining entities form joint ventures with the government. As a result, the Anglo-Swiss company entered into negotiations with Bolivian authorities about satisfying this requirement (Glencore 2012, p. 152). In 2016, Glencore (2017, p. 10) was still operating in the country but now under this new legal framework.

[56] Author's calculations based on Hajzler and Rosborough's (2016) database.

[57] See also D. Molinski, "Helmerich Warns Other Firms after Venezuela Seizes Oil Rigs," *Wall Street Journal*, 7 July 2010.

3.3.2 *Risks Related to Legal, Regulatory, and Judicial Environment*

There is a plethora of laws, regulatory rules, and judicial decisions that—wittingly or not—contribute to discouraging foreign investment. This section examines some of the most striking recent examples.

3.3.2.1 Inefficient Jurisdictional System

A basic risk for foreign investors is to operate in a country where bureaucracy, red tape, and lack of competence at the legislative, regulatory, and administrative levels hinder business opportunities and reduce productivity. These risks, which become acute when they preclude adequate contract enforcement and investor protection, have obliged corporate managers and researchers to take governance quality into account (see Kaufmann et al. 2002).

3.3.2.2 Subsidies to Local Firms[58]

Laws and business practices that favor local competitors and hamper foreign investors' operations are a major concern among MNCs (Chrysler Group 2014, p. 33; American Express 2017, p. 19). In 2010, amid trade discussions between the European Union and Turkey, the European Parliament urged Ankara to stop discriminating against non-Turkish firms by granting a 15% price advantage to local bidders for public procurement contracts.[59] China's support to its domestic firms was conducted on a much larger scale. During 1985–2005, total subsidies to Chinese manufacturing enterprises reached $310 billion (Haley and Haley 2013, pp. 2–3). These transfers of funds prevented foreign industrialists from garnering their expected share of the market.

3.3.2.3 Copyright and Intellectual Property Rights (IPR) Infringement

Copyrights and IPR violations are widespread in developing and emerging countries. In 2004, after the US copyright industry announced it had lost $785 million in Brazil the previous year, a controversy arose between the US and the Brazilian governments. The former promoted a strict enforcement of IPR, whereas the latter preferred "flexible" enforcement.[60] In the past years, many foreign companies sued

[58] This threat is part of protectionism risk; see Sect. 3.4.4.

[59] "EU-Turkey Trade Relations: More Functional Customs Union without Barriers," *US Fed News Service*, 15 July 2010.

[60] R. Colitt, "Brazil Warned over Copyright Violations," *Financial Times*, 22 September 2004.

local infringers in court to protect their industrial property (for summaries of the lawsuits filed in Bulgaria and China, see Hoekman and Djankov 2000 and Ross 2012, respectively). It is noteworthy that the violation of IPR may take extreme forms. In the early 2010s, for instance, Chinese police organized raids and copied computer hard drives in foreign firms' offices. These episodes convinced several MNCs to shift headquarters from Shanghai to Singapore.[61] Today, copyright and intellectual property protection is a key issue for all business sectors (Coca-Cola 2017, p. 17; IBM 2017, p. 13; Travelers 2017, p. 67; United Technologies 2017, p. 15).

3.3.2.4 Burdensome Taxes

Multinational companies may experience discrimination due to the host country's tax policy. In Saudi Arabia, foreign investors are subject to corporate income tax at the rate of 20%—when compared to 2.5% for local firms and entrepreneurs based in Gulf Cooperation Council states[62] (PWC 2015, pp. 8–10). Sometimes, an unexpected tax increase in a specific sector may jeopardize business operations abroad. In 2008, Zambia introduced a new tax regime that upset the copper mining industry. Some provisions of this law were removed after foreign companies asserted they were likely to face a marginal tax rate exceeding 100% for high-cost mines (World Bank 2011, pp. 16–22).

3.3.2.5 Shift in Legal Environment

A new legal framework may affect the operations of a foreign company to various degrees. In Angola, a new mining code became effective in 2011. Despite some business-friendly provisions, for certain contracts the code gives priority to local firms, workers, and technicians. It also distinguishes between "ordinary" and "strategic" mineral resources, where the latter are subject to more state intervention (Business Monitor International 2013, p. 22). On a much larger scale, Travelers expresses concern about "Solvency II"—the capital adequacy and risk management regulations implemented by the European Commission in 2016. This US insurance company states that, "under Solvency II, it is possible that the US parent of a European Union subsidiary could be subject to certain Solvency II requirements if the regulator determines that the subsidiary's capital position is dependent on the parent company and the US parent is not already subject to regulations deemed "equivalent" to Solvency II" (Travelers 2017, p. 65).

---

[61] K. Bradsher, "Looking beyond China, Some Companies Shift Personnel," *New York Times*, 10 September 2014.

[62] The Gulf Cooperation Council includes Bahrain, Kuwait, Oman, Qatar, Saudi Arabia, and the United Arab Emirates.

3.3.2.6 Prosecutions and Fines

Multinational firms may be sued and fined for failing to comply with all applicable laws and regulations relevant to their operations abroad. During fiscal years 2012 through 2016, BHP Billiton failed to comply with various environmental regulations and received 18 separate fines from outside Australia, its home country.[63] In 2015, BNP Paribas was sentenced for conspiring to violate the International Emergency Economic Powers Act and the Trading with the Enemy Act (see Sect. 3.1.2). The BNP Paribas case raises a tricky issue. An ineffective and unpredictable judiciary—as is characteristic of developing countries—raises red flags among foreign investors (Kaufmann et al. 2002). Yet a study of corporate prosecutions in the United States reveals that corporate fines levied against foreign firms are much larger than those against US firms (Garrett 2014, pp. 218–249). These findings suggest that the risks related to legal, regulatory, and judicial environment are complex and not systematically correlated with poor governance indicators. As described next, MNCs may seek to circumvent legal and judicial risks by opting for corruption.

3.3.3 Corruption Practices

Senior (2006, p. 27) offers an accurate and useful definition of corruption: "corruption occurs when a corruptor covertly gives a favour to a corruptee or to a nominee to influence action(s) that benefit the corruptor or a nominee, and for which the corruptee has authority." Corruption practices are a peculiar risk in the sense that they generally aim to reduce other types of risks—for example, political and jurisdiction risks (for discussion from a global perspective, see Svensson 2005; Senior 2006). Corruption may threaten foreign firms in three ways.

A first problem affects the foreign investors engaged in countries, where corruption is widespread but who want to *avoid* any involvement with such illegal practices. In the 1990s, Procter & Gamble preferred to close a Pampers plant in Nigeria rather than pay a bribe to a customs official (Doh et al. 2003, p. 116). The *Dow Jones Anti-Corruption Survey Results 2014* shows that 66% of companies consider that bribery should always be reported to authorities, but only 13% report ever having taken action against corrupt competitors (Dow Jones 2014, p. 4). A company seeking to pursue an ethical strategy may "blow the whistle" on wrongdoers by alerting the media or nongovernmental organizations (NGOs; e.g., Transparency International).

Foreign firms who adopt corruption practices may experience short-term gains, but in the longer term, they risk reputational damage and prosecution in the host country. Siemens is a good illustration. In the 1990s and 2000s, the German engineering giant bribed thousands of officials in dozens of countries. As a consequence,

[63] Author's calculations based on BHP Billiton (2012, p. 166; 2013, p. 193; 2014, p. 215; 2015, p. 203; 2016, p. 154).

Siemens was later banned from doing business in Singapore for 5 years and was fined by several nations (including the United States, Nigeria, and Israel).[64] Amid this turmoil, Transparency International suspended Siemens's membership in the nongovernmental watchdog group.[65] This large-scale bribery by the Munich-headquartered company is now a notorious case study for law and political science scholars (see Choudhary 2013; Klinkhammer 2013).

The third threat to a corrupt firm is the risk of being prosecuted in its home country. In the United States, for example, the Foreign Corrupt Practices Act (FCPA) of 1977[66] makes it illegal for American citizens, US companies, and certain non-US foreign companies to influence foreign officials with any personal payments, rewards, or bribes.[67] In past years, many US firms have paid fines and penalties to settle US charges for making illegal foreign payments (Sanyal and Samanta 2011, p. 155). In most cases, the incriminated companies neither admit nor deny the complaint's allegations (Doh et al. 2003, p. 116). Compliance with FCPA provisions appears to be a major issue for DJIA firms (see Appendix 3).

3.4 Macroeconomic Risks

All foreign investors are exposed to local or worldwide recessions or economic crises. Walmart (2017, p. 17) states that economic slowdown and other economic factors are likely to affect consumer demand for the products their stores sell in foreign markets. Although it owns no mine in China, BHP Billiton (2012, p. 7; 2016, p. 30) explains that reduced Chinese demand may have a negative effect on its results. The success of Coca-Cola (2017, p.12) depends on its ability to grow in emerging and developing markets. Doubts on that score are driven by macroeconomic uncertainties. The macroeconomic risks studied here include country-specific and international monetary, financial, debt, fiscal, and trade risks that affect the activity of MNCs abroad.

[64] L. Kramer, "The World's Second-Oldest Profession," *Institutional Investor*, September 1998, p. 49; S. Schubert and T. C. Miller, "Managing the Siemens Bribe Budget; Accountant Details Secret Life Distributing $50 Million a Year," *International Herald Tribune*, 20 December 2008; T. Soniyi, "Bribe Scandal: Siemens Fined N7 Billion," *This Day*, 23 November 2010; T. Pileggi, "Ex-Power Company Execs Charged in Massive Siemens Bribery Case," *The Times of Israel*, 3 May 2016.

[65] M. Esterl, "Corruption Probes Threaten Germany's Image; Siemens, DaimlerChrysler Get Caught Up in Inquiries; A Backlog of Court Cases," *Wall Street Journal*, 24 November 2006.

[66] See https://www.justice.gov/criminal-fraud/foreign-corrupt-practices-act.

[67] Since then, other governments have enacted similar laws (e.g., the Bribery Act in United Kingdom). See Sanyal and Samanta (2011).

3.4.1 *Foreign Currency and Monetary Issues*

3.4.1.1 Foreign Currency Risk and Foreign Exchange Controls

The most frequent and basic risk relates to foreign currency fluctuations and especially depreciation. This type of risk became a major concern following collapse of the Bretton Woods accord in 1971–1973.[68] Today, currency risk is highlighted by almost all DJIA companies in their 2016–2017 annual reports (see Appendix 4). This is not surprising when one considers that, in 2016, Coca-Cola (2017, p. 12) used 72 functional currencies in addition to the US dollar.

Currency risk may stem from an excessive appreciation of the home country's currency. Merck (1987, pp. 3–4) reported that the foreign currencies in which its sales abroad were made had declined an overall 40% during 1981–1985.[69] A more common disturbance to the operations of foreign investors is persistent depreciation of the host country's currency. After Venezuela announced the establishment of several alternative exchange rate systems in 2014–2016, the subsidiary of 3M in Caracas had to recast its financial statements accordingly and also carefully monitor its access to liquidity (3M 2017, pp. 60–61). A more striking example is that of Argentina's 2002 currency crisis: The currency board system was abandoned, and the peso lost 70% of its value against the dollar. Argentina simultaneously imposed exchange controls, which restricted the ability of foreign firms to repatriate funds (Monsanto 2003, p. 46).

It is noteworthy that, in some developing and emerging economies, exchange control is a policy tool often used when the goal is a more stable financial system. For example, Jaguar Land Rover's subsidiary in China is subject to such restrictions and so cannot freely transfer cash to other entities outside China (Tata Motors 2013, p. 79).

Foreign currency risk is also a plague for the investors who purchase corporate or government bonds denominated in a currency that depreciates vis-à-vis their home country's currency.

3.4.1.2 Inflation and Risks Related to the Monetary Policy

Foreign currency depreciation is partly determined by the difference between inflation rates in the home and the host countries. Inflation was a major concern of most MNCs during the 1974–1975 world stagflation (see L'Air Liquide 1975, pp. 10, 14; L'Oréal 1975, pp. 14–17; Wells Fargo 1975, p. 10), but it has become less feared in

[68] Foreign investors have since developed foreign exchange hedging strategies to minimize currency risk.

[69] Foreign currency depreciation is actually an opportunity for MNCs intending to purchase assets in the foreign country.

light of the disinflation trend evident since the 1980s.[70] In 2015, only four economies—those of Venezuela, South Sudan, Ukraine, and Malawi—experienced inflation in excess of 20%.[71]

Monetary policy and the communication among central bankers are increasingly scrutinized by foreign investors (Holmes 2014). Most investors view the capacity of a central bank to fight inflation and deflation, maintain the stability of the financial system, provide adequate financial services, regulate banking institutions, and influence market expectations about the future levels of interest rates as crucial to sustaining economic growth in the medium-long term. Note that perceptions of the risk implied by a foreign country's monetary policy might diverge across business sectors. Take, for example, two German companies that operate in the United States. In 2013–2014, after the Federal Reserve began to normalize its monetary policy and announced that it planned to increase interest rates soon, Daimler (2015, p. 134) expressed its fear that this move could slow down the pace of growth. However, Munich Re (2016, p. 136) believed that the less expansive monetary policy would benefit its long-term insurance activity.

Finally, another key issue is the credibility of top officials in charge of the host country's monetary policy. For instance, in 2013, those in business circles hailed the appointment of Raghuram Rajan, former chief economist of the International Monetary Fund, as head of India's central bank.[72]

3.4.2 Financial and Private Debt Issues

Regardless of the country, regulatory bodies and the central bank must trade-off preserving the financial system's stability against stimulating economic growth. Since the 1980s, however, most of the monetary policies implemented and financial regulations passed in developed and emerging countries reflect the priority of economic stimulus. In concrete terms, this tendency has led to a surge in private indebtedness and also to asset price bubbles—typically in the equity and real estate sectors.

As evidence, one may examine the evolution of the ratio of total credit to private non-financial sector (as a percentage of GDP) in the United States, China, and Japan—the world's three largest economies; see Fig. 3.6. This ratio, which reflects the importance of leverage in the economy, increased in Japan and in the United States until a major financial crisis erupted (respectively) in the early 1990s and in 2007–2008. These two episodes suggest that the present credit boom in China could trigger another financial and economic crisis. That the Chinese economy might overheat should therefore be a major concern of foreign investors, whether or not they

[70] The world inflation rate dropped from 14% in 1980 to 5.6% in 1997 and 1.4% in 2015 (World Development Indicators).

[71] World Development Indicators.

[72] P. Sahu, "Delhi Taps IMF Veteran to Run Central Bank; Raghuram Rajan Is Viewed as a Reform-Minded Outsider in a Policy-Making Role Long Held by Indian Bureaucrats," *Wall Street Journal*, 6 August 2013.

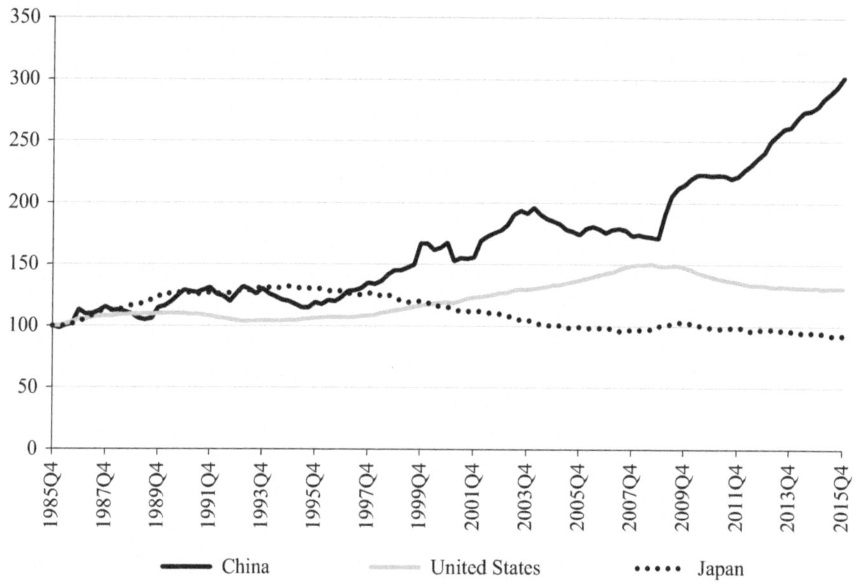

Fig. 3.6 Total credit to private nonfinancial sector as percentage of GDP (100 = 1985Q4). *Notes:* Quarterly data for China, Japan, and the United States. Credit is provided by domestic banks, all other sectors of the economy, and nonresidents. The "private non-financial sector" includes nonfinancial corporations, households, and nonprofit institutions that serve households. *Source:* https://fred.stlouisfed.org

operate in that country. HeidelbergCement (2014, p. 117; 2016, p. 129) seems to be among the few firms to worry *officially* about overheating and speculation, especially with respect to urban residential property. Other companies remain silent on this issue, perhaps because China is a such a large market and because the excessive lending and borrowing there mirror companies' own respective leverage strategies.

Financial crises may have many different causes. A surge in the proportion of nonperforming loans held by a bank, a drop in prices of a specific class of assets, and/or bad macroeconomic news (e.g., a poor GDP forecast, a disappointing manufacturing survey, a pessimistic speech delivered by a top policy maker) may lead bankers to reduce the supply of credit. The resulting increase in interest rates may trigger an economic slowdown or a recession. In this context, firms with greater short-term borrowing needs may face a liquidity or solvency crisis. If a financial institution is involved then strains in interbank lending markets may appear, which could well lead to a global banking crisis (for a review of banking crises, see Reinhart and Rogoff 2009, pp. 147–155). This scenario played out in the United States during 2007–2008, when Bear Stearns and Lehman Brothers went bankrupt. Had major central banks and the G7 governments not intervened as lenders of last resort, systemic risk would have materialized with consequences even more painful than those that did transpire.[73]

[73] Systemic risk is the possibility that an event at the bank or company level could trigger the collapse of an economy.

In addition to private debt issues, certain developing and emerging countries must cope with the risk of financial "openness." Financial liberalization is a double-edged sword: On the one hand, it is needed to attract foreign investors (especially *portfolio* investors), and on the other hand, it is likely to exacerbate a crisis if those investors lose confidence in the country or become risk averse. In their study of the 20th century's last three decades, Kaminsky and Reinhart (1999) show that financial liberalization frequently led to banking and currency crises. Such findings should encourage investors to monitor the financial openness of host countries. Chinn and Ito (2006) have developed and updated an index that measures the financial openness of most economies for the period 1970–2014. It seems that the richer the country, the greater its financial openness. However, the following low-income and lower-middle-income economies exhibit a financial openness index equal to that of rich industrialized countries and could therefore be more prone than expected to capital outflows and financial crises: Armenia, Gambia, Guatemala, Haiti, Liberia, Micronesia, Nicaragua, São Tomé and Principe, Uganda, Yemen, and Zambia.[74]

In their annual reports, multinational firms (including international banks) do not exhaustively analyze currency or banking crises. Yet they do express concerns about possible capital controls (Caterpillar 2017, p. 17; Goldman Sachs 2017, p. 43), which include the freezing of deposits, foreign currency controls, restrictions on certain transactions, tax measures, and tariffs. It is interesting that not all foreigners are equally affected by such risk. Thus, when Cyprus introduced capital controls in 2013, some foreign banks were exempt from the restrictions.[75]

With the advent of financial globalization, interdependence between economies has grown dramatically. A financial crisis in a major Latin American country may affect a foreign investor operating in an Asian economy. Contagion risk has become so high that it may be in the best interest of certain MNCs, especially those with long-term strategies, to conduct business in emerging countries that impose some (moderate) capital controls.

3.4.3 *Fiscal and Public Debt Issues*

The fiscal policy of a host country presents three challenges to MNCs. First, an excessively tight or orthodox fiscal policy may depress consumer spending and economic activity. The austerity programs implemented in eurozone countries during 2010–2012 were a source of concern for international investors (see Nissin Kogyo 2011, p. 1; Johnson & Johnson 2012, p. 4; Pirelli 2012, p. 32). A second challenge arises when fiscal policy affects the overall business climate or specific sectors through adverse tax measures, public expenditures aimed at supporting domestic companies, and so

[74] Author's classification based on Chinn and Ito's (2006) updated database and the World Bank list of economies as of September 2016.

[75] E. Hazou, "Call to Ease Restrictions to Stop Flight of Companies," *Cyprus Mail*, 29 May 2013.

forth (see also Sect. 3.3.2). In fact, the main risk in such circumstances is a continually expansionist fiscal policy and chronic fiscal deficits that might jeopardize the country's credit position and so lead to a major economic and financial crisis.

Figure 3.7 illustrates the distribution of sovereign defaults during 1975–2015. Their increase during the early and mid-1980s reflects the first widespread public debt crisis since WWII (see Sect. 4.2.1).[76] After a peak in the mid-1990s, the cases of distressed governments declined slowly; however, they were still nearly twice as numerous in 2015 as in the mid-1970s. Sub-Saharan Africa accounts for 44% of all observations, followed by Latin America and Caribbean countries (23%). The number of defaults in Europe and Central Asia increased by a factor of 6 between 1990 and 1995 because of the economic difficulties experienced by the states that gained independence from Yugoslavia and the Soviet Union.

A total of 21 countries remained in default during the entire period: Benin, Cambodia, Central African Republic, Chad, Democratic Republic of Congo, Republic of Congo, Ghana, Guinea, Guyana, Jordan, Madagascar, Mali, Mauritania, Nicaragua, Sierra Leone, Somalia, Tanzania, Togo, Uganda, Yemen, and Zambia. Because these governments are chronic defaulters, lenders (and, perhaps to a lesser extent, direct investors) are aware of the risks involved. Evidence spanning the past four decades indicates that sovereign risk is greatest for borrowers that regularly tap capital markets and thus are more likely to accumulate a large stock of debt.

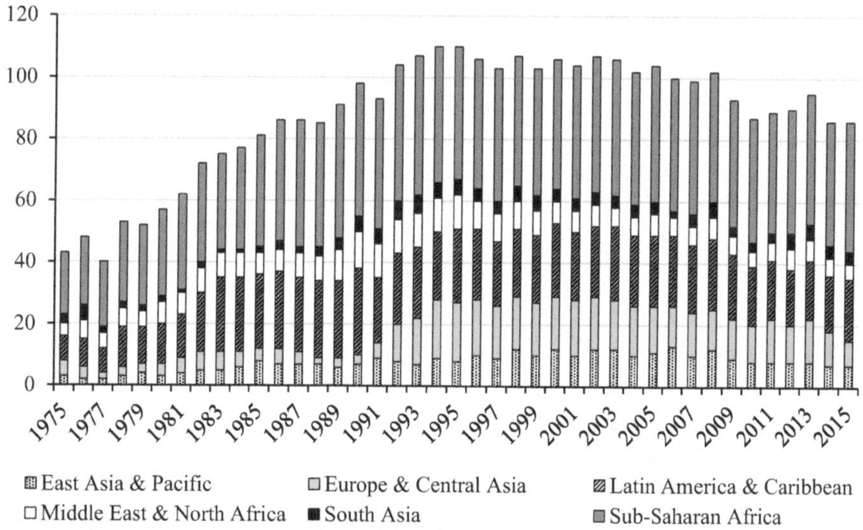

Fig. 3.7 Number of sovereign debt issuers in default by area, 1975–2015. *Notes:* Observations include all forms of default to all types of creditors; only those defaults of at least $500,000 are included. There was no sovereign default in North America during 1975–2015. *Sources:* Author's calculations based on Beers and de Leon-Manlagnit's (2019) database

[76] The total number of defaulting governments increased by 65% between 1979 and 1986.

During 1975–2015, the four most damaging "bankruptcies" (in terms of the total amounts of public debt in default for the period) were those in Argentina, Brazil, Greece, and Iraq.[77] The crisis of 1982–1983 obliged Buenos Aires and Brasilia to default on their FC bank loans. The haircuts imposed by the two governments on their foreign creditors averaged 20% and affected, respectively, $30 billion and $62 billion worth of debt (per Cruces and Trebesch's 2013 database).[78] The restructuring of Argentina's, Iraq's, and Greece's debts in (respectively) 2005, 2006, and 2012 led to haircuts far deeper than 50% (Cruces and Trebesch's 2013 database; Eurogroup 2012).

The riskiness of a sovereign "bankruptcy" is evidently linked to the domestic political context, the simultaneous occurrence of a currency or a banking crisis, and the form that the default takes.

If the default consists of a missed payment or a debt restructuring deal that is promptly negotiated and concluded, then risk is lower than in case of debt repudiation or unilateral debt restructuring (for a review, see Gaillard 2014, pp. 1–12). Also, political tensions may foreshadow a deep haircut on creditors (e.g., Poland in 1982, Iraq in 2006). Finally, a currency or banking crisis inevitably exacerbates any sovereign debt turmoil and vice versa: Domestic banks can no longer lend to their government, which in turn can no longer bail out distressed banks. The resulting collapse of the domestic currency puts both the government and banks in the position of desperately seeking foreign currencies, whose costs continue to rise.

The economic and financial crisis that hit Argentina in 2001–2002 is an illustration of this devastating spiral. The consequences were harsh for certain foreign bankers. For example, Citigroup (2003, p. 34) recorded a total of $1.7 billion in net pretax charges (60% of which represented net provisions for credit losses) for fiscal year 2002 alone. In addition, the peso's devaluation led to foreign currency translation losses that reduced Citigroup's equity by about $600 million. Foreign direct investors were also affected: The revenues of DaimlerChrysler Argentina S.A. tumbled 75%, from €698 million in 2000 to €176 million in 2002 (DaimlerChrysler 2001, p. 116; 2003, p. 144).

3.4.4 Trade Issues

Trade restrictions and protectionism can be serious impediments to exporters and direct investors. Under the auspices of the General Agreement on Tariffs and Trade (during 1948–1994) and the World Trade Organization (since 1995), many rules have been adopted to reduce tariffs and nontariff protective measures, to fight restrictive business practices, and to promote international investment and trade. These rules have been complemented by the signing of regional trade agreements and bilat-

[77] Author's classification based on Beers and de Leon-Manlagnit's (2019) database.

[78] The percentage reported here reflects the two main restructuring plans devised in 1987 and 1988 by, respectively, Argentina and Brazil.

eral investment treaties (Baldwin 2016). All such initiatives have contributed to stimulate international trade, whose average annual growth exceeded that of GDP for all regions during 1975–2015 (Fig. 3.8).

Despite this global evolution, many protectionist measures affecting foreign investors are still in force around the world. These include (among others) bailouts; state aid; competitive devaluation; consumption subsidies; export incentives; import bans, quotas, and tariffs; intellectual property protection; expropriation; restrictions on investment; localization requirements; "national content" preferences; sanitary and phytosanitary rules; technical barriers to trade; funding facilities; trade defense measures; and immigration restrictions.[79]

In June 2017, the economies that had implemented the highest number of protectionist rules were the United States (1438 rules enacted), India (904), Russia (878), Brazil (649), and Argentina (506). On average, there were 158 "anti-trade" measures in high-income countries as compared with 99, 53, and 3 measures in (respectively) upper-middle income, lower-middle income, and low-income countries.[80] Protectionism is unlike most other macroeconomic risks because it is characteristic

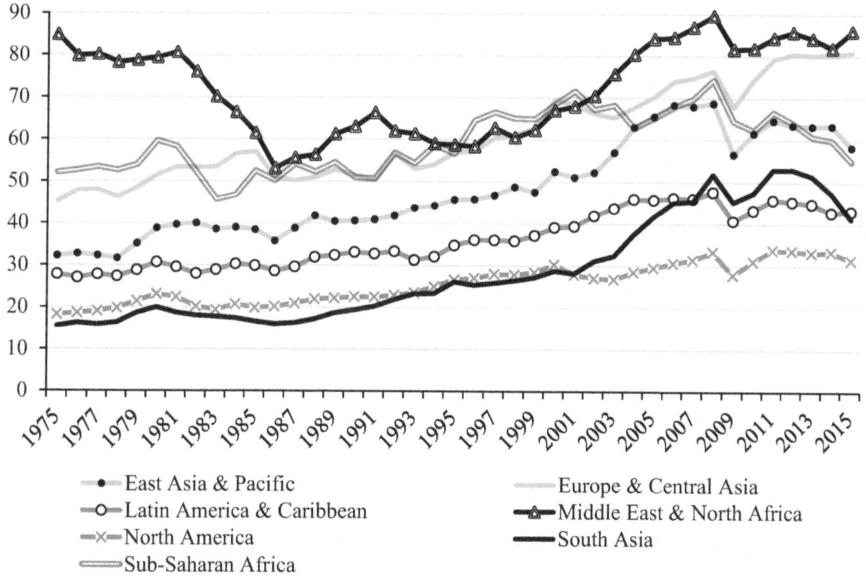

Fig. 3.8 Trade as percentage of GDP, 1975–2015. *Note:* Trade is the sum of exports and imports of goods and services measured as a share of gross domestic product. *Source:* World Development Indicators

[79] See http://www.globaltradealert.org for an exhaustive list of the different protectionist measures; that list identifies not only the implementing governments but also the affected trading partners (countries as well as firms).

[80] Author's calculations based on http://www.globaltradealert.org (data retrieved 16 June 2017).

of rich countries and not poor ones. The uncertainty related to the Brexit vote and President Trump's economic nationalism tends to support this view (Irwin 2017).

Most multinational companies express concerns about the risks of protectionism and potential trade disputes (see Appendix 4). For example, Caterpillar (2017, p. 10) views itself as being exposed to the imposition of burdensome tariffs or quotas and to changes in trade agreements. Boeing (2017, p. 10) fears that the raw materials on which it depends (e.g., aluminum and titanium) might become unavailable or available only at very high prices.

3.5 Microeconomic Risks

Microeconomic risks are ubiquitous as befits the multitude of components involved. Only the most significant supply- and demand-side risks are examined here. Supply-side risks (Sect. 3.5.1) are connected to the three basic factors of production: labor, capital, and land. Those demand-side risks that depend mainly on macroeconomic conditions (real income, inflation, prevailing interest rates, etc.) are addressed in Sect. 3.4. Hence Sect. 3.5.2 focuses on the demand-side risks driven by a shift in consumer preferences.

3.5.1 Supply-Side Risks

3.5.1.1 Social and Labor Risks

The first type of this social risk may be connected to the "obsolescing legitimacy" problem that can affect some MNCs abroad (Bucheli and Kim 2012). Foreign firms that violate human rights or overlook fundamental social norms are subject to labor riots that could disrupt their operations and tarnish their reputation. After decades of dreadful labor conditions on United Fruit Company's Colombian plantations, social tensions intensified throughout the country and encouraged local producers to organize and compete (successfully) with the Boston-based company (Bucheli 2004; Chomsky 2007).

In some cases, a foreign investor did not own manufacturing facilities abroad but stocked up at factories where workers were exploited. In the early 1990s, for example, Nike's general manager in Indonesia stated that it was not within the firm's scope to investigate allegations of labor violations in these factories.[81] Yet only a few years later, Nike had to accept the blame for those conditions and admit wrongdoing (see Sect. 3.5.2.2).

---

[81] A. Schwarz, "Shoe Manufacturers Accused of Exploiting Labour – Running a Business," *Far Eastern Economic Review*, 20 June 1991.

The second category of risk includes strikes and lockouts. Guillén (2000) conceptualizes how organized labor both responded to and shaped the presence of MNCs in newly industrialized economies. He identifies four images of multinationals (i.e., "villains," "necessary evils," "arm's-length collaborators," and "partners") that depend on the focal country's political regime and the economic attitudes of its organized labor segment. Authoritarian regimes, in which foreign investors are typically perceived as "villains," are more subject to labor riots; Argentina in the 1960s–1970s is an illustration (Guillén 2000, p. 428). The countries where foreign businesses are considered a "necessary evil" (e.g., Argentina in the 1990s) or "arm's-length collaborators" (e.g., South Korea) may be the scene of long strikes—for instance, the 5-month strike at a South Korean Nestlé plant in 2003.[82] In contrast, labor relations are generally less confrontational in "non-populist democracies" (e.g., Spain since the 1980s).

The third type of labor-related risk includes the cost of labor and the possibility of being unable to attract, hire, and retain a sufficiently qualified workforce. These fears *officially* top the list of social concerns among DJIA firms (see Appendix 5).

3.5.1.2 Capital-Related Risks

Insufficient access to credit and the difficulty of protecting intellectual capital are addressed in Sects. 3.4.2 and 3.3.2.3, respectively. Two additional risks are studied here: fraud and system failure.[83]

Internal fraud risks include, inter alia, the misappropriation of assets and fraudulent financial reporting in a foreign subsidiary. External fraud risks include (among others) industrial espionage, racketeering, blackmail, and violations of partnership agreements. For example, Danone discovered in 2007 that the Wahaha Group, its Chinese partner in a joint venture, had created secret companies that siphoned off profits. The French company filed a lawsuit in California but eventually exited the venture by selling its 51% stake in the Wahaha Group (Danone 2009, p. 99; 2010, p. 16).[84]

Two types of system failures are examined here: (1) blackouts and (2) ransomware, cyberattacks, and hacking.[85] Table 3.1 reports on the reliability of power supply. Electrical outages are a key constraint to doing business in South Asia, the Middle East, and North Africa. Moreover, the time required to obtain an electrical connection in these regions is exceedingly long.

---

[82] S. Len, "Long Strike at a Nestlé Plant in Korea Comes to an End," *New York Times*, 29 November 2003. It is remarkable that Nestlé (2004, 2005) did not mention this exceptionally long strike in its 2003 and 2004 annual reports.

[83] System failure and technological risk are here viewed as equivalents.

[84] D. Barboza, "Danone Exits China Venture after Years of Legal Dispute," *New York Times*, 30 September 2009.

[85] Ransomware, cyberattacks, and hacking are idiosyncratic in that their origins are seldom known with certainty. Thus, they cannot constitute a *systematic* component of country risk.

Table 3.1 Reliability of Electrical Connections

Region	Number of electrical outages in a typical month	Losses due to electrical outages (% of annual sales)	Days to obtain an electrical connection (after application)
East Asia and Pacific	5.0	1.3	27.6
Europe and Central Asia	2.0	1.2	31.5
Latin American and Caribbean	2.8	1.2	22.3
Middle East and North Africa	17.6	4.7	41.1
South Asia	25.4	6.6	55.1
Sub-Saharan Africa	8.3	5.2	36.8

Source: http://www.enterprisesurveys.org/data/exploretopics/infrastructure

Multinational companies are also concerned about cybersecurity incidents (see Appendix 6). The North Korean cyberattack on Sony in 2014 illustrates this phenomenon.[86] There is a risk that cyberattacks experienced by a firm or group of firms might be part of global technological warfare, referred to by Rid and Hecker (2009) as "War 2.0."

All these threats of business or supply chain disruptions require that foreign direct investors expend significant resources to enhance their control environment, processes, and practices (as advocated in DuPont 2017, p. 13).

3.5.1.3 Land

In addition to expropriation risk that may affect companies exploiting natural resources (see Sect. 3.3.1), the lack of access to land is a considerable challenge for foreigners who invest in small countries or territories like Dubai (Elbadawi 2016, pp. 299–303). The waiting period for property registration and construction permits can also complicate matters by causing expensive delays (World Bank 2016, pp. 62–69, 78–82).

[86] S. Sicard, "North Korean Cyber Attack on Sony Poses Tough Security Questions," *National Defense*, March 2015.

3.5.2 *Demand-Side Risks*

Beyond the changes in consumer tastes that are driven by international fashions and technological evolution, demand for goods and services supplied by MNCs may be jeopardized by adverse publicity and boycotts.

3.5.2.1 Adverse Publicity

Adverse publicity is often the result of content-related or quality risks.

Content-related risk usually involves public health issues. Since the 1990s, the tobacco industry has been held responsible for the illness and death of thousands of smokers. Tobacco firms have paid billions in fines and settlements in various countries.[87] They were also affected by many public health measures whose purpose was to reduce the consumption of tobacco products: increasing the taxes on cigarettes, prohibiting underage access to tobacco, launching anti-tobacco campaigns, expanding smoke-free areas, and so on (Britton and Bogdanovica 2013). More recently, Coca-Cola (2017, p. 10) has admitted that obesity and other health-related concerns could reduce demand for some of its products.

Quality risk has especially negative consequences; it is likely to tarnish a firm's reputation if not destroy its business altogether. During 2014–2016, several Japanese, European, and American automobile companies were obliged to recall millions of vehicles equipped with defective Takata airbags, which were responsible for many serious injuries and even deaths. Following an investigation led by the US Department of Justice, Takata—the Japanese original equipment manufacturer—paid $1 billion in criminal penalties and restitution to automakers that purchased the airbags[88] before filing, in June 2017, for bankruptcy protection in both the United States and Japan.[89]

3.5.2.2 Boycotts

Boycotts stem from ideological roots and are usually a response to perceived ethical lapses of the targeted company.

A striking illustration is the Arab League's boycott of Israeli companies, Israeli-made goods, non-Arab companies that do business with Israeli companies, and Arab entities that do business with blacklisted companies. This boycott, driven by an anti-

[87] See "Excerpts from Agreement between States and Tobacco Industry," *New York Times*, 25 June 1997.

[88] For a chronology, see http://www.consumerreports.org/cro/news/2016/05/everything-you-need-to-know-about-the-takata-air-bag-recall/index.htm.

[89] J. Soble, "Takata, Unable to Overcome Airbag Crisis, Files for Bankruptcy Protection," *New York Times*, 25 June 2017.

Zionist agenda, upsets the strategies of some Western MNCs. Shortly after opening a bottling franchise in Israel in 1966, Coca-Cola was expelled from Egypt—where it had been operating for decades (Labelle 2014).

Some boycotts are initiated by human rights groups. During 1996–2001, NGOs (e.g., Oxfam) worked with consumer and labor groups (e.g., the Clean Clothes Campaign) to organize boycotts of Nike goods after media revealed that the firm's production processes involved underpaid workers in Indonesia, child labor in Cambodia and Pakistan, and poor working conditions in China and Vietnam (Locke 2002). These boycotts damaged Nike's image and severely depressed its profitability: The firm's pretax income fell 36% in the United States and 98% abroad during fiscal year 1997–1998 (Nike 1998, p. 47). In May 1998, Nike's Chief Executive Officer announced a series of measures to improve factory working conditions (Nike 1998, p. 56).

Business circles have developed new tools to help reduce microeconomic risks. For example, more firms have begun to provide public statements discussing corporate social responsibility (CSR) and to codify business ethics (see Kitzmueller and Shimshack 2012). Present-day CSR principles aim not only to prevent social wrongdoing but also to reduce negative environmental effects.

3.6 Sanitary, Health, Industrial, and Environmental Risks

The main feature of sanitary, health, industrial, and environmental risks is that they endanger the lives of a firm's employees, its consumers, or a population group. Although some such risks are beyond the firm's control, others are the consequence of its activities.

3.6.1 Sanitary and Health Risks

One of the most dangerous health risks in the world is the human immunodeficiency virus (HIV), which causes acquired immune deficiency syndrome (AIDS). Firms that hire their workforce in regions where the HIV pandemic is severe (e.g., Southern Africa) are especially exposed.[90]

Ebola virus disease in sub-Saharan Africa and influenza A (H1N1) virus are extremely hazardous because they are likely to affect people traveling in contaminated zones. In 2009, a pandemic crisis management team at the Asian Development Bank (2010, p. 92) set up screening procedures and a medical hotline to respond to the outbreak of new influenza virus.

[90] See http://www.unaids.org.

Sanitary risk may be closely connected to the activities of a company. In 1990, Perrier—a French brand of natural bottled mineral water—had to recall its water in the United States after benzene was found in bottles.[91] However, some anticipated risks do not actually materialize. In 2013, for instance, China halted imports of all milk powder from New Zealand and Australia after dairy products were found to contain bacteria that could cause botulism. Fonterra, the New Zealand dairy giant, was held responsible for exporting these contaminated products. Yet it was announced just a few weeks later that the botulism scare was a false alarm (Fonterra 2013, pp. 10–11).[92]

3.6.2 *Industrial Risk*

Industrial risk generally reflects casualties resulting from a company's failure to comply with fundamental safety norms.

In April 2013, the collapse of the eight-story Rana Plaza building in Bangladesh killed more than 1100 people and injured thousands. The building housed several clothing factories that manufactured goods for Western retail companies (e.g., Benetton, Mango, Matalan, and Primark). In the months that followed, an accord was signed by more than 200 international brands toward the end of improving factory safety and labor conditions.[93]

The chemical tragedy in Bhopal had even stronger political repercussions because it affected civilian populations (and not just the firm's own employees), led to a long and controversial international judicial battle, and ultimately destroyed the company at fault. In December 1984, methyl isocyanate gas leaked from a tank at Union Carbide India Limited's Bhopal plant. Approximately 3800 people died, and thousands suffered permanent disabilities. Union Carbide Corporation (UCC) lost its reputation, paid $470 million in fines, and ended up being purchased by rival Dow Chemical in 1999 (Broughton 2005).[94]

---

[91] G. James, "Perrier Recalls Its Water in U.S. after Benzene Is Found in Bottles," *New York Times*, 10 February 1990.

[92] See also L. Craymer, "Fonterra Recall: New Zealand Dairy to Plead Guilty; Company Faces Maximum $425,000 Fine from Four Charges," *Wall Street Journal*, 13 March 2014.

[93] "Rising from the Rubble," *Sunday Times*, 24 April 2016.

[94] S. Warren, "Dow Chemical to Acquire Union Carbide—Deal, Valued at $8.89 Billion, Would Position Firm to Challenge DuPont," *Wall Street Journal*, 5 August 1999.

3.6.3 Environmental Risk

In addition to the numerous casualties it caused, the Bhopal accident irrevocably damaged the local environment. Two studies released in December 2009 confirmed the presence of toxic chemicals in the soil and groundwater around the abandoned UCC plant. Drinking water samples contained total pesticides as high as 59 times the levels permitted by the Bureau of Indian Standards.[95]

Such pollution cases are not uncommon in the mining sector. In 2001, cyanide waste contaminated the Asuman, a Ghanaian river, after a tailings dam ruptured at a mine operated by Goldfields Ltd. (a South African company). Thereafter, those living in the villages along the river no longer had clean drinking water and were prohibited from fishing; thus, this industrial catastrophe cost that population its main source of sustenance and revenue.[96]

Other environmental hazards include air pollution, oil spills, nuclear fallout, and deforestation. The repeated occurrence of hazardous events has progressively deteriorated overall working conditions in some areas. The toxic smog that has cloaked Beijing for several years documents the interconnectedness of health, industrial, and environmental risks, which can undermine the efficient operation of MNCs (see Appendix 6).

3.7 Natural and Climate Risks

Natural catastrophes were long overlooked by many investors until climate risk emerged as a new threat in business circles.[97]

3.7.1 Natural Risk

Natural risk may materialize in various forms. These include (among others) coastal erosion, drought, earthquake, extreme temperature, flood, insect infestation, hurricane, landslide, storm, volcanic activity, and wildfire.

In 1999, the Turkish industrial center of Izmit was hit by an earthquake. Biomeks, the Turkish distributor of Anika Therapeutics (a US firm), was obliged to postpone

[95] N. Jayaraman, "Bhopal: Generations of Poison," Special to CorpWatch, 2 December 2009, available at http://www.corpwatch.org/article.php?id=15485.

[96] M. Anane, "Ghana: Cyanide Spill Worst Disaster Ever in West African Nation," *Environment News Service*, 24 October 2001, available at http://www.corpwatch.org/article.php?id=744.

[97] A catalyst for this changed assessment may well have been publication of the *first* report by the Intergovernmental Panel on Climate Change (IPCC 1990).

product delivery to local customers, which caused disruption in sales and profits (Bouchet et al. 2003, p. 17).

An earthquake is likely to affect creditors, too. In 2010, the earthquake that devastated Haiti constrained the IMF to cancel the country's outstanding liabilities to the Fund, after which it approved a credit facility to support reconstruction (IMF 2010).

Natural disasters can also have indirect consequences. BHP Billiton (2010, p. 11) expressed concern when the Chilean government announced an increase in the corporate income tax rate and a change in the mining code to fund the reconstruction of the areas destroyed by an earthquake.

3.7.2 Climate Risk

Climate risk has become a key component of country risk, and it is likely to worsen the business environment for all companies regardless of sector and geographical location.

The 2007 Fourth Assessment Report of the Intergovernmental Panel on Climate Change (IPCC) presents empirical evidence linking human economic activities to the emission of greenhouse gases (IPCC 2007). These conclusions are confirmed in the 2014 Fifth Assessment Report. Climatic evolution will have negative consequences on social and economic life worldwide. By 2030–2040, IPCC experts fear reduced crop productivity associated with heat and drought stress in Africa; increased water restrictions and extreme heat events in Europe; wildfire-induced loss of ecosystem integrity, property loss, and human mortality in North America; decreased food production and the spread of vector-borne diseases in Central and South America; and increased risk of heat-related mortality in Central and South Asia. Moreover, if the global mean sea level continues to rise then low-lying coastal areas will be threatened while biodiversity and the abundance of fisheries will decline (IPCC 2014, pp. 21–25).

Climate-related hazards exacerbate natural risks, yet they might also affect political stability. The IPCC (2014, p. 20) indicates that climate-induced population displacement, and hence violent conflict, may spread in several regions throughout the twenty-first century.

Although all business activities are threatened by climate risk (see Appendix 6), the insurance and reinsurance sectors are especially vulnerable (Mills 2009; Travelers 2017, pp. 109–110). Beyond corporate concerns, a huge challenge for capitalist societies is to avert those catastrophes against which it may well be impossible to insure.

Appendix 1: International Political Risks Perceived by DJIA Firms, 2016–2017

Firm	Relations between the recipient country and the investor's country	International sanctions and embargoes	International tensions and warfare
3M	No	No	Yes. Reference to "geopolitical risks"
American Express	Yes. Concern about "a negative perception of the United States" abroad	No	Yes
Apple	No	No	Yes. Reference to "geopolitical uncertainties"
Boeing	No	Yes	Yes (e.g., reference to "political unrest involving Russia and Ukraine")
Caterpillar	No	Yes	Yes
Chevron	No	No	Yes. Reference to war
Cisco	Partly. Concern about retaliations to "intelligence gathering methods of the U.S. government"	No	No
Coca-Cola	Not explicit	Yes	Yes
Disney	No	No	Yes, but in general terms
DuPont	No	No	No
Exxon Mobil	Not explicit	Yes	No
General Electric	No	No	Yes. Reference to "geopolitical risks"
Goldman Sachs	Not explicit	Yes	Yes, but in general terms
Home Depot	No	No	Yes. Reference to war
IBM	No	No	Yes
Intel	No	No	Yes
Johnson & Johnson	No	No	Yes. Reference to war
JPMorgan Chase	No	Yes	Yes. Reference to "geopolitical instabilities"
McDonald's	No	No	No
Merck	No	No	Yes. Reference to war
Microsoft	Not explicit	Yes	Yes. Reference to war
Nike	No	No	Yes. Reference to military conflicts
Pfizer	No	No	Yes
Procter & Gamble	No	No	Yes. Reference to war
Travelers	No	No	No

Firm	Relations between the recipient country and the investor's country	International sanctions and embargoes	International tensions and warfare
United Technologies	Not explicit	Yes	Yes. Reference to "geopolitical risks"
UnitedHealth	No	No	No
Verizon	No	No	Yes. Reference to war
Visa	No	No	Yes
Walmart	No	Yes	Yes

Sources: Author's analysis based on "Item 1A. Risk Factors" of US Securities and Exchange Commission (SEC) Form 10-K as filed by the 30 DJIA companies for the fiscal year ended between April 2016 and March 2017

Appendix 2: Domestic Political Risks Perceived by DJIA Firms, 2016–2017

Firm	Political instability	Domestic tensions and warfare
3M	Yes, but in general terms: political conditions in specific countries	
American Express	Yes	Yes. Reference to "nationalism"
Apple	Yes. Reference to war and terrorism	
Boeing	Yes (e.g., "changes in non-U.S. national priorities and budgets")	Yes, but in general terms
Caterpillar	Yes	Yes
Chevron	Yes, but in general terms	
Cisco	Yes, but in general terms	
Coca-Cola	Yes	Yes
Disney	Yes, but in general terms	
DuPont	Yes	Not explicit
Exxon Mobil	Yes	Yes. Reference to "civil unrest"
General Electric	Yes, but in general terms	Yes. Reference to "populism" and "nationalism"
Goldman Sachs	Yes, but in general terms	
Home Depot	Yes, but in general terms	
IBM	Yes, but in general terms	
Intel	Yes	Yes
Johnson & Johnson	Yes, but in general terms	
JPMorgan Chase	Yes, but in general terms	
McDonald's	Yes, but in general terms	
Merck	Yes, but in general terms	
Microsoft	Yes, but in general terms	
Nike	Yes	Yes. Reference to "political unrest"

Firm	Political instability	Domestic tensions and warfare
Pfizer	Yes	Yes. Reference to "political unrest"
Procter & Gamble	Yes	Yes. Reference to political upheaval
Travelers	Yes, but in general terms	
United Technologies	Yes, but in general terms	
UnitedHealth	Yes, but in general terms	
Verizon	Yes, but in general terms	
Visa	Yes, but in general terms	
Walmart	Yes, but in general terms	

Sources: Author's analysis based on "Item 1A. Risk Factors" of SEC Form 10-K as filed by the 30 DJIA companies for the fiscal year ended between April 2016 and March 2017

Appendix 3: Jurisdiction Risks Perceived by DJIA Firms, 2016–2017

Firm	Expropriation	Unstable legal, regulatory, or judiciary environment	Corruption
3M	No	Yes	Yes, reference to the FCPA
American Express	No	Yes (e.g., "laws and business practices that favor local competitors")	Yes, reference to the FCPA
Apple	No	Yes	Yes, but in general terms
Boeing	No	Yes	No
Caterpillar	No	Yes	Yes, reference to the FCPA
Chevron	Yes	Yes	No
Cisco	Yes. Major concern	Yes	No
Coca-Cola	No	Yes	Yes, reference to the FCPA
Disney	Yes. Reference to "ownership restrictions"	Yes	Yes
DuPont	No	Yes	No
Exxon Mobil	Yes	Yes	No
General Electric	No	Yes	No
Goldman Sachs	Yes	Yes	Yes, reference to the FCPA
Home Depot	No	Yes	Yes, reference to the FCPA

Firm	Expropriation	Unstable legal, regulatory, or judiciary environment	Corruption
IBM	Yes. Reference to the "ownership and protection of patents"	Yes	Yes
Intel	Yes	Yes	Yes, reference to the FCPA
Johnson & Johnson	Yes. Major concern	Yes	Yes, reference to the FCPA
JPMorgan Chase	Yes	Yes	Yes, implicit reference to the FCPA
McDonald's	No	Yes	Yes
Merck	Yes	Yes	No
Microsoft	No	Yes	Yes, reference to the FCPA
Nike	No	Yes	No
Pfizer	Yes	Yes	Yes, reference to the FCPA
Procter & Gamble	No	Yes	Yes, reference to the FCPA
Travelers	Yes	Yes. Major concern	Yes, reference to the FCPA
United Technologies	Yes. Reference to the protection of "intellectual property"	Yes	Yes, reference to the FCPA
UnitedHealth	Yes	Yes	No
Verizon	No	Yes	No
Visa	No	Yes	No
Walmart	No	Yes	Yes, reference to the FCPA

Sources: Author's analysis based on "Item 1A. Risk Factors" of SEC Form 10-K as filed by the 30 DJIA companies for the fiscal year ended between April 2016 and March 2017

Appendix 4: Macroeconomic Risks Perceived by DJIA Firms, 2016–2017

Firm	Foreign currency exchange rates and fluctuations	Economic or financial crisis	Trade disputes; availability and cost of energy and raw materials	Deposit freeze, foreign exchange control, or sovereign default
3M	Yes	Yes	Yes	Yes
American Express	Yes	Yes	Yes	Yes
Apple	Yes	Yes	Yes	Yes

Firm	Foreign currency exchange rates and fluctuations	Economic or financial crisis	Trade disputes; availability and cost of energy and raw materials	Deposit freeze, foreign exchange control, or sovereign default
Boeing	Yes	Yes	Yes	Unclear
Caterpillar	Yes	Yes	Yes. Changes in trade rules are a major concern	Yes
Chevron	Not explicit	Not explicit	Yes	Yes
Cisco	Yes	Yes	Yes	No
Coca-Cola	Yes	Yes	Yes. Major concern	Not explicit
Disney	Yes	Yes	Yes	Yes
DuPont	Yes	Yes	Yes	Yes
Exxon Mobil	Yes	Yes	Yes	Yes
General Electric	Yes	Yes	Yes	Yes
Goldman Sachs	Yes	Yes	Not explicit	Yes
Home Depot	Yes	Yes	Yes	Not explicit
IBM	Yes	Yes	Yes	Yes
Intel	Yes	Yes	Yes	Yes
Johnson & Johnson	Yes	Yes	Yes	Not explicit
JPMorgan Chase	Yes	Yes	Yes	Yes
McDonald's	Yes	Yes	Yes	Yes
Merck	Yes	Yes	Yes	Not explicit
Microsoft	Yes	Yes	Yes	Not explicit
Nike	Yes	Yes	Yes	Yes
Pfizer	Yes	Yes	Yes	Yes
Procter & Gamble	Yes	Yes	Yes	Yes
Travelers	Yes	Yes	Not explicit	Yes
United Technologies	Yes	Yes	Yes	Yes
UnitedHealth	Yes	Yes	No	Yes
Verizon	No	Yes	No	No
Visa	Yes	Yes	Yes	Yes
Walmart	Yes	Yes	Yes	Not explicit

Sources: Author's analysis based on "Item 1A. Risk Factors" of SEC Form 10-K as filed by the 30 DJIA companies for the fiscal year ended between April 2016 and March 2017

Appendix 5: Microeconomic Risks Perceived by DJIA Firms, 2016–2017

Firm	Fraud	Negative publicity or boycotts	Adverse labor conditions
3M	No	No	Yes
American Express	Partly and indirectly: fear that third-party service providers may act in ways that "could result in regulatory actions, fines, sanctions or economic and reputational harm"		Yes, but in very general terms
Apple	Yes	No	Yes
Boeing	No	No	Yes (e.g., the hiring of "non-U.S. representatives and consultants")
Caterpillar	No	Yes. "Negative publicity" in connection with cost reduction actions	Yes, major concern (e.g., "business culture" problems, "union disputes")
Chevron	No	Partly. Reference to "societal pressures"	No
Cisco	Yes. Fear of counterfeit products	No	Yes
Coca-Cola	Not explicit	Yes. Major concern	Yes
Disney	Implicit reference	No	Yes
DuPont	No	No	No
Exxon Mobil	No	No	No
General Electric	No	No	Yes
Goldman Sachs	Yes	Yes, reference to "negative publicity"	No
Home Depot	Yes	No	Yes
IBM	Yes	No	Yes
Intel	Yes	No	Yes
Johnson & Johnson	Not explicit	No	Yes
JPMorgan Chase	Implicit reference	Yes, reference to "adverse publicity"	Yes
McDonald's	Not explicit	Yes	Yes
Merck	Yes	Partly. Reference to the role of certain "social media platforms"	Yes
Microsoft	Yes	No	Yes

Firm	Fraud	Negative publicity or boycotts	Adverse labor conditions
Nike	Yes. Fear of counterfeit products	Yes ("negative publicity")	Yes
Pfizer	Yes	No	Not explicit
Procter & Gamble	Yes	Yes ("negative publicity")	Yes
Travelers	Yes	Yes ("negative publicity")	Yes
United Technologies	Not explicit	Yes ("adverse publicity")	Yes
UnitedHealth	Yes	Yes ("negative publicity")	Yes
Verizon	Not explicit	No	Yes
Visa	Yes. Major concern	No	Yes
Walmart	Yes	No	Yes

Sources: Author's analysis based on "Item 1A. Risk Factors" of SEC Form 10-K as filed by the 30 DJIA companies for the fiscal year ended between April 2016 and March 2017

Appendix 6: Sanitary, Health, Industrial, Technological, Environmental, Natural, and Climate Risks Perceived by DJIA Firms, 2016–2017

Firm	Technological, industrial, sanitary, or environmental risks	Natural or climate risks
3M	Partly: reference to "natural and *other* disasters" and to "cybersecurity risks"	Yes
American Express	Yes	Yes
Apple	Yes	Yes
Boeing	Yes	Yes
Caterpillar	Yes	Yes
Chevron	Yes	Yes
Cisco	Yes	Yes
Coca-Cola	Main concern relates to cyberattacks	Yes. Long-term adverse impact
Disney	Yes	Yes
DuPont	Main concern relates to cyberattacks	Yes
Exxon Mobil	Yes	Yes
General Electric	Main concern relates to cyberattacks	Not explicit
Goldman Sachs	Yes	Yes
Home Depot	Yes	Yes
IBM	Yes	Yes
Intel	Yes	Yes

Firm	Technological, industrial, sanitary, or environmental risks	Natural or climate risks
Johnson & Johnson	Yes	Yes
JPMorgan Chase	Yes	Yes
McDonald's	Yes	Yes
Merck	Yes	Yes
Microsoft	Yes	Yes
Nike	Yes	Yes
Pfizer	Yes	Yes
Procter & Gamble	Yes	Yes
Travelers	Yes. Major concern	Yes. Major concern
United Technologies	Yes	Yes
UnitedHealth	No	No
Verizon	Yes	Yes
Visa	Yes	Yes
Walmart	Yes	Yes

Sources: Author's analysis based on "Item 1A. Risk Factors" of SEC Form 10-K as filed by the 30 DJIA companies for the fiscal year ended between April 2016 and March 2017

References

3M (2017). *Annual Report Pursuant to Section 13 or 15(d) of the Securities Exchange Act of 1934 for the fiscal year ended December 31, 2016*, Form 10–K.

African Mining (2002a, May–June). Country updates—Burundi: African Mining, 7(3).

African Mining (2002b, July–August). Country updates—Burundi: African Mining, 7(4).

African Mining (2002c, September–October). Country updates—Burundi: African Mining, 7(5).

American Express (2017). *Annual Report Pursuant to Section 13 or 15(d) of the Securities Exchange Act of 1934 for the fiscal year ended December 31, 2016*, Form 10–K.

Apple (2016). *Annual Report Pursuant to Section 13 or 15(d) of the Securities Exchange Act of 1934 for the fiscal year ended September 24, 2016*, Form 10–K.

Areva (2014). *2013 Annual report.*

Asian Development Bank (2001). *Annual report 2000.*

Asian Development Bank (2002). *Annual report 2001.*

Asian Development Bank (2010). *Annual report 2009.*

Assemblée Nationale (2007). *Rapport d'information déposé en application de l'article 145 du Règlement par la Commission des Affaires Etrangères en conclusion des travaux d'une mission d'information constituée le 13 décembre 2006 sur la situation des Français rapatriés de Côte d'Ivoire*, Rapport d'information No. 3694, 13 février.

Attijariwafa Bank (2012). *2011 Annual report.*

Attijariwafa Bank (2013). *2012 Annual report.*

Attijariwafa Bank (2014). *2013 Annual report.*

Baldwin, R. (2016). The World Trade Organization and the future of multilateralism. *Journal of Economic Perspectives, 30*(1).

Beers, D., & de Leon-Manlagnit, P. (2019). The BoC-BoE sovereign default database: What's new in 2019? *Bank of Canada Staff Working Paper 2019-39.*

Bellamy, C. (1998, February). If You can't stand the heat: New concepts of conflict intensity. *Royal United Services Institute Journal, 143*(1).

BHP Billiton (2010). *Annual report 2010.*

BHP Billiton (2012). *Annual report 2012.*

BHP Billiton (2013). *Annual report 2013.*

BHP Billiton (2014). *Annual report 2014.*

BHP Billiton (2015). *Annual report 2015.*

BHP Billiton (2016). *Annual report 2016.*

Billingsley, A. (2010). *Political succession in the Arab world: Constitutions, family loyalties and Islam.* London and New York: Routledge.

Boeing (2017). *Annual Report Pursuant to Section 13 or 15(d) of the Securities Exchange Act of 1934 for the fiscal year ended December 31, 2016*, Form 10–K.

Bouchet, M. H., Clark, E., & Groslambert, B. (2003). *Country risk assessment—A guide to global investment strategy.* Chichester: Wiley.

Britton, J., & Bogdanovica, I. (2013). Tobacco control efforts in Europe. *The Lancet, 381.*

Broughton, E. (2005). The Bhopal disaster and its aftermath: A review. *Environmental Health: A Global Access Science Source, 4*(6).

Bucheli, M. (2004). Enforcing business contracts in South America: The United Fruit company and Colombian banana planters in the twentieth century. *Business History Review, 78*(2).

Bucheli, M., & Kim, M.-Y. (2012). Political institutional change, obsolescing legitimacy, and multinational corporations: The case of the Central American banana industry. *MIR: Management International Review, 52*(6).

Business Monitor International (2013). *Angola —Mining report*, Q4 2013.

Casino Group (2011). *Registration document 2010.*

Caterpillar (2017). *Annual Report Pursuant to Section 13 or 15(d) of the Securities Exchange Act of 1934 for the fiscal year ended December 31, 2016*, Form 10–K.

Centerra Gold Inc. (2015). *Annual report 2014.*

Chevron (2017). *Annual Report Pursuant to Section 13 or 15(d) of the Securities Exchange Act of 1934 for the fiscal year ended December 31, 2016*, Form 10–K.

Chinn, M. D., & Ito, H. (2006). What matters for financial development? Capital controls, institutions, and interactions. *Journal of Development Economics, 81*(1).

Chomsky, A. (2007). Globalization, labor, and violence in Colombia's banana zone. *International Labor and Working-Class History, 72*(1).

Choudhary, A. (2013). Anatomy and impact of bribery on Siemens AG. *Journal of Legal, Ethical and Regulatory Issues, 16*(2).

Chrysler Group (2014). *Annual Report Pursuant to Section 13 or 15(d) of the Securities Exchange Act of 1934 for the fiscal year ended December 31, 2013*, Form 10–K.

Cisco (2016). *Annual Report Pursuant to Section 13 or 15(d) of the Securities Exchange Act of 1934 for the fiscal year ended July 30, 2016*, Form 10–K.

Citigroup (2003). *Annual Report, 2002.*

Coca-Cola (2017). *Annual Report Pursuant to Section 13 or 15(d) of the Securities Exchange Act of 1934 for the fiscal year ended December 31, 2016*, Form 10–K.

Colgate-Palmolive Company (1990). *1989 Annual report.*

Cruces, J. J., & Trebesch, C. (2013). Sovereign defaults: The price of haircuts. *American Economic Journal: Macroeconomics, 5*(3).

Daimler (2015). *Annual report 2014.*

DaimlerChrysler (2001). *Annual report 2000.*

DaimlerChrysler (2003). *Annual report 2002.*

Danone (2009). *Registration document 2008.*

Danone (2010). *Registration document 2009.*

Disney (2016). *Annual Report Pursuant to Section 13 or 15(d) of the Securities Exchange Act of 1934 for the fiscal year ended October 1, 2016*, Form 10–K.
Doh, J. P., Rodriguez, P., Uhlenbruck, K., Collins, J., Edenand, L., & Shekshnia, S. (2003). Coping with corruption in foreign markets. *Academy of Management Executive, 17*(3).
Dow Jones (2014). *Anti-corruption survey results 2014.*
DuPont (2017). *Annual Report Pursuant to Section 13 or 15(d) of the Securities Exchange Act of 1934 for the fiscal year ended December 31, 2016*, Form 10–K.
Elbadawi, I. (2016). Access to land and the investment behavior of firms. In A. Al Faris & R. Soto (Eds.), *The economy of Dubai*. Oxford: Oxford University Press.
Eurogroup (2012). *Eurogroup statement*. 21 February.
Export-Import Bank of the United States (1981). *Fiscal 1980 annual report*, Washington, DC.
Exxon Mobil (2017). *Annual Report Pursuant to Section 13 or 15(d) of the Securities Exchange Act of 1934 for the fiscal year ended December 31, 2016*, Form 10–K.
Fonterra (2013). *Annual review 2013.*
Frynas, J. G. (1998). Political instability and business: Focus on Shell in Nigeria. *Third World Quarterly, 19*(3).
Gaillard, N. (2014). *When sovereigns go bankrupt*. Cham: Springer.
Garrett, B. L. (2014). *Too big to jail: How prosecutors compromise with corporations*. Cambridge: Harvard University Press.
General Electric (2017). *Annual Report Pursuant to Section 13 or 15(d) of the Securities Exchange Act of 1934 for the fiscal year ended December 31, 2016*, Form 10–K.
Glencore (2012). *Annual report 2011.*
Glencore (2017). *Annual report 2016.*
Goldman Sachs (2017). *Annual Report Pursuant to Section 13 or 15(d) of the Securities Exchange Act of 1934 for the fiscal year ended December 31, 2016*, Form 10–K.
Goldstein, E. (1992). *Wars and peace treaties, 1816–1991*. London: Routledge.
Grimaud, N. (1972). Le conflit pétrolier franco-algérien. *Revue française de science politique, 22*(6).
Guillén, M. (2000). Organized labor's images of multinational enterprise: Divergent foreign investment ideologies in Argentina, South Korea, and Spain. *Industrial and Labor Relations Review, 53*(3).
Hajzler, C., & Rosborough, J. (2016). Government corruption and foreign direct investment under the threat of expropriation. *Bank of Canada Staff Working Paper 2016-13.*
Haley, U. C. V., & Haley, G. T. (2013). *Subsidies to Chinese industry: State capitalism, business strategy and trade policy*. Oxford: Oxford University Press.
Hartleb, F. (2015). Here to stay: Anti-establishment parties in Europe. *European View, 14*(1).
HeidelbergCement (2014). *Annual report 2013.*
HeidelbergCement (2016). *Annual report 2015.*
Helmerich & Payne, Inc. (2010). *Annual report 2010.*
Helmerich & Payne, Inc. (2016). *Annual report for 2016.*
Hilton Hotels (1964). *Annual report 1963.*
Hira, A., & Gaillard, N. (2011). The bottom line: The fundamental weaknesses of Latin American Finance. *Bulletin of Latin American Research, 30*(2).
Hoekman, B., & Djankov, S. (2000). Competition law in post-central-planning Bulgaria. *Antitrust Bulletin, 45*(1).
Holmes, D. R. (2014). *Economy of words: Communicative imperatives in central banks*. Chicago: Chicago University Press.
Home Depot (2017). *Annual Report Pursuant to Section 13 or 15(d) of the Securities Exchange Act of 1934 for the fiscal year ended January 29, 2017*, Form 10–K.
Huntington, S. P. (1968). *Political order in changing societies*. New Haven: Yale University Press.
IBM (2017). *Annual Report Pursuant to Section 13 or 15(d) of the Securities Exchange Act of 1934 for the fiscal year ended December 31, 2016*, Form 10–K.

Intel (2017). *Annual Report Pursuant to Section 13 or 15(d) of the Securities Exchange Act of 1934 for the fiscal year ended December 31, 2016*, Form 10–K.
Intergovernmental Panel on Climate Change (1990). *Climate change: The IPCC impacts assessment*. In W. J. M. G. Tegart, G. W. Sheldon, & D. C. Griffiths (Eds.), *Report prepared for IPCC by Working Group II*. Canberra: Australian Government Publishing Service.
Intergovernmental Panel on Climate Change (2007). *Climate change 2007: Impacts, adaptation and vulnerability*. In M. Parry, O. Canziani, J. Palutikof, P. van der Linden, & C. Hanson (Eds.), *Contribution of Working Group II to the fourth assessment report of the intergovernmental panel on climate change*. Cambridge: Cambridge University Press.
Intergovernmental Panel on Climate Change (2014). Summary for policymakers. In C. B. Field, V. R. Barros, D. J. Dokken, K. J. Mach, M. D. Mastrandrea, T. E. Bilir, M. Chatterjee, K. L. Ebi, Y. O. Estrada, R. C. Genova, B. Girma, E. S. Kissel, A. N. Levy, S. MacCracken, P. R. Mastrandrea, & L. L. White (Eds.), *Climate change 2014: Impacts, adaptation, and vulnerability. Part A: Global and sectoral aspects, Contribution of Working Group II to the fifth assessment report of the intergovernmental panel on climate change*. Cambridge/New York, NY: Cambridge University Press.
International Finance Corporation (various years). *Annual report*, Washington, DC.
International Monetary Fund (2010). IMF Executive Board cancels Haiti's debt and approves new three-year program to support reconstruction and economic growth. *Press Release No. 10/299*, 21 July.
Irwin, D. A. (2017). The false promise of protectionism—Why Trump's trade policy could backfire. *Foreign Affairs, 96*(3).
Johnson, L. L. (1965). U.S. business interests in Cuba and the rise of Castro. *World Politics, 17*(3).
Johnson & Johnson (2012). *Annual report 2011*.
Johnson & Johnson (2017). *Annual Report Pursuant to Section 13 of the Securities Exchange Act of 1934 for the fiscal year ended January 1, 2017*, Form 10–K.
JPMorgan Chase (2017). *Annual Report Pursuant to Section 13 or 15(d) of the Securities Exchange Act of 1934 for the fiscal year ended December 31, 2016*, Form 10–K.
Kaminsky, G. L., & Reinhart, C. M. (1999). The twin crises: The causes of banking and balance-of-payments problems. *American Economic Review, 89*(3).
Kaufmann, D., Kraay, A., & Zoido-Lobatón, P. (2002). Governance matters II: Updated indicators for 2000–01. *World Bank Policy Research Working Paper No. 2772*.
Kitzmueller, M., & Shimshack, J. (2012). Economic perspectives on corporate social responsibility. *Journal of Economic Literature, 50*(1).
Klinkhammer, J. (2013). On the dark side of the code: Organizational challenges to an effective anti-corruption strategy. *Crime, Law and Social Change, 60*(2).
Kobrin, S. J. (1984). Expropriation as an attempt to control foreign firms in LDCs: Trends from 1960 to 1979. *International Studies Quarterly, 28*(3).
L'Air Liquide (1975). *L'Air Liquide 1974*.
L'Oréal (1975). *L'Oréal 1974*.
Labelle, M. M. (2014). De-coca-colonizing Egypt: Globalization, decolonization, and the Egyptian boycott of Coca-Cola, 1966–68. *Journal of Global History, 9*(1).
Lancaster, T. D. (2017). The Spanish general elections of 2015 and 2016: A new stage in democratic politics? *West European Politics, 40*(4).
Locke, R. M. (2002, July). The promise and perils of globalization: The case of Nike. *MIT Working Paper IPC-02-00*.
Losman, D. L. (1998, April). Economic sanctions: An emerging business menace. *Business Economics, 33*(2).
Luttwak, E. (1969). *Coup d'Etat—A practical handbook*. New York: Knopf.
Marriott International Inc. (2014). *2013 Annual report*.
McDonald's (2017). *Annual Report Pursuant to Section 13 or 15(d) of the Securities Exchange Act of 1934 for the fiscal year ended December 31, 2016*, Form 10–K.
Melia Hotels International (2014). *Annual report and CSR 2013*.

Merck (1987). *1986 Annual report.*

Merck (2017). *Annual Report Pursuant to Section 13 or 15(d) of the Securities Exchange Act of 1934 for the fiscal year ended December 31, 2016*, Form 10–K.

Microsoft (2016). *Annual Report Pursuant to Section 13 or 15(d) of the Securities Exchange Act of 1934 for the fiscal year ended June 30, 2016*, Form 10–K.

Mills, E. (2009). A global review of insurance industry responses to climate change. *Geneva Papers on Risk and Insurance. Issues and Practice. Special Issue on Climate Change and Insurance, 34*(3).

Minor, M. S. (1994). The demise of expropriation as an instrument of LDC policy, 1980–1992. *Journal of International Business Studies, 25*(1).

Monsanto (2003). *2002 Annual report.*

Moody's Investors Service (1963). *Moody's municipal and government manual—American and foreign*. New York: Moody's Investors Service.

Moody's Investors Service (1970). *Moody's municipal and government manual—American and foreign*. New York: Moody's Investors Service.

Moody's Investors Service (2015a). Sovereign default and recovery rates, 1983–2014. *Special comment*, 27 April.

Moody's Investors Service (2015b). Moody's upgrades Ukraine's sovereign rating to Caa3, Outlook stable. *Rating Action*, 19 November.

Munich Re (2016). *Group annual report 2015.*

National Association of Manufacturers (1997). *A catalog of new US unilateral economic sanctions for foreign policy purposes 1993–96*. Available at http://archives.usaengage.org/archives/studies/nam2.html

Nestlé (2004). *Management report 2003.*

Nestlé (2005). *Management report 2004.*

Nike (1998). *1998 Annual report.*

Nike (2016). *Annual Report Pursuant to Section 13 or 15(d) of the Securities Exchange Act of 1934 for the fiscal year ended May 31, 2016*, Form 10–K.

Nissin Kogyo (2011). *Annual review 2011 for the year ended March 31, 2011.*

Nye, J. S. (1974). Multinational corporations in world politics. *Foreign Affairs, 53*(1).

O'Brien, K. A. (2000). Private military companies and African security 1990–1998. In A.-F. Musah & J. K. Fayemi (Eds.), *Mercenaries: An African security dilemma*. London and Sterling (VA): Pluto Press.

Peterson Institute for International Economics (2011). Case 60-3, US v. Cuba (1960: Castro). *Case studies in economic sanctions and terrorism*, Washington, DC.

Pfizer (2017). *Annual Report Pursuant to Section 13 or 15(d) of the Securities Exchange Act of 1934 for the fiscal year ended December 31, 2016*, Form 10–K.

Pirelli (2012). *Volume A—Annual financial report at December 31, 2011.*

Powell, J. M., & Thyne, C. L. (2011). Global instances of coups from 1950 to 2010: A new dataset. *Journal of Peace Research, 48*(2).

Procter & Gamble (2016). *Annual Report Pursuant to Section 13 or 15(d) of the Securities Exchange Act of 1934 for the fiscal year ended June 30, 2016*, Form 10–K.

PWC (2015). *Doing business in the Kingdom of Saudi Arabia—A tax and legal guide.*

Reinhart, C. M., & Rogoff, K. (2009). *This time is different—Eight centuries of financial folly*. Princeton: Princeton University Press.

Rid, T., & Hecker, M. (2009). *War 2.0: Irregular warfare in the information age*. Westport, CT: Praeger Security International.

Robock, S. H. (1971). Political risk: Identification and assessment. *Columbia Journal of World Business, 6*(4).

Rood, L. L. (1976). Nationalisation and indigenisation in Africa. *Journal of Modern African Studies, 14*(3).

Root, F. R. (1968). The expropriation experience of American companies. *Business Horizons, 11*(2).

Ross, T. I. (2012). Enforcing intellectual property rights in China. *China Business Review, 39*(4).
Sada, H. (1990). Les intérêts militaires et stratégiques en Afrique austral. In D. Bach (Ed.), *La France et l'Afrique du Sud: histoire, mythes et enjeux contemporains*. Paris: Khartala.
Sanyal, R., & Samanta, S. (2011). Trends in international bribe-giving: Do anti-bribery laws matter? *Journal of International Trade Law and Policy, 10*(2).
Saunders, E. N. (2006). Setting boundaries: Can international society exclude 'Rogue States'? *International Studies Review, 8*(1).
Senior, I. (2006). *Corruption—The World's Big C: Cases, causes, consequences, cures*. London: Institute of Economic Affairs.
Seymour Whitaker, J. (1983). Africa beset. *Foreign Affairs, 62*(3).
Suter, C. (1990). *Schuldenzyklen in der Dritten Welt: Kreditaufnahme, Zahlungskrisen und Schuldenregelungen peripherer Länder im Weltsystem von 1820 bis 1986*. Frankfurt am Main: Anton Hain.
Svensson, J. (2005). Eight questions about corruption. *Journal of Economic Perspectives, 19*(3).
Tabaar, M. A. (2013). Assessing (In) security after the Arab spring: The case of Egypt. *PS: Political Science and Politics, 46*(4).
Tata Motors (2013). *68th Annual report 2012–13*.
Taylor, M., & Herman, V. M. (1971). Party systems and government stability. *American Political Science Review, 65*(1).
Texaco Inc. (1991). *Annual report 1990*.
Texaco Inc. (1992). *Annual report 1991*.
The Williams Companies, Inc. (2003). *Annual Report Pursuant to Section 13 or 15(d) of the Securities Exchange Act of 1934 for the fiscal year ended December 31, 2002*, Form 10–K.
The Williams Companies, Inc. (2004). *Annual Report Pursuant to Section 13 or 15(d) of the Securities Exchange Act of 1934 for the fiscal year ended December 31, 2003*, Form 10–K.
Thompson Coburn LLP (2017). *Checklists of foreign countries subject to sanctions*. Retrieved from http://thompsoncoburn.com/docs/default-source/publication-documents/country-chart.pdf
Travelers (2017). *Annual Report Pursuant to Section 13 or 15(d) of the Securities Exchange Act of 1934 for the fiscal year ended December 31, 2016*, Form 10–K.
Truitt, J. F. (1970). Expropriation of foreign investment: Summary of the post world war II experience of American and British investors in the less developed countries. *Journal of International Business Studies, 1*(2).
Ukraine (2016). Notes Due 2019-2027 and GDP-linked Securities. *Listing Prospectus*, 28 April.
United Technologies (2017). *Annual Report Pursuant to Section 13 or 15(d) of the Securities Exchange Act of 1934 for the fiscal year ended December 31, 2016*, Form 10–K.
UnitedHealth (2017). *Annual Report Pursuant to Section 13 or 15(d) of the Securities Exchange Act of 1934 for the fiscal year ended December 31, 2016*, Form 10–K.
Vashchilko, T. (2011). *Three essays on foreign direct investment and bilateral investment treaties*. Dissertation in Political Science, Pennsylvania State University, Graduate School College of the Liberal Arts.
Vasquez, J. A., & Valeriano, B. (2010). Classification of interstate wars. *Journal of Politics, 72*(2).
Verizon (2017). *Annual Report Pursuant to Section 13 or 15(d) of the Securities Exchange Act of 1934 for the fiscal year ended December 31, 2016*, Form 10–K.
Visa (2016). *Annual Report Pursuant to Section 13 or 15(d) of the Securities Exchange Act of 1934 for the fiscal year ended September 30, 2016*, Form 10–K.
Walmart (2017). *Annual Report Pursuant to Section 13 or 15(d) of the Securities Exchange Act of 1934 for the fiscal year ended January 31, 2017*, Form 10–K.
Weeks, J. (1977). The sphere of production and the analysis of crisis in capitalism. *Science & Society, 41*(3).
Wells Fargo & Company (1975). *1974 Annual report*.
Wells Fargo & Company (1980). *1979 Annual report*.
Williams, M. L. (1975). The extent and significance of the nationalization of foreign-owned assets in developing countries, 1956–1972. *Oxford Economic Papers, New Series, 27*(2).

World Bank (2011). Zambia—What would it take for Zambia's copper mining industry to achieve its potential? Finance & Private Sector Development Unit, Africa Region, *Report No. 62378-ZM*.
World Bank (2016). *Doing Business 2016*, Washington, DC.
Wyndham Worldwide Corporation (2008). *Annual Report Pursuant to Section 13 or 15(d) of the Securities Exchange Act of 1934 for the fiscal year ended December 31, 2007*, Form 10–K.
Wyndham Worldwide Corporation (2012). *Annual Report Pursuant to Section 13 or 15(d) of the Securities Exchange Act of 1934 for the fiscal year ended December 31, 2011*, Form 10–K.
Wyndham Worldwide Corporation (2016). *Annual Report Pursuant to Section 13 or 15(d) of the Securities Exchange Act of 1934 for the fiscal year ended December 31, 2015*, Form 10–K.
Xerox Corporation (1988). *1987 Annual report*.
Young, Jr., K. T. (1961). New politics in new states. *Foreign Affairs, 39*(3).

Part II
Sovereign and Country Risk Indicators

Chapter 4
Sovereign Risk Indicators

Starting in the mid-1970s, an increasing number of economists began using the term "country risk" to refer to "sovereign risk" (see Chap. 1). At the time of this writing, that confusion has not yet completely dissipated and so the two terms are sometimes used interchangeably. This chapter focuses on what is known as "type-3 country risk" (CR3)—in other words, the risk that a sovereign borrower might fail to fulfill its financial obligations to a foreign creditor.[1] This emphasis is motivated by the high likelihood of sovereign risk exacerbating all the other risks that affect international investors.

Section 4.1 presents the sovereign rating methodologies used by Moody's, S&P, *Institutional Investor*, and *Euromoney*. Section 4.2 measures and compares the performances of these four raters since the early 1980s. Two fundamental criteria are examined: the consistency and the accuracy of sovereign ratings. Section 4.3 offers three extended comments. First, it identifies some weaknesses of these sovereign risk indicators. Next, it names the countries whose credit positions improved or weakened most significantly during the globalization era and advances some explanations for those trends. Finally, it explores on the major disagreements between raters as of September 1, 2016.

4.1 Sovereign Rating Methodologies

This section investigates the sovereign rating methodologies implemented by Moody's, S&P, *Institutional Investor,* and *Euromoney*. Moody's and S&P are the two major CRAs, and they have rated sovereign borrowers for a century. *Institutional Investor* and *Euromoney* are well-known monthly periodicals that focus on business and finance; both started assessing sovereign risk in 1979.

[1] See Gaillard (2014c) for an overview of sovereign risk.

N. Gaillard, *Country Risk*, https://doi.org/10.1007/978-3-030-45788-4_4

4.1.1 Sovereign Ratings Issued by Moody's and Standard & Poor's

Sovereign ratings first appeared in 1918 in *Moody's Analyses of Investments—Government and Municipal Securities*. By 1929, Moody's and its three competitors—Poor's, Standard Statistics, and Fitch[2]—rated most of the foreign government securities issued worldwide. Sovereign rating activity declined following the Great Depression and did not rebound until the financial globalization of the 1980s–1990s. The growth in borrowing needs of both developed and industrialized countries, combined with the establishment of market-based macroeconomic policies (Williamson 1990), reinvigorated government bond markets and spurred the resumption of sovereign ratings. Moody's and S&P rated (respectively) 11 and 14 countries in 1986, 89 and 87 countries in 2001, and 133 and 131 countries in 2016.[3]

The significance of a sovereign credit rating has not changed since 1918: it consists of an opinion regarding the relative ability and willingness of a government to meet its financial commitments in the medium term. Today, CRAs assign long-term and short-term credit ratings with regard to both foreign currency and local currency. Table 4.1 summarizes Moody's and S&P's long-term rating scales.[4]

The methods by which these two CRAs assign their ratings have been substantially revised since the interwar years.

Starting in the 1980s, Moody's and S&P have each used committees to assign ratings. The committee process is intended to limit the influence of a single analyst as most such committees include four to ten analysts. Their deliberations are based on data and information either provided by the debt issuer or gathered by the analysts themselves. In the former case, the sovereign rating assignment is solicited by the country in question; in the latter, it is not. Today, nearly all sovereign ratings are assigned on a solicited basis—in contrast to the interwar period, during which sovereign issuers did *not* participate in the rating process.[5]

Ratings are now reviewed at least once a year,[6] but a CRA may initiate a rating review whenever it considers that economic, fiscal, financial, political, or any other information is likely to affect the issuer's creditworthiness. In practice, upgrades and downgrades are not frequent. During 1987–2010, an S&P rating was modified every 3.7 years, on average, as compared with every 5.2 years for a Moody's rating (Gaillard 2011, p. 125).

---

[2] Poor's and Standard Statistics merged in 1941 to form Standard & Poor's (S&P).

[3] Author's calculations based on moodys.com and spglobal.com.

[4] In the rest of this book, Moody's and S&P ratings refer to Moody's and S&P *long-term FC* ratings.

[5] For a more detailed analysis of the sovereign rating process, see Gaillard (2011, Chap. 4) and Nye (2014, Chaps. 4 and 5).

[6] The ratings assigned to European Union (EU) members must be reviewed at least once every six months, per Article 8 of Regulation (EC) No. 1060/2009 as amended by Regulation (EU) No. 462/2013.

Table 4.1 Current meanings of ratings issued by Moody's and S&P

Category	Moody's ratings	S&P ratings	Significance
Investment grade	Aaa	AAA	Lowest credit risk
	Aa1	AA+	Very low credit risk
	Aa2	AA	
	Aa3	AA−	
	A1	A+	Low credit risk
	A2	A	
	A3	A−	
	Baa1	BBB+	Moderate credit risk
	Baa2	BBB	
	Baa3	BBB−	
Speculative grade	Ba1	BB+	Substantial credit risk
	Ba2	BB	
	Ba3	BB−	
	B1	B+	High credit risk
	B2	B	
	B3	B−	
	Caa1	CCC+	Very high credit risk
	Caa2	CCC	
	Caa3	CCC−	
		CC	
Default	Ca	SD	SD designates issuers that have defaulted on part of their debt; Ca designates defaulting issuers for which there is some prospect of recovering the principal and interest
	C	D	D designates issuers that have defaulted on all of their debt; C designates defaulting issuers for which there is little prospect of recovering the principal or interest

Sources: Author's classification based on moodys.com and spglobal.com

In fact, the most noticeable feature involves sovereign rating *methodologies*. The paradox here is that the fundamental determinants of sovereign ratings have remained the same since the 1920s. Thus Moody's and S&P ratings have always been a function of the same macroeconomic and institutional variables: the ratio of gross domestic product (GDP) per capita and of foreign currency debt to exports (or revenues), inflation, default history, and institutional stability (Cantor and Packer 1996, pp. 39–43; Gaillard 2011, pp. 50–60). That said, sovereign rating methodologies have been refined considerably and have become more transparent and quantitative.

The first step was Moody's decision to open its "black box" by publishing quantitative models for both LC and FC ratings (Moody's 2003, 2004). The objective of these two studies was to alleviate criticism that the firm lacked transparency (see

SEC 2003). In 2008, Moody's redrafted its methodology and implemented a mechanistic process to assign its sovereign ratings. The agency identified four broad determining factors: the focal country's economic strength (Factor 1), its institutional strength (Factor 2), its financial strength (Factor 3), and its "susceptibility to event risk" (Factor 4). These four factors, which are assessed via various quantitative and qualitative indicators,[7] are combined to establish a rating range. Determination of the final rating relies on the analysts' own opinions (Moody's 2008).

Five years later, Moody's (2013) published an updated methodology. Each of the four broad factors just described is now decomposed into several rating subfactors, for which Moody's provides at least one indicator each. After these subfactors are calculated (or estimated), the outcomes are mapped to one of the 15 ranking categories: very high plus (VH+), very high (VH), very high minus (VH−), high plus (H+), high (H), high minus (H−), medium plus (M+), medium (M), medium minus (M−), low plus (L+), low (L), low minus (L−), very low plus (VL+), very low (VL), and very low minus (VL−). These mappings are used to determine the score for the subfactors and also for the broader rating factors. Finally, Factors 1, 2, 3, and 4 are combined to obtain a provisional FC credit rating. It is noteworthy that Factor 4 follows a maximum function. Moody's explains that, "as soon as one area of risk warrants an assessment of elevated risk, the country's overall susceptibility to event risk is scored at that specific, elevated level." This approach is indicative of a more conservative rating policy. Moody's (2015) subsequently revised its rating criteria but without making any major amendments (see Table 4.2).

Table 4.2 Moody's sovereign rating criteria, 2015

Broad rating factors	Rating subfactors	Subfactor weighting within factor	Subfactor indicators
Factor 1: Economic strength	Growth dynamics	50%	Average real GDP growth$_{t-4\ to\ t+5}$
			Volatility in real GDP growth$_{t-9\ to\ t}$
			WEF Global Competitiveness Index$_t$
	Scale of the economy	25%	Nominal GDP (US$)$_t$
	National income	25%	GDP per capita (PPP, US$)$_t$
	Adjustment factors	1–6 scores	Diversification
			Credit boom

(continued)

[7] For instance, economic strength is based mainly on GDP per capita, the economy's size and diversification, and long-term economic trends.

Table 4.2 (continued)

Broad rating factors	Rating subfactors	Subfactor weighting within factor	Subfactor indicators
Factor 2: Institutional strength	Institutional framework and effectiveness	75%	World Bank Government Effectiveness Index
			World Bank Rule of Law Index
			World Bank Control of Corruption Index
	Policy credibility and effectiveness	25%	Inflation level$_{t-4\ to\ t+5}$
			Inflation volatility$_{t-9\ to\ t}$
	Adjustment factor	1–6 scores	Track record of default
Factor 3: Fiscal strength	Debt burden	50%	General gov. debt/GDP$_t$
			General gov. debt/revenue$_t$
	Debt affordability	50%	General gov. interest payments/revenue$_t$
			General gov. interest payments/GDP$_t$
	Adjustment factors	1–6 scores	Debt trend$_{t-4\ to\ t+1}$
			General gov. FC debt/gen. gov. debt$_t$
			Other public sector debt/GDP$_t$
			Public sector financial assets or SWFs/GDP$_t$
Factor 4: Susceptibility to event risk	Political risk	Max. function	Domestic political risk
			Geopolitical risk
	Government liquidity risk	Max. function	Fundamental metrics
			Market funding stress
	Banking sector risk	Max. function	Strength of banking system
			Size of banking system
			Funding vulnerabilities
	External vulnerability risk	Max. function	(Current account balance + FDI)/GDP$_t$
			External vulnerability indicator (EVI)$_{t+2}$
			Net international investment position/GDP$_t$

Notes: *FDI* foreign direct investment, *PPP* purchasing power parity, *SWF* sovereign wealth fund, *WEF* World Economic Forum
Source: Moody's (2015)

What about S&P? In the early 2000s, S&P stated that its analytical framework for sovereign borrowers was divided into ten categories: political risk, income and economic structure, economic growth prospects, fiscal flexibility, general government debt burden, offshore and contingent liabilities, monetary stability, external liquidity, public-sector external debt burden, and private-sector external debt burden (S&P 2002). Each category consisted of a list of factors, and a country was ranked on a scale of 1 (best) to 6 (worst) for each of these categories. However, S&P acknowledged that there was no exact formula for combining the scores to determine ratings.

In 2011, this rating agency adopted a multistep analytical process (S&P 2011). After grouping the major criteria listed in its traditional methodology into five broad categories, S&P then assigns a score to each on a 6-point scale ranging from 1 (the strongest) to 6 (the weakest). Next, the five scores are grouped into two profiles. The political and economic scores are combined to form the *political and economic* profile; the external, fiscal, and monetary scores are combined to form the *flexibility and performance* profile. The two profiles are then combined to yield an initial sovereign rating level, although exceptional adjustments may be made prior to assigning the final FC rating. Thereafter, S&P (2013a, 2014) made some minor amendments to its 2011 methodology. Table 4.3 presents the five broad categories along with their respective key factors.

Table 4.3 S&P sovereign rating criteria, 2014

Broad categories	Key factors
Institutional assessment	Effectiveness, stability, and predictability of the sovereign's policymaking and political institutions (primary factor)
	Transparency and accountability of institutions, data, and processes as well as coverage and reliability of statistical information (secondary factor)
	Sovereign's debt payment culture (potential adjustment factor)
	External security risks (potential adjustment factor)
Economic assessment	Income levels
	Growth prospects
	Economic diversity and volatility
External assessment	Status of a sovereign's currency in international transactions
	External liquidity, which provides an indication of the economy's ability to generate the foreign exchange necessary to meet its public- and private-sector obligations to nonresidents
	External position, or residents' assets and liabilities (in both FC and LC) relative to the rest of the world
Fiscal assessment	Fiscal flexibility
	Long-term fiscal trends and vulnerabilities
	Debt structure and funding access
	Potential risk arising from contingent liabilities

(continued)

Table 4.3 (continued)

Broad categories	Key factors
Monetary assessment	Ability to coordinate monetary policy with fiscal and other economic policies to support sustainable economic growth
	Credibility of monetary policy, as measured by inflation trends over an economic cycle
	Market-oriented monetary mechanisms' effect on the real economy, which is largely a function of the depth and diversification of the country's financial system and capital markets

Source: Author's classification based on S&P (2014)

4.1.2 Institutional Investor Ratings

Institutional Investor is a leading international business-to-business publisher of magazines, newsletters, journals, research, directories, books, and maps. The *Institutional Investor* magazine (hereafter simply "Institutional Investor") debuted in 1967 but did not publish its first country credit ratings until September 1979. Institutional Investor ratings are updated twice a year and published in the March and September issues. Countries were initially rated on a scale of 0–10, where 0 represents the least creditworthy countries and 10 the most creditworthy. In 1980, the scale was modified so that the top credit rating was 100. This 0–100 scale was still in use in 2016.

Since 1979, Institutional Investor's country credit ratings have been based on information provided by senior economists and sovereign risk analysts at leading international banks and—for ratings issued since the late 1990s—at money management and securities firms. These respondents grade each country on the 0–100 scale. Participant responses are then weighted according to their respective institutions' global exposure. All participants in the surveys are assured that their opinions will be kept strictly confidential. Starting in September 1999, however, Institutional Investor mentioned the names of sovereign risk experts in the analyses accompanying their classification, which suggested that they were part of Institutional Investor's panel.[8] In addition to the opinions delivered by financial institutions' experts, it is worth mentioning the prominent role played by Harvey D. Shapiro. Mr. Shapiro—a writer, consultant, and senior contributing editor at Institutional Investor—has supervised most surveys since the mid-1980s.[9]

Institutional Investor ratings are unsolicited. The magazine rated 93 countries in 1979, 135 in 1996, and 179 in 2016. Academic research has established no clear consensus about the determinants of these ratings. In their study of the ratings

[8] *Institutional Investor*, September 1999, pp. 197–200.

[9] See for example *Institutional Investor*, September 1984, p. 293; September 2002, p. 167; and September 2016, p. 104. For more information, readers may refer to https://www.conference-board.org/bio/index.cfm?bioid=3099.

published in September 1987, Cosset and Roy (1991) find that gross national product per capita, propensity to invest, and the ratio of net foreign debt to exports are key explanatory variables. Haque et al. (1996) extend the coverage of ratings to the period 1982–1993 but focus exclusively on developing countries; they conclude that Institutional Investor ratings are driven by the ratios of current account balance to GDP and of international reserves to imports, the three-month US Treasury bill rate, and GDP growth. In a follow-up article, Butler and Fauver (2006) show that the determinants of Institutional Investor ratings published in March 2004 are GDP per capita, the ratio of foreign debt to GDP, default history, the underdevelopment index, and the legal environment—thereby highlighting the importance of institutional issues.

4.1.3 Euromoney Country Risk Ratings

Euromoney magazine (hereafter, "Euromoney") was launched in 1969 to cover the reemergence of international cross-border capital markets.[10] Euromoney published its first country risk survey in October 1979. The magazine showed how the international banking community, through its lending activities, rated the countries that borrowed that year. Euromoney pointed out that the ratings disclosed were those "assigned" by the market. That is, they were the result of "statistical analysis of the terms and conditions for all sovereign borrowers that tapped the Eurodollar and floating rate Deutschemark syndicated loan market in 1979."[11] In fact, a country's ranking was completely driven by its weighted average interest rate spread (i.e., the gap between a given country's interest rate and that of a "risk-free" country). The lower the spread, the higher the ranking. In addition, Euromoney divided borrowers into seven categories. The best risks got seven stars and the worst received just one. Seven-star countries had a weighted average spread no higher than 0.50%; those that were granted six stars had a weighted average spread no higher than 0.75%, and so forth. Borrowers suffering a spread higher than 1.75% were rated as one star. A few months later, Euromoney replaced its seven-star rating system by a seven-grade system under which EM-I referred to the most creditworthy countries and EM-VII to the least creditworthy.

Euromoney amended its methodology again in 1982. Country risk ratings, henceforth established on a 0–100 scale (equivalent to Institutional Investor's), were now based on three criteria: access to eurocredit and all bond markets (40% weighting), terms obtained in the current year (30%), and selldown performance (30%)—where the last criterion assesses whether loans had a successful, normal, or poor syndication. Extra points were awarded if loans had been oversubscribed and the

[10] See http://www.euromoney.com/AboutUs.aspx?copyrightInfo=true.

[11] *Euromoney*, October 1979, p. 130.

amounts raised were considerable.[12] For the first time, Euromoney's methodology had not only quantitative but also qualitative features. This tendency was confirmed in subsequent years. For instance, in 1986, the criteria and weighting were as follows: access to markets (20% weighting), access to trade finance (10%), payment record (15%), difficulties in rescheduling (5%), political risk (20%), and selldown (30%).[13] A further step was taken in 1987 when Euromoney announced that several experts were asked to give their opinions on each country. The number of key variables was then expanded to eight: political risk (15% weighting), economic risk (10%), economic indicators (15%),[14] payment record (15%), ease of rescheduling (5%), access to bond markets (15%), selldown on short-term paper (10%), and access to and discount available on forfeiting (15%).[15]

In March 1993, Euromoney responded to increased international volatility by announcing that its country risk surveys would be carried out every 6 months: not only in September but also in March. Nine criteria were identified, and the opinions of experts were involved in assessing the first two of them (viz., economic data and political risk). Unless these analysts wished to remain anonymous, their names were published. Six months later, Euromoney's methodology was updated once again. The nine criteria were kept but the weightings of economic and political risks were revised from 10% and 20% to 25% and 25%, respectively (see Table 4.4).

In September 2010, the survey weightings were changed to increase the influence of the focal country's political risk and economic performance. So to obtain the overall country risk score, Euromoney assigned a weighting to six rating categories. The three *qualitative* expert opinions are political risk (30% weighting), economic performance (30%), and structural assessment (10%); the three *quantitative* values are debt indicators (10%), credit ratings (10%), and access to bank finance and/or capital markets (10%). This methodology, as summarized in Table 4.5, was still being used in 2016.

Unlike Moody's, S&P, and Institutional Investor, which focus solely on sovereign risk, Euromoney Country Risk (ECR) evaluates several aspects of a country's investment risk: the risk of default on a bond, the risk of losing direct investment, the risk to global business relations, and so forth.[16] This particular feature should be borne in mind when comparing and analyzing the performance of the four raters (see Sects. 4.2 and 4.3). The ECR ratings are unsolicited, and Euromoney rated 66 countries in 1979, 178 in 1996, and 186 in 2016.

[12] *Euromoney*, September 1982, pp. 71–74.

[13] *Euromoney*, September 1986, p. 364.

[14] The economic indicators consisted of three ratios: debt service to exports, balance of payments to gross national product (GNP), and external debt to GNP.

[15] *Euromoney*, September 1988, p. 233.

[16] See https://www.euromoneycountryrisk.com/Methodology.

Table 4.4 Euromoney country risk criteria, September 1993

Criteria	Weighting	Explanation
Economic data	25%	Data are taken from Euromoney global economic projections.
Political risk	25%	Euromoney polls risk analysts, risk insurance brokers, and bank credit officers, who are asked to give each country a score from 0 to 10. A score of 10 indicates no risk of nonpayment; a score of 0 indicates that there is no chance of payments being made.
Debt indicators	10%	Scores are calculated from the following ratios: debt service to export, current account balance to GNP, and external debt to GNP.
Debt in default or rescheduled	10%	A score from 0 to 10 based on the amount of debt in default or that had to be rescheduled during the last 3 years.
Credit ratings	10%	Average of sovereign ratings from Moody's and S&P. Countries without credit ratings or with less than BB—score 0.
Access to bank finance	5%	Scores are calculated from disbursements of long-term private nonguaranteed debt as a percentage of GNP. All OECD countries automatically score 10.
Access to short-term finance	5%	Score is calculated based on the OECD "consensus group" to which the country belongs—i.e., whether the country is covered by the US Export-Import Bank or by Nederlandsche Credietverzekering Maatschappij N.V.
Access to international bond and syndicated loan markets	5%	Analysis by Euromoney of syndicated loan and international bond issues since January 1989 and a judgment concerning how easy it would be for that country to tap the market now.
Access to and discount on forfeiting	5%	Scores are a combination of the maximum tenor available and the forfeiting spread over riskless countries such as the United States.

Note: Each criterion is scored on a 0–10 scale
Source: Author's classification based on *Euromoney* (September 1993)

Table 4.5 Euromoney country risk methodology, September 2016

Broad rating category	Weighting	Criteria
Economic assessment	30%	Bank stability/risk
		Economic/GNP outlook
		Employment/unemployment
		Government finances
		Monetary policy/currency stability
Political assessment	30%	Corruption
		Government nonpayments/non-repatriation
		Government stability
		Information access/transparency
		Institutional risk
		Regulatory and policy environment

(continued)

Table 4.5 (continued)

Broad rating category	Weighting	Criteria
Structural assessment	10%	Demographics
		Hard infrastructure
		Labor market/industrial relations
		Soft infrastructure
Debt indicators	10%	Calculated using the following ratios: total debt stocks to GNP, debt service to exports, and current account balance to GNP. Developing countries that do not report complete debt data receive a score of 0
Credit ratings	10%	Nominal values are assigned to sovereign ratings from Moody's, S&P, and Fitch Ratings. The ratings are converted into a score using a preestablished scoring chart; this score is then averaged
Access to bank finance or capital markets	10%	Accessibility to international markets

Note: Each criterion is scored on a 0–10 scale
Source: Author's classification based on euromoneycountryrisk.com

4.2 Performance of Sovereign Risk Indicators

This section analyzes the consistency and accuracy of sovereign ratings issued by Moody's, S&P, Institutional Investor, and Euromoney during the globalization era. Three specific periods are scrutinized: the wave of defaults in LDCs during 1982–1984 (Sect. 4.2.1), the Eurozone crisis during 2009–2013 (Sect. 4.2.2), and the "sovereign bond years" during 1995–2013 (Sect. 4.2.3). The selection of the first two periods is underpinned by the surge in total public debt in default, as shown in Fig. 4.1.[17] The third period encompasses the most recent and active years on bond markets; it starts in 1995 because, for the first time since the interwar years, the sovereign rating coverage by the two CRAs exceeded 50 issuers, of which more than half were nonindustrialized countries.

[17] Of the total sovereign debt in default in 1984 (resp., 2013), 100% (resp., 68%) had been issued by emerging and developing countries (resp., eurozone members). Author's calculation based on Beers and de Leon-Manlagnit's (2019) database.

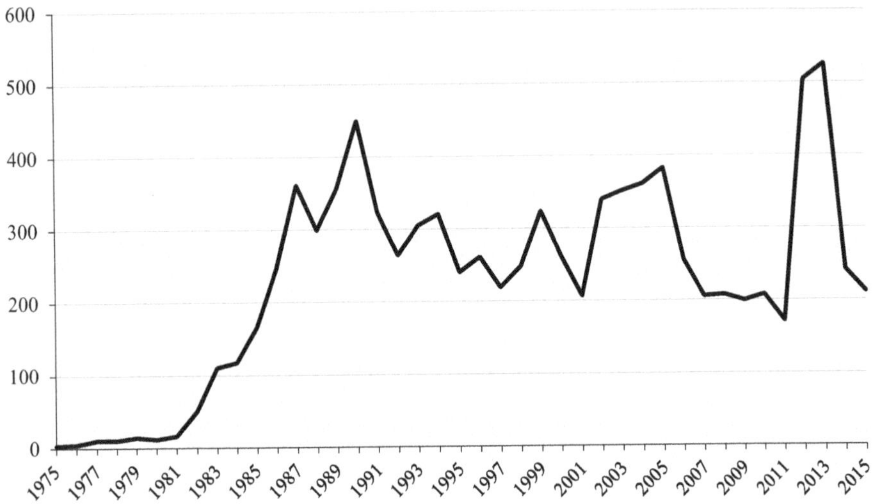

Fig. 4.1 Total sovereign debt in default (US$ bn) by year. *Source:* Beers and de Leon-Manlagnit's (2019) database

4.2.1 The Debt Crisis of 1982

Between 1973 and 1981, the total external debt of oil-importing developing countries increased from $96.8 billion to $436.9 billion (IMF 1982, p. 36). This rise was driven by the oil crises of 1973 and 1979 and by the surge in international interest rates that followed the 1979 shift in US monetary policy. Although US banks lending abroad had implemented specific country risk assessments in the second part of the 1970s,[18] they failed to anticipate the LDC debt crisis that erupted in 1982. Fishlow (1978) was one of the few who raised doubts about the sustainability of Latin American public debt. His concerns spread to international financial institutions a couple of years later (BIS 1980, p. 111; IMF 1981, p. 53). A few countries defaulted between mid-1981 and mid-1982 (see below), but the financial crisis in LDCs was sparked in August 1982 when Mexico's Treasury Secretary Jesus Silva Herzog informed the country's foreign creditors that his government had to suspend principal payments on its debt.[19] Between 1981 and 1984, the amount of sovereign debt in default soared from $16.4 billion to $117.4 billion.[20]

[18] See Friedman (1977) and Wilson (1979) for a presentation of the country risk rating systems established by Citicorp and Bank of America, respectively. For an overview, see Heffernan (1986).

[19] L. Rout and J. Salamon, "Bankers Tentatively Agree to Let Mexico Delay Repayment of Some Debt Principal," *Wall Street Journal*, 23 August 1982.

[20] Based on Beers and de Leon-Manlagnit's (2019) database.

This section offers the first-ever analysis of the performance of sovereign risk indicators during the debt crisis of 1982–1984. Considering that Moody's and S&P rated barely a dozen sovereign debt issuers in the early 1980s (Gaillard 2011, pp. 8–9), this examination focuses on Institutional Investor and Euromoney ratings. The performance of these ratings is assessed by observing those assigned prior to default, computing accuracy ratios (ARs), and studying the stability of ratings.

4.2.1.1 Ratings Prior to Default

The Institutional Investor ratings examined here are those published in March 1982, which reported the credit risk of 105 countries at the end of 1981. Euromoney ratings are those published in February 1982; these gave the average credit risk of 69 countries for the year 1981. I shall assess the accuracy of sovereign ratings at the 3-year horizon.

My list of sovereign defaults includes the countries that defaulted on their foreign currency bank loans during 1982–1984. My source is Beers and de Leon-Manlagnit's (2019) database. The rankings and ratings assigned by Institutional Investor and Euromoney to countries that defaulted during 1982–1984 are shown in Table 4.6.

Table 4.6 Rankings and ratings assigned by Institutional Investor and Euromoney to countries that defaulted during 1982–1984

Institutional Investor			Euromoney		
Rank	Country	Rating	Rank	Country	Rating
28	Venezuela	63.3	27	Mexico	EM-II
29	Mexico	62.8	33	Uruguay	EM-III
43	Nigeria	52.3	34	Chile	EM-III
44	Chile	52.1	37	Philippines	EM-IV
48	Argentina	50.5	38	Argentina	EM-IV
49	Brazil	50.3	39	Ecuador	EM-IV
50	Ecuador	46.9	43	Nigeria	EM-IV
59	Peru	41.0	45	Cuba	EM-V
60	Panama	40.5	47	Peru	EM-V
61	Yugoslavia	40.3	52	Ivory Coast	EM-VI
62	Philippines	40.2	53	Morocco	EM-VI
63	Uruguay	40.1	56	Panama	EM-VI
64	Ivory Coast	39.8	58	Yugoslavia	EM-VI
71	Morocco	33.4	61	Venezuela	EM-VI
76	Dominican Rep.	23.3	62	Brazil	EM-VI
78	Cuba	20.5	66	Zambia	EM-VII
79	Malawi	20.2	69	Niger	EM-VII
94	Zambia	12.8			
95	Tanzania	11.9			
105	North Korea	4.3			

Notes: For Institutional Investor, rankings and ratings are those published in March 1982. For Euromoney, rankings and ratings are those published in February 1982. Institutional Investor and Euromoney rated then 105 and 69 countries, respectively

Sources: Institutional Investor (March 1982), *Euromoney* (February 1982), and Beers and de Leon-Manlagnit's (2019) database

The top quarter and top third of, respectively, the Institutional Investor and Euromoney classifications are default-free; this suggests that the two raters made no major mistakes when ranking countries. However, the highest rating assigned to a sovereign issuer that defaulted in the following 3 years (i.e., Venezuela for Institutional Investor and Mexico for Euromoney) was too kind: 63.3 out of 100 for Institutional Investor and the second highest (EM-II) of seven rating categories for Euromoney. Other countries were also assigned excessively high ratings: the Institutional Investor scores for Mexico, Nigeria, Chile, Argentina, and Brazil were all above 50; and Uruguay and Chile were each rated EM-III by Euromoney. Notwithstanding these exceptions, the majority of defaulting countries was assigned low or very low scores.[21]

4.2.1.2 Accuracy Ratios

The second evaluative measure is derived by tracing cumulative accuracy profile (CAP) curves and then computing ARs. Both CAPs and ARs are designed to establish whether raters manage to assign low ratings to issuers that default and high ratings to issuers that do not. A CAP is constructed by sorting the countries from lowest to highest rating and then plotting, for each rating category, the percentage of defaults due to sovereigns with the same or a lower rating against the percentage of all sovereigns with the same or a lower rating. The further the CAP curve bows toward the graph's upper left corner, the greater the fraction of all defaults that are accounted for by the lowest rating categories (for an illustration, see Gaillard 2011, pp. 141–142).

Figures 4.2 and 4.3 plot the 3-year CAP curves for the countries rated by, respectively, Institutional Investor and Euromoney. The countries already in default in 1981 are excluded.[22] Hence the two respective samples consist of 90 and 63 countries.

The two CAPs illustrated in these figures are "above" the curve that would be plotted for a random assignment of ratings—that is, a 45° line from the origin. The AR compresses the information encoded by a CAP curve into a single summary statistic: the ratio of the area between the CAP curve and the 45° line to the total area above the 45° line. Accuracy ratios range between −1 and 1, where 1 represents maximum accuracy (all defaulters are assigned the lowest rating) and −1 represents

[21] It is worth mentioning that Venezuela was the only defaulting borrower rated by Moody's and S&P. The country was ranked in the triple-A category by these CRAs both in 1981, which indicates that the ratings assigned by Institutional Investor and Euromoney were reasonably accurate. See Moody's (1981) and S&P (2013b).

[22] The countries removed from the Institutional Investor sample are Bolivia, Costa Rica, Honduras, Iran, Jamaica, Liberia, Nicaragua, Poland, Romania, Senegal, Sierra Leone, Sudan, Turkey, Uganda, and Zaire. Those removed from the Euromoney sample are Bolivia, Honduras, Jamaica, Romania, Senegal, and Turkey.

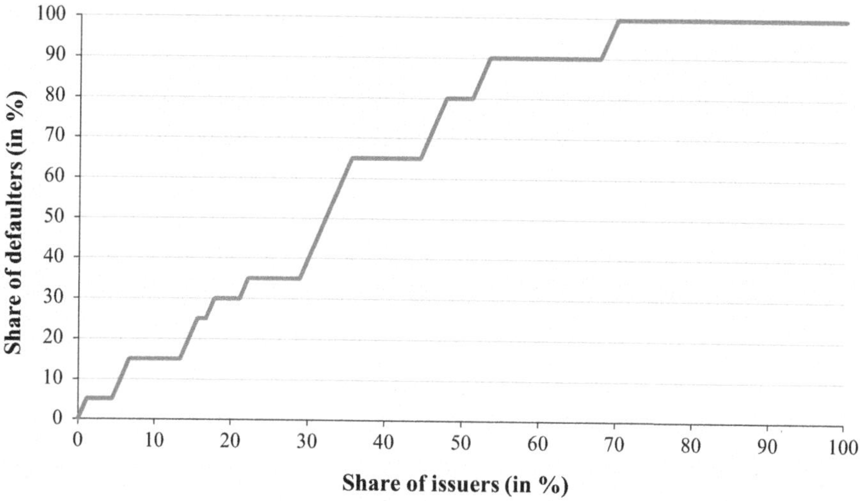

Fig. 4.2 Three-year cumulative accuracy profiles (CAPs), Institutional Investor, January 1982–December 1984. *Source*: Author's computations

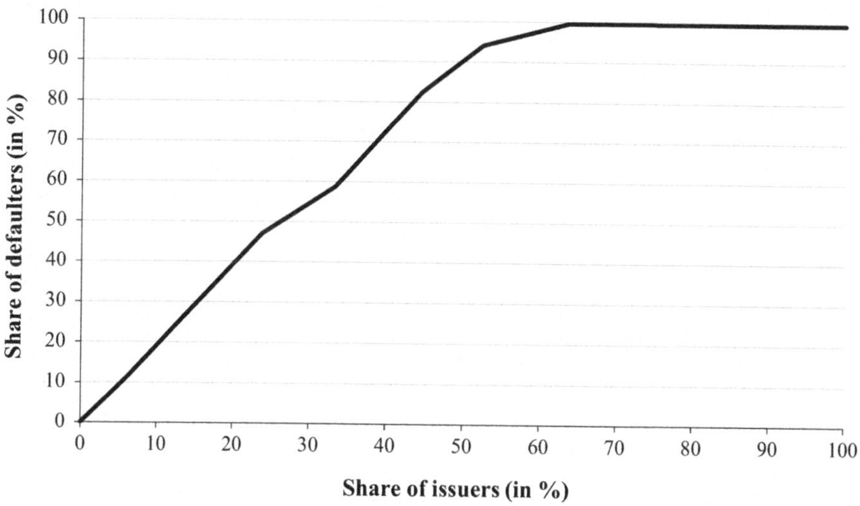

Fig. 4.3 Three-year cumulative accuracy profiles (CAPs), Euromoney, January 1982–December 1984. *Source*: Author's computations

the worst possible performance (all defaulters are assigned the highest rating). The formula for calculating an AR is as follows:

$$AR = 2\left[\left[\sum_{R_i = R_1,\ldots,R_{\max}} \frac{\left(D_{R_i} + D_{R_{i-1}}\right)\left(N_{R_i} + N_{R_{i-1}}\right)}{2DN}\right] - 0.5)\right]$$

where

D = total number of defaults;
N = total number of issuers;
R_i = rating of given rater;
D_{R_i} = total number of defaults rated R_i and less;
N_{R_i} = total number of issuers rated R_i and less;
$D_0 = 0$;
$N_0 = 0$.

The 3-year ARs for Institutional Investor and Euromoney are 0.347 and 0.454, respectively. Three comments can be made. First, ARs are significantly greater than zero, which confirms that these two raters generally managed to distinguish between good and bad debtors. Second, although the two ratios are not strictly comparable (recall that the samples under consideration differ), the Institutional Investor performance is worse than that of Euromoney. Two reasons may be advanced. On the one hand, half of the defaults are concentrated on the bottom 33% of the issuers included in Institutional Investor's sample as compared with the bottom 25% of those in Euromoney's sample. On the other hand, there are no defaults in the top 30% of the International Investor sample as compared with the top 38% of the Euromoney sample. Third, Institutional Investor's and Euromoney's performance with respect to the 1982 LDC crisis is somewhat worse than the performance posted by CRAs during the interwar sovereign debt debacle (Flandreau et al. 2011, pp. 527–529). It seems that CRAs in that earlier period were better able to rank relative risks. Perhaps more surprising is that the Institutional Investor and Euromoney ARs are reduced because half of all emerging and developing countries did *not* default in 1982–1984 despite having been assigned intermediate or low ratings. This outcome is in contrast with the 1930s, when more than two thirds of Latin American and Eastern European countries lapsed into default during a single 3-year period (1931–1933).[23]

4.2.1.3 Ratings Stability

Given that Euromoney's rating scale was completely changed in 1982 (see Sect. 4.1.3), the examination here of sovereign ratings stability focuses exclusively on Institutional Investor ratings. After collecting the ratings it issued in September of

[23] Author's computations based on Gaillard (2011, apx. 1 and 3).

1981, 1982, 1983, and 1984, I identified each country whose rating was lowered by 15 points or more within a year. This 15-point downgrade is roughly equivalent to a three-notch downgrade on CRAs' rating scales (see Table 4.7), which reflects a major change in creditworthiness of the rated country.[24]

Three major downgrades are observed for 1982—Romania (−25 points), Argentina (−19.7 points), and Costa Rica (−18 points)—and another three for 1983: Mexico (−20.8 points), Venezuela (−16.9 points), and Chile (−16.6 points). No country lost 15 points or more between 1983 and 1984. These results indicate that only a few Institutional Investor ratings were excessively high when the debt crisis erupted in 1982. Between September 1981 and September 1984, however, the overall adjustment of sovereign ratings was dramatic: within 3 years, they lost on average 7.2 points. Fourteen countries were downgraded by at least 15 points, of which seven (Ecuador, Nigeria, Iraq, Chile, Venezuela, Mexico, and Argentina) lost 25 points or more.

The seriousness of the 1982 debt crisis is reflected not only in the lowered Institutional Investor ratings between 1981 and 1984 but also in their subsequent slow recovery. In 1989, *none* of the seven countries just mentioned had a rating higher than it did in 1981.

Table 4.7 Equivalence table for rating scales used by Institutional Investor, Moody's, and S&P

Institutional Investor	Moody's	S&P
100	Aaa	AAA
95	Aa1	AA+
90	Aa2	AA
85	Aa3	AA−
80	A1	A+
75	A2	A
70	A3	A−
65	Baa1	BBB+
60	Baa2	BBB
55	Baa3	BBB−
50	Ba1	BB+
45	Ba2	BB
40	Ba3	BB−
35	B1	B+
30	B2	B
25	B3	B−
20	Caa1	CCC+
15	Caa2	CCC
10	Caa3	CCC− and CC
5	Ca and C	SD and D

Source: Author's classifications

[24] See Gaillard (2011, p. 78).

4.2.2 The Eurozone Crisis of 2009–2013

The eurozone debt crisis was triggered in October 2009 when the newly elected Prime Minister of Greece, George Papandreou, revised the country's forecasted budget deficit upward to 12.5%—more than double the previous forecast. In the months that followed, Greek bond yields and credit default swaps soared while the country's credit rating was downgraded by CRAs, Institutional Investor, and Euromoney (see Gaillard 2011, Chap. 10, for a description of the actions undertaken by CRAs during October 2009–June 2010). In May 2010, in the context of a 3-year program set up jointly by the European Monetary Union and the International Monetary Fund (IMF), a €110 billion financial package was offered to help Greece meet its financing needs.

In June 2010, the European Financial Stability Facility (EFSF) was established to rescue two additional countries: Ireland and Portugal (in 2010 and 2011, respectively). Greece was bailed out again in 2012. The European Stability Mechanism (ESM), which was set up in October 2012 as a successor to the EFSF, rescued Spain in 2012 and Cyprus in 2013.

This section analyzes the ability of Moody's, S&P, Institutional Investor, and Euromoney to anticipate these five bailout packages.[25] Absent their implementation, the countries of Ireland, Portugal, and Spain would have become insolvent and the defaults of Greece and Cyprus would have had far more severe consequences. Gaillard (2017) documents that bailouts undermine a government's financial credibility and therefore dictate that sovereign ratings be lowered.[26] As in Sect. 4.2.1, ratings performance is assessed by examining the ratings prior to default, computing ARs, and evaluating the stability of ratings. The time horizon for this assignment is again 3 years.

4.2.2.1 Ratings Prior to Default

Tables 4.8 and 4.9 report eurozone sovereign ratings as of (respectively) September 1, 2009 and September 1, 2010.[27] Institutional Investor and Euromoney scores are transformed into CRA ratings via the equivalences given in Table 4.7. For example, a score ranging between 85.01 and 90.00 would be rounded up to the higher score in the table's first column (i.e., 90), which is then converted to AA on the S&P rating scale. Countries that were bailed out in the three subsequent years are printed in boldface type.

---

[25] The second bailout of Greece, implemented in 2012, is not accounted for here.

[26] Greece's and Cyprus's defaults on their FC bonds have been estimated at $312.4 billion and $1.7 billion, respectively (Beers and de Leon-Manlagnit's 2019 database).

[27] Unless otherwise stated, Euromoney ratings are rounded to the first decimal place to facilitate comparisons with Institutional Investor ratings.

Table 4.8 Eurozone sovereign ratings, 1 September 2009

	Institutional Investor	*Institutional Investor*	Euromoney	*Euromoney*	Moody's	S&P
Austria	87.6	*AA*	88.5	*AA*	Aaa	AAA
Belgium	87.2	*AA*	84.8	*AA−*	Aa1	AA+
Cyprus	74.9	*A*	77.9	*A+*	Aa3	A+
Finland	90.6	*AA+*	89.1	*AA*	Aaa	AAA
France	90.2	*AA+*	86.0	*AA*	Aaa	AAA
Germany	91.5	*AA+*	85.7	*AA*	Aaa	AAA
Greece	**74.9**	***A***	**77.4**	***A+***	**A1**	**A−**
Ireland	**80.0**	***A+***	**83.4**	***AA−***	**Aa1**	**AA**
Italy	78.5	*A+*	78.3	*A+*	Aa2	A+
Luxembourg	92.6	*AA+*	96.3	*AAA*	Aaa	AAA
Malta	76.8	*A+*	77.8	*A+*	A1	A
Netherlands	91.7	*AA+*	88.0	*AA*	Aaa	AAA
Portugal	**80.1**	***AA−***	**76.7**	***A+***	**Aa2**	**A+**
Slovakia	75.4	*A+*	75.1	*A+*	A1	A+
Slovenia	82.6	*AA−*	77.7	*A+*	Aa2	AA
Spain	**81.6**	***AA−***	**81.7**	***AA−***	**Aaa**	**AA+**

Notes: Institutional Investor and Euromoney scores are those published in September 2009. Institutional Investor and Euromoney scores that have been converted to CRA ratings are *italicized*. Countries that were bailed out during the period from 1 September 2009 to 1 September 2012 are shown in **boldface**

Sources: Author's classifications based on *Institutional Investor* (September 2009), *Euromoney* (September 2009), moodys.com, and spglobal.com

On the two dates in question, Moody's assigned the highest ratings whereas Institutional Investor followed the most conservative policy. In September 2009, Greece was ranked in the single-A broad rating category by all four raters; however, Euromoney was much slower to downgrade after the bailout was announced in May 2010. For all the other countries to be rescued, Moody's posted the poorest performance. Institutional Investor and Euromoney outperformed the two CRAs in terms of assessing the creditworthiness of Ireland and Spain. Two distinct reasons can be advanced. First, Moody's and S&P realized that the credit position of the two countries was weakening yet they were reluctant to lower their ratings. In fact, the two CRAs feared that multi-notch downgrades would trigger massive sales of sovereign bonds and thereby exacerbate the debt crisis. That concern stemmed from the institutional overreliance on CRA ratings through their incorporation into regulatory rules and investors' "prudential" rules (for an exhaustive analysis, see Gaillard 2014a). This factor did not apply to the ratings issued by the two magazines. Second, Institutional Investor and Euromoney may have benefited from the greater granularity of their rating scales. As risk aversion increased in 2007–2008, for instance, they managed to assign Germany a rating higher than Spain and Ireland. In contrast, the 20-notch rating scale used by Moody's and S&P might have been too narrow to enable distinguishing among different eurozone members (e.g., Germany and Spain).

Table 4.9 Eurozone sovereign ratings, 1 September 2010

	Institutional Investor	*Institutional Investor*	Euromoney	*Euromoney*	Moody's	S&P
Austria	85.2	*AA*	85.8	*AA*	Aaa	AAA
Belgium	81.4	*AA−*	80.2	*AA−*	Aa1	AA+
Cyprus	**71.4**	***A***	**80.0**	***A+***	**Aa3**	**A+**
Finland	88.6	*AA*	88.6	*AA*	Aaa	AAA
France	85.6	*AA*	82.0	*AA−*	Aaa	AAA
Germany	90.8	*AA+*	84.5	*AA−*	Aaa	AAA
Greece	**43.9**	***BB***	**60.3**	***BBB+***	**Ba1**	**BB+**
Ireland	**67.5**	***A−***	**77.9**	***A+***	**Aa2**	**AA−**
Italy	70.4	*A*	74.0	*A*	Aa2	A+
Luxembourg	90.1	*AA+*	88.3	*AA*	Aaa	AAA
Malta	75.5	*A+*	75.7	*A+*	A1	A
Netherlands	90.5	*AA+*	88.2	*AA*	Aaa	AAA
Portugal	**62.2**	***BBB+***	**73.8**	***A***	**A1**	**A−**
Slovakia	71.2	*A*	76.3	*A+*	A1	A+
Slovenia	84.4	*AA−*	78.7	*A+*	Aa2	AA
Spain	**66.7**	***A−***	**72.3**	***A***	**Aaa**	**AA**

Notes: Institutional Investor and Euromoney scores are those published in September 2010. Institutional Investor and Euromoney scores that have been converted to CRA ratings are *italicized*. Countries that were bailed out during the period from 1 September 2010 to 1 September 2013 are shown in **boldface**. On 1 September 2010, Greece had already been bailed out but was rescued again in 2012

Sources: Author's classifications based on *Institutional Investor* (September 2010), *Euromoney* (September 2010), moodys.com, and spglobal.com

4.2.2.2 Accuracy Ratios

Figures 4.4 and 4.5 present the 3-year CAP curves for eurozone countries as rated by Institutional Investor, Euromoney, Moody's, and S&P on September 1, 2009 and September 1, 2010, respectively.[28] Because Greece was bailed out in May 2010, it has been excluded from the second sample. The resulting two samples comprise 16 and 15 countries.

For the two periods under consideration (i.e., September 1, 2009–September 1, 2012 and September 1, 2010–September 1, 2013), the Institutional Investor and the Moody's CAP curves are (respectively) the first and the last to reach the uppermost line, which suggests that Institutional Investor performed much better than Moody's. The Euromoney and S&P CAP curves are fairly similar, and the performance of these raters seems to be intermediate. The concavity of the curves is more pronounced for ratings issued in September 2010, which means that the four raters lowered the credit ratings of those countries that were about to be bailed out by the EFSF or the ESM.

[28] The Institutional Investor and Euromoney ratings used here are their original scores (i.e., on the 0–100 scale).

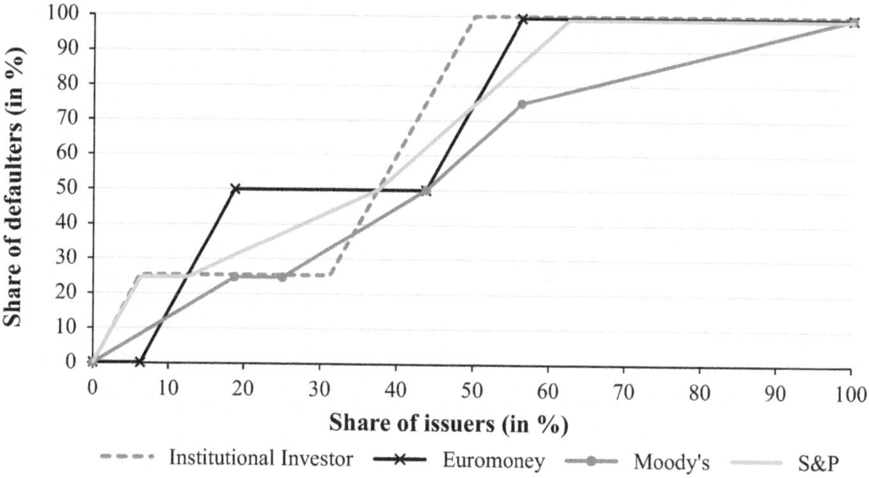

Fig. 4.4 Three-year CAPs: Eurozone countries as of 1 September 2009. *Source:* Author's computations

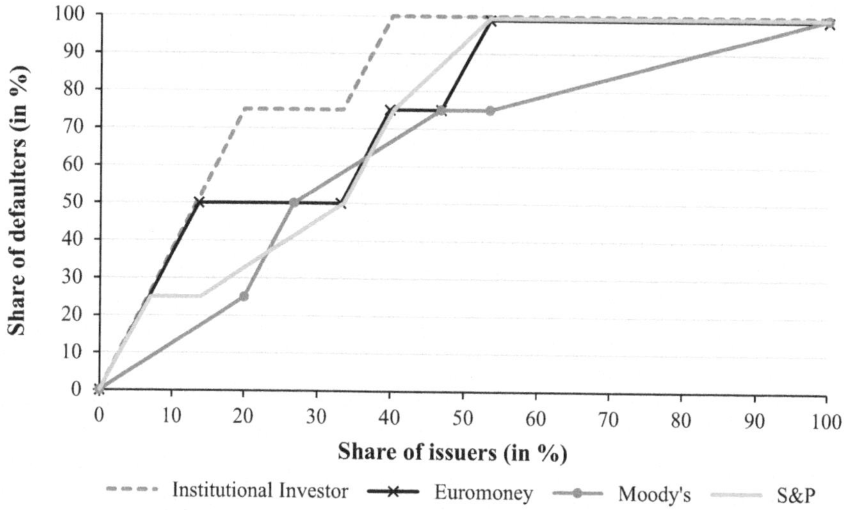

Fig. 4.5 Three-year CAPs: Eurozone countries as of 1 September 2010. *Source:* Author's computations

These results are reflected in the accuracy ratios (see Table 4.10). Moody's ARs are the lowest for the two periods. Two main reasons can be proposed. The firm assigned its highest rating (i.e., Aaa) to Spain, which was bailed out in 2012. More fundamentally, Moody's failed to discriminate between creditworthy and distressed issuers in the eurozone. S&P came in with the next-to-worst performance. For the ratings issued in September 2009, its ARs are comparable to those of Institutional Investor and

Table 4.10 Three-year accuracy ratios, Eurozone countries

	Three-year accuracy ratio, 1 September 2009–1 September 2012	Three-year accuracy ratio, 1 September 2010–1 September 2013
Institutional Investor	0.375	0.667
Euromoney	0.375	0.500
Moody's	0.141	0.267
S&P	0.359	0.450

Sources: Author's computations

Euromoney; for its September 2010 ratings, however, S&P is penalized because of the high proportion of *non*-distressed countries (e.g., Italy, Malta, and Slovakia) in the lower rating categories. Euromoney exhibits better performance but suffers from its overly optimistic scores assigned to Greece and Ireland in September 2009 and to Cyprus in September 2010. Institutional Investor shows an impressive capacity to assign high ratings only to creditworthy debt issuers. Moreover, its scores exhibit efficient adjustments between September 2009 and September 2010: thus Institutional Investor's AR increased by 0.29 points during this period, as compared with 0.13 points for both Euromoney and Moody's and only 0.09 points for S&P. The sharp downgrades of Ireland, Portugal, and Spain in 2010 are emblematic of Institutional Investor's winning strategy.

4.2.2.3 Ratings Stability

After collecting the ratings issued in September of 2009, 2010, 2011, and 2012, I identified the countries whose ratings were lowered—within a year—by 15 points or more by Institutional Investor and Euromoney (Table 4.11) and by three notches or more by Moody's and S&P (Table 4.12).

These two tables merit several comments. First, Moody's and S&P's major downgrades outnumber those made by Institutional Investor and Euromoney: nine cases (seven countries) versus four cases (three countries), respectively. These results suggest that the ratings assigned by the two CRAs were excessively high in 2009 and so had to be lowered dramatically. In the cases of Greece and Cyprus, there is an additional explanation. During 2011 and 2012 (respectively), the two countries became increasingly likely to restructure their debt in the short term. That prospect obliged Moody's and S&P to lower their ratings to the default level (Ca/C and SD/D, resp.) or to near-default levels (Caa1, Caa2, Caa3 and CCC+, CCC, CCC−, CC, resp.). Such specific categories are absent from the Institutional Investor and Euromoney rating scales. Hence these two raters could dispense with massive downgrades of distressed debt issuers.

Second, the more-than-two-notch downgrades announced by Moody's and S&P hit exactly the same set of countries: Cyprus, Greece, Ireland, Italy, Portugal, Slovenia, and Spain. Similar comments can be made for Institutional Investor and

Table 4.11 Eurozone members that experienced a major downgrade by Institutional Investor and Euromoney, 1 September 2009–1 September 2012

Institutional investor			Euromoney		
Country	Period	Downgrade (in points)	Country	Period	Downgrade (in points)
Greece	Sept. 2009–Sept. 2010	31.0	Greece	Sept. 2009–Sept. 2010	17.1
Portugal	Sept. 2009–Sept. 2010	17.9	Greece	Sept. 2010–Sept. 2011	21.5
Greece	Sept. 2010–Sept. 2011	16.7	Ireland	Sept. 2010–Sept. 2011	16.8
Ireland	Sept. 2010–Sept. 2011	18.5	Portugal	Sept. 2010–Sept. 2011	17.7

Source: Author's computations and classifications

Table 4.12 Eurozone members that experienced a major downgrade by Moody's and S&P, 1 September 2009–1 September 2012

Moody's			S&P		
Country	Period	Downgrade (in notches)	Country	Period	Downgrade (in notches)
Greece	Sept. 2009–Sept. 2010	6	Greece	Sept. 2009–Sept. 2010	4
Cyprus	Sept. 2010–Sept. 2011	4	Cyprus	Sept. 2010–Sept. 2011	3
Greece	Sept. 2010–Sept. 2011	9	Greece	Sept. 2010–Sept. 2011	9
Ireland	Sept. 2010–Sept. 2011	8	Ireland	Sept. 2010–Sept. 2011	4
Portugal	Sept. 2010–Sept. 2011	7	Portugal	Sept. 2010–Sept. 2011	3
Cyprus	Sept. 2011–Sept. 2012	5	Cyprus	Sept. 2011–Sept. 2012	4
Italy	Sept. 2011–Sept. 2012	6	Italy	Sept. 2011–Sept. 2012	3
Slovenia	Sept. 2011–Sept. 2012	6	Slovenia	Sept. 2011–Sept. 2012	3
Spain	Sept. 2011–Sept. 2012	7	Spain	Sept. 2011–Sept. 2012	5

Source: Author's computations and classifications

Euromoney: Greece, Ireland, and Portugal were massively downgraded by the two magazines. These observations support the view that the two CRAs and the two magazines had converging opinions about the creditworthiness of eurozone sovereign issuers. Their disagreements and performance gaps mainly reflect the timing and magnitude of the downgrades. For instance, Institutional Investor was more prompt in downgrading Portugal and lowered Greece's rating to a much greater extent than did Euromoney. Moody's adjustments were more dramatic than S&P's primarily because its ratings were higher when the eurozone debt crisis began in 2009. Moody's had rated the four countries that requested a bailout in 2010–2012 (i.e., Greece, Ireland, Portugal, and Spain) 1.5 notches higher, on average, than S&P had.

Third, unlike Institutional Investor and Euromoney, Moody's and S&P announced major downgrades of two countries (Italy and Slovenia) that ultimately would *not* need to be rescued. The two CRAs might have overestimated the risk of contagion to other eurozone members, which rendered the credit ratings—especially those by Moody's—more procyclical during 2011–2012. This assumption is partly corroborated when one compares the eurozone ratings issued in September 2012 with those assigned 3 years earlier. The steepest downgrades are observed for Moody's: 4.3 notches as compared with 2.9 notches for S&P, 13.2 points for Institutional Investor (the equivalent of 2.6 notches), and 15.4 points for Euromoney (3.1 notches).

The eurozone debt crisis would have been worse if the IMF, the EFSF, and the ESM had not intervened as lenders of last resort. Despite these bailouts, it is possible to assess the relative performance of Institutional Investor, Euromoney, Moody's, and S&P. The ratings published by Institutional Investor were the most accurate essentially because the magazine refrained from assigning top scores to countries that had to default or be rescued during the three subsequent years. At the other extreme, Moody's poor performance resulted from its failure to discriminate adequately among eurozone countries' creditworthiness.

4.2.3 The Sovereign Bond Years (1995–2013)

The debt crisis experienced by many emerging and developing economies in the 1980s was partly solved by the Brady Plan. Implemented in 1989 under the auspices of US Secretary of Treasury Nicholas Brady, this plan helped distressed sovereign borrowers to reach debt reduction agreements with their commercial bank creditors and to exchange their discounted bank loans for so-called "Brady bonds." Mexico was the first country to restructure its debt. Other emerging countries followed suit (see Vásquez 1996 for an overview). In 1992, JP Morgan created the Emerging Markets Bond Index (EMBI), a "total return" index that tracked the traded market for Brady bonds. The market trading volume for this type of security grew from $247 billion in 1992 to $2.69 trillion in 1996 (Emerging Markets Traders Association 1996, 1999). These Brady deals attracted many investors and had the effect of increasing the size of emerging bond and equity markets (Erb et al. 1999). They also enabled many middle- and low-income countries to tap capital markets for the first time (Grigorian 2003).

This section studies foreign government bond markets during 1995–2013. Only two measures of ratings performance are used: the assigned ratings prior to default; and ratings stability. As in previous sections, the time horizon considered is 3 years.

Accuracy ratios are not computed because fewer than half of the countries that defaulted on their FC bond debt were rated simultaneously by Institutional Investor, Euromoney, Moody's, and S&P.

4.2.3.1 Ratings Prior to Default

Using Beers and de Leon-Manlagnit's (2019) database, I compiled a list of the countries that lapsed into default on their foreign currency bond debt during 1995–2013; the resulting sample comprised 31 defaults.[29] Several countries defaulted twice or more.[30] Tables 4.13, 4.14, and 4.15 report the ratings issued by Institutional Investor, Euromoney, Moody's, and S&P 1, 2, and 3 years prior to default.[31] As in Sect. 4.2.2.1, Institutional Investor and Euromoney scores are transformed into CRA ratings.

For the ratings assigned 3 years before default, Table 4.13 shows that three countries were rated in the investment-grade category by all four raters: Uruguay, Greece, and Cyprus. The highest rating was given either by Euromoney or by Moody's. Euromoney was the only firm to rank Argentina in the investment-grade category. Of the 27 sovereign debt issuers rated both by Institutional Investor and by Euromoney, 25 were rated lower by the former than by the latter. The implication is that Institutional Investor performed significantly better than Euromoney. Of the 13 sovereign debt issuers rated by both Moody's and S&P, 6 were assigned the same rating. Of the seven remaining defaults, S&P ratings were lower for five of them. Once the Institutional Investor scores are transformed into CRA ratings, its performance is seen to be worse than both Moody's and S&P's. On average, however, the rating gap between Institutional Investor and S&P amounts to less than one notch. For the period 1995–2013, then, S&P was the most accurate rater over 3-year time horizons.

Two years prior to default (Table 4.14), Cyprus is the only country still placed in the investment-grade category by all four raters. Institutional Investor was the first to downgrade Uruguay's rating to the speculative-grade category, while Euromoney was the last to maintain Greece's rating in the investment-grade category. Observe also that Euromoney assigned a score above 50 points to two other countries that defaulted 2 years later: Argentina and the newly rated Antigua and Barbuda. As emphasized previously, Institutional Investor's ratings are more conservative (and hence generally more accurate) than Euromoney's but end up being slightly less accurate than either Moody's or S&P's. The ratings issued by the two CRAs 2 years prior to default are strongly similar.

---

[29] Saint Kitts and Nevis defaulted on its FC bond debt in 2011 but is excluded from the sample because it was not evaluated by any of the four raters.

[30] When a country is in default for at least two consecutive years, only the first year is considered.

[31] Moody's and S&P ratings are as of September 1. Institutional Investor and Euromoney ratings are those published in their respective September issues. For a country that defaulted in year *y*, the ratings studied are those published on September 1 of years $y-3$, $y-2$, and $y-1$.

Table 4.13 Institutional Investor, Euromoney, Moody's, and S&P ratings 3 years prior to default, 1995–2013

	Year of default	Institu. Investor	*Institu. Investor*	Euromoney	*Euromoney*	Moody's	S&P
Moldova	1998	N.R.	*N.R.*	27.5	*B*	N.R.	N.R.
Russia	1998	19.4	*CCC+*	27.4	*B*	N.R.	N.R.
Ukraine	1998	15.7	*CCC+*	28.0	*B*	N.R.	N.R.
Ecuador	1999	26.4	*B*	45.0	*BB*	N.R.	N.R.
Pakistan	1999	29.2	*B*	49.8	*BB+*	B1	B+
Ivory Coast	2000	20.1	*B−*	37.0	*BB−*	N.R.	N.R.
Argentina	2001	41.8	*BB*	61.3	*BBB+*	Ba3	BB
Nigeria	2001	16.4	*CCC+*	33.6	*B+*	N.R.	N.R.
Moldova	2002	N.R.	*N.R.*	31.0	*B+*	B2	N.R.
Cameroon	2003	16.3	*CCC+*	29.7	*B*	N.R.	N.R.
Dominica	2003	N.R.	*N.R.*	38.6	*BB−*	N.R.	N.R.
Nicaragua	2003	21.8	*B−*	26.3	*B*	B2	N.R.
Paraguay	2003	32.5	*B+*	41.3	*BB*	B2	B
Uruguay	2003	53.5	*BBB−*	56.8	*BBB*	Baa3	BBB−
Grenada	2004	27.7	*B*	37.9	*BB−*	N.R.	N.R.
Moldova	2004	16.2	*CCC+*	26.0	*B*	Caa1	N.R.
Nigeria	2004	18.3	*CCC+*	28.8	*B*	N.R.	N.R.
Venezuela	2004	33.3	*B+*	44.7	*BB*	B2	B
Antigua and Barb.	2005	N.R.	*N.R.*	33.7	*B+*	N.R.	N.R.
Dominican Rep.	2005	38.1	*BB−*	47.3	*BB+*	Ba2	BB−
Belize	2006	37.4	*BB−*	32.0	*B+*	Ba3	B+
Ecuador	2008	28.0	*B*	35.1	*BB−*	Caa1	CCC+
Nicaragua	2008	23.1	*B−*	29.0	*B*	Caa1	N.R.
Seychelles	2008	26.1	*B*	37.8	*BB−*	N.R.	N.R.
Zimbabwe	2009	7.0	*CCC−*	19.9	*CCC+*	N.R.	N.R.
Jamaica	2010	36.2	*BB−*	42.6	*BB*	B1	B
Belize	2012	28.2	*B*	43.2	*BB*	B3	B
Greece	2012	74.9	*A*	77.4	*A+*	A1	A−
Cyprus	2013	71.4	*A*	80.0	*AA−*	Aa3	A+
Grenada	2013	33.0	*B+*	16.4	*CCC+*	N.R.	B−
Jamaica	2013	31.1	*B+*	34.1	*B+*	B3	B−

Notes: Institutional Investor and Euromoney scores that have been transformed into CRA ratings are *italicized*. N.R. = not rated

Sources: Author's classifications based on *Institutional Investor* (various issues), *Euromoney* (various issues), moodys.com, and spglobal.com

Table 4.14 Institutional Investor, Euromoney, Moody's, and S&P ratings 2 years prior to default, 1995–2013

	Year of default	Institu. investor	*Institu. investor*	Euromoney	*Euromoney*	Moody's	S&P
Moldova	1998	N.R.	*N.R.*	31.5	*B+*	N.R.	N.R.
Russia	1998	21.4	*B–*	42.6	*BB*	N.R.	N.R.
Ukraine	1998	16.6	*CCC+*	29.5	*B*	N.R.	N.R.
Ecuador	1999	26.3	*B*	37.1	*BB–*	B1	N.R.
Pakistan	1999	27.2	*B*	44.5	*BB*	B2	B+
Ivory Coast	2000	22.2	*B–*	34.0	*B+*	N.R.	N.R.
Argentina	2001	42.4	*BB*	53.8	*BBB–*	Ba3	BB
Nigeria	2001	17.9	*CCC+*	31.2	*B+*	N.R.	N.R.
Moldova	2002	15.8	*CCC+*	29.2	*B*	B3	N.R.
Cameroon	2003	17.0	*CCC+*	29.7	*B*	N.R.	N.R.
Dominica	2003	N.R.	*N.R.*	32.5	*B+*	N.R.	N.R.
Nicaragua	2003	18.9	*CCC+*	28.7	*B*	B2	N.R.
Paraguay	2003	28.9	*B*	38.8	*BB–*	B2	B
Uruguay	2003	49.5	*BB+*	57.0	*BBB*	Baa3	BBB–
Grenada	2004	37.9	*BB–*	33.0	*B+*	N.R.	BB–
Moldova	2004	15.7	*CCC+*	26.2	*B*	Ca	N.R.
Nigeria	2004	17.6	*CCC+*	24.5	*B–*	N.R.	N.R.
Venezuela	2004	30.6	*B+*	39.9	*BB–*	B2	B
Antigua and Barb.	2005	N.R.	*N.R.*	52.5	*BBB–*	N.R.	N.R.
Dominican Rep.	2005	36.6	*BB–*	43.4	*BB*	Ba2	B+
Belize	2006	35.1	*BB–*	41.2	*BB*	B2	B–
Ecuador	2008	30.2	*B+*	34.5	*B+*	Caa1	CCC+
Nicaragua	2008	19.5	*CCC+*	30.0	*B+*	Caa1	N.R.
Seychelles	2008	23.0	*B–*	42.5	*BB*	N.R.	N.R.
Zimbabwe	2009	8.0	*CCC–*	19.8	*CCC+*	N.R.	N.R.
Jamaica	2010	37.4	*BB–*	40.8	*BB*	B1	B
Belize	2012	28.7	*B*	44.7	*BB*	B3	B
Greece	2012	43.9	*BB*	60.3	*BBB+*	Ba1	BB+
Cyprus	2013	65.8	*A–*	70.0	*A–*	Baa1	BBB+
Grenada	2013	27.1	*B*	17.4	*CCC+*	N.R.	B–
Jamaica	2013	32.0	*B+*	32.2	*B+*	B3	B–

Notes: Institutional Investor and Euromoney scores that have been transformed into CRA ratings are *italicized*. N.R. = not rated

Sources: Author's classifications based on *Institutional Investor* (various issues), *Euromoney* (various issues), moodys.com, and spglobal.com

In September of the year preceding a default (Table 4.15), three countries were still rated as investment grade by at least one rater: Argentina, Antigua and Barbuda (both scored above 50 points by Euromoney), and Cyprus (which was scored at 51 points and 59.7 points by Institutional Investor and Euromoney, respectively). All ratings assigned by Moody's and S&P were in the speculative-grade category, and

Table 4.15 Institutional Investor, Euromoney, Moody's, and S&P ratings 1 year prior to default, 1995–2013

	Year of default	Institu. Investor	*Institu. Investor*	Euromoney	*Euromoney*	Moody's	S&P
Moldova	1998	N.R.	*N.R.*	36.3	*BB−*	Ba2	N.R.
Russia	1998	27.5	*B*	49.7	*BB+*	Ba2	BB−
Ukraine	1998	19.8	*CCC+*	29.7	*B*	N.R.	N.R.
Ecuador	1999	26.1	*B*	44.8	*BB*	B1	N.R.
Pakistan	1999	25.3	*B*	35.9	*BB−*	B3	CCC
Ivory Coast	2000	22.7	*B−*	31.2	*B+*	N.R.	N.R.
Argentina	2001	45.8	*BB+*	55.0	*BBB−*	B1	BB
Nigeria	2001	18.1	*CCC+*	32.1	*B+*	N.R.	N.R.
Moldova	2002	16.2	*CCC+*	26.0	*B*	Caa1	N.R.
Cameroon	2003	19.7	*CCC+*	29.6	*B*	N.R.	N.R.
Dominica	2003	N.R.	*N.R.*	29.3	*B*	N.R.	N.R.
Nicaragua	2003	17.6	*CCC+*	30.8	*B+*	B2	N.R.
Paraguay	2003	29.7	*B*	36.8	*BB−*	B2	B
Uruguay	2003	41.9	*BB*	43.1	*BB*	B3	B
Grenada	2004	33.9	*B+*	48.2	*BB+*	N.R.	BB−
Moldova	2004	18.7	*CCC+*	31.5	*B+*	Caa1	N.R.
Nigeria	2004	20.2	*B−*	33.5	*B+*	N.R.	N.R.
Venezuela	2004	27.1	*B*	34.6	*B+*	Caa1	B−
Antigua and Barb.	2005	N.R.	*N.R.*	50.4	*BBB−*	N.R.	N.R.
Dominican Rep.	2005	26.3	*B*	37.6	*BB−*	B3	CC
Belize	2006	31.4	*B+*	39.6	*BB−*	B3	CCC−
Ecuador	2008	33.0	*B+*	34.2	*B+*	Caa2	CCC
Nicaragua	2008	20.9	*B−*	31.2	*B+*	Caa1	N.R.
Seychelles	2008	29.0	*B*	41.9	*BB*	N.R.	B
Zimbabwe	2009	7.6	*CCC−*	14.6	*CCC*	N.R.	N.R.
Jamaica	2010	37.1	*BB−*	43.6	*BB*	B2	CCC+
Belize	2012	33.2	*B+*	36.6	*BB−*	B3	B−
Greece	2012	27.2	*B*	38.9	*BB−*	Ca	CC
Cyprus	2013	51.0	*BBB−*	59.7	*BBB*	Ba3	BB
Grenada	2013	31.1	*B+*	13.5	*CCC*	N.R.	B−
Jamaica	2013	30.1	*B+*	31.1	*B+*	B3	B−

Notes: Institutional Investor and Euromoney scores that have been transformed into CRA ratings are *italicized*. N.R. = not rated

Sources: Author's classifications based on *Institutional Investor* (various issues), *Euromoney* (various issues), moodys.com, and spglobal.com

more than three-fourths were rated B1/B+ or below (i.e., the bottom of that category). These results suggest that the two CRAs were more prompt to reassess credit risk as the likelihood of default increased. This finding is in line with the evolution of ratings observed between the third and the last year preceding default. Moody's and S&P downgraded distressed debt issuers by 2.7 and 3.3 notches, respectively, compared with 2.2 and 2.5 points for Euromoney and Institutional Investor. These gaps are substantial because one notch on CRAs' rating scale is equivalent to 5 points on Euromoney's and Institutional Investor's scoring scale.

A detailed analysis reveals that Moody's and S&P ratings 1 year prior to default were never more than those assigned 3 years prior to default. In contrast, only 61% and 48% of the scores published by (respectively) Euromoney and Institutional Investor 1 year prior to default were lower than those issued 2 years earlier. These percentages reveal that the two magazines failed to realize that the credit position of some economies was weakening. For example, the scores given by Euromoney to Russia, Antigua and Barbuda, and Grenada were increased by 22.3, 16.7, and 10.3 points. There may have been methodological flaws behind these upgrades (see Sect. 4.3.1). A second explanation, which likely accounts for most of the untimely upgrades announced by Institutional Investor, is that a more granular rating scale increases the probability of a (modest) upgrade for a country that will default in the short term.

4.2.3.2 Ratings Stability

After collecting the ratings issued on September 1 in each year from 1995 to 2012, I identified the countries whose ratings were lowered—within a year's time—by 15 points or more by Institutional Investor (Table 4.16) and Euromoney (Table 4.17) and by three notches or more by Moody's (Table 4.18) and S&P (Table 4.19).

Observe first of all that the number of major downgrades differs across raters: 14 by Institutional Investor, 25 by Moody's, 31 by S&P, and 62 by Euromoney. These downgrades account for (respectively) 0.5%, 1.5%, 1.9%, and 2% of all observations.[32] Institutional Investor's ratings are far more stable than those of its three

Table 4.16 Major downgrades by Institutional Investor, 1 September 1995–1 September 2012

Country	Period	Country	Period	Country	Period
Indonesia	1997–1998	Latvia	2008–2009	Greece	2010–2011
South Korea	1997–1998	Ukraine	2008–2009	Ireland	2010–2011
Argentina	2001–2002	Greece	2009–2010	Libya	2010–2011
Ecuador	2008–2009	Portugal	2009–2010	Vanuatu	2010–2011
Iceland	2008–2009	Bahrain	2010–2011		

Source: Author's calculations and classifications

[32] Here an observation is the evolution of a rating between year y and year $y+1$.

Table 4.17 Major downgrades by Euromoney, 1 September 1995–1 September 2012

Country	Period	Country	Period	Country	Period
Barbados	1996–1997	Bermuda	2009–2010	Nepal	2009–2010
Cambodia	1996–1997	Bhutan	2009–2010	Rwanda	2009–2010
Central Afric. Rep.	1996–1997	Botswana	2009–2010	Samoa	2009–2010
Tonga	1996–1997	Brunei	2009–2010	Sao Tome and Princ.	2009–2010
Bahamas	1997–1998	Burundi	2009–2010	Solomon Islands	2009–2010
Bermuda	1997–1998	Cambodia	2009–2010	St Lucia	2009–2010
Brunei	1997–1998	Cape Verde	2009–2010	St Vincent and Gren.	2009–2010
Indonesia	1997–1998	Central Afr. Rep.	2009–2010	Swaziland	2009–2010
Malaysia	1997–1998	Dominica	2009–2010	Tajikistan	2009–2010
Mauritius	1997–1998	Dominican Rep.	2009–2010	Tonga	2009–2010
South Korea	1997–1998	Equatorial Guinea	2009–2010	Trinidad and Tobago	2009–2010
Tonga	1999–2000	Eritrea	2009–2010	Turkmenistan	2009–2010
Zaire	2000–2001	Fiji	2009–2010	Vanuatu	2009–2010
Argentina	2001–2002	Greece	2009–2010	Bahrain	2010–2011
Estonia	2008–2009	Grenada	2009–2010	Greece	2010–2011
Iceland	2008–2009	Laos	2009–2010	Ireland	2010–2011
Mali	2008–2009	Lesotho	2009–2010	Libya	2010–2011
Niger	2008–2009	Maldives	2009–2010	Pakistan	2010–2011
Antigua and Barb.	2009–2010	Marshall Isl.	2009–2010	Portugal	2010–2011
Bahamas	2009–2010	Mauritius	2009–2010	Yemen	2010–2011
Barbados	2009–2010	Micronesia	2009–2010		

Source: Author's calculations and classifications

Table 4.18 Major downgrades by Moody's, 1 September 1995–1 September 2012

Country	Period	Country	Period	Country	Period
Indonesia	1997–1998	Uruguay	2001–2002	Ireland	2010–2011
Moldova	1997–1998	Dominican Rep.	2003–2004	Portugal	2010–2011
Russia	1997–1998	Belize	2005–2006	Belize	2011–2012
South Korea	1997–1998	Ecuador	2008–2009	Cyprus	2011–2012
Thailand	1997–1998	Iceland	2008–2009	Italy	2011–2012
Romania	1998–1999	Latvia	2008–2009	Slovenia	2011–2012
Argentina	2000–2001	Greece	2009–2010	Spain	2011–2012
Argentina	2001–2002	Cyprus	2010–2011		
Moldova	2001–2002	Greece	2010–2011		

Source: Author's calculations and classifications

Table 4.19 Major downgrades by S&P, 1 September 1995–1 September 2012

Country	Period	Country	Period	Country	Period
Indonesia	1997–1998	Dominican Rep.	2003–2004	Greece	2010–2011
Malaysia	1997–1998	Belize	2004–2005	Ireland	2010–2011
Pakistan	1997–1998	Cameroon	2004–2005	Portugal	2010–2011
Russia	1997–1998	Grenada	2004–2005	Belize	2011–2012
South Korea	1997–1998	Seychelles	2007–2008	Cyprus	2011–2012
Indonesia	1999–2000	Iceland	2008–2009	Egypt	2011–2012
Argentina	2000–2001	Latvia	2008–2009	Italy	2011–2012
Argentina	2001–2002	Ukraine	2008–2009	Slovenia	2011–2012
Indonesia	2001–2002	Greece	2009–2010	Spain	2011–2012
Paraguay	2002–2003	Bahrain	2010–2011		
Uruguay	2002–2003	Cyprus	2010–2011		

Source: Author's calculations and classifications

counterparts. It is noteworthy that about half of Euromoney's major downgrades involve small states or microstates, which suggests that the credit position of such issuers is quite unpredictable. Moreover, 60% of Euromoney's major downgrades occurred in 2010: this concentration reflects that year's change in the ECR methodology (see Sect. 4.1.3).

Second, 28% of all major downgrades follow two events: the Asian debt crisis of 1997–1998 and the eurozone turmoil of 2009–2012. This proportion is lower than one might expect because many countries experienced idiosyncratic economic and financial difficulties. Several of them defaulted (e.g., Russia in 1998; Moldova in 1998, 2002, and 2004; Argentina in 2001; Belize in 2006 and 2012), but others managed to remain solvent thanks to a bailout (e.g., Iceland and Latvia in 2008).

Third, these tables show that 39% of the countries that defaulted on their FC debt bonds during 1995–2013 were not severely downgraded within the year preceding and following their bankruptcy. In fact, these debt issuers typically had a poor credit rating one or 2 years prior to default, which made it unnecessary for raters to issue significant downgrades. This dynamic is evidenced in particular by Institutional Investor and Euromoney. However, there is one puzzling exception: Antigua and Barbuda. This twin-island country was scored at 50.4 points by Euromoney in September 2004 and at 53.2 points in September 2005 (i.e., the year of its default). A year later, the score was lowered by only 2.1 points. It is possible that Euromoney overlooked Antigua and Barbuda's default and so maintained its intermediate score. This anomaly illustrates how Euromoney ratings may assess not strictly *sovereign* risk but also—and more globally—*country* risk (see Sect. 4.1.3).

Finally, the profile of those countries that suffered a major downgrade evolved during the period under consideration. During 1995–2008, high-income countries accounted for the smallest portion of that subsample, but during 2008–2012 they represented no less than 46% of major downgrades—a larger share than that of either middle- or low-income countries. This shift, which was driven by the debt crisis that shook the eurozone, Iceland, and Bahrain, calls into question the debt sustainability of wealthy sovereign issuers. In the medium–long term, this counterintuitive possibility may constitute the main challenge for Institutional Investor, Euromoney, Moody's, and S&P.

4.3 General Comments

This section is home to many globally applicable comments that should help foreign creditors grasp the limits of sovereign ratings, appreciate some historical background, and assess sovereign risk more efficiently. Section 4.3.1 identifies some flaws in Institutional Investor's, Euromoney's, Moody's, and S&P's sovereign rating methodologies, and it emphasizes some important yet overlooked factors in the medium- and long-term creditworthiness of sovereign borrowers. Section 4.3.2 studies the evolution of sovereign ratings during the globalization era and focuses on countries whose respective credit positions either improved or weakened the most. Section 4.3.3 examines the main disagreements across the four raters as of September 1, 2016 and attempts to account for those differences.

4.3.1 Redrafting Sovereign Rating Methodologies

4.3.1.1 Why Neither Transparency Nor a Quantitative Approach Is a Panacea

The first lesson that can be drawn from Sect. 4.2 is that transparency does not entail accuracy. In this respect, the eurozone debt crisis is especially telling. Institutional Investor, the least transparent rater, exhibited the best performance; whereas Moody's, which had recently opened the "black box" of its methodology, assigned excessively high ratings to countries that defaulted or were bailed out in the following 3 years. This finding should convince investors to keep a critical eye on sovereign rating methodologies or, even better, to develop their own tools for assessing credit risk.

Sovereign rating methodologies have also become increasingly quantitative. Euromoney opened the way to this new pattern as early as the 1980s; Moody's and S&P followed suit, albeit not until the late 2000s. The main problem is that rating analysts are now ensnared in quantitative risk assessments that allow little room to maneuver when adjusting ratings upward or downward. Furthermore, the quantitative criteria do not always permit one to anticipate debt crises. The reasons are that (a) most such indicators (e.g., the WEF Global Competitiveness Index and the unemployment rate) assess a country's *structural* strengths and weaknesses and (b) most ratios are stated relative to GNP or GDP (e.g., current account balance to GNP, public debt to GDP) and so are insufficiently sensitive to current events. As a result, sovereign ratings tend to be too "sticky."

Because a credit rating is an opinion about the willingness and ability of a borrower to repay its debt in the *medium term*, it would be hazardous to transform that rating into an early warning indicator. A more relevant way to enhance rating methodologies would therefore be to focus on the *sustainability* of the rated sovereign's public debt, of its economic framework, and of its institutional and political system. These factors will be discussed in turn.

4.3.1.2 Sustainability of Public Debt

Despite the extensive research dealing with debt sustainability (e.g., Reinhart et al. 2003; Collard et al. 2015),[33] Euromoney, Moody's, and S&P have difficulty in addressing this issue.

The "debt indicators" score (which accounts for 10% of the final rating) assigned by Euromoney to sovereign borrowers 1 year, 2 years, and 3 years prior to their default during 1995–2013 (see Tables 4.13–4.15 for the list of defaulting countries) have systematically contributed to the inflation of final ratings. For the three countries that were still rated above 50 points the year prior to their default—namely, Cyprus, Argentina, and Antigua and Barbuda—this factor was set at a high or very high level: respectively 7.6, 7.7, and 10 out of 10. Part of the relatively poor performance of Euromoney ratings (see Sect. 4.2.3) was driven by this "mis-scoring" of the debt indicators.

The problem with Moody's and S&P's methodologies is that they have traditionally placed too much emphasis on the ratio of general government debt to GDP *without* distinguishing between industrialized economies, on the one hand, and emerging and developing economies, on the other. Yet the former enjoy a higher "debt intolerance" threshold than do the latter. Hence it is fruitless to classify countries on a risk scale that is based on this ratio, as Moody's (2015, p. 16) currently does. The traditional *quantitative* measures used by rating analysts include public debt ratios, the maturity structure of the debt, whether it is indexed or not, whether the debt is denominated in foreign or domestic currency, whether it has fixed or floating rates, by whom it is held, and so forth. However, the less than stellar past performance of these raters confirms the indispensability of also conducting *qualitative* analyses in three principal areas.

First, in the present era of moral hazard, assessing sovereign risk requires that one examines the credit position of all borrowers that could apply for a government bailout: local debt issuers, government-related firms, and especially "systemically important financial institutions" (SIFIs). Growing debt and liabilities in any of these entities may indicate an increased risk of future contingent liabilities for the central or federal government. Rating analysts have persistently downplayed these chal-

[33] See also the debt sustainability assessments (DSAs) of low-income countries undertaken by the IMF and the World Bank since 2005 (http://www.imf.org/external/pubs/ft/dsa/lic.aspx).

lenges, which have led them to assign inflated ratings to developed countries (Gaillard 2017).

Second, a country's fiscal balance must be carefully monitored. A fiscal deficit or surplus is a poor indicator unless it is analyzed over time and in relation to GDP growth. A government that posts fiscal deficits after several years of high GDP growth (e.g., Argentina in the late 1990s, Greece in the mid-2000s) will be vulnerable in the event of an economic slowdown. By the same token, fiscal or primary surpluses during a recession—which are often run to reduce the debt/GDP ratio—may prove to be counterproductive. Austerity measures are likely to fail if they are not accompanied by a strong social consensus and/or a significant debt restructuring (e.g., Greece in the 2010s).

Third, an exhaustive analysis of debt sustainability requires that one focus on the quality of public spending and the tax system's efficiency. A high level of public spending does not threaten a country's credit position *provided* those expenditures stimulate growth, education, and competitiveness. Scandinavian countries embody this truism. At the same time, a tax system's capacity to collect revenues fairly and efficiently and to increase taxes with no risk of evasion, avoidance, or revolt is imperative because otherwise indebtedness will almost surely follow. That China's ratio of general government revenue to GDP doubled between 1995 and 2015 reflects not only that country's rapid economic growth but also its government's increasing ability to extract revenues from all taxpayers.[34]

4.3.1.3 Sustainability of a Country's Economic Structure

The eurozone debt crisis serves as a reminder that also rich countries may default. Between 1890 and 2010, there were 13 defaults involving high-income countries (Gaillard 2014b). All European countries included in this sample became insolvent for political reasons: they either entered a world war or were authoritarian regimes that refused to meet their financial commitments. However, the debt restructurings of Greece in 2012 and of Cyprus in 2013 did *not* have political roots. In this sense, the eurozone crisis was both unprecedented and idiosyncratic. Hence it should oblige all raters to revise their methodologies because sovereign ratings have always been strongly correlated to income per capita and to GDP per capita (Cantor and Packer 1996; Gaillard 2011). This correlation was still high in September 2016 (see Table 4.20). In fact, the economic framework of industrialized countries may be threatened by an unsustainable exchange rate and/or the creation of asset bubbles.[35]

First of all, exchange rate sustainability vis-à-vis major foreign currencies has become a key factor in assessing the credit positions of emerging *and* developed countries. The default of Greece in 2012 and the financial difficulties experienced

---

[34] Author's computation based on Moody's data.

[35] These two risks were leading causes in the default of emerging economies (e.g., Indonesia in 1999 and Argentina in 2001). Yet the 2008–2012 financial turmoil in Iceland and the eurozone demonstrated that they could trigger a solvency crisis in developed countries as well.

Table 4.20 Correlation coefficients for sovereign ratings versus GDP per capita, September 2016

	GDP per capita, PPP (constant 2011 international $)	GDP per capita, PPP (current international $)
Institutional Investor ratings	0.78	0.77
Euromoney ratings	0.75	0.75
Moody's ratings	0.73	0.72
S&P ratings	0.76	0.75

Notes: The GDP per capita figures used are the latest available. A country is excluded from the sample if the latest figure available is from prior to 2009. Moody's and S&P ratings are transformed into numerical values following the equivalents listed in Table 4.7. There are 174, 180, 129, and 119 pairs for (respectively) Institutional Investor, Euromoney, Moody's, and S&P
Sources: Author's computations based on the World Bank's World Development Indicators as of November 2016, *Institutional Investor* (September 2016), *Euromoney* (September 2016), moodys.com, and spglobal.com

by peripheral eurozone members were partly driven by high appreciation of the euro, which undermined the economic competitiveness of those countries. During the 20 years preceding their eurozone membership, the currencies of Greece, Portugal, and Spain depreciated by (respectively) 9%, 6.5%, and 4% per annum against the US dollar. In contrast, from 2001 to 2009 the euro appreciated, on average, 5% each year against the US dollar.[36] Southern European economies suffered from losing their monetary sovereignty because their competitiveness depended in large part on being able to let their currency depreciate over time. The implementation of austerity measures since the early 2010s is thus the steep price they have paid for adopting an international currency.[37]

Two crucial questions then arise for foreign creditors. Will peripheral eurozone countries be able to remain in the monetary union? If not, then the exiting countries are likely to default. If these peripheral countries do remain, the second question is: Will they manage to stay solvent? Countries can address this challenge by improving their non-price competitiveness, diversifying their economies, rationalizing public spending, limiting the painful effects of austerity, and—to the extent that this is even possible—encouraging eurozone governance bodies to adopt remedies that reflect a more Keynesian perspective.

As regards the second factor affecting economic structure, the ability of high-income countries to prevent credit-fueled asset bubbles from arising should be given greater weight. Over the past three decades, homes and financial assets have increasingly been acquired by means of leverage and quite often with the intention of selling them later at a higher price. The problem is that asset bubbles exacerbate business cycles; thus their appearance tends to reduce risk aversion only to magnify

[36] Author's calculations based on World Bank's World Development Indicators.

[37] It is interesting that Greece's former Finance Minister Yanis Varoufakis, who opposed German Chancellor Angela Merkel regarding the austerity measures imposed on his country, admitted that a "Grexit" would be too hazardous (Varoufakis 2016, pp. 205–206).

it when they burst (Reinhart and Rogoff 2009, pp. 158–162). More dramatically, debt—and especially mortgage debt—increases inequality and acts as "anti-insurance," concentrating risks on the middle class (Mian and Sufi 2014, p. 30). In concrete terms, these considerations dictate that specific indicators be more carefully examined. For instance, stock exchange indices and real estate prices that rise at least three times as fast as GDP growth for several consecutive years are good indicators of speculation. A prolonged surge in the ratio of average domestic private-sector credit to GDP (or of bank assets to GDP) is also cause for alarm. If these indicators had been properly taken into account by Institutional Investor, Euromoney, Moody's, and S&P in the 2000s, then distressed eurozone countries would have been rated lower when the Greek debt crisis broke out in 2009.

4.3.1.4 Sustainability of Institutional and Political Systems

The sustainability of a country's institutional and political system is evidently contingent on four parameters: the legitimacy of the institutional regime; its capacity to yield stable government and administration; the *absence* of powerful "anti-system" parties in the political landscape; and, more importantly, the preservation of the rule of law. The last factor will be analyzed in Chap. 5 because it has turned out to be even more important for *country* risk than for *sovereign* risk.

4.3.2 *Evolution of Sovereign Ratings during the Globalization Era*

The world economy has changed substantially during the past 35 years. Between 1982 and 2016, world GDP and total exports of goods and services rose by factors of 6.5 and 9.5, respectively. In the meantime, life expectancy at birth increased by more than 8 years.[38] As Deaton (2013) states, "life is better now than at almost any time in history." However, growth and development were accompanied by a soaring world public debt (+2300% between 1982 and 2016).[39] This context helps explain why some countries managed to improve their credit position while others failed to do so.

4.3.2.1 The Worst-Performing Borrowers

Table 4.21 lists the five countries whose credit position deteriorated the most during 1982–2016 (as measured by Institutional Investor and Euromoney ratings) and during 1995–2016 (as measured by Moody's and S&P ratings).

[38] Author's calculations based on World Bank's World Development Indicators.

[39] Author's calculations based on Beers and de Leon-Manlagnit's (2019) database.

Table 4.21 Five worst-performing countries during the globalization era

Institutional Investor		Euromoney		Moody's		S&P	
Country	Downg. (in points)	Country	Downg. (in points)	Country	Downg. (in notches)	Country	Downg. (in notches)
Venezuela	−43.8	Greece	−38.9	Greece	−9	Cyprus	−9
Greece	−30.1	Libya	−37.2	Portugal	−6	Italy	−7
Zimbabwe	−17.9	Venezuela	−30.5	Spain	−6	Portugal	−7
Japan	−15.4	France	−30.3	Venezuela	−6	Greece	−6
Papua N.G.	−14.2	Fiji	−29.6	Barbados	−5	Spain	−5

Notes: For Institutional Investor and Euromoney, the ratings published in September 2016 are compared with those published in September 1982. For Moody's and S&P, the ratings as of 1 September 2016 are compared with those as of 1 September 1995

Sources: Author's calculations and classifications based on *Institutional Investor* (September 1982 and September 2016), *Euromoney* (September 1982 and September 2016), moodys.com, and spglobal.com

I first examine the countries that were massively downgraded by Institutional Investor and Euromoney. Only two sovereign borrowers are on both lists: Greece and Venezuela. In total, there are eight different countries, yet only three of them (Greece, Venezuela, and Zimbabwe) defaulted massively on their FC debt during 1982–2016. All three experienced more than a debt crisis: they were embroiled in (and are still undergoing) major social and political crises with little hope for recovery in the medium term. Papua New Guinea and Fiji share several fundamental weaknesses, including political instability and their respective economies' lack of diversification. The consequence is that their sovereign ratings have traditionally been volatile. The other three severely downgraded sovereign issuers—Libya, France, and Japan—were solvent during the entire period. Libya's rating fell sharply as early as 1983–1984, although it rebounded in the late 2000s before plummeting again during the 2011 war. In France and Japan, the ratio of general government debt to GDP increased fourfold over the past 35 years; even so, their rating did not decline significantly until the Great Recession. To date, neither nation has been able to achieve fiscal deficit reduction goals or to curb public debt. Sovereign rating analysts and investors should pay close attention not only to debt sustainability but also to the capacity of these countries to implement reforms that will reduce unemployment (in France) and cut deflationary pressures (in Japan).

Turning now to Moody's and S&P ratings, we can see that the sovereign borrowers whose credit position deteriorated the most during 1995–2016 are eurozone countries. These downgrades, which are mainly concentrated in the period 2009–2013, were analyzed extensively in Sect. 4.2.2. The last pending case is Barbados. After being rated in the investment-grade category for more than a decade, this Caribbean island's rating was subjected to multiple downgrades. The main causes are the continued increase in government debt and the limited prospects of fiscal reform. Barbados ultimately defaulted on its LC and FC debt in 2018.[40]

[40] See Beers and de Leon-Manlagnit's (2019) database.

4.3.2.2 The Best-Performing Borrowers

Table 4.22 presents the five countries whose credit position improved the most during 1982–2016 (as measured by Institutional Investor and Euromoney ratings) and during 1995–2016 (as measured by Moody's and S&P ratings).

In several instances, the best "performers" are countries that, at the beginning of the period under consideration, were already in default (e.g., Costa Rica, Poland, and Romania in 1982) or were then experiencing—or had recently experienced—a severe economic and financial crisis (e.g., Mexico, Sweden, and Turkey in 1995). By and large, the sovereign borrowers that enhanced their credit position enjoyed strong GDP growth, implemented pro-business measures to attract foreign investors, and were unaffected by any political crises. In addition, the Czech Republic, Malta, Poland, Romania, and Slovakia all took advantage (until the mid-2000s) of the prospect of EU membership and of that membership itself in the following years.

4.3.3 Ratings Convergence and Divergence

As of September 1, 2016, the ratings issued by Institutional Investor, Euromoney, Moody's, and S&P were strongly correlated with one another. Table 4.23 reports the correlation coefficients and Appendix provides the ratings lists.

Table 4.22 Five best-performing countries during the globalization era

Institutional Investor		Euromoney		Moody's		S&P	
Country	Upg. (in points)	Country	Upg. (in points)	Country	Upg. (in notches)	Country	Upg. (in notches)
Poland	+63.7	Malta	+45.1	Mexico	+6	Slovakia	+6
Costa Rica	+40.6	Israel	+40.3	Chile	+4	China	+5
Israel	+37.6	Poland	+38.3	Poland	+4	Hong Kong	+5
Romania	+37.1	Botswana	+32.7	Slovakia	+4	Czech Rep.	+4
Mauritius	+33.6	Romania	+26.6	China	+3	Mexico	+4
				Czech Rep.	+3	Poland	+4
				Philippines	+3		
				Sweden	+3		
				Turkey	+3		

Notes: For Institutional Investor and Euromoney, the ratings published in September 2016 are compared with those published in September 1982. For Moody's and S&P, the ratings as of 1 September 2016 are compared with those as of 1 September 1995

Sources: Author's calculations and classifications based on *Institutional Investor* (September 1982 and September 2016), *Euromoney* (September 1982 and September 2016), moodys.com, and spglobal.com

Table 4.23 Correlation coefficients among sovereign risk indicators, September 1, 2016

	Institutional Investor ratings	Euromoney ratings	Moody's ratings	S&P ratings
Institutional Investor ratings	1 (179)	N.R.	N.R.	N.R.
Euromoney ratings	0.96 (175)	1 (186)	N.R.	N.R.
Moody's ratings	0.97 (126)	0.95 (128)	1 (133)	N.R.
S&P ratings	0.97 (119)	0.96 (119)	0.98 (117)	1 (131)

Notes: Moody's and S&P ratings are transformed into numerical values using the equivalents given in Table 4.7. The number of pairwise observations is reported in parentheses. N.R. = not relevant
Sources: Author's computations based on *Institutional Investor* (September 2016), *Euromoney* (September 2016), moodys.com, and spglobal.com

However, these strong correlations obscure some major disagreements between raters. After transforming Moody's and S&P ratings into numerical values (per Table 4.7), the following pairs are evaluated: Institutional Investor–Euromoney, Institutional Investor–Moody's, Institutional Investor–S&P, Euromoney–Moody's, Euromoney–S&P, and Moody's–S&P. Table 4.24 lists the countries with large split ratings—that is, those countries for which the ratings gap is at least 15 points or 3 notches. There are 69 such splits, which account for 8.8% of the observations. These data support the following conclusions.

First, Euromoney is the rater that disagrees most frequently with its competitors (nearly 80% of all large split ratings). The most striking pattern is that Euromoney underrates high-income sovereign borrowers and China. In particular, Euromoney's assigned economic performance score, structural assessment score, and debt indicators all contribute to deflate the ratings of these countries (cf. Table 4.5). An economy rated Aaa/AAA or Aa1/AA+ by Moody's or S&P is typically scored at about 80 points or less by Euromoney.

Second, Moody's and S&P assign lower ratings to sovereign debt issuers that defaulted during the past 5 years (i.e., Belize, Cyprus, Greece, Jamaica, and Ukraine). These findings are in line with academic research showing that CRAs traditionally place considerable emphasis on default history.

Finally, Table 4.24 shows that there is no major divergence—with the exception of China—across the four raters regarding the credit position of emerging economies. Most disagreements involve developed economies, in contrast to what was observed during the 1990s and the 2000s (Gaillard 2011, Chap. 6). These results support the view that the credit positions of some high-income countries are more at risk than they were a decade ago and hence the sustainability of their debt should be questioned.

Table 4.24 Countries with large split ratings

	Institu. Investor–Euromoney	Institutional Investor–Moody's	Institutional Investor–S&P	Euromoney–Moody's	Euromoney–S&P	Moody's–S&P
Countries for which Institu. Investor rating is lower	Cyprus, Guinea-Bissau, and Liberia	Kuwait and Botswana	Kuwait and Hong Kong	N.A.	N.A.	N.A.
Countries for which Euromoney rating is lower	Djibouti, China, France, and USA	N.A.	N.A.	China, UK, USA, Kuwait, UAE, France, Saudi Arabia, South Korea, New Zealand, Macau, Australia, Bermuda, Qatar, Germany, Canada, Mauritius, Botswana, Sweden, Denmark, Luxembourg, and Netherlands	China, Bermuda, Kuwait, France, Hong Kong, South Korea, Australia, UK, USA, Qatar, Germany, Canada, Estonia, Sweden, Belgium, Denmark, Luxembourg, and Netherlands	N.A.
Countries for which Moody's rating is lower	N.A.	Barbados, Greece, Jamaica, and Belize	N.A.	Greece, Cyprus, Barbados, Mozambique, Belize, Jamaica, and Ukraine	N.A.	Slovenia, Greece, Jamaica, Trinidad and Tobago, and Ukraine
Countries for which S&P rating is lower	N.A.	N.A.	Barbados	N.A.	Cyprus and Mozambique	No country

Notes: Moody's and S&P ratings are transformed into numerical values in accordance with Table 4.7. N.A. = not applicable

Sources: Author's computations based on *Institutional Investor* (September 2016), *Euromoney* (September 2016), moodys.com, and spglobal.com

Appendix: Ratings Assigned by Institutional Investor, Euromoney Country Risk, Moody's, and S&P as of 1 September 2016

Country	Institutional Investor rating	ECR rating	Moody's rating	S&P rating
Abu Dhabi	N.R.	N.R.	Aa2	AA
Afghanistan	14.2	26.63	N.R.	N.R.
Albania	41.0	36.28	B1	B+
Algeria	46.6	38.37	N.R.	N.R.
Andorra	N.R.	N.R.	N.R.	BBB–
Angola	32.5	32.62	B1	B
Antigua and Barbuda	N.R.	29.13	N.R.	N.R.
Argentina	35.1	36.47	B3	B–
Armenia	35.2	43.32	B1	N.R.
Aruba	N.R.	N.R.	N.R.	BBB+
Australia	90.5	81.17	Aaa	AAA
Austria	87.2	80.29	Aa1	AA+
Azerbaijan	45.3	42.89	Ba1	BB+
Bahamas	57.1	49.51	Baa3	BBB–
Bahrain	50.5	49.39	Ba2	BB
Bangladesh	33.2	30.63	Ba3	BB–
Barbados	48.1	41.76	Caa1	B
Belarus	26.0	26.04	Caa1	B–
Belgium	83.3	74.19	Aa3	AA
Belize	32.0	35.12	Caa2	B–
Benin	26.8	23.25	N.R.	N.R.
Bermuda	71.2	56.92	A2	A+
Bhutan	30.0	21.89	N.R.	N.R.
Bolivia	42.0	39.54	Ba3	BB
Bosnia and Herzegovina	33.9	25.20	B3	B
Botswana	58.8	58.25	A2	A–
Brazil	55.7	51.20	Ba2	BB
Brunei	N.R.	57.32	N.R.	N.R.
Bulgaria	55.2	52.26	Baa2	BB+
Burkina Faso	20.6	28.20	N.R.	B–
Burundi	15.5	12.05	N.R.	N.R.
Cambodia	29.6	21.14	B2	N.R.
Cameroon	29.4	30.75	B2	B
Canada	93.3	82.31	Aaa	AAA
Cape Verde	25.5	37.07	N.R.	B
Cayman Islands	N.R.	N.R.	Aa3	N.R.
Central African Republic	10.5	10.21	N.R.	N.R.
Chad	15.3	10.66	N.R.	N.R.
Chile	78.0	75.80	Aa3	AA–

Country	Institutional Investor rating	ECR rating	Moody's rating	S&P rating
China	75.9	58.15	Aa3	AA–
Colombia	62.9	58.10	Baa2	BBB
Comoros	17.7	N.R.	N.R.	N.R.
Congo	22.7	32.65	B3	B–
Cook Islands	N.R.	N.R.	N.R.	B+
Costa Rica	54.8	47.10	Ba1	BB–
Croatia	52.3	49.34	Ba2	BB
Cuba	20.8	19.60	Caa2	N.R.
Curacao	N.R.	N.R.	N.R.	A–
Cyprus	37.8	58.30	B1	BB–
Czech Republic	78.7	71.53	A1	AA–
Democratic Rep. of Congo	15.0	26.71	B3	B–
Denmark	91.3	84.28	Aaa	AAA
Djibouti	28.0	5.72	N.R.	N.R.
Dominica	N.R.	30.80	N.R.	N.R.
Dominican Republic	43.1	37.13	B1	BB–
East Timor	23.4	N.R.	N.R.	N.R.
Ecuador	29.7	34.20	B3	B
Egypt	32.3	33.14	B3	B–
El Salvador	38.7	40.74	B1	B+
Equatorial Guinea	24.4	21.24	N.R.	N.R.
Eritrea	13.2	10.47	N.R.	N.R.
Estonia	76.5	68.38	A1	AA–
Ethiopia	22.7	35.42	B1	B
Fiji	28.9	23.88	B1	B+
Finland	90.3	81.06	Aa1	AA+
France	85.0	68.66	Aa2	AA
Gabon	36.0	43.54	B1	N.R.
Gambia	18.2	28.69	N.R.	N.R.
Georgia	40.2	44.97	Ba3	BB–
Germany	94.6	82.22	Aaa	AAA
Ghana	31.9	36.01	B3	B–
Greece	27.1	33.93	Caa3	B–
Grenada	20.7	34.31	N.R.	N.R.
Guatemala	41.8	39.79	Ba1	BB
Guernsey	N.R.	N.R.	N.R.	AA–
Guinea	12.3	20.84	N.R.	N.R.
Guinea-Bissau	14.7	32.95	N.R.	N.R.
Guyana	31.5	33.59	N.R.	N.R.
Haiti	16.0	16.60	N.R.	N.R.
Honduras	31.2	35.78	B2	B+
Hong Kong	83.9	80.28	Aa1	AAA
Hungary	57.4	51.93	Ba1	BB+

Country	Institutional Investor rating	ECR rating	Moody's rating	S&P rating
Iceland	61.0	63.88	A3	BBB+
India	62.3	53.91	Baa3	BBB−
Indonesia	56.9	50.69	Baa3	BB+
Iran	26.3	31.97	N.R.	N.R.
Iraq	21.4	28.37	N.R.	B−
Ireland	74.6	66.59	A3	A+
Isle of Man	N.R.	N.R.	Aa1	N.R.
Israel	71.2	66.29	A1	A+
Italy	66.2	55.98	Baa2	BBB−
Ivory Coast	35.6	37.24	Ba3	N.R.
Jamaica	32.1	33.90	Caa2	B
Japan	80.5	69.36	A1	A+
Jersey	N.R.	N.R.	N.R.	AA−
Jordan	41.5	44.26	B1	BB−
Kazakhstan	49.3	46.85	Baa3	BBB−
Kenya	32.6	34.93	B1	B+
Kiribati	25.1	N.R.	N.R.	N.R.
Kuwait	73.7	67.96	Aa2	AA
Kyrgyzstan	28.8	23.97	B2	B
Laos	23.4	19.37	N.R.	N.R.
Latvia	69.0	57.68	A3	A−
Lebanon	29.8	31.95	B2	B−
Lesotho	30.0	27.22	N.R.	N.R.
Liberia	17.7	34.70	N.R.	N.R.
Libya	27.7	22.58	N.R.	N.R.
Liechtenstein	N.R.	N.R.	N.R.	AAA
Lithuania	69.5	60.17	A3	A−
Luxembourg	93.3	84.54	Aaa	AAA
Macau	N.R.	66.04	Aa3	N.R.
Macedonia	43.3	38.68	N.R.	BB−
Madagascar	22.0	33.00	N.R.	N.R.
Malawi	20.2	33.50	N.R.	N.R.
Malaysia	67.2	61.32	A3	A−
Maldives	N.R.	22.97	N.R.	N.R.
Mali	19.7	24.98	N.R.	N.R.
Malta	71.3	69.14	A3	BBB+
Marshall Islands	N.R.	5.21	N.R.	N.R.
Mauritania	17.9	21.57	N.R.	N.R.
Mauritius	53.5	48.07	Baa1	N.R.
Mexico	70.6	61.10	A3	BBB+
Micronesia	N.R.	1.00	N.R.	N.R.
Moldova	24.8	28.77	B3	N.R.
Mongolia	39.4	33.72	B3	B−

Country	Institutional Investor rating	ECR rating	Moody's rating	S&P rating
Montenegro	39.9	33.28	B1	B+
Montserrat	N.R.	N.R.	N.R.	BBB−
Morocco	50.2	46.96	Ba1	BBB−
Mozambique	18.0	30.64	Caa3	CCC
Myanmar	25.3	30.06	N.R.	N.R.
Namibia	47.0	51.20	Baa3	N.R.
Nepal	24.2	24.06	N.R.	N.R.
Netherlands	90.8	84.98	Aaa	AAA
New Caledonia	N.R.	4.00	N.R.	N.R.
New Zealand	87.1	80.73	Aaa	AA
Nicaragua	24.4	30.93	B2	B+
Niger	16.6	31.29	N.R.	N.R.
Nigeria	35.6	37.20	B1	B+
North Korea	7.2	7.77	N.R.	N.R.
Norway	93.8	88.62	Aaa	AAA
Oman	62.2	60.03	Baa1	BBB−
Pakistan	29.3	31.26	B3	B−
Panama	59.6	55.67	Baa2	BBB
Papua New Guinea	28.4	30.46	B2	B+
Paraguay	41.3	43.60	Ba1	BB
Peru	65.5	59.47	A3	BBB+
Philippines	61.7	54.04	Baa2	BBB
Poland	72.5	63.70	A2	BBB+
Portugal	56.6	55.66	Ba1	BB+
Qatar	76.3	72.18	Aa2	AA
Ras Al Khaimah	N.R.	N.R.	N.R.	A
Romania	57.2	53.22	Baa3	BBB−
Russia	54.4	45.70	Ba1	BB+
Rwanda	29.9	29.40	B2	B+
Saint Lucia	N.R.	34.49	N.R.	N.R.
St Vincent and the Grenadines	N.R.	35.11	B3	N.R.
Samoa	N.R.	16.31	N.R.	N.R.
Sao Tome and Principe	14.0	21.05	N.R.	N.R.
Saudi Arabia	71.1	59.24	A1	A−
Senegal	33.7	37.44	B1	B+
Serbia	41.0	42.81	B1	BB−
Seychelles	30.6	43.03	N.R.	N.R.
Sharjah	N.R.	N.R.	A3	A
Sierra Leone	15.9	30.06	N.R.	N.R.
Singapore	93.2	86.62	Aaa	AAA
Sint Maarten	N.R.	N.R.	Baa2	N.R.
Slovakia	73.6	69.22	A2	A+

Country	Institutional Investor rating	ECR rating	Moody's rating	S&P rating
Slovenia	66.8	63.37	Baa3	A
Solomon Islands	27.6	13.82	B3	N.R.
Somalia	5.7	13.85	N.R.	N.R.
South Africa	51.9	52.26	Baa2	BBB−
South Korea	83.5	70.70	Aa2	AA
South Sudan	7.5	N.R.	N.R.	N.R.
Spain	65.9	58.33	Baa2	BBB+
Sri Lanka	34.5	44.96	B1	B+
Sudan	8.3	20.83	N.R.	N.R.
Suriname	32.5	36.01	B1	B+
Swaziland	20.8	23.44	N.R.	N.R.
Sweden	93.6	83.75	Aaa	AAA
Switzerland	95.4	87.86	Aaa	AAA
Syria	8.7	15.24	N.R.	N.R.
Taiwan	81.6	71.49	Aa3	AA−
Tajikistan	21.7	21.07	N.R.	N.R.
Tanzania	29.7	36.38	N.R.	N.R.
Thailand	62.0	54.32	Baa1	BBB+
Togo	22.6	31.68	N.R.	N.R.
Tonga	27.9	15.09	N.R.	N.R.
Trinidad and Tobago	58.9	55.05	Baa3	A−
Tunisia	41.8	40.88	Ba3	N.R.
Turkey	51.0	51.92	Baa3	BB
Turkmenistan	29.3	26.76	N.R.	N.R.
Turks and Caicos Islands	N.R.	N.R.	N.R.	BBB+
Uganda	30.4	34.27	B1	B
Ukraine	24.0	28.04	Caa3	B−
United Arab Emirates	76.1	68.50	Aa2	N.R.
United Kingdom	85.8	71.49	Aa1	AA
United States	93.3	77.06	Aaa	AA+
Uruguay	57.8	56.01	Baa2	BBB
Uzbekistan	27.5	27.91	N.R.	N.R.
Vanuatu	28.2	26.59	N.R.	N.R.
Venezuela	16.5	24.65	Caa3	CCC
Vietnam	48.6	43.43	B1	BB−
Yemen	17.5	21.65	N.R.	N.R.
Zambia	31.4	34.19	B3	B
Zimbabwe	8.3	15.82	N.R.	N.R.

Notes: N.R. = not rated

Sources: *Institutional Investor* (September 2016), *Euromoney* (September 2016), moodys.com and spglobal.com

References

Bank for International Settlements (1980). *Fiftieth Annual Report*, Basel.

Beers, D., & de Leon-Manlagnit, P. (2019). The BoC-BoE sovereign default database: What's new in 2019? *Bank of Canada Staff Working Paper 2019–39*.

Butler, A. W., & Fauver, L. (2006). Institutional environment and sovereign credit ratings. *Financial Management, 35*(3).

Cantor, R., & Packer, F. (1996, Spring). Determinants and impact of sovereign credit ratings. *Economic Policy Review, Federal Reserve Bank of New York, 2*.

Collard, F., Habib, M., & Rochet, J.-C. (2015). Sovereign debt sustainability in advanced economies. *Journal of the European Economic Association, 13*(3).

Cosset, J.-C., & Roy, J. (1991). The determinants of country risk ratings. *Journal of International Business Studies, 22*(1).

Deaton, A. (2013). *The great escape: Health, wealth, and the origins of inequality*. Princeton: Princeton University Press.

Emerging Markets Traders Association (1996). *1995 Annual report*, New York City.

Emerging Markets Traders Association (1999). *1998 annual report*, New York City.

Erb, C. B., Harvey, C. R., & Viskanta, T. E. (1999, Winter). New perspectives on emerging market bonds. *Journal of Portfolio Management, 25*(2).

Euromoney (various years). *Euromoney*.

Fishlow, A. (1978, Spring). Debt remains a problem. *Foreign Policy, 30*.

Flandreau, M., Gaillard, N., & Packer, F. (2011). To err is human: Rating agencies and the interwar foreign government debt crisis. *European Review of Economic History, 15*(3).

Friedman, I. S. (1977). *Evaluation of risk in international lending: A lender's perspective. Key issues in international banking, conference series no. 18*. Boston: Federal Reserve Bank of Boston.

Gaillard, N. (2011). *A century of sovereign ratings*. New York: Springer.

Gaillard, N. (2014a). How and why credit rating agencies missed the Eurozone debt crisis. *Capital Markets Law Journal, 9*(2).

Gaillard, N. (2014b). Assessing sovereign risk: The case of rich countries. *Journal of Financial Economic Policy, 6*(3).

Gaillard, N. (2014c). *When sovereigns go bankrupt—A study on sovereign risk*. Cham: Springer.

Gaillard, N. (2017). Credible sovereign ratings: Beyond statistics and regulations. *European Business Law Review, 28*(1).

Grigorian, D. A. (2003). On the determinants of first-time sovereign bond issues. *IMF Working Paper WP/03/184*.

Haque, N. U., Kumar, M. S., Mark, N., & Mathieson, D. J. (1996, December). The economic content of indicators of developing country creditworthiness. *IMF Staff Papers, 13*(4).

Heffernan, S. (1986). *Sovereign risk analysis*. London: Allen & Unwin.

Institutional Investor (various years). *Institutional Investor*.

International Monetary Fund (1981). *Annual report 1981*, Washington, DC.

International Monetary Fund (1982). *Annual report 1982*, Washington, DC.

Mian, A., & Sufi, A. (2014). *House of Debt: How they (and you) caused the great recession, and how we can prevent it from happening again*. Chicago: University of Chicago Press.

Moody's Investors Service (1981). *Moody's bond survey*, 27 April.

Moody's Investors Service (2003, September). *A quantitative model for local currency government bond ratings*.

Moody's Investors Service (2004, February). *A quantitative model for foreign currency government bond ratings*.

Moody's Investors Service (2008, September). *Sovereign bond ratings*.

Moody's Investors Service (2013, 12 September). *Sovereign bond ratings*.

Moody's Investors Service (2015, 18 December). *Sovereign bond ratings*.

Nye, R. P. (2014). *Understanding and managing the credit rating agencies*. London: Euromoney Books.

Reinhart, C., & Rogoff, K. (2009). *This time is different—Eight centuries of financial folly*. Princeton: Princeton University Press.

Reinhart, C., Rogoff, K., & Savastano, M. (2003). Debt intolerance. *Brookings Papers on Economic Activity, 34*(1).

Securities and Exchange Commission (2003, January). *Report on the role and function of credit rating agencies in the operation of the securities markets*.

Standard & Poor's (2002, 3 April). *Sovereign credit ratings: A primer*.

Standard & Poor's (2011, 30 June). *Government rating methodology and assumptions*.

Standard & Poor's (2013a, 24 June). *Sovereign government rating methodology and assumptions*.

Standard & Poor's (2013b, 6 November). *Sovereign rating and country T&C assessment histories*.

Standard & Poor's (2014, 23 December). *Sovereign rating methodology*.

Varoufakis, Y. (2016). *Et les faibles subissent ce qu'ils doivent ?* Paris: Les liens qui libèrent.

Vásquez, I. (1996). The Brady plan and market-based solutions to debt crises. *Cato Journal, 16*(2).

Williamson, J. (1990). What Washington means by policy reform. In J. Williamson (Ed.), *Latin American adjustment: How much has happened?* Washington, DC: Peterson Institute for International Economics.

Wilson, J. O. (1979). Measuring country risk in a global context. *Business Economics, 14*(1).

Chapter 5
Country Risk Indicators

This chapter studies the various indicators used to assess type-1, type-2, type-4, type-5, and type-6 country risks (i.e., CR1, CR2, CR4, CR5, and CR6)—in other words, the risks likely to affect exporters, importers, foreign creditors of corporate entities, foreign shareholders, and foreign direct investors, respectively. The purpose is to assess the extent to which country risk indicators are able to anticipate major shocks.

Section 5.1 presents the country risk rating methodologies used by six major raters: International Country Risk Guide (ICRG), Credendo, the Organisation for Economic Co-operation and Development (OECD), the Fraser Institute, the Heritage Foundation, and the World Economic Forum (WEF). Section 5.2 discusses eight types of shocks, which reflect the main components of country risk analyzed in Chap. 3. Each type of shock has occurred a number of times since the early 1980s, resulting in *country risk crises* (or simply "crises"). Section 5.3 measures the capacity of Euromoney and the six raters examined in Sect. 5.1 to anticipate these crises. The criteria used are the ratings and rankings assigned to a country 1, 2, and 3 years before it encountered a crisis as well as the percentage of what I call *crisis countries* whose scores put them in the top rating categories and were classified in the top tier of the rankings 1, 2, and 3 years prior to their respective crises. Sect. 5.4 gives four extended comments. First, it identifies the strengths and weaknesses of these country risk indicators and provides some comparisons between the raters. Second, it makes recommendations to improve country risk methodologies. Third, it names the countries whose country risk positions improved or weakened most significantly during the globalization era and then offers some explanations for those trends. Finally, it examines correlations among country risk scores.

N. Gaillard, *Country Risk*, https://doi.org/10.1007/978-3-030-45788-4_5

5.1 Country Risk Rating Methodologies

It would clearly be impossible to conduct an exhaustive investigation of all the political and country risk methodologies that have flourished since the 1960s. As a result, this section focuses on a small set of the most significant raters. Four generations of raters are studied here. The first generation includes the external country risk assessors that emerged *before* the globalization years—namely, Euromoney (see Sect. 4.1.3) and ICRG (Sect. 5.1.1). The second generation is represented by export credit agencies, such as Credendo (Sect. 5.1.2), and the OECD through its "country risk classification" (Sect. 5.1.3). The third generation comprises what I call the "neoliberal indicators." Launched in the mid-1990s, the indices of the Heritage Foundation (Sect. 5.1.4) and the Fraser Institute (Sect. 5.1.5) put considerable emphasis on economic freedom. The fourth generation, which gained influence in the 2000s, scrutinizes competitiveness and the business environment; the *Global Competitiveness Reports* published by the WEF are emblematic of this generation (Sect. 5.1.6).

5.1.1 ICRG Methodology

The ICRG model for forecasting political, financial, and economic risk was created in 1980 by the editors of *International Reports*, the newsletter dealing with international finance and economic issues. In 1992, ICRG analysts moved from *International Reports* to The PRS Group (Howell 2001, p. 19).[1] Very little information is provided about the ICRG team. Yet it seems that Professor Howard Howell, senior advisor to ICRG for more than three decades, played a prominent role in the design of its rating methodologies.[2]

The ICRG approach incorporates 22 variables in three subcategories of risk: political, financial, and economic. A specific index is created for each subcategory. The *political risk* index is based on a 100-point scale, whereas the *financial risk* and *economic risk* indices are each based on a 50-point scale. For the three indices, 0 represents the maximum risk. The three scores are aggregated and then divided by 2 to yield the *composite risk score*. The composite scores, which range from 0 to 100, are then broken into five categories: "very high risk" (0–49.9 points), "high risk" (50–59.9 points), "moderate risk" (60–69.9 points), "low risk" (70–79.9 points), and "very low risk" (80–100 points); see Howell (1998, pp. 185–188; 2001, pp. 19–22) and The PRS Group (2012, p. 15; 2014, p. 15). The scores are updated on a monthly basis.

The political risk index is composed of 12 criteria with different weightings (see Table 5.1). "Government stability" measures a government's ability to carry out its program and remain in office. The "socioeconomic conditions" component assesses "general public satisfaction, or dissatisfaction, with the government's economic policies." "Investment profile" reflects four risks: expropriation, taxation, repatriation,

[1] The PRS Group is headquartered in East Syracuse, New York.

[2] See https://isearch.asu.edu/profile/2593007/cv

Table 5.1 Political risk components

Components	Maximum points
Government stability	12
Socioeconomic conditions	12
Investment profile	12
Internal conflict	12
External conflict	12
Corruption	6
Military in politics	6
Religious tensions	6
Ethnic tensions	6
Law and order	6
Democratic accountability	6
Bureaucracy quality	4
Maximum total points	**100**

Sources: Howell (1998, 2001), The PRS Group (2012, 2014)

and labor costs. The factors measured by the "internal conflict," "external conflict," "corruption," "military in politics," "religious tensions," and "ethnic tensions" components are self-evident. "Law and order" reflect the strength and impartiality of the legal system, on the one hand, and popular observance of the law, on the other hand. "Democratic accountability" focuses on the government's responsiveness to its citizens, and "bureaucracy quality" measures the bureaucracy's "strength and expertise to govern without drastic changes in policy or interruptions in government services" (Howell 1998, 2001; The PRS Group 2012, 2014).

The ICRG model's financial risk index consists of five criteria with different weightings (see Table 5.2): the ratios of foreign debt to GDP, foreign debt service to exports of goods and services, and current account to exports of goods and services; the net international liquidity position (measured as months of import cover); and the country's exchange rate stability. For each component, ICRG establishes a scale whereby performance is transformed into a point score (see Tables 5.3, 5.4, and 5.5).

The economic risk index is determined by five criteria with different weightings (see Table 5.6): GDP per capita, real GDP growth, annual inflation rate, and the ratios of current account to GDP and of central government budget balance to GDP. Here, too, ICRG establishes a scale whereby performance is transformed into a point score (see Tables 5.7 and 5.8).

In addition to these current political, financial, economic, and composite risk scores, ICRG also uses the same methodology to produce a "worst-case forecast" (WCF) and a "best-case forecast" (BCF) at the 1- and 5-year horizons (The PRS Group 2012).[3]

[3] In the early 2000s, ICRG issued a "most probable forecast" (MPF) (Howell 2001, pp. 33–34). The MPF, which was neither the mean nor the median of the BCF and WCF, assumed that the government would take action to reduce the risks identified by the current scores. However, the MPF was discontinued shortly after its implementation.

Table 5.2 Financial risk components

Components	Points (maximum)
Foreign debt as a percentage of GDP	10
Foreign debt service as a percentage of exports of goods and services	10
Current account as a percentage of exports of goods and services	15
Net international liquidity as months of import cover	5
Exchange rate stability	10
Maximum total points	**50**

Notes: ICRG indicates that figures are converted into US dollars at the average exchange rate for the given year. The appreciation or depreciation of a currency against the US dollar (against the German mark/Euro in the case of the United States) over a calendar year or the most recent 12-month period is calculated as a percentage change
Sources: Howell (1998, 2001), The PRS Group (2012, 2014)

Table 5.3 Foreign debt as a percentage of GDP and foreign debt service as a percentage of exports of goods and services: Point scores

Foreign debt as a percentage of GDP		Foreign debt service as a percentage of exports of goods and services	
Ratio (%)	Points	Ratio (%)	Points
0.0–4.9	10.0	0.0–4.9	10.0
5.0–9.9	9.5	5.0–8.9	9.5
10.0–14.9	9.0	9.0–12.9	9.0
15.0–19.9	8.5	13.0–16.9	8.5
20.0–24.9	8.0	17.0–20.9	8.0
25.0–29.9	7.5	21.0–24.9	7.5
30.0–34.9	7.0	25.0–28.9	7.0
35.0–39.9	6.5	29.0–32.9	6.5
40.0–44.9	6.0	33.0–36.9	6.0
45.0–49.9	5.5	37.0–40.9	5.5
50.0–59.9	5.0	41.0–44.9	5.0
60.0–69.9	4.5	45.0–48.9	4.5
70.0–79.9	4.0	49.0–52.9	4.0
80.0–89.9	3.5	53.0–56.9	3.5
90.0–99.9	3.0	57.0–60.9	3.0
100.0–109.9	2.5	61.0–65.9	2.5
110.0–119.9	2.0	66.0–70.9	2.0
120.0–129.9	1.5	71.0–75.9	1.5
130.0–149.9	1.0	76.0–79.9	1.0
150.0–199.9	0.5	80.0–84.9	0.5
≥ 200.0	0.0	≥ 85.0	0.0

Source: The PRS Group (2012)

Table 5.4 Current account as a percentage of exports of goods and services and net international liquidity position as months of import cover: Point scores

Current account as a percentage of exports of goods and services		Net international liquidity as months of import cover	
Ratio (%)	Points	Net liquidity in months	Points
≥25.0	15.0	≥15	5.0
20.0–24.9	14.5	12.0–14.9	4.5
15.0–19.9	14.0	9.0–11.9	4.0
10.0–14.9	13.5	6.0–8.9	3.5
5.0–9.9	13.0	5.0–5.9	3.0
0.0–4.9	12.5	4.0–4.9	2.5
−4.9 to −0.1	12.0	3.0–3.9	2.0
−9.9 to −5.0	11.5	2.0–2.9	1.5
−14.9 to −10.0	11.0	1.0–1.9	1.0
−19.9 to −15.0	10.5	0.6–0.9	0.5
−24.9 to −20.0	10.0	≤0.5	0.0
−29.9 to −25.0	9.5		
−34.9 to −30.0	9.0		
−39.9 to −35.0	8.5		
−44.9 to −40.0	8.0		
−49.9 to −45.0	7.5		
−54.9 to −50.0	7.0		
−59.9 to −55.0	6.5		
−64.9 to −60.0	6.0		
−69.9 to −65.0	5.5		
−74.9 to −70.0	5.0		
−79.9 to −75.0	4.5		
−84.9 to −80.0	4.0		
−89.9 to −85.0	3.5		
−94.9 to −90.0	3.0		
−99.9 to −95.0	2.5		
−104.9 to −100.0	2.0		
−109.9 to −105.0	1.5		
−114.9 to −110.0	1.0		
−119.9 to −115.0	0.5		
≤ −120.0	0.0		

Source: The PRS Group (2012)

Table 5.5 Exchange rate stability: Point scores

Depreciation (%)	Points	Appreciation (%)	Points
0.1–4.9	10.0	0.0–9.9	10.0
5.0–7.4	9.5	10.0–14.9	9.5
7.5–9.9	9.0	15.0–19.9	9.0
10.0–12.4	8.5	20.0–22.4	8.5
12.5–14.9	8.0	22.5–24.9	8.0
15.0–17.4	7.5	25.0–27.4	7.5
17.5–19.9	7.0	27.5–29.9	7.0
20.0–22.4	6.5	30.0–34.9	6.5
22.5–24.9	6.0	35.0–39.9	6.0
25.0–29.9	5.5	40.0–49.9	5.5
30.0–34.9	5.0	≥ 50.0	5.0
35.0–39.9	4.5		
40.0–44.9	4.0		
45.0–49.9	3.5		
50.0–54.9	3.0		
55.0–59.9	2.5		
60.0–69.9	2.0		
70.0–79.9	1.5		
80.0–89.9	1.0		
90.0–99.9	0.5		
100.0	0.0		

Source: The PRS Group (2012)

Table 5.6 Economic risk components

Components	Maximum points
Annual inflation rate	10
Real GDP growth	10
GDP per capita	5
Current account as a percentage of GDP	15
Budget balance as a percentage of GDP	10
Maximum total points	**50**

Notes: ICRG indicates that figures are converted into US dollars at the average exchange rate for the given year. GDP per capita is expressed as a percentage of the average of all the countries covered by ICRG. The annual inflation rate is the unweighted average of the Consumer Price Index

Sources: Howell (1998, 2001), The PRS Group (2012)

Table 5.7 Annual inflation rate, real GDP growth, and GDP per capita: Point scales

Annual inflation rate		Real GDP growth		GDP per capita	
Change (%)	Points	Change (%)	Points	% of average	Points
<2.0	10.0	≥6.0	10.0	≥250.0	5.0
2.0–2.9	9.5	5.0–5.9	9.5	200.0–249.9	4.5
3.0–3.9	9.0	4.0–4.9	9.0	150.0–199.9	4.0
4.0–5.9	8.5	3.0–3.9	8.5	100.0–149.9	3.5
6.0–7.9	8.0	2.5–2.9	8.0	75.0–99.9	3.0
8.0–9.9	7.5	2.0–2.4	7.5	50.0–74.9	2.5
10.0–11.9	7.0	1.5–1.9	7.0	40.0–49.9	2.0
12.0–13.9	6.5	1.0–1.4	6.5	30.0–39.9	1.5
14.0–15.9	6.0	0.5–0.9	6.0	20.0–29.9	1.0
16.0–18.9	5.5	0.0–0.4	5.5	10.0–19.9	0.5
19.0–21.9	5.0	−0.4 to −0.1	5.0	≤9.9	0.0
22.0–24.9	4.5	−0.9 to −0.5	4.5		
25.0–30.9	4.0	−1.4 to −1.0	4.0		
31.0–40.9	3.5	−1.9 to −1.5	3.5		
41.0–50.9	3.0	−2.4 to −2.0	3.0		
51.0–65.9	2.5	−2.9 to −2.5	2.5		
66.0–80.9	2.0	−3.4 to −3.0	2.0		
81.0–95.9	1.5	−3.9 to −3.5	1.5		
96.0–110.9	1.0	−4.9 to −4.0	1.0		
111.0–129.9	0.5	−5.9 to −5.0	0.5		
≥130.0	0.0	≤ −6.0	0.0		

Source: The PRS Group (2012)

Table 5.8 Current account as a percentage of GDP and budget balance as a percentage of GDP: Point scales

Current account as a percentage of GDP		Budget balance as a percentage of GDP	
Ratio (%)	Points	Ratio (%)	Points
≥10.0	15.0	≥4.0	10.0
8.0–9.9	14.5	3.0–3.9	9.5
6.0–7.9	14.0	2.0–2.9	9.0
4.0–5.9	13.5	1.0–1.9	8.5
2.0–3.9	13.0	0.0–0.9	8.0
1.0–1.9	12.5	−0.9 to −0.1	7.5
0.0–0.9	12.0	−1.9 to −1.0	7.0
−0.9 to −0.1	11.5	−2.9 to −2.0	6.5
−1.9 to −1.0	11.0	−3.9 to −3.0	6.0
−3.9 to −2.0	10.5	−4.9 to −4.0	5.5
−5.9 to −4.0	10.0	−5.9 to −5.0	5.0
−7.9 to −6.0	9.5	−6.9 to −6.0	4.5
−9.9 to −8.0	9.0	−7.9 to −7.0	4.0
−11.9 to −10.0	8.5	−8.9 to −8.0	3.5
−13.9 to −12.0	8.0	−9.9 to −9.0	3.0

(continued)

Table 5.8 (continued)

Current account as a percentage of GDP		Budget balance as a percentage of GDP	
Ratio (%)	Points	Ratio (%)	Points
−15.9 to −14.0	7.5	−11.9 to −10.0	2.5
−16.9 to −16.0	7.0	−14.9 to −12.0	2.0
−17.9 to −17.0	6.5	−19.9 to −15.0	1.5
−18.9 to −18.0	6.0	−24.9 to −20.0	1.0
−19.9 to −19.0	5.5	−29.9 to −25.0	0.5
−20.9 to −20.0	5.0	≤ −30.0	0.0
−21.9 to −21.0	4.5		
−22.9 to −22.0	4.0		
−23.9 to −23.0	3.5		
−24.9 to −24.0	3.0		
−26.9 to −25.0	2.5		
−29.9 to −27.0	2.0		
−32.5 to −30.0	1.5		
−34.9 to −32.5	1.0		
−39.9 to −35.0	0.5		
≤ −40.0	0.0		

Source: The PRS Group (2012)

5.1.2 *Credendo's Country Risk Methodologies*

In 1921, the Belgian Ministry of Economic Affairs set up the Delcredere Committee to guarantee Belgian export transactions. Eighteen years later, this Committee was transformed into the Office nationale du ducroire (ONDD), an autonomous public financial body with a state guarantee. As an export credit agency, ONDD expanded its operations in the postwar decades, providing a range of services that covered risks worldwide (see Sect. 2.3.5.2). The ONDD became a private limited company in 2004 and was renamed Credendo in 2013 (SA Ducroire 2006; Credendo Group 2014).[4]

For export transactions, the agency has developed three rating systems that aim to assess short-term political risk, medium/long-term political risk, and commercial risk.[5]

For assessing short-term political risk, Credendo uses a quantitative model based on the host country's short-term external liabilities, foreign exchange reserves, current account balance, and refinancing capabilities. For medium/long-term political risk assessment, the firm employs a quantitative model to measure the country's solvency. This model includes external debt ratios and liquidity indicators, yet it also considers the country's fiscal and monetary policies, external balances and structural reforms, potential growth, export diversification, aid dependency, political situation, and payment experience. For both political risk classifications, countries are rated on a scale of 1 to 7, where 1 corresponds to the least risky countries and 7 to the riskiest.

[4] Credendo is headquartered in Brussels.

[5] See https://www.credendo.com/rating-explanation

Commercial risk assessment consists mainly of case-by-case microeconomic assessments of the buyer/obligor, its business sector, and the country in which it is active. The model used is based on economic and financial indicators affecting all companies in the country (e.g., inflation, GDP growth, volatility in exchange rates, etc.) and on the institutional context in which the companies operate. Countries are rated on a three-grade scale: A, B, and C indicate (respectively) low, average, and high commercial risk.

For FDI, Credendo has implemented three rating systems that assess the risk of (i) political violence, (ii) expropriation, and (iii) currency inconvertibility and transfer restrictions.[6] Political violence risk includes wars, terrorist acts, and political violence damages. Expropriation risk encompasses the quality of the country's legal system as well as all measures taken by a host government that discriminate against foreign investors without adequate compensation. It seems that no quantitative model is used to assess these two types of risk. In contrast, Credendo indicates that the risk of currency inconvertibility and transfer restrictions is driven by essentially the same factors underlying medium/long-term political risk. For all three risk types, host countries are rated on a scale of 1 (least risky) to 7 (most risky).

All Credendo country risk ratings are updated on a regular basis and subject to immediate review as circumstances warrant.

5.1.3 OECD's Country Risk Classification

In 1997, the Participants to the Arrangement on Officially Supported Export Credits established a methodology for assessing country credit risk and classifying countries accordingly. These classifications were produced solely for the purpose of setting minimum premium rates for transactions. They reflect country risk, which includes transfer and convertibility risk as well as what the OECD considers "cases of *force majeure*"—for example, war, expropriation, revolution, civil disturbance, floods, and earthquakes.[7]

Countries are rated on a scale of 0 to 7—where 0 represents the least risky countries and 7 the riskiest—via application of a two-step methodology. The Country Risk Assessment Model (CRAM) yields a quantitative evaluation of country credit risk that is based on a set of indicators (e.g., the country's financial and economic circumstances and payment experience reported by the participants). Next, the CRAM ratings are adjusted upward or downward following a qualitative analysis by OECD experts. Any adjustment requires a consensus among these experts.

The OECD released its first country risk ratings in January 1999. Since then, the ratings have been updated quarterly. It is noteworthy that the rating of high-income OECD and eurozone countries was discontinued in 2013.

[6] See https://www.credendo.com/rating-explanation

[7] See http://www.oecd.org/trade/xcred/crc.htm

5.1.4 The Heritage Foundation's Index of Economic Freedom

The Heritage Foundation is a conservative think tank founded in 1973. It gained significant influence under the Reagan administration and has since maintained a tight relationship with the Republican Party.[8] It was ranked #12 in the *2016 Global Go to Think Tank Index Report* (McGann 2017, p. 46). The mission of the Heritage Foundation is to "formulate and promote conservative public policies based on the principles of free enterprise, limited government, individual freedom, traditional American values, and a strong national defense."[9]

In December 1994, the Heritage Foundation launched its Index of Economic Freedom (IEF) in collaboration with the *Wall Street Journal*.[10] Its purpose was to measure economic freedom in ten key areas: trade policy, tax policy, government intervention in the economy, monetary policy, capital flows and foreign investment, banking policy, wage and price controls, property rights, regulations, and "black market" activity. For each category, countries are rated on a scale that ranges from 1 to 5. A score of 1 (resp. 5) indicates that the focal policy is most (resp. least) conducive to economic freedom. The ten categories are weighted equally to yield the average overall score. Countries that exhibit an overall score in the 1.00–1.99 bracket are considered "free" economies; those with an overall score in the 2.00–2.99, 3.00–3.99, and 4.00–5.00 brackets are viewed as being (respectively) "mostly free," "mostly unfree," and "repressive" economies.

Table 5.9 presents the key components of the ten categories used by the IEF in year 2003. For each of these components, Heritage Foundation experts set boundaries that enable them to assign specific "sub-scores." For example, a country receives a sub-score of 1 on the "weighted average tariff rate" component if that rate does not exceed 4%. The sub-score falls to 2 if the rate is higher than 4% but does not exceed 9%; the next boundaries are 14% and 19% (Heritage Foundation 2002, p. 53). The key components and their associated boundaries have changed frequently since 1995.

The methodology was amended substantially in the IEF for 2007 (Heritage Foundation 2007, pp. 37–55). First, the ten main categories were reorganized and renamed as follows: business freedom, trade freedom, fiscal freedom, freedom from government, monetary freedom, investment freedom, financial freedom, property rights, freedom from corruption, and labor freedom. Second, an equation-based approach replaced the bracket scores for several key components. Third, the 1–5 scoring scale was converted to a 0–100 scale, with 100 representing the most free business environment. Finally, the assessments of economic freedom were expanded from four categories to five (Table 5.10).

---

[8] See https://www.heritage.org/conservatism/commentary/reagan-and-heritage-unique-partnership and https://www.heritage.org/article/timeline-heritage-successes

[9] See https://www.heritage.org/about-heritage/mission

[10] K. R. Holmes, "In Search of Free Markets," *Wall Street Journal*, 12 December 1994.

Table 5.9 Methodology for the 2003 IEF

Broad categories	Key components
Trade policy	Weighted average tariff rate
	Nontariff barriers
	Corruption in the customs service
Fiscal burden of government	Top income tax rate and marginal rate for the average taxpayer
	Corporate tax rate
	Government expenditures as a percentage of GDP
Government intervention in the economy	Government consumption as a percentage of the economy
	Government ownership of businesses and industries
	Share of government revenues from state-owned enterprises and gov. ownership of property
	Economic output produced by the government
Monetary policy	Weighted average inflation rate from 1992 to 2001
Capital flows and foreign investment	Foreign investment code
	Restrictions on foreign ownership of business
	Restrictions on the industries and companies open to foreign investors
	Restrictions and performance requirements on foreign companies
	Foreign ownership of land
	Equal treatment under the law for both foreign and domestic companies
	Restrictions on repatriation of earnings
	Availability of local financing for foreign companies
Banking and finance	Government ownership of banks
	Restrictions on the ability of foreign banks to open branches and subsidiaries
	Government influence over the allocation of credit
	Government regulations
	Freedom to offer all types of financial services, securities, and insurance policies
Wages and prices	Minimum wage laws
	Freedom to set prices privately without government influence
	Government price controls and the extent to which government price controls are used
	Government subsidies to businesses that affect prices
	Government role in setting wages
Property rights	Freedom from government influence over the judicial system
	Commercial code defining contracts
	Sanctioning of foreign arbitration of contract disputes
	Government expropriation of property and legally granted and protected private property
	Corruption within the judiciary and delays in receiving judicial decisions

(continued)

Table 5.9 (continued)

Broad categories	Key components
Regulations	Licensing requirements to operate a business and ease of obtaining a business license
	Corruption within the bureaucracy
	Labor regulations
	Environmental, consumer safety, and worker health regulations
	Regulations that impose a burden on business
Black market	Smuggling
	Piracy of intellectual property in the black market
	Agricultural production, manufacturing, services, transportation, and labor supplied on the black market

Source: Heritage Foundation (2002, pp. 49–69)

Table 5.10 Revised assessment categories in the 2007 IEF

Broad rating categories	Brackets
Free	80.0–100
Mostly free	70.0–79.9
Moderately free	60.0–69.9
Mostly unfree	50.0–59.9
Repressed	0.0–49.9

Source: Heritage Foundation (2007, p. 3)

The methodology did not change fundamentally in subsequent years. It is worth mentioning, however, that the 2017 IEF measured 12 broad categories: property rights, judicial effectiveness, government integrity, tax burden, government spending, fiscal health, business freedom, labor freedom, monetary freedom, trade freedom, investment freedom, and financial freedom (Heritage Foundation 2017, pp. 455–469).

The Index of Economic Freedom is published every year—during November/December until 2002 (in each case for the *following* year) and during January since 2004 (in each case for that *same* year). Its experts and contributors have included diplomats (e.g., Kim R. Holmes and Terry Miller) and senior economists (e.g., Gerald P. O'Driscoll, Jr., and Anthony B. Kim).

5.1.5 *The Fraser Institute's Economic Freedom of the World Index*

The Fraser Institute is an independent, Vancouver-headquartered think tank founded in 1974. It was ranked #19 in the *2016 Global Go to Think Tank Index Report* (McGann 2017, p. 46). The mission of the Fraser Institute is to "improve the quality of life for Canadians, their families, and future generations by studying, measuring, and broadly communicating the effects of government policies, entrepreneurship, and choice on their well-being."[11]

The Fraser Institute launched its Economic Freedom of the World (EFW) report in January 1996.[12] Its goal was to "construct an index that is (a) a good indicator of economic freedom across countries and (b) based on objective components that can be updated regularly and used to track future changes in economic freedom" (Fraser Institute 1996, p. xv). The report's neoliberal inspiration was recounted in its Introduction, which stated that "the current volume is the culmination of a process which began at the 1984 meetings of the Mont Pelerin Society in Cambridge, England" (ibid., p. 1).

The EFW index for 1996 had 17 components distributed among four major areas: money and inflation; government operations and regulations; takings and discriminatory taxation; and international exchange (Table 5.11). Every component is rated on a scale of 0–10, where 10 corresponds to the most economic freedom. The index is based on three distinct assessment methods. The first one, which is used for 7 of the 17 components, establishes a grading scale and then transforms indicators and qualitative assessments into specific ratings. The second method (used for another seven components) involves arranging the data from best to worst and then dividing them into 11 groups that each contains an equal number of countries. Countries ranked in the top 11th are assigned a rating of 10; those in the second eleventh, a rating of 9; and so forth. The third method is a binary assessment whereby the country is given a rating of 10 or 0 according as whether a focal condition consistent with economic freedom is or is not present—for example, key component #3 is evaluated by answering this question: Are citizens free to own a foreign currency bank account domestically? The Fraser Institute provides three alternative summary indices that assign different weights to the 17 components (Fraser Institute 1996, pp. 11–46).

During 1997–2001, there were fluctuations in the index's number of key components and their respective weights (see Table 5.12). Starting in 2002, the EFW index used a simple average to combine the key components into broad category ratings and then to express those ratings as "summary" ratings.

In 2017, the EFW index was changed again to consist of 24 key items grouped in five major areas. Several components themselves comprise a number of subcomponents. Altogether, the index now incorporates 42 distinct variables. Each component is still evaluated on a 0–10 scale that reflects the underlying data's distribution. In the case of subcomponents, their ratings are averaged to yield the main component's rating. The component ratings within each broad category are then averaged to

[11] See https://www.fraserinstitute.org/about

[12] Several think tanks were copublishers of the report: the Cato Institute, the Centro de Investigaciones Económicas Nacionales (Guatemala), the Centro de Investigaciones Sobre la Libre Empresa (Mexico), the Free Market Foundation of Southern Africa (South Africa), the Hong Kong Centre for Economic Research (Hong Kong), the Institute of Economic Affairs (England), the Institute of Economic Affairs (Ghana), the Institute of Public Affairs (Australia), the Israel Center for Social and Economic Progress (Israel), and the Liberales Institut (Germany).

Table 5.11 Methodology used to construct the EFW index: 1996

Broad categories	Key components
Money and inflation	Average annual growth rate of the money supply during the last 5 years minus the potential growth rate of real GDP
	Standard deviation of the annual inflation rate during the last 5 years
	Freedom of citizens to own a foreign currency bank account domestically
	Freedom of citizens to maintain a bank account abroad
Government operations and regulations	Government general consumption expenditures as a percentage of GDP
	Role and presence of government-operated enterprises
	Price controls
	Freedom of private businesses and cooperatives to compete in markets
	Equality of citizens under the law and access of citizens to a nondiscriminatory judiciary
	Freedom from government regulations and policies that cause negative real interest rates
Takings and discriminatory taxation	Transfers and subsidies as a percentage of GDP
	Top marginal tax rate
	Use of conscripts to obtain military personnel
Restraints on international exchange	Taxes on international trade as a percentage of exports plus imports
	Difference between the official exchange rate and the black market rate
	Actual size of trade sector compared to the expected size
	Restrictions on the freedom of citizens to engage in capital transactions with foreigners

Source: Fraser Institute (1996, pp. 11–46)

derive ratings for each of the five broad categories. In turn, those five ratings are averaged to obtain the summary rating for each country (Table 5.13).

The EFW is published on a yearly basis—at different times of the year until 2004 and in September since 2005. Experts and contributors include a variety of senior economists. Since 1996, professors James Gwartney (Florida State University) and Robert Lawson (Southern Methodist University) have served as chief editors of the EFW annual report.

Table 5.12 Methodology used to construct the EFW index: 2001

Broad categories (overall weighting)	Key components (weighting within the broad category)
Size of government: consumption, transfers, and subsidies (11%)	General government consumption expenditures as a percentage of total consumption (50%)
	Transfers and subsidies as a percentage of GDP (50%)
Structure of the economy and use of markets (14.2%)	Government enterprises and investment as a percentage of the economy (32.7%)
	Price controls: extent to which businesses are free to set their own prices (33.5%)
	Top marginal tax rate (25%)
	Use of conscripts to obtain military personnel (8.8%)
Monetary policy and price stability (9.2%)	Average annual growth rate of the money supply during the last 5 years minus the growth rate of real GDP during the last 10 years (34.9%)
	Standard deviation of the annual inflation rate during the last 5 years (32.6%)
	Annual inflation rate during the most recent year (32.5%)
Freedom to use alternative currencies (14.6%)	Freedom of citizens to own foreign currency bank accounts domestically and abroad (50%)
	Difference between the official exchange rate and the black market rate (50%)
Legal structure and property rights (16.6%)	Legal security of private ownership rights (50%)
	Rule of law (50%)
International exchange: freedom to trade with foreigners (17.1%)	Revenue from taxes on international trade as a percentage of exports and imports (28.2%)
	Mean tariff rate (29.4%)
	Standard deviation of tariff rates (28.4%)
	Actual size of trade sector compared to the expected size (14%)
Freedom of exchange in capital and financial markets (17.2%)	Ownership of banks: percentage of deposits held in privately owned banks (27.1%)
	Extension of credit: percentage of credit extended to private sector (21.2%)
	Interest rate controls and regulations that lead to negative interest rates (24.7%)
	Restrictions on the freedom of citizens to engage in capital transactions with foreigners (27.1%)

Source: Fraser Institute (2001, p. 6)

Table 5.13 Methodology used to construct the EFW index: 2017

Broad categories	Key components
Size of government	Government consumption
	Transfers and subsidies
	Government enterprises and investment
	Top marginal tax rate
Legal system and property rights	Judicial independence
	Impartial courts
	Protection of property rights
	Military interference in rule of law and politics
	Integrity of the legal system
	Legal enforcement of contracts
	Regulatory costs of the sale of real property
	Reliability of police
	Business costs of crime
Sound money	Money growth
	Standard deviation of inflation
	Inflation: most recent year
	Freedom to own foreign currency bank accounts
Freedom to trade internationally	Tariffs
	Regulatory trade barriers
	Black-market exchange rates
	Controls of the movement of capital and people
Regulation	Credit market regulations
	Labor market regulations
	Business regulations

Source: Fraser Institute (2017, p. 4)

5.1.6 The World Economic Forum's Growth Competitiveness Index and Global Competitiveness Index

The World Economic Forum was established as a foundation by Klaus Schwab in 1971.[13] The WEF is famous for organizing annual symposiums that gather top policy makers and business leaders in Davos, Switzerland.

In 1979, the Forum launched the *Report on the Competitiveness of European Industry*. A few years later, this publication became the annual *Global Competitiveness Report*. Klaus Schwab's seminal study was clearly innovative in the sense that it did not define competitiveness exclusively in terms of productivity and production costs. For him, many other factors had to be considered: "the internal dynamism of a country, its socio-political consensus, the quality of its human resources, its commercial spirit, the manner in which it prepares for the future, etc." (The World Economic Forum 2009, p. 29). Ten key drivers of competitiveness were

[13] The foundation's original name was the European Management Forum, but it was changed to the World Economic Forum in 1987 (The World Economic Forum 2009, p. 71).

identified: the economy's "dynamism," industrial efficacy and cost of production, the dynamics of the market, financial dynamism, human resources, the role of the state, the infrastructural dimension, outward orientation, forward orientation, and sociopolitical consensus and stability.

During the 1980s and 1990s, the report expanded its coverage to include non-European economies and newly industrialized countries. The number of economies under consideration increased from 32 in 1989 to 59 in 2000.

In 2001, the WEF ranked 75 countries and developed its Growth Competitiveness Index (Growth CI). The methodology is based on a multi-step process.[14] First, the 75 economies are classified into "core" and "noncore" groups according to their level of technological sophistication. The 24 core countries are Australia, Austria, Belgium, Canada, Denmark, Finland, France, Germany, Hong Kong, Iceland, Ireland, Israel, Italy, Japan, the Netherlands, New Zealand, Norway, Singapore, South Korea, Sweden, Switzerland, Taiwan, the United Kingdom, and the United States (World Economic Forum 2001, p. 30). Second, three major indices are constructed: the technology index, the public institutions index, and the macroeconomic environment index.

For core economies, the technology index is a simple average of its innovation subindex and the information and communication technology (ICT) subindex. For noncore economies, the technology index is a weighted average of the innovation subindex (accounting for 12.5%), the ICT subindex (50%), and the technology transfer subindex (37.5%). The innovation subindex is based on hard data (e.g., gross tertiary enrollment rate) and survey questions (e.g., "What is your country's position in technology relative to world leaders?")[15]; the ICT subindex is also based on hard data (e.g., number of mobile telephone and Internet users per capita) and survey questions (e.g., "How extensive is Internet access in schools?"). The technology transfer subindex is derived from of a "technology in trade" analysis and the following survey question: "Is FDI in your country an important source of new technology?"

The Growth CI's public institutions index relies on two series of survey data, each accounting for 50%. The first series addresses contracts and law issues (e.g., "Is the judiciary independent from the government and/or parties to dispute?"); the second addresses corruption issues (e.g., "How common are bribes paid in connection to export and import permits?").

The macroeconomic environment index is a weighted average of the *Institutional Investor* rating as of March 2001 (accounting for 25%), the ratio of general government expenditure to GNP (25%), and a macroeconomic stability subindex (50%). That subindex is based on hard data (the real exchange rate relative to the United States, the interest rate spread between deposits and loans, the ratio of general government budget balance to GNP, the consumer price index, and the national savings rate) and survey questions (e.g., "Is your country's economy likely to be in recession next year?").

---

[14] This methodology was developed by economists Jeffrey Sachs and John McArthur.

[15] The Executive Opinion Survey conducted annually by the WEF records the perspectives of business leaders around the world by asking them to compare aspects of their local business environment with global standards.

Table 5.14 Thresholds for establishing stages of development for WEF's GCI

Stage of development	GDP per capita (in US$)
Stage 1: Factor-driven stage	<2000
Transition from stage 1 to stage 2	*2000–3000*
Stage 2: Efficiency-driven stage	3000–9000
Transition from stage 2 to stage 3	*9000–17,000*
Stage 3: Innovation-driven stage	>17,000

Source: World Economic Forum (2006, p. 12)

The information derived from these two steps is then used to compute overall Growth CI scores. For core countries, the Growth CI is weighted as follows: technology index (50%), public institutions index (25%), and macroeconomic environment index (25%). For noncore countries, the Growth CI is the simple average of the three major indices (World Economic Forum 2001, pp. 28–51).

The maximum possible score on the Growth CI is 7, and the lowest is 1. Note that all component variables—whether taken from the Executive Opinion Survey or from hard data sources—are "rebased" so that the highest score is always equal to 7 and the lowest score is always equal to 1.

In 2006, the WEF amended its methodology (World Economic Forum 2006, p. 5) and thus the *Growth* Competitiveness Index was replaced by the *Global* Competitiveness Index (GCI).[16] The GCI introduced the "stages of development" concept into the index's calculation. Stage 1 is the factor-driven stage, stage 2 is the efficiency-driven stage, and stage 3 is the innovation-driven stage. The 125 countries covered are classified into these stages of development as a function of their per capita GDP at market exchange rates (Table 5.14).

The GCI methodology establishes three subindices based on nine "pillars" and a list of key component variables (Table 5.15). As before, all the component variables are "rebased" so that the highest (resp. lowest) score is always 7 (resp. 1). The conversion formula is:

$$\text{Component variable} = 6 \times \left[\frac{\text{country value} - \text{sample min.}}{\text{sample max.} - \text{sample min.}} \right] + 1$$

where "sample min." and "sample max." are (respectively) the variable's minimum and maximum values observed in the sample.

Each pillar score is the simple average of its component variables, and each subindex score is the simple average of its pillar scores; finally, the subindex scores are weighted to yield the GCI score. Those weightings differ depending on the focal country's developmental stage (Table 5.16). For countries "in transition," the weights change smoothly as the economy develops and thus reflect the transition from one stage of development to the next.

[16] The new competitiveness model was implemented by economist Xavier Sala-i-Martin.

Table 5.15 Composition of the Global Competitiveness Index for 2006

Subindices	Pillars	Component variables
Basic requirements	Institutions	Public institutions: property rights; ethics and corruption; undue influence; government inefficiency; and security
		Private institutions: corporate ethics and accountability
	Infrastructure	Overall infrastructure quality; railroad infrastructure development; quality of port and air transport infrastructures; quality of electricity supply; and telephone lines
	Macroeconomy	Government fiscal balance; national savings rate; inflation; interest rate spread; government debt; and real effective exchange rate
	Health and primary education	Health: medium-term business impact of malaria, tuberculosis, and HIV/AIDS; infant mortality; life expectancy; tuberculosis, malaria, and HIV prevalence
		Primary education: primary enrolment
Efficiency enhancers	Higher education and training	Quantity of education: secondary and tertiary enrolment ratios
		Quality of education: quality of the educational system, math and science education, and management schools
		On-the-job-training: local availability of specialized research and training services and extent of staff training
	Market efficiency	Good markets: distortions, competition, and size
		Labor markets: flexibility and efficiency
		Financial markets: sophistication and openness
	Technological readiness	Firm-level technology absorption; laws relating to ICT; FDI and technology transfer; cellular telephones; Internet users; personal computers
Innovation and sophistication factors	Business sophistication	Networks and supporting industries: local supplier quantity and quality
		Sophistication of firms' operations and strategy
	Innovation	Quality of scientific research institutions; company spending on R&D; university/industry research collaboration; government procurement of advanced technology products; availability of scientists and engineers; utility patents; intellectual property protection; capacity of innovation

Source: World Economic Forum (2006, pp. 3–50)

Since 2006, there have been few changes in the GCI methodology. A brief comparison between the *Global Competitiveness Reports* published in 2006 and 2017 shows that the "efficiency enhancers" subindex is now composed of six pillars (viz., higher education and training, goods market efficiency, labor market efficiency, financial market development, technological readiness, and market size). Also, some component variables are now weighted differently within the corresponding pillar. Another change is that a country's developmental stage depends not

Table 5.16 Weighting of GCI subindices by the country's developmental stage

	Basic requirements (%)	Efficiency enhancers (%)	Innovation and sophistication factors (%)
Factor-driven stage countries	50	40	10
Efficiency-driven stage countries	40	50	10
Innovation-driven stage countries	30	40	30

Source: World Economic Forum (2006, p. 12)

only on its GDP per capita but also on the share of raw materials among all exports (World Economic Forum 2017).

Global Competitiveness Reports are published in September every year. Prominent roles are played in this publication by Professor Klaus Schwab and by Professor Xavier Sala-i-Martín, its Chief Advisor for more than a decade.

5.2 Country Risk Shocks

This section describes eight types of shocks that reflect the main components of country risk analyzed in Chap. 3. In Sect. 5.2.1, I discuss the selection methodology. Each of Sects. 5.2.2–5.2.9 is devoted to one of these eight selected shocks: major episodes of international political violence, major episodes of domestic political violence, expropriation acts, high-inflation peaks, deep economic depressions, significant restrictions on capital flows, sovereign debt crises, and exceptional natural disasters. Section 5.2.10 concludes with some additional comments.

5.2.1 Methodology

Recall from Chap. 3 that country risk consists of both *shocks* and *latent hazards*. The rest of this chapter focuses on the shocks that may affect firms involved in business relations abroad. There are three main reasons for studying shocks. First, they are an observable embodiment of country risk. Second, they can be identified and measured more easily than latent risks, whose effects may be difficult to perceive or may become evident only in the long term. Third, shocks enable one to test the accuracy of country risk indicators.

Selecting a country risk component as a *potential* shock is based on the analysis conducted in Chap. 3. The selection is contingent on four factors: (i) the availability of reliable information about the focal component; (ii) the extent to which such information can be quantified; (iii) the possibility of observing a sharp decline in the component's measure within a short period of time (typically a year or less); and

(iv) the shock's capacity to affect the business operations of a wide array of firms or sectors in the short to medium term.[17]

I find that eight components—accounting for five of the seven broad components of country risk analyzed in Chap. 3—satisfy these four criteria. For each component, I shall determine a specific threshold beyond which its measure's decline is significant enough that one can reasonably deem the component to have been affected by an *actual* shock. My efforts to set unbiased thresholds will be supported by academic research, professional publications, and press articles.

The eight shocks materialized several times during the period under consideration (1985–2014), resulting in a number of country risk crises.[18] In the discussion to follow, one such *crisis* corresponds to one specific shock experienced by one country a given year. The crises identified will allow me to test, in Sect. 5.3, the accuracy of country risk indicators.

5.2.2 *Major Episodes of International Political Violence*

For this type of shock, I use the data and analyses performed by the Center for Systemic Peace (CSP). This Virginia-based nonprofit corporation has been studying international and civil wars since 1997.[19]

The CSP defines major episodes of political violence as the "systematic and sustained use of lethal violence by organized groups that result in at least 500 directly-related deaths over the course of the episode." Episodes are coded for time span and magnitude and are assigned to one of six categories of armed conflict: international violence, international war, civil violence, civil war, ethnic violence, and ethnic war. Each episode is designated as spanning a certain number of years and is assessed as being of a certain "magnitude of societal-systemic impact." The CSP measures such magnitude on an 11-point scale (where 0 represents no major episode of political violence and 10 the most violent episodes). Scores are consistent and comparable across categories. Components of the two *interstate* categories (i.e., international violence and international war) and of the four *intrastate* categories (i.e., civil violence, civil war, ethnic violence, and ethnic war) are combined to yield, respectively, the CSP's INTTOT and CIVTOT scores. These scores, which are also measured on a 0–10 scale, reflect the magnitude of total international political violence and of total domestic political violence.

---

[17] Here I exclude not only latent risks but also threats that are likely to affect only a particular firm or a limited set of firms: most microeconomic risks; protectionist measures; and industrial risks. These "asymmetric shocks" can be more reliably anticipated by corporate-level risk analyses than by the global country risk ratings presented in Sect. 5.1.

[18] Determining the period to be examined is constrained by the availability of (i) country risk ratings and (ii) data on the country risk components.

[19] See www.systemicpeace.org

The analysis presented here employs only the INTTOT scores. However, it is difficult to establish the threshold score beyond which an episode of international political violence constitutes a shock. In order to perform this task, I analyze how the *New York Times* and the *Wall Street Journal* covered the different international conflicts listed by the CSP. I find that a country's business environment is significantly affected by an international political violence episode when its INTTOT score exceeds 3, so I list all country-year observations that are assigned a score higher than 3 during 1985–2014. When there are several consecutive country-year observations with a score higher than 3, I retain only the first observation of the series because my objective is to identify the year of the shock.[20] When the first observation is for an episode that occurred prior to 1985, it is removed along with the following observations in that series.[21] This procedure identifies five crises: Eritrea:1998, Ethiopia:1998, Iraq:1990, Iraq:2003, and Kuwait:1990.

5.2.3 *Major Episodes of Domestic Political Violence*

To identify episodes of domestic political violence, I use the CIVTOT scores computed by the CSP (cf. Sect. 5.2.2). As in the case of international episodes, I list all country-year observations that scored higher than 3 during 1985–2014 (and retain only the first in any *series* of such observations). As before, pre-1985 episodes (and their sequelae) are omitted from the sample. I thus identify the 21 crises listed in Table 5.17.

Table 5.17 Crises caused by a major episode of domestic political violence

Algeria:1991	Kenya:2008	Russia:1994
Bosnia and Herzegovina:1992	Liberia:1990	Russia:1999
Burundi:1993	Libya:2011	Rwanda:1994
Dem. Republic of Congo:1996	Mexico:2006	Somalia:1988
Indonesia:1999	Nigeria:2001	South Sudan:2013
Iraq:1996	Nigeria:2009	Syria:2011
Iraq:2011	Pakistan:2004	Yugoslavia (Fed. Rep.):1999

Sources: Author's classification based on the major episodes of political violence listed by the Center for Systemic Peace; available at http://www.systemicpeace.org/inscr/MEPV2015.xls

[20] For example: because the INTTOT score of Iraq is 5 in 1990 and also in 1991, I retain only the "Iraq:1990" observation.

[21] In the case of Lebanon, for example, the INTTOT score is 4 during 1982–1990 and so none of the nine observations for that country is retained.

5.2.4 Expropriation Acts

Any forced divestment constitutes a major shock because it indicates that the host government does not respect property rights and has little interest in enforcing them.

The sources used to track nationalizations are Minor (1994) for the period 1985–1988 and Hajzler and Rosborough (2016) for 1989–2014. For each year, I compile a list of expropriating countries. When a country expropriates foreign investors during consecutive years, I retain only the first because (as mentioned previously) it is the one most directly related to the notion of a shock. This selection method results in 81 crises, which are listed in Table 5.18.

Table 5.18 Crises caused by expropriations

Antigua and Barbuda:2002	Georgia:2007	Mongolia:2009
Argentina:2001	Ghana:2011	Nigeria:2012
Argentina:2009	Guinea:2008	Pakistan:2011
Azerbaijan:2005	Guinea:2011	Pakistan:2013
Belarus:2011	Guinea:2013	Papua New Guinea:2011
Belize:2009	Hungary:2002	Peru:1985
Belize:2011	Hungary:2010	Peru:2011
Bolivia:2000	Hungary:2014	Romania:2009
Bolivia:2006	Indonesia:1998	Russia:2006
Bolivia:2012	Indonesia:2011	Sri Lanka:1990
Bulgaria:2014	Indonesia:2013	Togo:2014
China:2011	Ivory Coast:2003	Trinidad and Tobago:2010
Costa Rica:2007	Kazakhstan:1992	Turkey:2011
Costa Rica:2012	Kazakhstan:1999	Turkmenistan:1996
Dem. Republic of Congo:1993	Kazakhstan:2003	Turkmenistan:2007
Dem. Republic of Congo:1997	Kazakhstan:2007	Turkmenistan:2010
Dem. Republic of Congo:2010	Kenya:1998	Ukraine:2007
Dominican Republic:1994	Kyrgyzstan:2004	Ukraine:2009
Ecuador:2006	Kyrgyzstan:2010	Uzbekistan:2006
Ecuador:2008	Laos:2012	Uzbekistan:2011
Egypt:1989	Latvia:2008	Venezuela:2001
Egypt:1991	Lesotho:1992	Venezuela:2005
Egypt:1995	Libya:2009	Yemen:2005
Egypt:2014	Maldives:2012	Yugoslavia (Fed. Rep.):1999
El Salvador:2008	Mexico:1995	Zimbabwe:2004
Gambia:2008	Mexico:1998	Zimbabwe:2007
Georgia:1996	Mexico:2001	Zimbabwe:2010

Sources: Author's classification based on Minor (1994) for 1985–1988 and on Hajzler and Rosborough's (2016) updated database for 1989–2014

5.2.5 *High-Inflation Peaks*

One might suppose that the threshold beyond which an inflation rate will likely disrupt a country's business environment is the "hyperinflation" level. The problem is that Cagan's (1956) traditional definition of hyperinflation (i.e., monthly rates above 50%, corresponding to a 5-digit annual inflation rate) may not be appropriate because foreign operations are undoubtedly disturbed by much lower inflation rates (see Sect. 3.4.1.2). Furthermore, the 1985–2014 period was characterized by a worldwide disinflation trend, from which it follows that what constitutes "high" inflation has changed since the 1980s.

The threshold adopted here is an annual inflation rate of 100%. This boundary is used by Dornbusch (1990) and Bruno (1991) to identify hazardous high-inflation episodes in the 1980s. To obtain inflation rates, I use the consumer price index provided by the International Financial Statistics database maintained by the IMF. When a country posts an annual inflation rate of 100% for several consecutive years, I retain only the first year's observation (unless it is before 1985, in which case I omit both that observation and the series that it initiates).

The cases of the Soviet Union and the Socialist Federal Republic of Yugoslavia require specific comments. The two federations were already experiencing high inflation (as defined here) when they broke up in 1991. In the following months and years, hyperinflation spread throughout most of the territories that had just gained their independence (see Filatochev and Bradshaw 1992; Petrovic et al. 1999). Yet because the initial shocks occurred during 1987 in Yugoslavia and during 1991 in the Soviet Union, the high-inflation episodes observed in the newly independent countries during 1992–1995 are not counted (based on the "series" criterion described previously). Thus, I identify a total of 32 crises due to high inflation (see Table 5.19).

Table 5.19 Crises caused by high-inflation episodes

Albania:1992	Laos:1999	Sudan:1996
Angola:1992	Mexico:1987	Suriname:1993
Argentina:1987	Mongolia:1993	Turkey:1994
Belarus:1999	Nicaragua:1985	Uganda:1985
Bulgaria:1991	Peru:1988	Uruguay:1990
Bulgaria:1996	Poland:1989	USSR:1991
Dem. Republic of Congo:1989	Romania:1991	Yugoslavia (Soc. Fed. Rep.):1987
Dem. Republic of Congo:1991	Romania:1997	Zambia:1989
Dem. Republic of Congo:1999	Sierra Leone:1987	Zambia:1992
Iraq:1991	Sierra Leone:1990	Zimbabwe:2002
Iraq:1993	Sudan:1991	

Sources: Author's classification based on the IMF's International Financial Statistics database

5.2.6 *Deep Economic Depressions*

For the purposes of this analysis, a "deep" economic depression is defined as a decline in real GDP of 10% or more within a calendar year. This definition has been widely adopted and is consistent with other research that addresses major macroeconomic shocks (e.g., Barro and Jin 2011).

My main source for data on this factor is the World Bank's World Development Indicators. When a country's GDP contracts by at least 10% for consecutive years, I retain the first year's observation only; if that is a pre-1985 observation, then (as before) it is removed from the sample and the following observations are also removed.

For the Soviet Union and the Socialist Federal Republic of Yugoslavia, I use Angus Maddison's historical statistics.[22] In 1991, Yugoslavia was in depression, but the Soviet Union was not. Hence, I do *not* count as shocks the depressions observed in Bosnia and Herzegovina, Croatia, and the Federal Republic of Yugoslavia (including Kosovo, Montenegro, and Serbia) in 1992. In contrast, the countries that became independent of the Soviet Union and posted GDP growth rates worse than −10% in 1992 *are* viewed as being crisis countries; they are included in the total of 68 crises listed by Table 5.20.

Table 5.20 Crises caused by deep economic depressions

Albania:1991	Jordan:1989	Romania:1991
Albania:1997	Kazakhstan:1994	Russia:1992
Angola:1993	Kuwait:1988	Russia:1994
Antigua and Barbuda:2009	Kyrgyzstan:1992	Rwanda:1994
Argentina:2002	Latvia:1992	Sierra Leone:1992
Armenia:1992	Latvia:2009	Solomon Islands:2000
Armenia:2009	Lebanon:1989	South Sudan:2012
Azerbaijan:1992	Liberia:1989	Suriname:1987
Belarus:1994	Liberia:2003	Tajikistan:1992
Central African Republic:2013	Libya:2011	Togo:1993
Chad:1993	Lithuania:1992	Turkmenistan:1992
Cuba:1991	Lithuania:2009	Turkmenistan:1994
Czechoslovakia:1991	Madagascar:2002	Turkmenistan:1997
Dem. Republic of Congo:1992	Malawi:1994	Ukraine:1993
Estonia:1992	Marshall Islands:1996	Ukraine:2009
Estonia:2009	Moldova:1992	United Arab Emirates:1986
Ethiopia:1985	Moldova:1994	Uzbekistan:1992
Gabon:1987	Myanmar:1988	Yemen:2011
Georgia:1992	Nicaragua:1988	Yugoslavia (Fed. Rep.):1999

(continued)

[22] See www.ggdc.net/maddison/historical_statistics/horizontal-file_02-2010.xls

Table 5.20 (continued)

Guinea-Bissau:1998	Nigeria:1987	Yugoslavia (Soc. Fed. Rep.):1991
Indonesia:1998	Palau:1993	Zimbabwe:2003
Iraq:1991	Panama:1988	Zimbabwe:2008
Iraq:2003	Peru:1989	

Sources: Author's classification based on the World Bank's World Development Indicators and Angus Maddison's database; the latter is retrieved from www.ggdc.net/maddison/historical_statistics/horizontal-file_02-2010.xls

5.2.7 *Significant Restrictions on Capital Flows*

In order to identify significant restrictions in cross-border financial transactions, I use Chinn and Ito's (2006) updated index (see Sect. 3.4.2). This index captures the extent of capital controls based on information culled from the IMF's *Annual Report on Exchange Arrangements and Exchange Restrictions*. Countries are scored each year on a scale from 0 to 1; here 0 (resp. 1) corresponds to the lowest (resp. highest) level of financial openness, which is reduced by such restrictions.

Because Chinn and Ito's study does not specify any thresholds, its results cannot be used to determine how much of a decline in the focal country's score would constitute a significant restriction on capital flows. I therefore compute and compare the average world scores, for the years 1985 and 2014, toward the end of measuring the average increase in financial openness among countries that were not fully liberalized in 1985. Hence I define a shock in this context as any country-year's decrease in financial openness that is of at least the same magnitude as the average world *increase* in financial openness observed during 1985–2014.

My sample excludes the 22 countries that were assigned a score of 1 in 1985, and all missing country-year observations for 1985 and 2014 are assigned a score of 0. The resulting sample includes 160 countries. I find that the average world score increased by 0.30 points, rising from 0.17 points in 1985 to 0.47 points in 2014. Therefore, a decline in financial openness is considered a shock if the reduction amounts to at least 0.30 points within a year. When a country announces a major restriction on capital flows in consecutive years (as Egypt did in 2012 and 2013), only the first year's observation is retained. Thus Table 5.21 lists a total of 16 crises.

Table 5.21 Crises caused by a significant restriction on capital flows

Argentina:2001	Dominican Republic:1996	Liberia:1986
Bosnia and Herzegovina:2012	Ecuador:2011	Seychelles:2004
Botswana:1996	Egypt:2012	Sierra Leone:2009
Cambodia:1996	Iceland:2008	Venezuela:2002
Chile:1996	Kyrgyzstan:2012	
Cyprus:2012	Lebanon:2001	

Sources: Author's classification based on Chinn and Ito's (2006) updated database

5.2.8 *Sovereign Debt Crises*

Using Beers and de Leon-Manlagnit's (2019) database, I compile a list of countries that lapsed into default on their FC bank loans, FC bonds, or LC debt—or that failed to fulfill their financial obligations to private creditors—during 1985–2014. Defaults affecting less than $100 million of debt are excluded for the purpose of this classification.

This list also includes the countries already in default whose debt arrears soared dramatically.[23] After analyzing Beers and de Leon-Manlagnit's database and browsing the *New York Times* and the *Wall Street Journal*, I conclude that a tenfold increase (within a single year) in the defaulted debt owed to foreign or private creditors causes serious alarm among investors. Table 5.22 lists the 64 sovereign debt crises so identified.[24]

Table 5.22 Crises caused by sovereign debt turmoil

Albania:1991	Grenada:2004	Saint Kitts and Nevis:2011
Algeria:1991	Indonesia:1999	Sierra Leone:2005
Angola:1989	Indonesia:2002	Slovenia:1992
Antigua and Barbuda:1996	Iraq:1988	South Africa:1985
Argentina:1987	Ivory Coast:2000	South Africa:1989
Argentina:2001	Jamaica:1987	South Africa:1993
Belarus:1994	Jamaica:2010	South Sudan:2013
Belize:2006	Jamaica:2013	Syria:1995
Belize:2012	Jordan:1989	Tajikistan:2010
Bosnia and Herzegovina:1992	Kazakhstan:1998	Trinidad and Tobago:1988
Bosnia and Herzegovina:1999	Kazakhstan:2014	Turkey:1999
Bulgaria:1990	Kuwait:1990	Ukraine:2012
Cameroon:1985	Macedonia:1992	Ukraine:2014
Chad:2014	Morocco:1989	Uruguay:1988
Colombia:1988	Mozambique:1985	Uruguay:1990
Croatia:1992	Mozambique:2007	Uruguay:2003
Cyprus:2013	Mozambique:2013	USSR:1991
Dominican Republic:2005	Myanmar:1985	Venezuela:1992
Ecuador:1999	Myanmar:1987	Yemen:2001
Ecuador:2008	Pakistan:1998	Yugoslavia (Fed. Rep.):1992
Egypt:1986	Paraguay:1986	
Greece:2012	Romania:1986	

Sources: Author's classification based on Beers and de Leon-Manlagnit's (2019) database

[23] The objective here is to include all defaulting countries whose debt arrears may become unsustainable.

[24] Newly independent countries are included in the list if they satisfy the stipulated conditions.

5.2.9 Exceptional Natural Disasters

I use the Emergency Events Database (EM-DAT) to identify natural disasters that had the most damaging economic effects. The EM-DAT, launched in 1988 by the Centre for Research on the Epidemiology of Disasters, contains essential core data on the occurrence and effects of more than 22,000 disasters worldwide since 1900.[25] Natural disasters include geophysical, meteorological, hydrological, climatological, biological, and extraterrestrial calamities. I focus on country-year observations and examine two series of data: the cost of natural disasters and the percentage of a country's population affected.

The threshold beyond which I consider the annual cost of natural disasters to be "exceptional" is 10% of a country's GDP, which is the same threshold used in Sect. 5.2.6 to identify deep economic depressions. I analyze the EM-DAT and the newspapers available through ProQuest to determine the proportion—of a country's inhabitants affected by a natural disaster—beyond which economic and social life is devastated. I conclude that an appropriate threshold is one-third of the population. Based on these two criteria, I identify the 11 crises listed in Table 5.23.

Table 5.23 Crises caused by an exceptional natural disaster

El Salvador:2001	Honduras:1998	Samoa:1991
Grenada:2004	Jamaica:1988	Tajikistan:2008
Guyana:2005	Liberia:1990	Vanuatu:1985
Haiti:2010	Samoa:1990	

Sources: Author's classification based on the EM-DAT and www.proquest.com

5.2.10 Comments on the Country Risk Crises Identified

The eight idiosyncratic shocks named at the start of this section resulted in 298 country risk crises. The next step is to aggregate the data so that no country-year observation is counted more than once. For example, Albania was hit by two distinct shocks in 1991—a deep economic depression and a sovereign debt crisis—but only one crisis is counted: "Albania:1991." Hence my final sample consists of 272 observations, which are listed (chronologically) in Appendix.

An examination of these 272 crises reveals that 117 nations were hit by at least one of the eight shocks. There were 23 countries that experienced at least four crises during 1985–2014: Argentina, Belize, Bulgaria, the Democratic Republic of Congo, Ecuador, Egypt, Indonesia, Iraq, Jamaica, Kazakhstan, Kyrgyzstan, Liberia, Mexico, Nigeria, Pakistan, Peru, Romania, Russia, Sierra Leone, Turkmenistan, Ukraine, Venezuela, and Zimbabwe.

[25] See www.emdat.be

Observe that several low-income and lower-middle–income nations do not appear in the sample. This does not mean that these countries posed no risks to foreign investors. Rather, it simply means that—despite their economic backwardness and/or weak political system—these countries managed to avoid any major shocks and to meet (at least roughly) the expectations of investors.

5.3 Performance of Country Risk Indicators

This section analyzes how well the ratings—issued during 1984–2013 by Euromoney, ICRG, Credendo, the OECD, the Heritage Foundation, the Fraser Institute, and the World Economic Forum—anticipated the country risk crises observed during 1985–2014. After presenting the methodology in Sect. 5.3.1, I examine the performance of each rater in Sects. 5.3.2–5.3.8.

5.3.1 Methodology

The tools used to measure the performance of country risk indicators are different from those applied in Sect. 4.2.

Here, examining the *stability* of country risk ratings is not relevant for two reasons. First, several rating data sets (e.g., those contained in the Heritage Foundation's Index of Economic Freedom and the Fraser Institute's Economic Freedom of the World) were not issued on a regular basis. Thus, the time that elapsed between the two consecutive "annual" rating data sets could be anywhere between 10 and 16 months. Second, the very nature of some ratings differs: the ICRG metric is the annual average of monthly ratings, whereas the metric used by other raters is a "point in time" rating. These two factors would bias any analysis of ratings stability.

Neither are the accuracy ratios (ARs) used in Sect. 4.2 operative in this context. The reason is that in this chap. I test the performance of country risk indicators in terms of eight types of risks, whereas sovereign risk indicators were tested exclusively in terms of sovereign default risk. In particular, the computation of ARs in Sect. 4.2 required the ratings of countries already in default at the start of the time interval t be *removed* from the cohort whose performance is measured over time t. If the same procedure was applied to this chapter's country risk crises, then a large number of observations would have to be omitted. For example, the CIVTOT score of the Democratic Republic of Congo exceeded 3 (i.e., the threshold beyond which an episode of domestic political violence is viewed as major) in 1996 and remained at that high level until 2014. Removing all country risk crises experienced by this nation during 1997–2014 would oblige me also to drop three observations: the expropriations of 1997 and 2010 and the high-inflation episode of 1999 (see Appendix). Similar removals would affect other countries, which would substantially reduce the total number of country risk crises.

As a result, I focus on six simple criteria to measure the performance of country risk indicators:

- The average rating assigned to a country 1, 2, and 3 years before it was hit by a shock.
- The average percentile ranking assigned to a country 1, 2, and 3 years before it was hit by a shock.
- The percentage of countries in the "risk-free" rating category 1, 2, and 3 years before they were hit by a shock.
- The percentage of countries in the top 25% of all ranked countries 1, 2, and 3 years before they were hit by a shock.[26]
- The percentage of countries in the "safe" and "relatively safe" rating categories 1, 2, and 3 years before they were hit by a shock.
- The percentage of countries in the top 50% of all ranked countries 1, 2, and 3 years before they were hit by a shock.[27]

The decision to focus on rankings as well as ratings is supported by the emphasis that most raters—namely, Euromoney, the Heritage Foundation, the Fraser Institute, and the World Economic Forum—place on both measurements. The country risk crises used for testing are the ones listed in Appendix.

In what follows I measure the performance of each rater in terms of all six criteria. I also identify the country risk crises that raters failed to anticipate and account for those lapses in light of the methodologies analyzed in Sect. 5.1.

5.3.2 *Performance of Euromoney's Country Risk Ratings*

I test how well Euromoney ratings issued during 1988–2013 anticipated the country risk crises that occurred during 1989–2014. The ratings 1, 2, and 3 years prior to the crisis observed in year y are those published in September of (respectively) year $y-1$, $y-2$, and $y-3$.

For many years, Euromoney did not use broad rating categories as ICRG did (e.g., "moderate risk," "low risk," and "very low risk"). Starting in the early 2010s, however, Euromoney divided countries into five groups. Countries labeled Tier 1 are those rated in the 80–100 range. Its Tier 2, Tier 3, Tier 4, and Tier 5 countries are those with ratings in the ranges of (respectively) 65–79.9, 50–64.9, 36–49.9, and 0–35.9. I therefore consider as "risk-free" the countries assigned a score of 80 or higher. By the same token, I consider as "safe" and "relatively safe" the countries assigned a score of at least 50.[28]

[26] The selection of this threshold is supported by discussions I had with economists and analysts.

[27] Idem.

[28] My analysis is based on various internal briefs retrieved from www.euromoneycountryrisk.com

Table 5.24 Euromoney ratings performance 1, 2, and 3 years before a crisis

Performance criterion	Year y–1	Year y–2	Year y–3
Average rating of the crisis countries	36.7	38.3	39.6
Average percentile ranking of the crisis countries	63rd	62nd	61st
Percentage of crisis countries rated in the "risk-free" category	0.5	0.5	1.1
Percentage of crisis countries ranked in the top 25%	4.3	5.7	7.1
Percentage of crisis countries rated in the "safe"/"relatively safe" categories	19.0	23.7	23.6
Percentage of crisis countries ranked in the top 50%	34.1	36.6	37.4

Notes: Euromoney ratings are established on a 0–100 scale, where 0 (resp. 100) corresponds to countries that are the most (resp. least) risky. The samples 1, 2, and 3 years prior to a crisis consist of (respectively) 211, 194, and 182 observations. A crisis is a country-year pair in which a shock occurred, and an observation is a crisis-rating pair. I view Russia and the Federal Republic of Yugoslavia (FRY) as being the sole legal successors to the Soviet Union and the Socialist Federal Republic of Yugoslavia (SFRY), respectively. As a result, the pre-1992 ratings of Russia and the FRY are those of the Soviet Union and the SFRY, respectively
Source: Author's computations based on Euromoney ratings

Table 5.24 displays the performance of Euromoney ratings as measured by the six criteria detailed previously. One, two, and three years prior to a crisis, the average ratings and percentile rankings were especially accurate, as they were located in the lower end of the Tier 4 category and in the 62nd percentile, respectively. The overall good performance of Euromoney is confirmed by the very low percentages of crisis countries rated in the "risk-free" category: 0.5%, 0.5%, and 1.1% (respectively) 1, 2, and 3 years before a crisis. The percentages of crisis countries ranked in the top 25% were higher (between 4.3% and 7.1%) but still relatively modest.

The percentages of crisis countries rated in the "safe" and "relatively safe" rating categories are good, and the percentages of crisis countries ranked in the top 50% are acceptable. As one might expect, all the metrics are increasingly accurate as the country risk crises near.

Table 5.25 presents the few mistakes made by Euromoney. It shows that as many as 2 (resp. 13) crisis countries were rated (resp. ranked) excessively high 3 years before a crisis.

The capital controls implemented by Iceland in 2008 led to the most dramatic instance of misrating. A deeper analysis reveals that Iceland enjoyed very high scores on all the criteria emphasized in Euromoney's methodology (see Sect. 4.1.3). However, this failure should be put into perspective given that many top economists were highly optimistic about the stability of Iceland's financial system on the eve of the 2007–2008 crisis (e.g., Mishkin and Herbertsson 2006).

The excessively high rating assigned to the Soviet Union until 1988 and its elevated ranking until 1989 are more puzzling because that country had long rejected the fundamental rules of capitalism. In September 1988, Euromoney supported its views by referencing the positive effects expected from the perestroika reforms championed by Gorbachev and by describing the Soviet Union as an "oil- and cash-rich" nation.[29]

[29] *Euromoney*, September 1988, p. 232.

Table 5.25 Euromoney's misratings

	Year y−1	Year y−2	Year y−3
Crisis countries rated in the "risk-free" category (types of shocks in parentheses)	Iceland:2008 (restriction on capital flows)	Iceland:2008 (restriction on capital flows)	Iceland:2008 (restriction on capital flows); USSR:1991 (high inflation, sovereign debt crisis)
Crisis countries ranked in the top 25% (types of shocks in parentheses)	Iceland:2008 (restriction on capital flows); Cyprus:2012 (restriction on capital flows); Chile:1996 (restriction on capital flows); Hungary:2002 (expropriation); China:2011 (expropriation); Cyprus:2013 (sovereign debt crisis); Indonesia:1998 (economic depression, expropriation); Peru:2011 (expropriation); Mexico:2001 (expropriation)	Iceland:2008 (restriction on capital flows); Cyprus:2012 (restriction on capital flows); Cyprus:2013 (sovereign debt crisis); USSR:1991 (high inflation, sovereign debt crisis); Hungary:2002 (expropriation); Turkey:1994 (high inflation); Chile:1996 (restriction on capital flows); Indonesia:1998 (economic depression, expropriation); Indonesia:1999 (major domestic political violence episode, sovereign debt crisis); China:2011 (expropriation); Estonia:2009 (economic depression)	Iceland:2008 (restriction on capital flows); Cyprus:2013 (sovereign debt crisis); Cyprus:2012 (restriction on capital flows); USSR:1991 (high inflation, sovereign debt crisis); Greece:2012 (sovereign debt crisis); Russia:1992 (economic depression); Indonesia:1998 (economic depression, expropriation); Estonia:2009 (economic depression); Hungary:2002 (expropriation); Indonesia:1999 (major domestic political violence episode, sovereign debt crisis); Hungary:2010 (expropriation); Chile:1996 (restriction on capital flows); Lithuania:2009 (economic depression)

Note: The higher the rating or ranking of a crisis country, the higher its position in the classification
Source: Author's classifications based on Euromoney ratings

In fact, Euromoney seems to have greater difficulty in anticipating stringent capital controls and sovereign debt crises; these two types of shocks account for more than half of its "mis-rankings" and for all of its misratings. I am therefore led to draw two series of conclusions. On the one hand, Euromoney experts tend to underestimate the riskiness of current account deficits and of inadequate prudential regulations in countries exhibiting a high level of financial openness (cf. the crises experienced by Iceland and Cyprus in 2008 and 2012, respectively). On the other hand, Euromoney should pay more attention to the public debt's sustainability and public spending's efficiency (see the sovereign debt crises in the Soviet Union in 1991, Greece in 2012, and Cyprus in 2013). Recall that the "debt indicators" criteria for Greece and Cyprus were scored at the maximum (10 out of 10) 3 years prior to their default.

5.3.3 Performance of ICRG's Country Risk Ratings

Here I test how well ICRG ratings issued during 1984–2013 anticipated the country risk crises that occurred during 1985–2014. The ratings 1, 2, and 3 years prior to a crisis observed in year y are the average annual composite ratings for years $y-1$, $y-2$, and $y-3$, respectively.

I consider as "risk-free" countries those that are assigned a score of 80 or higher, and I consider as "safe" and "relatively safe" those countries that are assigned a score of 60 or higher. This categorization is based on ICRG methodology (see Sect. 5.1.1).

Table 5.26 displays the performance of ICRG ratings. One, two, and three years prior to a crisis, the average ratings (at the upper end of its "high risk" category) and percentile rankings (67th percentile) are especially good. The relative accuracy of ICRG is confirmed by the low percentages of crisis countries rated in the "risk-free" category: 0.6%, 1.9%, and 2.5% for 1, 2, and 3 years prior to a crisis. The percentages of crisis countries ranked in the top 25% are slightly higher (between 3.6% and 5.1%).

The percentages of crisis countries ranked in the top 50% are satisfactory. In contrast, more than half of the crisis countries were rated in the "safe" and "relatively safe" categories, which reflects poor performance. Note that the number of crisis countries included in the "moderate risk," "low risk," and "very low risk" rating categories actually exceeds those in the "high risk" and "very high risk" categories. In fact, the "low-risk" and "moderate-risk" rating categories are insufficiently safe, which suggests that ICRG should do a better job of discriminating among countries rated in those two categories and should probably downgrade some of them to the "high-risk" category. These findings differ substantially from what I observe for Euromoney ratings.

Table 5.26 ICRG ratings performance 1, 2, and 3 years before a crisis

Performance criterion	Year y–1	Year y–2	Year y–3
Average rating of the crisis countries	57.8	58.6	58.6
Average percentile ranking of the crisis countries	68th	66th	66th
Percentage of crisis countries rated in the "risk-free" category	0.6	1.9	2.5
Percentage of crisis countries ranked in the top 25%	3.6	3.7	5.1
Percentage of crisis countries rated in the "safe"/"relatively safe" categories	54.4	54.3	51.3
Percentage of crisis countries ranked in the top 50%	24.3	28.4	27.8

Notes: ICRG ratings are established on a 0–100 scale, where 0 (resp. 100) corresponds to countries that are the most (resp. least) risky. The samples 1, 2, and 3 years prior to a crisis consist of (respectively) 169, 162, and 158 observations. A crisis is a country-year pair in which a shock occurred, and an observation is a crisis-rating pair

Source: Author's computations based on ICRG ratings

Table 5.27 ICRG's misratings

	Year y−1	Year y−2	Year y−3
Crisis countries rated in the "risk-free" category (types of shocks in parentheses)	Libya:2009 (expropriation)	Iceland:2008 (restriction on capital flows); Trinidad and Tobago:2010 (expropriation); Libya:2009 (expropriation)	Iceland:2008 (restriction on capital flows); Libya:2011 (major domestic political violence episode, economic depression); Trinidad and Tobago:2010 (expropriation); Libya:2009 (expropriation)
Crisis countries ranked in the top 25% (types of shocks in parentheses)	Trinidad and Tobago:2010 (expropriation); Venezuela:1992 (sovereign debt crisis); Libya:2011 (major domestic political violence episode, economic depression); Libya:2009 (expropriation); Chile:1996 (restriction on capital flows); China:2011 (expropriation)	Iceland:2008 (restriction on capital flows); Trinidad and Tobago:2010 (expropriation); Libya:2009 (expropriation); China:2011 (expropriation); El Salvador:2001 (natural disaster); Chile:1996 (restriction on capital flows)	Iceland:2008 (restriction on capital flows); Cyprus:2012 (restriction on capital flows); Libya:2011 (major domestic political violence episode, economic depression); Trinidad and Tobago:2010 (expropriation); Chile:1996 (restriction on capital flows); Libya:2009 (expropriation); Hungary:2002 (expropriation); China:2011 (expropriation)

Note: The higher the rating or ranking of a crisis country, the higher its position in the classification
Source: Author's classifications based on ICRG ratings

Finally, the metrics are increasingly accurate as a country risk crisis nears—except for the percentages of crisis countries rated in the "safe" and "relatively safe" categories.

Table 5.27 presents ICRG's misratings. There were a total of four and eight crisis countries that were (respectively) rated and ranked excessively high 3 years prior to a crisis. The four crises that ICRG failed to anticipate were the controls on capital flows announced by Iceland in 2008, the expropriations that occurred in Libya during 2009 and in Trinidad and Tobago during 2010, and the political and economic turmoil that shook Libya in 2011.

The rating of Libya was an utter failure and merits closer examination. The generous rating granted during 2006–2008 was mainly driven by the country's high economic and financial scores: on average, 46.4 and 48.4 out of 50 (see Tables 5.2 and 5.6). These flaws suggest that even outstanding macroeconomic scores are really no protection against a major economic shock. This ratings debacle also highlights the limits of scores that rely exclusively on quantitative data. If the composite score of Libya had been set at the same level as its political score, no misrating would have occurred.

In sum, ICRG failed to foresee capital controls and nationalizations (nearly 80% of all misratings) but had no problem anticipating the major sovereign debt crises that occurred since the 1980s.

5.3.4 Performance of Credendo's Country Risk Ratings

Most of the metrics used by Credendo are not tested because they aim to measure a specific type of shock that did not occur often enough to assess predictions (i.e., short-term and medium/long-term political risks, political violence risk, and the risk of currency inconvertibility and transfer restrictions) or because the metric reflects case-by-case microeconomic assessments (i.e., commercial risk).

However, I can test the predictive accuracy of Credendo's expropriation risk scores issued during 2002–2013 with regard to the nationalizations that occurred during 2003–2014.[30] The scores 1, 2, and 3 years prior to the expropriation observed in year *y* are the scores as of 31 December in (respectively) years $y-1$, $y-2$, and $y-3$.

Countries that are assigned an expropriation risk score of 1 are considered to be "risk free." Because Credendo does not indicate the risk inherent to each score category, I assume that "safe" and "relatively safe" countries are those with a score of 3 or lower.

Table 5.28 reports the performance of Credendo's ratings. One, two, and three years prior to a crisis, the average ratings and percentile rankings are adequate, falling in the middle rating category and around the 59th percentile.

Table 5.28 Credendo ratings performance 1, 2, and 3 years before an expropriation

	Year y−1	Year y−2	Year y−3
Average rating of the expropriating countries	4.3	4.2	4.0
Average percentile ranking of the expropriating countries	60th	59th	57th
Percentage of expropriating countries rated in the "risk-free" category	7.3	5.8	8.2
Percentage of expropriating countries ranked in the top 25%	7.3	5.8	8.2
Percentage of expropriating countries rated in the "safe"/"relatively safe" categories	30.9	40.4	36.7
Percentage of expropriating countries ranked in the top 50%	30.9	42.3	36.7

Notes: Credendo expropriation risk scores are established on a 1–7 scale, where 7 (resp. 1) corresponds to countries that are the most (resp. least) risky. The samples 1, 2, and 3 years prior to a crisis consist of (respectively) 55, 52, and 49 observations. A crisis is a country-year pair in which an expropriation occurred, and an observation is a crisis-rating pair

Source: Author's computations based on Credendo scores

[30] The list of expropriating countries is based on Table 5.18.

Table 5.29 Credendo's misratings

	Year y−1	Year y−2	Year y−3
Expropriating countries rated in the "risk-free" category	Latvia:2008; Romania:2009; Hungary:2010; Bulgaria:2014	Latvia:2008; Hungary:2010; Bulgaria:2014	Latvia:2008; Hungary:2010; Bulgaria:2014; Hungary:2014
Expropriating countries ranked in the top 25%	Latvia:2008; Romania:2009; Hungary:2010; Bulgaria:2014	Latvia:2008; Hungary:2010; Bulgaria:2014	Latvia:2008; Hungary:2010; Bulgaria:2014; Hungary:2014

Note: The higher the rating or ranking of a crisis country, the higher its position in the classification
Source: Author's classifications based on Credendo scores

The percentages of expropriating countries rated in the "risk-free" category, on the one hand, and ranked in the top 25%, on the other hand, are the same because the countries that are assigned a score of 1 (the "risk-free" category) generally account for a fourth of the total number of countries rated. That percentage is relatively high (7.3%) 1 year prior to expropriation. However, I proceed cautiously in this analysis because the three samples of expropriating countries are quite small (only 49–55 observations in total). The percentages of expropriating countries rated in the "safe" and "relatively safe" rating categories and ranked in the top 50% are quite high.

The expropriating countries that were overrated and over-ranked by Credendo are Bulgaria, Hungary (twice), Latvia, and Romania (see Table 5.29). The five nationalizations in those countries were observed during 2008–2014. Credendo's excessive optimism about these nations could perhaps be explained by their membership in the European Union and/or their classification as upper–middle-income or even high-income economies. It is also worth mentioning that all five of the expropriation cases were brought to arbitration, which gave investors some hope of eventually being compensated.[31]

5.3.5 *Performance of OECD's Country Risk Ratings*

I test the capacity of OECD country risk ratings issued during 1999–2013 to anticipate the country risk crises that occurred during 2000–2014. The ratings 1, 2, and 3 years prior to a crisis observed in year *y* are the ratings as of 1 September in years *y*−1, *y*−2, and *y*−3.

Countries that are assigned a score of 0 are considered "risk free." Since the OECD does not indicate the risk inherent to each score category, I assume that "safe" and "relatively safe" countries are those with a score of 3 or lower.

[31] See Hajzler and Rosborough's (2016) updated database and https://icsid.worldbank.org/en/Pages/cases/casedetail.aspx?CaseNo=ARB/15/43

Table 5.30 OECD ratings performance 1, 2, and 3 years before a crisis

	Year y−1	Year y−2	Year y−3
Average rating of the crisis countries	5.6	5.6	5.6
Average percentile ranking of the crisis countries	52nd	51st	52nd
Percentage of crisis countries rated in the "risk-free" category	4.2	4.3	4.6
Percentage of crisis countries ranked in the top 25%	11.0	11.2	13.8
Percentage of crisis countries rated in the "safe"/"relatively safe" categories	16.1	16.4	16.5
Percentage of crisis countries ranked in the top 50%	36.4	37.9	34.9

Notes: OECD country risk ratings are established on a 0–7 scale, where 7 (resp. 0) corresponds to countries that are the most (resp. least) risky. The samples 1, 2, and 3 years prior to a crisis consist of (respectively) 118, 116, and 109 observations. A crisis is a country-year pair in which a shock occurred, and an observation is a crisis-rating pair
Source: Author's computations based on OECD country risk ratings

Table 5.30 summarizes the performance of OECD ratings. One, two, and three years prior to a crisis, the average ratings are very accurate (around 5.6); in contrast, the average percentile rankings are too high (at about the 52nd percentile). This schizophrenic performance reflects the conservative policy followed by the OECD: on average, more than 57% of countries are assigned to its three riskiest rating categories (i.e., with scores of 5, 6, or 7). It follows that many countries with low ratings are not affected by a major shock, which inflates the average percentile ranking of crisis countries.[32]

The reason that the percentages of crisis countries rated in the "risk-free" category are significantly lower than those of crisis countries ranked in the top 25% is that only a small proportion of countries is rated in the top category. The same comments apply as regards the percentages of crisis countries rated in the "safe" and "relatively safe" categories and of those ranked in the top 50%.

It turns out that OECD country risk ratings are relatively accurate metrics. The poorer predictive power of rankings is of secondary concern given that this international institution's rating policy does not incorporate that tool.

The OECD country risk rating system failed to forecast six crises: the capital controls announced in Iceland during 2008 and in Cyprus during 2012, the sovereign defaults suffered by Greece in 2012 and by Cyprus in 2013, and the nationalizations by Hungary's government in 2010 and 2014 (Table 5.31). The OECD membership (except for Cyprus) and the "high-income economy" status enjoyed by these countries could have been key factors in the OECD's decision to place them in its top rating category.

The longer lists of "mis-ranked" crisis countries reflect that the percentage of countries rated in the "risk-free" category is much lower than 25%. This fact mechanically increases the rank of countries in the second, third, and fourth highest

[32] On average, a country that was assigned a rating of 5 before being hit by a major shock was ranked at about the 43rd percentile.

Table 5.31 OECD's misratings

	Year y−1	Year y−2	Year y−3
Crisis countries rated in the "risk-free" category (types of shocks in parentheses)	Iceland:2008 (restriction on capital flows); Hungary:2010 (expropriation); Cyprus:2012 (restriction on capital flows); Greece:2012 (sovereign debt crisis); Cyprus:2013 (sovereign debt crisis)	Iceland:2008 (restriction on capital flows); Cyprus:2012 (restriction on capital flows); Greece:2012 (sovereign debt crisis); Cyprus:2013 (sovereign debt crisis); Hungary:2014 (expropriation)	Iceland:2008 (restriction on capital flows); Cyprus:2012 (restriction on capital flows); Greece:2012 (sovereign debt crisis); Cyprus:2013 (sovereign debt crisis); Hungary:2014 (expropriation)
Crisis countries ranked in the top 25% (types of shocks in parentheses)	Iceland:2008 (restriction on capital flows); Hungary:2010 (expropriation); Cyprus:2012 (restriction on capital flows); Greece:2012 (sovereign debt crisis); Cyprus:2013 (sovereign debt crisis); Hungary:2002 (expropriation); Mexico:2006 (major domestic political violence episode); Estonia:2009 (economic depression); Lithuania:2009 (economic depression); Trinidad and Tobago:2010 (expropriation); China:2011 (expropriation); Mexico:2001 (expropriation); Bulgaria:2014 (expropriation)	Iceland:2008 (restriction on capital flows); Cyprus:2012 (restriction on capital flows); Greece:2012 (sovereign debt crisis); Cyprus:2013 (sovereign debt crisis); Hungary:2014 (expropriation); Hungary:2002 (expropriation); Latvia:2008 (expropriation); Estonia:2009 (economic depression); Lithuania:2009 (economic depression); Trinidad and Tobago:2010 (expropriation); China:2011 (expropriation); Uruguay:2003 (sovereign debt crisis); Mexico:2006 (major domestic political violence episode)	Iceland:2008 (restriction on capital flows); Cyprus:2012 (restriction on capital flows); Greece:2012 (sovereign debt crisis); Cyprus:2013 (sovereign debt crisis); Hungary:2014 (expropriation); Latvia:2008 (expropriation); Estonia:2009 (economic depression); Latvia:2009 (economic depression); Lithuania:2009 (economic depression); Trinidad and Tobago:2010 (expropriation); China:2011 (expropriation); Hungary:2002 (expropriation); Uruguay:2003 (sovereign debt crisis); Mexico:2006 (major domestic political violence episode); Costa Rica:2007 (expropriation)

Note: The higher the rating or ranking of a crisis country, the higher its position in the classification
Source: Author's classifications based on OECD country risk ratings

rating categories and so enables them to join the top 25% for some years. In this respect, there is substantial divergence between the methodology used by Credendo to assess expropriation risk and the one used by OECD to assess country risk.

5.3.6 *Performance of IEF's Country Risk Ratings*

The Heritage Foundation's Index of Economic Freedom has been published at different times of the year since being launched in 1994. For 1995–1999, ratings were reported in December of the previous year. The indices for 2000, 2001, 2002,

Table 5.32 IEF ratings performance 1, 2, and 3 years before a crisis

	Year y−1	Year y−2	Year y−3
Average rating of the crisis countries (ratings issued during 1995–2006)	3.4	3.4	3.3
Average rating of the crisis countries (ratings issued during 2007–2014)	56.2	56.9	56.8
Average percentile ranking of the crisis countries	62nd	61st	61st
Percentage of crisis countries rated in the "risk-free" category	0.7	0.0	0.8
Percentage of crisis countries ranked in the top 25%	12.8	10.3	10.2
Percentage of crisis countries rated in the "safe"/"relatively safe" categories	31.2	32.4	31.3
Percentage of crisis countries ranked in the top 50%	32.6	33.8	32.8

Notes: IEF ratings are established on a 1–5 scale during 1995–2006, where 5 (resp. 1) corresponds to countries that are the most (resp. least) risky, and on a 0–100 scale during 2007–2014, where 0 (resp. 100) corresponds to countries that are the most (resp. least) risky. The samples 1, 2, and 3 years prior to a crisis consist of (respectively) 141, 136, and 128 observations. A crisis is a country-year pair in which a shock occurred, and an observation is a crisis-rating pair
Source: Author's classifications based on the IEF's ratings

and 2003 were released in (respectively) January 2000, November 2000, November 2001, and December 2002. For 2004–2014, the IEF was reported in January of the corresponding year.

I test how well the scores published in the 1995–2014 reports anticipated the country risk crises that occurred during 1995–2014. The scores 1, 2, and 3 years prior to the crisis observed in year y are those given in the IEF for years y, $y-1$, and $y-2$, respectively.

Here, I view the IEF's "free economies" as corresponding to "risk-free" countries. Recall that these are the economies observed in the countries rated from 1.00 to 1.99 during 1995–2006 and from 80 to 100 during 2007–2014 (see Sect. 5.1.4). I consider as "safe" and "relatively safe" the countries that are assigned a score of less than 3 during 1995–2006 and of at least 60 during 2007–2014.

Table 5.32 gives the performance of IEF ratings. One, two, and three years prior to a crisis, the average ratings (near the top of its "mostly unfree economies" category) and also the average percentile rankings (around the 61st percentile) are quite good.

In particular, the percentages of crisis countries rated in the "risk-free" category are remarkably low. These findings reflect the conservative policy followed by the Heritage Foundation: on average, barely ten countries (accounting for just 6% of all the nations rated) are classified as "free economies" in a given year. However, the percentages of crisis countries ranked in the top 25% are higher, an outcome indicating that the category of "mostly free economies" (i.e., the second highest rating category) includes a significant number of risky nations.

The percentages of crisis countries rated in the "safe" and "relatively safe" rating categories are similar to the percentages of those ranked in the top 50%, which reflects that the proportion of nations classified as having "free," "mostly free," and (since 2007) "moderately free" economies accounts for roughly half of the samples. These percentages—around 32%—are satisfactory.

It is interesting that the IEF's performances 1, 2, and 3 years prior to a crisis are the same. This could mean that the Heritage Foundation's index has some difficulty perceiving the weakened political and/or economic position of countries that are about to encounter a shock.

Two countries that were rated in the "risk-free" category before being hit by a shock are El Salvador and Iceland (see Table 5.33). The nature of the shock suffered by El Salvador (two earthquakes and subsequent landslides occurred in 2001) hardly allows a test of whether that country's "free economy" status was appropriately granted. A less understandable misrating was the failure of Heritage Foundation experts to anticipate the capital controls implemented by the Icelandic government in 2008.

The crisis countries ranked in the top 25% have various profiles. Putting aside the shocks resulting from the Great Recession of 2008–2009, I identify two facts that deserve further comment. First, the IEF did not anticipate a number of nationalizations that occurred in Argentina, Costa Rica, El Salvador, Georgia, Hungary, Latvia, Peru, and Trinidad and Tobago. This shortcoming casts doubt on an index that claims to assess economic freedom. Second, Argentina was unquestionably overrated during the few years preceding its economic turmoil of 2001–2002. For instance, this country was rated at the very top of the "mostly free economies" category in 1999–2000. The Heritage Foundation was evidently way too optimistic about the free-market reforms implemented under the Menem presidency. Yet in December 2001, at the dawn of Argentina's economic depression, the Heritage Foundation admitted that this Latin American country still had many problems to solve: a high cost of doing business, the insufficient protection of property rights, and fragility of the rule of law.[33]

Table 5.33 IEF's misratings

	Year y−1	Year y−2	Year y−3
Crisis countries rated in the "risk-free" category (types of shocks in parentheses)	El Salvador:2001 (natural disaster)	No misrating	Iceland:2008 (restriction on capital flows)

(continued)

[33] See https://www.heritage.org/americas/commentary/dont-blame-capitalism-argentina. It is not surprising that the IEF rating of Argentina plummeted in the 2000s.

Table 5.33 (continued)

	Year y−1	Year y−2	Year y−3
Crisis countries ranked in the top 25% (types of shocks in parentheses)	Estonia:2009 (economic depression); El Salvador:2001 (natural disaster); Iceland:2008 (restriction on capital flows); Cyprus:2012 (restriction on capital flows); Lithuania:2009 (economic depression); Armenia:2009 (economic depression); Argentina:2001 (expropriation, restriction on capital flows, sovereign debt crisis); Hungary:2002 (expropriation); El Salvador:2008 (expropriation); Georgia:2007 (expropriation); Chile:1996 (restriction on capital flows); Uruguay:2003 (sovereign debt crisis); Peru:2011 (expropriation); Cyprus:2013 (sovereign debt crisis); Latvia:2008 (expropriation); Argentina:2002 (economic depression); Costa Rica:2012 (expropriation); Turkey:1999 (sovereign debt crisis)	El Salvador:2001 (natural disaster); Estonia:2009 (economic depression); Iceland:2008 (restriction on capital flows); Cyprus:2012 (restriction on capital flows); Argentina:2001 (expropriation, restriction on capital flows, sovereign debt crisis); Cyprus:2013 (sovereign debt crisis); Lithuania:2009 (economic depression); Armenia:2009 (economic depression); El Salvador:2008 (expropriation); Argentina:2002 (economic depression); Chile:1996 (restriction on capital flows); Trinidad and Tobago:2010 (expropriation); Latvia:2009 (economic depression); Hungary:2010 (expropriation)	Iceland:2008 (restriction on capital flows); Estonia:2009 (economic depression); Argentina:2001 (expropriation, restriction on capital flows, sovereign debt crisis); Cyprus:2013 (sovereign debt crisis); Argentina:2002 (economic depression); El Salvador:2001 (natural disaster); Cyprus:2012 (restriction on capital flows); Lithuania:2009 (economic depression); Trinidad and Tobago:2010 (expropriation); Armenia:2009 (economic depression); El Salvador:2008 (expropriation); Uruguay:2003 (sovereign debt crisis); Latvia:2008 (expropriation)

Note: The higher the rating or ranking of a crisis country, the higher its position in the classification
Source: Author's classifications based on the IEF's ratings

5.3.7 *Performance of EFW's Country Risk Ratings*

Publication of the Fraser Institute's Economic Freedom of the World report was irregular for several years. I test the predictive accuracy of the EFW scores published during 1995–2013 with respect to the country risk crises that occurred during 1996–2014. The sources of the scores 1, 2, and 3 years prior to a crisis-inducing shock observed in year *y* are presented in Table 5.34.

Unlike the Heritage Foundation's IEF, the Fraser Institute's EFW does not use broad rating categories to label "free economies." Hence I assume that "risk-free"

Table 5.34 Shocks and sources of EFW ratings

Year of the crisis	Name of the EFW report used (date of publication)		
	Year y−1	Year y−2	Year y−3
1996	*EFW 1995* (Jan. 1996)	Not Applicable	Not Applicable
1997	*EFW 1995* (Jan. 1996)	*EFW 1995* (Jan. 1996)	Not Applicable
1998	*EFW 1997* (May 1997)	*EFW 1995* (Jan. 1996)	*EFW 1995* (Jan. 1996)
1999	*EFW 1998–1999* (Nov. 1998)	*EFW 1997* (May 1997)	*EFW 1995* (Jan. 1996)
2000	*EFW 2000* (Jan. 2000)	*EFW 1998–1999* (Nov. 1998)	*EFW 1997* (May 1997)
2001	*EFW 2000* (Jan. 2000)	*EFW 2000* (Jan. 2000)	*EFW 1998–1999* (Nov. 1998)
2002	*EFW 2001* (April 2001)	*EFW 2000* (Jan. 2000)	*EFW 2000* (Jan. 2000)
2003	*EFW 2002* (June 2002)	*EFW 2001* (April 2001)	*EFW 2000* (Jan. 2000)
2004	*EFW 2003* (July 2003)	*EFW 2002* (June 2002)	*EFW 2001* (April 2001)
2005	*EFW 2004* (July 2004)	*EFW 2003* (July 2003)	*EFW 2002* (June 2002)
2006	*EFW 2005* (Sept. 2005)	*EFW 2004* (July 2004)	*EFW 2003* (July 2003)
2007	*EFW 2006* (Sept. 2006)	*EFW 2005* (Sept. 2005)	*EFW 2004* (July 2004)
2008	*EFW 2007* (Sept. 2007)	*EFW 2006* (Sept. 2006)	*EFW 2005* (Sept. 2005)
2009	*EFW 2008* (Sept. 2008)	*EFW 2007* (Sept. 2007)	*EFW 2006* (Sept. 2006)
2010	*EFW 2009* (Sept. 2009)	*EFW 2008* (Sept. 2008)	*EFW 2007* (Sept. 2007)
2011	*EFW 2010* (Sept. 2010)	*EFW 2009* (Sept. 2009)	*EFW 2008* (Sept. 2008)
2012	*EFW 2011* (Sept. 2011)	*EFW 2010* (Sept. 2010)	*EFW 2009* (Sept. 2009)
2013	*EFW 2012* (Sept. 2012)	*EFW 2011* (Sept. 2011)	*EFW 2010* (Sept. 2010)
2014	*EFW 2013* (Sept. 2013)	*EFW 2012* (Sept. 2012)	*EFW 2011* (Sept. 2011)

Source: Author's classification based on the Fraser Institute's EFW reports (various years)

countries are those that are given a rating higher than 7.5.[34] Because setting a threshold with respect to which countries can be reliably labeled as "safe" and "relatively safe" is too uncertain an undertaking, I do not report data for this performance criterion.

Because no EFW ratings clearly correspond to a "safe" and "relatively safe" category, the average ratings of crisis countries convey less relevant information than do the average percentile rankings; as reported in Table 5.35, those are adequate (at about the 58th percentile).

Although the percentages of crisis countries rated in the "risk-free" category are higher than those observed for the IEF, the percentages of such countries ranked in the top 25% are much the same as those seen for the IEF. The EFW underperforms against its neoliberal counterpart in terms of the proportion of crisis countries ranked in the top 50%, which suggests that the EFW ranking's second quartile is not very accurate.

[34] I set this threshold so that the rating assigned to the United States is always in the "risk-free" category. For the period under consideration, the lowest US rating was 7.6 (see *EFW 1995*, p. xxi; *EFW 2011*, p. 9).

Table 5.35 EFW ratings performance 1, 2, and 3 years before a crisis

	Year y−1	Year y−2	Year y−3
Average rating of the crisis countries	6.1	6.1	6.1
Average percentile ranking of the crisis countries	58th	58th	57th
Percentage of crisis countries rated in the "risk-free" category	10.4	8.9	8.3
Percentage of crisis countries ranked in the top 25%	13.2	13.9	12.5
Percentage of crisis countries rated in the "safe"/"relatively safe" categories	N.A.	N.A.	N.A.
Percentage of crisis countries ranked in the top 50%	41.5	42.6	42.7

Notes: EFW ratings are established on a 0–10 scale, where 0 (resp. 10) corresponds to countries that are the most (resp. least) risky. The samples 1, 2, and 3 years prior to a crisis consist of (respectively) 106, 101, and 96 observations. A crisis is a country-year pair in which a shock occurred, and an observation is a crisis-rating pair. N.A. denotes Not Applicable
Source: Author's computations based on EFW ratings

The EFW's performance is much the same at 1, 2, and 3 years before a crisis. A close examination of these ratings reveals that they are "sticky" and therefore do not adjust as country risks approach a crisis point.

The misratings by the EFW are presented in Table 5.36. Most are primarily the same as those observed for the IEF: the global crises in Argentina (2001–2002) and Cyprus (2012–2013), and the restriction on capital flows in Iceland (2008). I examine these three cases in turn.

In its *EFW 2000* report, the Fraser Institute lauded Argentina's widespread privatization of state-owned firms, decontrol of prices, and implementation of a currency board that reduced 1990's 4-digit inflation rate to only 1% by the end of that decade (Fraser Institute 2000, p. 22). These key factors underpinned the rating of 8.4 granted to the country and its 12th place in the year 2000 ranking. The Fraser Institute was even more enthusiastic than the Heritage Foundation about Argentina's "economic freedom," so in that respect it failed completely.

The case of Cyprus is clearly different. The subcomponent rating this country received on the "access to sound money" rating criterion in 2010 and 2011 (9.3–9.4 out of 10) is so high that it compensates for other categories (whose ratings range from 6.7 to 7.5) and yields a final rating above 7.5. These findings question the relevance of that criterion's components—namely, money growth, the standard deviation of inflation, the most recent inflation rate, and the freedom to own foreign currency bank accounts (Fraser Institute 2010, p. 56; 2011, p. 60).

The misrating of Iceland raises another important issue. Examination of the *EFW 2007* report reveals that its "international capital market controls" score—a component of the "freedom to trade internationally" rating category—was especially low. However, it was offset by the high level of other sub-scores (Fraser Institute 2007, p. 99). That failure illustrates how a rating system based on weightings is likely to underestimate an economy's true weaknesses. I shall return to this issue in Sect. 5.4.2.1.

Table 5.36 EFW's misratings

	Year y−1	Year y−2	Year y−3
Crisis countries rated in the "risk-free" category (types of shocks in parentheses)	Argentina:2001 (expropriation, restriction on capital flows, sovereign debt crisis); El Salvador:2001 (natural disaster); Argentina:2002 (economic depression); Bolivia:2000 (expropriation); Estonia:2009 (economic depression); Iceland:2008 (restriction on capital flows); Mexico:2001 (expropriation); Cyprus:2013 (sovereign debt crisis); El Salvador:2008 (expropriation); Hungary:2014 (expropriation); Cyprus:2012 (restriction on capital flows)	Argentina:2001 (expropriation, restriction on capital flows, sovereign debt crisis); Argentina:2002 (economic depression); El Salvador:2001 (natural disaster); Estonia:2009 (economic depression); Iceland:2008 (restriction on capital flows); Bolivia:2000 (expropriation); Mexico:2001 (expropriation); Cyprus:2012 (restriction on capital flows); Cyprus:2013 (sovereign debt crisis)	Argentina:2001 (expropriation, restriction on capital flows, sovereign debt crisis); Argentina:2002 (economic depression); El Salvador:2001 (natural disaster); Iceland:2008 (restriction on capital flows); Estonia:2009 (economic depression); Costa Rica:2012 (expropriation); Cyprus:2013 (sovereign debt crisis); Hungary:2014 (expropriation)
Crisis countries ranked in the top 25% (types of shocks in parentheses)	Iceland:2008 (restriction on capital flows); Estonia:2009 (economic depression); Argentina:2002 (economic depression); Argentina:2001 (expropriation, restriction on capital flows, sovereign debt crisis); El Salvador:2001 (natural disaster); El Salvador:2008 (expropriation); Cyprus:2012 (restriction on capital flows); Cyprus:2013 (sovereign debt crisis); Latvia:2008 (expropriation); Hungary:2014 (expropriation); Bolivia:2000 (expropriation); Lithuania:2009 (economic depression); Peru:2011 (expropriation); Costa Rica:2007 (expropriation)	Estonia:2009 (economic depression); Iceland:2008 (restriction on capital flows); Argentina:2001 (expropriation, restriction on capital flows, sovereign debt crisis); Argentina:2002 (economic depression); El Salvador:2001 (natural disaster); Cyprus:2013 (sovereign debt crisis); Cyprus:2012 (restriction on capital flows); Latvia:2009 (economic depression); Lithuania:2009 (economic depression); Costa Rica:2007 (expropriation); Costa Rica:2012 (expropriation); Hungary:2010 (expropriation); Armenia:2009 (economic depression); El Salvador:2008 (expropriation)	Argentina:2001 (expropriation, restriction on capital flows, sovereign debt crisis); Estonia:2009 (economic depression); Argentina:2002 (economic depression); Iceland:2008 (restriction on capital flows); Hungary:2014 (expropriation); Costa Rica:2012 (expropriation); Cyprus:2013 (sovereign debt crisis); El Salvador:2001 (natural disaster); Hungary:2010 (expropriation); Bulgaria:2014 (expropriation); Bolivia:2000 (expropriation); El Salvador:2008 (expropriation)

Note: The higher the rating or ranking of a crisis country, the higher its position in the classification
Source: Author's classifications based on EFW ratings

5.3.8 Performance of the Growth CI and the GCI

Finally, I test how well the World Economic Forum's Growth Competitiveness Index and Global Competitiveness Index scores issued during 2001–2013 anticipated the country risk crises that occurred during 2002–2014. The scores 1, 2, and 3 years prior to the crisis observed in year *y* are those published in the *Global Competitiveness Reports* of (respectively) years *y*–1, *y*–2, and *y*–3.

Global Competitiveness Reports do not use broad rating categories to label the "most" or "very" competitive economies. Consequently, I assume that "risk-free" countries are those that are assigned a rating higher than 5.00.[35] Once again (cf. my remarks concerning the EFW ratings), establishing a threshold for "safe" and "relatively safe" countries is too uncertain to allow evaluation based on that performance criterion.

As in Sect. 5.3.7, this absence of "safe" and "relatively safe" rating categories lessens the relevance of the average ratings of the crisis countries referenced in Table 5.37. In contrast, it is crucial to examine average percentile rankings because the *Global Competitiveness Reports* place great emphasis on rankings. The table shows that the average percentile rankings are especially satisfactory: around the 66th percentile.

The proportion of crisis countries rated in the "risk-free" category and ranked in the top 25% is low, which means that those indices are very accurate. These findings are confirmed by the low percentages (26.5%, on average) of crisis countries ranked in the top 50%.

Table 5.37 Growth CI and GCI rating performance 1, 2, and 3 years before a crisis

	Year y–1	Year y–2	Year y–3
Average rating of the crisis countries	3.8	3.8	3.8
Average percentile ranking of the crisis countries	67th	65th	65th
Percentage of crisis countries rated in the "risk-free" category	1.3	1.5	3.1
Percentage of crisis countries ranked in the top 25%	3.9	4.4	4.7
Percentage of crisis countries rated in the "safe"/"relatively safe" categories	N.A.	N.A.	N.A.
Percentage of crisis countries ranked in the top 50%	26.3	26.5	26.6

Notes: Growth and *Global Competitiveness Indices* ratings are established on a 1–7 scale, where 1 (resp. 7) corresponds to countries that are the most (resp. least) risky. The samples 1, 2, and 3 years prior to a crisis consist of (respectively) 76, 68, and 64 observations. A crisis is a country-year pair in which a shock occurred, and an observation is a crisis-rating pair. N.A. denotes Not Applicable
Source: Author's computations based on Growth CI and GCI scores

[35] I set this threshold so that the rating assigned to the United States is always in the "risk-free" category. For the period under consideration, the lowest US rating was 5.43 (World Economic Forum 2010, p. 15; 2011, p. 15).

Table 5.38 Growth CI's and GCI's misratings

	Year y−1	Year y−2	Year y−3
Crisis countries rated in the "risk-free" category (types of shocks in parentheses)	Iceland:2008 (restriction on capital flows)	Iceland:2008 (restriction on capital flows)	Iceland:2008 (restriction on capital flows); Estonia:2009 (economic depression)
Crisis countries ranked in the top 25% (types of shocks in parentheses)	Iceland:2008 (restriction on capital flows); China:2011 (expropriation); Estonia:2009 (economic depression)	Iceland:2008 (restriction on capital flows); Estonia:2009 (economic depression); China:2011 (expropriation)	Iceland:2008 (restriction on capital flows); Estonia:2009 (economic depression); China:2011 (expropriation)

Note: The higher the rating or ranking of a crisis country, the higher its position in the classification
Source: Author's classifications based on Growth CI and GCI scores

The WEF ratings failed to anticipate three crises: the controls on capital flows in Iceland (2008), the economic depression in Estonia (2009), and the expropriation announced by China (2011); see Table 5.38.

The excessively high ranking of China is driven by the high scores granted to the "macroeconomic environment" and "health and primary education" pillars. However, this error is not entirely attributable to the GCI rating system. In fact, China was ranked 38th and assigned a score of 5.1 (out of 7) in terms of property rights protection in 2010—at the same level as the United States (World Economic Forum, 2010, pp. 128–129, 366). This mis-ranking and misrating reflect the poor judgment of business executives who participated in the WEF's annual opinion survey and expressed positive views about the quality of property rights protection in China.

The GCI rating of Estonia was inflated by the high scores given to the pillars of "macroeconomic environment," "health and primary education," "higher education and training," and "technological readiness" (World Economic Forum 2006, p. 214). This index echoed other raters in viewing Estonia favorably despite its vulnerability to an international economic downturn.

The case of Iceland is perhaps less informative about GCI's accuracy given that *no* raters foresaw the sudden restriction on capital flows in 2008. Further remarks on this matter are given in Sect. 5.4.2.3.

5.4 General Comments

This section offers a series of comments that should help foreign investors grasp the limits of country risk ratings, appreciate some historical background, and assess country risk more accurately. Section 5.4.1 details the lessons drawn from Sect. 5.3 and makes some useful comparisons between Euromoney, ICRG, Credendo, the

OECD, the Heritage Foundation's IEF, the Fraser Institute's EFW, and the World Economic Forum's GCI. Section 5.4.2 explains how a conservative rating system can improve the capacity of country risk scores to anticipate crises; it also points to some important yet overlooked factors that could enhance rating methodologies. Section 5.4.3 studies the evolution of country risk ratings during the globalization era and examines economies whose positions have improved (or weakened) the most. Section 5.4.4 looks at the correlations across raters at the end of 2013.

5.4.1 *Country Risk Indicators and Types of Risks*

5.4.1.1 Do All Types of Shocks Really Matter for Country Risk Raters?

A first lesson from Sect. 5.3 is that certain types of shocks are much harder to anticipate than others. Table 5.39 shows which types of shocks most frequently led to a misrating.

More than 60% of misratings were caused either by an expropriation or by a sudden control of capital flows. The latter is extremely difficult for country risk raters to anticipate when one considers that it accounts for only 5.4% of the 298 shocks observed during 1985–2014 (see Sect. 5.2.10).[36] In Sects. 5.4.2.2 and 5.4.2.3, I make some recommendations that can facilitate better anticipation of these two shocks.

Table 5.39 Misratings and types of shocks

	Misratings by causal type of shock (raw number)	Misratings by causal type of shock (as % of all misratings)
Major episode of international political violence	0	0.0
Major episode of domestic political violence	1	1.4
Expropriation	19	27.5
High inflation	1	1.4
Deep economic depression	8	11.6
Restriction on capital flows	23	33.3
Sovereign debt crisis	13	18.8
Exceptional natural disaster	4	5.8

Note: A *misrating* occurs when a crisis country is assigned a rating in the "risk-free" category (Credendo's ratings are excluded because they measure only expropriation risk). The six country risk raters considered were responsible for a total of 69 misratings that occurred either 1, 2, or 3 years prior to a crisis. Several misratings were due to more than one shock. Values in the last column do not total 100% because of rounding
Source: Author's calculations

[36] All the misratings caused by capital controls involved the same countries (i.e., Argentina in 2001, Iceland in 2008, and Cyprus in 2012).

Deep economic depressions and sovereign debt crises, which caused 30% of misratings, remain a source of concern. In contrast, the four other types of shocks seem to be minor threats to the accuracy of country risk ratings. Of the raters examined in this chapter, ICRG is the only one to overrate an economy (Libya's) that was subsequently affected by a major episode of domestic political violence (see Sect. 5.3.3). Euromoney is the only rater that failed to forecast an episode of high inflation (in the Soviet Union; see Sect. 5.3.2). Finally, on four occasions the two neoliberal think tanks rated a country (El Salvador) as "risk free" prior to it suffering an exceptional natural disaster.

In fact, it is fair to assume that Euromoney, ICRG, the OECD, the Heritage Foundation, the Fraser Institute, and the World Economic Forum all managed to anticipate political shocks, high-inflation episodes, and exceptional natural disasters *mainly* because these crises affected low- and middle-income economies—which are seldom assigned a "risk-free" rating in the first place. However, history has taught us that developed nations are not immune to major political shocks (see Gaillard 2014). In addition, global warming and the ensuing natural disasters could pose a major threat to high-income countries in the years to come.

5.4.1.2 Comparisons Between Raters

Section 5.3 showed that the indicators designed to measure economic freedom and competitiveness can serve as accurate metrics for assessing country risk. This statement holds especially for the Heritage Foundation's Index of Economic Freedom and the World Economic Forum's Global Competitiveness Index. That key finding—which was far from evident when I started this research—is good news for investors who are considering the use of alternative country risk indicators.

Although a strict comparison of the seven raters is impossible, their relative performance (as described in Sect. 5.3) enables some judgments about the ratings' relative accuracy.

Credendo requires a separate examination because its ratings measure only expropriation risk.[37] The performance of this Belgian export credit agency was quite satisfactory. Only four countries were classified in the top rating category 1, 2, or 3 years before they announced an expropriation act. For two of these countries (Bulgaria and Latvia), the nationalization was the only one observed within three decades. Romania and Hungary seized foreign investors' assets twice and four times, respectively. The rating of Romania has remained unchanged since the first nationalization, but Hungary's rating was downgraded after its third expropriation. It is also worth noting that Credendo managed to anticipate the wave of expropriations in Bolivia, Ecuador, and Venezuela by downgrading these three "Bolivarian" economies as early as 2005–2006.

[37] Recall that Credendo also issues other ratings intended to measure other types of risks (see Sect. 5.1.2).

Examining the accuracy of the ratings assigned by the six other raters reveals some performance gaps. It appears that the Fraser Institute's Economic Freedom of the World index is less accurate than other indicators owing to the high proportion of crisis countries in its top ratings and rankings. The OECD country risk ratings are probably only the fifth best. The main weaknesses of the OECD metrics are the same as those observed for the Fraser Institute. Discriminating between the four remaining raters is more difficult. That said, the accuracy of ICRG ratings and of the Heritage Foundation's IEF ratings is compromised by their excessively high percentages of crisis countries in the "safe" and "relatively safe" categories. For these reasons, Euromoney and the World Economic Forum's Global Competitiveness Index outperform (if only slightly) their counterparts. Euromoney's "risk-free" rating category and the GCI's top-ranked group (i.e., the top 25%) are especially reliable.

5.4.1.3 Ratings Versus Rankings

Four of the raters examined in Sect. 5.3—Euromoney, the Heritage Foundation, the Fraser Institute, and the World Economic Forum—put emphasis on both the ratings and the rankings of the countries they study. A rating reflects the risk inherent to a country and can be compared to the rating of another country; a ranking only makes this comparison easier. So the natural question that arises is: Do rankings really matter?

In fact, they do for a foreign investor who examines the Fraser Institute's EFW index or the World Economic Forum's GCI. Because these two raters do not use broad rating categories to label "risk-free," "safe," and "relatively safe" economies, the rankings they assign are decidedly relevant. For the other raters, rankings are a secondary consideration and, moreover, may be misleading. In the case of Euromoney, which has rated and ranked no fewer than 180 countries for two decades, a good ranking does not entail a "risk-free" status. For example, a country to which Euromoney assigns a rating of 50 or higher is less likely to be affected by a shock than is a country whose Euromoney's percentile rank is 50 or lower (see Sect. 5.3.2).

5.4.2 Improving Country Risk Methodologies

I investigate now how country risk methodologies could yield more accurate ratings. Section 5.4.2.1 addresses the rating systems; Sects. 5.4.2.2 and 5.4.2.3 advance two series of proposals to amend rating criteria.

5.4.2.1 Why a Conservative Rating System Is an Option

Like sovereign rating methodologies, country risk rating methodologies are essentially quantitative (see Sect. 4.3.1.1). The problem is that quantitative risk assessments go hand in hand with weighting or averaging methods. When intermediate ratings or subcomponent ratings are weighted (equally or not) to yield a final overall rating, the impact of the riskiest broad categories (i.e., those that are assigned the lowest intermediate ratings) is systematically diluted. In fact, the weighting and averaging methods used by raters may well explain their inability to anticipate country risk crises.

In order to test this assumption, I examine the 44 observations of crisis countries rated in the "risk-free" category 1, 2, and 3 years before a crisis by every rater (excepting Credendo and the OECD, which do not provide intermediate ratings).[38] For every observation, I define a new final rating that is not a *combination* of the intermediate ratings but rather the *lowest* intermediate rating.

Following this "weakest link" approach has the effect of removing 41 out of the 44 crisis-country observations from the misratings lists. The only three cases that remain in the "risk-free" category are Iceland:2008 twice (still over-rated by Euromoney and the WEF respectively 1 and 3 years before the crisis) and Argentina:2001 (still overrated by the Fraser Institute 3 years prior to this crisis). These striking results should convince country risk raters to apply their methodologies in a more conservative manner.

Next, for each of the 41 observations, I check for whether the broad category that yielded the lowest intermediate rating—and thus my new final rating—includes the area in which the shock actually materialized. I find that, in close to half (44%) of the cases, the shock occurred in the "right" area.

It is noteworthy that the value is 100% for Euromoney's, ICRG's, and the Heritage Foundation's misratings. This outcome supports the view that these three raters are able to identify which of a country's weaknesses is most likely to trigger a major shock. The corresponding proportion is only 25% for the EFW's misratings, which indicates that the Fraser Institute has greater difficulty in identifying potential crises. All these results are consistent with the conclusions drawn in Sect. 5.4.1.2. The World Economic Forum's GCI is in a peculiar position: *none* of the lowest intermediate ratings assigned to the misrated countries falls in the "right" area. This anomaly is driven mainly by the inclusion—in GCI's pillars—of many microeconomic criteria that are not closely connected to the shocks suffered by those countries.[39] These findings reflect the idiosyncratic methodology employed by the WEF.

---

[38] Two crisis countries are excluded from this grouping because no intermediate rating is available: USSR:1991 (misrated by Euromoney) and El Salvador:2001 (misrated by the Heritage Foundation).

[39] For example, the lowest intermediate ratings of Estonia and Iceland in 2006–2007 affected the "innovation" and "market size" pillars.

However, the soundness of a "weakest link" approach should not prevent country risk raters from implementing other revisions that would improve the predictive accuracy of their methodologies' output. Two areas in particular merit examination.

5.4.2.2 The Rule of Law: A Key Driver of Political and Economic Confidence

The rule of law is a cornerstone of any legitimate, long-lasting regime. It is also necessary for the enforcement of property rights.

The Glorious Revolution of 1688 and the subsequent passage of the Bill of Rights in 1689 extended the powers of the English Parliament at the expense of the monarch's. This event was a watershed in the political and economic history of Western societies. In the decades that followed, Parliament expanded the granting of property rights to private individuals and companies and committed to secure those rights (North and Weingast 1989; Bogart and Richardson 2011). This new institutional order paved the way for the rise and domination of liberal capitalism.

My argument here is that the rule of law is certainly the most simple and reliable indicator for an investor seeking to assess expropriation risk and/or political risk. Following Kaufmann et al. (2010), I view the rule of law as reflecting "perceptions of the extent to which agents have confidence in and abide by the rules of society, and in particular the quality of contract enforcement, property rights, the police, and the courts, as well as the likelihood of crime and violence."

The rule of law in a country is explicitly considered by the two neoliberal raters of country risk (see Fraser Institute 2017, pp. 3–5; Heritage Foundation 2017, p. 455) but is considered in only an implicit way by Euromoney, ICRG, and the World Economic Forum.[40] Euromoney highlights "government stability," "institutional risk," and "regulatory and policy environment".[41] Similarly, ICRG (The PRS Group 2014, p. 3) focuses on the "government stability," "law and order," and "democratic accountability" components and measures the involvement of military and religious powers in politics. The WEF's *Global Competitiveness Report* (2017, p. 322) includes, as part of its "institutions" pillar, "judicial independence" as well as "efficiency of [the] legal framework in settling disputes" and "challenging regulations." Yet, these approaches have several shortcomings.

First, a government's stability does not convey reliable information about its impartiality or about the executive's relations with legislative and judicial branches of government. For example, the Russian and Turkish authoritarian regimes have proved especially stable (so far), but each is a far cry from exemplifying the rule of law. The same statement applies to many "populist" regimes (e.g., Hungary under Viktor Orban).

---

[40] Neither the OECD nor Credendo discloses the methodologies it employs to assess country risk.

[41] See www.euromoneycountryrisk.com

Second, democratic accountability and (more globally) the respect of democratic values do not preclude political interference in judicial and regulatory processes. Such interference is rife in Latin American democracies.

Third, even neoliberal methodologies exhibit some flaws on this account. The Heritage Foundation and the Fraser Institute each have a fairly narrow view of the rule of law; that is, both consider it almost exclusively through the lens of protecting property rights. This errant perspective is a consequence of the two think tanks' tendency to dissociate *economic* freedom from *political* freedom.

Country risk rating methodologies would yield better results if they incorporated the "rule of law" score proposed by Kaufmann et al. (2010). For example, when I test this indicator against all the countries that were affected by a jurisdictional or political shock (i.e., an expropriation or a major episode of domestic or international political violence),[42] I find that the maximum score assigned to a crisis country is 0.91 on a scale that ranges from −2.5 to +2.5 (where +2.5 is the best score) and that the maximum percentile ranking is 18%. The average score and percentile ranking assigned to a crisis country are each highly appropriate: respectively −0.59 and the 75th percentile. Only 3 of the 83 observations (3.6%) have a percentile ranking in the top 25%. For the three specific shocks considered here, the "rule of law" indicator outperforms all country risk raters but one: the World Economic Forum's GCI, whose capacity to anticipate political and jurisdictional shocks is unparalleled.

5.4.2.3 Optimal Level of Financial Openness

Increasing financial openness has been a key factor of the financial globalization that began in the 1980s. The problem is that country risk raters have not sufficiently investigated the pace at which—or the extent to which—a country should liberalize its financial sector.

A quick look at the average annual GDP growth and the evolution of financial openness during 1985–2014 reveals no correlation between the two series of data.[43] On the one hand, some countries that removed restrictions on capital and current account transactions enjoyed high GDP growth (e.g., Botswana, Israel, and Uganda) while others stagnated (e.g., Greece and Nicaragua). On the other hand, the few countries that reduced their financial openness posted diverging performances: the annual GDP growth of Malaysia was almost three times that of Gabon. Furthermore, the economies that grew most rapidly during the past three decades (China and India) did not change their respective levels of financial openness.

---

[42] I use Kaufmann et al.'s updated database (released in 2016). For a crisis observed in year y, I examine the "rule of law" score assigned to year $y-2$ (or the one assigned to $y-3$ if the $y-2$ score is not available). Scores are available for all years since 1996 *except* for 1997, 1999, and 2001.

[43] The adjusted R^2 value is 0.01. I define the "evolution of financial openness" as the score on this trait in 2014 *minus* the score in 1985. The sample includes 117 countries. Author's computations are based on World Development Indicators and Chinn and Ito's (2006) updated index.

The equivocal relationship between economic growth and the liberalization of capital and current accounts should encourage country risk raters to implement analyses of a more qualitative nature when assessing the likelihood that a government will impose restrictions on capital flows.[44] First of all, I believe that a high degree of financial openness is a positive sign *provided* the country has a diversified economy, a robust banking sector, and sophisticated domestic capital markets. These three factors mitigate the risk that a sudden stop in capital flows could trigger a major financial and economic crisis. In addition, raters should monitor the types of inflows absorbed by a country with high financial openness. For instance, a high proportion of short-term portfolio investments are cause for alarm, especially if they feed credit-fueled asset bubbles (see Sect. 4.3.1.3). In the second place, a precipitate liberalization of capital account transactions—as occurred in Argentina during the mid-1990s and in Cyprus during the mid-2000s—may be counterproductive and could ultimately oblige a government to impose significant restrictions on capital flows.

Finally, an extremely large current account deficit (i.e., exceeding 10% of GDP) could spell serious trouble. Such a deficit is the other side of massive capital inflows, and it renders the country vulnerable in the event of a sharp economic downturn. The crises experienced by Iceland and the Baltic states in 2008–2009 are illustrations of this vulnerability.

Combined with the "weakest link" approach and the recommendations advanced in Sect. 4.3.1, an accurate assessment of the focal country's rule of law and financial stability is likely to enhance country risk methodologies and (in most cases) to deflate country ratings.

5.4.3 *Evolution of Country Risk Ratings During the Globalization Era*

5.4.3.1 Worst-Performing Countries

Table 5.40 lists the five economies whose country risk ratings fell the most dramatically during 1988–2013 (as measured by Euromoney and ICRG ratings) and during 2001–2013 (as measured by the World Economic Forum's GCI scores).

It is noteworthy that only 4 of the 16 worst-performing countries presented in Table 5.40—Greece, Hungary, Iceland, and Venezuela—were hit by a major shock (as defined in Sect. 5.2) during the globalization era. When one considers that the countries most severely downgraded by Euromoney, ICRG, and the WEF are developed economies, it is clear that those countries experienced (and continue to experience) a *slow* decline in their economic and financial position.

That half of the worst performers are eurozone members is consistent with Sect. 4.3.2.1. The three raters were more concerned about the weakening of these

[44] See Prasad and Rajan (2008) for a more thorough analysis of how and when capital accounts should be liberalized.

Table 5.40 Five worst-performing countries during the globalization era—according to Euromoney, ICRG, and the GCI

Euromoney		ICRG		GCI	
Country	Downg. (in points)	Country	Downg. (in points)	Country	Downg. (in points)
Greece	−38.8	Spain	−9.5	Iceland	−0.74
Spain	−33.6	Japan	−9.1	Canada	−0.67
Italy	−30.9	United Kingdom	−8.0	Australia	−0.65
Japan	−29.8	Venezuela	−6.5	Hungary	−0.62
Portugal	−27.7	France	−5.1	Spain	−0.60
				Ireland	−0.60

Notes: For Euromoney and the World Economic Forum's GCI, the ratings published in September 2013 are compared with those published in September 1988 and September 2001, respectively. For ICRG, the average ratings of 2013 are compared with those of 1988
Sources: Author's calculations and classifications based on *Euromoney* (September 1988 and September 2013), the ICRG database, and World Economic Forum (2001, 2013)

eurozone members' credit position than about the significance of any deterioration in their respective business climates. Japan provides a good illustration of the poorly performing countries more generally. This country was at the top of Euromoney's rankings in the late 1980s, but its credibility faded after more than two decades of economic stagnation, deflation, and rising debt.

Table 5.41 lists the five economies whose associated country risk ratings declined the most during 1994–2013 (as measured by Credendo's expropriation risk ratings), during 1995–2013 (as measured by IEF ratings), during 1996–2013 (as measured by EFW ratings), and during 1999–2013 (as measured by OECD scores).

Three-fourths of worst-performing economies presented in Table 5.41 were hit by a major shock during the globalization era. The profile of these countries differs radically from those listed in Table 5.40. In fact, the most severe downgrades announced by Credendo, the Heritage Foundation, the Fraser Institute, and the OECD involved the ratings of developing and emerging economies only.

For example, the Latin American states that opted for Bolivarian-style policies (Argentina, Bolivia, Ecuador, and Venezuela) as well as several African countries (e.g., Gambia, Guinea, Zimbabwe) frightened international investors by nationalizing foreign assets. Other economies were shaken by wars, revolutions, or noxious political atmospheres (e.g., Bahrain, the Central African Republic, Egypt, Sudan, Syria, Yemen). One can conclude that Credendo, the Heritage Foundation, the Fraser Institute, and the OECD lowered the ratings of countries in which the business climate had deteriorated the most.

Tables 5.40 and 5.41 are instructive because they reveal two distinct paths in the assessment of country risk. On the one hand, Euromoney, ICRG, and the World Economic Forum tend to penalize countries that are unable to preserve their credit position and competitiveness. On the other hand, Credendo, the Heritage Foundation, the Fraser Institute, and the OECD tend to be ruthless when rating economies that challenge the most fundamental capitalist rules (especially the enforcement of property rights).

Table 5.41 Five worst-performing countries during the globalization era—according to Credendo, the IEF, EFW, and OECD

Credendo		IEF		EFW		OECD	
Country	Downg. (in notches)	Country	Downg. (in points)	Country	Downg. (in points)	Country	Downg. (in notches)
Bolivia	−5	Argentina	−22.7	Argentina	−0.61	Argentina	−2
Ecuador	−4	Venezuela	−21.6	Venezuela	−0.57	Egypt	−2
Argentina	−3	Zimbabwe	−12.3	Thailand	−0.36	Jamaica	−2
Namibia	−3	Thailand	−8.3	Hong Kong	−0.23	Lebanon	−2
Bahrain	−2	Ecuador	−6.9	Ecuador	−0.05	Maldives	−2
C. Afr. R.	−2					Venezuela	−2
Gabon	−2						
Gambia	−2						
Guinea	−2						
Yemen	−2						
Sudan	−2						
Syria	−2						
Thailand	−2						
Tunisia	−2						
Venezuela	−2						

Notes: For Credendo, the ratings as of 31 December 2013 are compared with those as of 31 December 1994. For the IEF, the ratings published in January 2014 are compared with those published in December 1994. For the EFW, the ratings published in September 2013 are compared with those published in January 1996. For the OECD, the ratings as of 1 September 2013 are compared with those as of 1 September 1999. The IEF ratings published in December 1994 are converted to the 0–100 scale (see Heritage Foundation 2007, pp. 400–405). "C. Afr. R." denotes Central African Republic
Sources: Author's calculations and classifications based on the Credendo database, Heritage Foundation (1994, 2014), Fraser Institute (1996, 2013), and the OECD database

5.4.3.2 Best-Performing Countries

Tables 5.42 and 5.43 list the five economies whose country risk ratings rose the most dramatically during the globalization era. The respective raters and periods considered are the same as in Tables 5.40 and 5.41.

Several comments are in order with respect to these two tables. First, the upgrades by the Fraser Institute and ICRG are much greater in magnitude than their downgrades (see Tables 5.40 and 5.41). These results mirror the inflation of the two raters' country risk scores since the 1990s. The average rating assigned by the Fraser Institute's EFW and by ICRG soared by 1.7 and 11.4 points, amounts corresponding to 17% and 11.4% of the span of their respective rating scales.[45] This pattern explains the excessively high percentage of crisis countries rated in the "safe" and "relatively safe" rating categories by ICRG (see Sect. 5.3.3) and also the poor performance posted by the Fraser Institute (see Sect. 5.3.7).

[45] Author's computations are based on the samples used for Tables 5.40, 5.41, 5.42, and 5.43. The Fraser Institute and ICRG samples consist of 101 and 92 countries, respectively.

Table 5.42 Five best-performing countries during the globalization era—according to Euromoney, ICRG, and the GCI

Euromoney		ICRG		GCI	
Country	Upg. (in points)	Country	Upg. (in points)	Country	Upg. (in points)
Peru	+40.2	Nicaragua	+36.9	Indonesia	+0.84
Lebanon	+26.7	Myanmar	+36.3	Nicaragua	+0.83
Panama	+26.4	El Salvador	+32.4	Ecuador	+0.82
Chile	+22.1	Peru	+32.3	Ukraine	+0.79
Uganda	+22.0	Zambia	+31.4	Bangladesh	+0.67

Notes: For Euromoney and the World Economic Forum's GCI, the ratings published in September 2013 are compared with those published in September 1988 and September 2001, respectively. For ICRG, the average ratings of 2013 are compared with those of 1988

Sources: Author's calculations and classifications based on *Euromoney* (September 1988 and September 2013), the ICRG database, and World Economic Forum (2001, 2013)

Table 5.43 Five best-performing countries during the globalization era—according to Credendo, the IEF, EFW, and OECD

Credendo		IEF		EFW		OECD	
Country	Upg. (in notches)	Country	Upg. (in points)	Country	Upg. (in points)	Country	Upg. (in notches)
Colombia	+3	Moldova	+24.3	Romania	+4.42	Russia	+4
Albania	+2	Romania	+22.6	Hungary	+4.29	Algeria	+3
Brunei	+2	Albania	+20.5	Iran	+3.95	Brazil	+3
Dom. Rep.	+2	Angola	+20.5	Nicaragua	+3.93	Indonesia	+3
El Salvador	+2	Nicaragua	+18.9	Rwanda	+3.76	Angola	+2
Croatia	+2			Slovakia	+3.76	Azerbaijan	+2
Liberia	+2					Bulgaria	+2
Mauritius	+2					Kazakhstan	+2
Romania	+2					Lithuania	+2
Slovakia	+2					Macedonia	+2
Slovenia	+2					Mongolia	+2
Turkey	+2					Nigeria	+2
Uruguay	+2					Oman	+2
						Peru	+2
						Romania	+2
						Zambia	+2

Notes: For Credendo, the ratings as of 31 December 2013 are compared with those as of 31 December 1994. For the IEF, the ratings published in January 2014 are compared with those published in December 1994. For the EFW, the ratings published in September 2013 are compared with those published in January 1996. For the OECD, the ratings as of 1 September 2013 are compared with those as of 1 September 1999. The IEF ratings published in December 1994 are converted to the 0–100 scale (see Heritage Foundation 2007, pp. 400–405). "Dom. Rep." denotes Dominican Republic

Sources: Author's calculations and classifications based on the Credendo database, Heritage Foundation (1994, 2014), Fraser Institute (1996, 2013), and the OECD database

Second, contrary to what is observed for the worst-performing countries, there is no dichotomy between the upgrades by Euromoney, ICRG, and the WEF on the one hand and, on the other hand, the upgrades by Credendo, the OECD, and the two neoliberal raters. In fact, all the "best performers" are developing and emerging economies. Several of these countries were slowly recovering from painful economic and political crises (e.g., Angola, Indonesia, Nicaragua, Peru, Rwanda, Uganda). Others (e.g., Bulgaria, Croatia, Hungary, Lithuania, Romania, Slovakia, Slovenia) took advantage of the prospect of EU membership and, later, of that membership itself.

Finally, almost two-thirds of the countries that significantly improved their country risk position experienced no major shock during 2007–2014. This observation suggests that, if a country can manage to avert a major shock, then it can reasonably expect a substantial surge in its country risk rating in the long term.

5.4.4 Ratings Correlations

This section focuses on the correlations between country risk scorings. In contrast to Sect. 4.3.3, I do not analyze the major disagreements between the six raters because it is impossible to determine a standard rating interval across all the rating scales.

Table 5.44 reports the correlation coefficients between the country risk raters' scores.[46] The ratings examined are those contained in the last yearly cohort used in Sect. 5.3 (i.e., those released between September 2013 and January 2014).

Although these correlations between the country risk ratings are strong, they are weaker than those observed for sovereign risk indicators (see Sect. 4.3.3). This outcome is not surprising. After all, the multidimensional nature of country risk obliges raters to take many more risk components into account and, inevitably, to prioritize different criteria.

The IEF and EFW ratings are highly correlated with each other but much less so with the other four raters. This finding supports the view that assessing economic freedom and assessing country risk are two distinct tasks. By the same token, one might also view the Heritage Foundation and the Fraser Institute as exhibiting a "neoliberal pattern." These conclusions are confirmed when correlation coefficients are calculated for the previous years.

[46] I exclude Credendo's expropriation risk ratings because they measure only a single aspect of country risk.

Table 5.44 Correlation coefficients among country risk indicators, end 2013

	Euromoney ratings	ICRG ratings	OECD ratings	IEF ratings	EFW ratings	GCI ratings
Euromoney ratings	1 (186)	N.R.	N.R.	N.R.	N.R.	N.R.
ICRG ratings	0.85 (140)	1 (140)	N.R.	N.R.	N.R.	N.R.
OECD ratings	−0.89 (134)	−0.80 (104)	1 (137)	N.R.	N.R.	N.R.
IEF ratings	0.77 (175)	0.69 (135)	−0.62 (128)	1 (178)	N.R.	N.R.
EFW ratings	0.72 (151)	0.63 (130)	−0.57 (113)	0.88 (152)	1 (152)	N.R.
GCI ratings	0.89 (146)	0.83 (126)	−0.78 (110)	0.76 (146)	0.74 (141)	1 (148)

Notes: The number of pairwise observations is reported in parentheses. N.R. = not relevant. Euromoney, EFW, and GCI ratings are those published in September 2013. OECD ratings are as of 1 September 2013. ICRG scores are the average ratings of 2013. IEF ratings are those published in January 2014. Contrary to the other country risk ratings, OECD high scores are associated with high risk

Sources: Author's calculations based on *Euromoney* (September 2013), the ICRG database, the OECD database, Heritage Foundation (2014), Fraser Institute (2013), and World Economic Forum (2013)

Appendix: List of the 272 "Country Risk Crises," 1985–2014

Year	Country	Type of shock
1985	Cameroon	Sovereign debt crisis
	Ethiopia	Deep economic depression
	Mozambique	Sovereign debt crisis
	Myanmar	Sovereign debt crisis
	Nicaragua	High inflation
	Peru	Expropriation
	South Africa	Sovereign debt crisis
	Uganda	High inflation
	Vanuatu	Exceptional natural disaster
1986	Egypt	Sovereign debt crisis
	Liberia	Significant restriction on capital flows
	Paraguay	Sovereign debt crisis
	Romania	Sovereign debt crisis
	United Arab Emirates	Deep economic depression

Year	Country	Type of shock
1987	Argentina	High inflation and sovereign debt crisis
	Gabon	Deep economic depression
	Jamaica	Sovereign debt crisis
	Mexico	High inflation
	Myanmar	Sovereign debt crisis
	Nigeria	Deep economic depression
	Sierra Leone	High inflation
	Suriname	Deep economic depression
	Yugoslavia (Soc. Fed. Rep.)	High inflation
1988	Colombia	Sovereign debt crisis
	Iraq	Sovereign debt crisis
	Jamaica	Exceptional natural disaster
	Kuwait	Deep economic depression
	Myanmar	Deep economic depression
	Nicaragua	Deep economic depression
	Panama	Deep economic depression
	Peru	High inflation
	Somalia	Major episode of domestic political violence
	Trinidad and Tobago	Sovereign debt crisis
	Uruguay	Sovereign debt crisis
1989	Angola	Sovereign debt crisis
	Dem. Rep. of Congo	High inflation
	Egypt	Expropriation
	Jordan	Deep economic depression and sovereign debt crisis
	Lebanon	Deep economic depression
	Liberia	Deep economic depression
	Morocco	Sovereign debt crisis
	Peru	Deep economic depression
	Poland	High inflation
	South Africa	Sovereign debt crisis
	Zambia	High inflation
1990	Bulgaria	Sovereign debt crisis
	Iraq	Major episode of international political violence
	Kuwait	Major episode of international political violence and sovereign debt crisis
	Liberia	Major episode of domestic political violence and exceptional natural disaster
	Samoa	Exceptional natural disaster
	Sierra Leone	High inflation
	Sri Lanka	Expropriation
	Uruguay	High inflation and sovereign debt crisis

Year	Country	Type of shock
1991	Albania	Deep economic depression and sovereign debt crisis
	Algeria	Major episode of domestic political violence and sovereign debt crisis
	Bulgaria	High inflation
	Cuba	Deep economic depression
	Czechoslovakia	Deep economic depression
	Dem. Rep. of Congo	High inflation
	Egypt	Expropriation
	Iraq	Deep economic depression and high inflation
	Romania	Deep economic depression and high inflation
	Samoa	Exceptional natural disaster
	Sudan	High inflation
	USSR	High inflation and sovereign debt crisis
	Yugoslavia (Soc. Fed. Rep.)	Deep economic depression
1992	Albania	High inflation
	Angola	High inflation
	Armenia	Deep economic depression
	Azerbaijan	Deep economic depression
	Bosnia and Herzegovina	Major episode of domestic political violence and sovereign debt crisis
	Croatia	Sovereign debt crisis
	Dem. Rep. of Congo	Deep economic depression
	Estonia	Deep economic depression
	Georgia	Deep economic depression
	Kazakhstan	Expropriation
	Kyrgyzstan	Deep economic depression
	Latvia	Deep economic depression
	Lesotho	Expropriation
	Lithuania	Deep economic depression
	Macedonia	Sovereign debt crisis
	Moldova	Deep economic depression
	Russia	Deep economic depression
	Sierra Leone	Deep economic depression
	Slovenia	Sovereign debt crisis
	Tajikistan	Deep economic depression
	Turkmenistan	Deep economic depression
	Uzbekistan	Deep economic depression
	Venezuela	Sovereign debt crisis
	Yugoslavia (Fed. Rep.)	Sovereign debt crisis
	Zambia	High inflation

Year	Country	Type of shock
1993	Angola	Deep economic depression
	Burundi	Major episode of domestic political violence
	Chad	Deep economic depression
	Dem. Rep. of Congo	Expropriation
	Iraq	High inflation
	Mongolia	High inflation
	Palau	Deep economic depression
	South Africa	Sovereign debt crisis
	Suriname	High inflation
	Togo	Deep economic depression
	Ukraine	Deep economic depression
1994	Belarus	Deep economic depression and sovereign debt crisis
	Dominican Rep.	Expropriation
	Kazakhstan	Deep economic depression
	Malawi	Deep economic depression
	Moldova	Deep economic depression
	Russia	Major episode of domestic political violence and deep economic depression
	Rwanda	Major episode of domestic political violence and deep economic depression
	Turkey	High inflation
	Turkmenistan	Deep economic depression
1995	Egypt	Expropriation
	Mexico	Expropriation
	Syria	Sovereign debt crisis
1996	Antigua and Barbuda	Sovereign debt crisis
	Botswana	Significant restriction on capital flows
	Bulgaria	High inflation
	Cambodia	Significant restriction on capital flows
	Chile	Significant restriction on capital flows
	Dem. Rep. of Congo	Major episode of domestic political violence
	Dominican Rep.	Significant restriction on capital flows
	Georgia	Expropriation
	Iraq	Major episode of domestic political violence
	Marshall Islands	Deep economic depression
	Sudan	High inflation
	Turkmenistan	Expropriation
1997	Albania	Deep economic depression
	Dem. Rep. of Congo	Expropriation
	Romania	High inflation
	Turkmenistan	Deep economic depression

Year	Country	Type of shock
1998	Eritrea	Major episode of international political violence
	Ethiopia	Major episode of international political violence
	Guinea-Bissau	Deep economic depression
	Honduras	Exceptional natural disaster
	Indonesia	Deep economic depression and expropriation
	Kazakhstan	Sovereign debt crisis
	Kenya	Expropriation
	Mexico	Expropriation
	Pakistan	Sovereign debt crisis
1999	Belarus	High inflation
	Bosnia and Herzegovina	Sovereign debt crisis
	Dem. Rep. of Congo	High inflation
	Ecuador	Sovereign debt crisis
	Indonesia	Major episode of domestic political violence and sovereign debt crisis
	Kazakhstan	Expropriation
	Laos	High inflation
	Russia	Major episode of domestic political violence
	Turkey	Sovereign debt crisis
	Yugoslavia (Fed. Rep.)	Major episode of domestic political violence, expropriation, and deep economic depression
2000	Bolivia	Expropriation
	Ivory Coast	Sovereign debt crisis
	Solomon Islands	Deep economic depression
2001	Argentina	Expropriation, significant restriction on capital flows, and sovereign debt crisis
	El Salvador	Exceptional natural disaster
	Lebanon	Significant restriction on capital flows
	Mexico	Expropriation
	Nigeria	Major episode of domestic political violence
	Venezuela	Expropriation
	Yemen	Sovereign debt crisis
2002	Antigua and Barbuda	Expropriation
	Argentina	Deep economic depression
	Hungary	Expropriation
	Indonesia	Sovereign debt crisis
	Madagascar	Deep economic depression
	Venezuela	Significant restriction on capital flows
	Zimbabwe	High inflation

Year	Country	Type of shock
2003	Iraq	Major episode of international political violence and deep economic depression
	Ivory Coast	Expropriation
	Kazakhstan	Expropriation
	Liberia	Deep economic depression
	Uruguay	Sovereign debt crisis
	Zimbabwe	Deep economic depression
2004	Grenada	Sovereign debt crisis and exceptional natural disaster
	Kyrgyzstan	Expropriation
	Pakistan	Major episode of domestic political violence
	Seychelles	Significant restriction on capital flows
	Zimbabwe	Expropriation
2005	Azerbaijan	Expropriation
	Dominican Rep.	Sovereign debt crisis
	Guyana	Exceptional natural disaster
	Sierra Leone	Sovereign debt crisis
	Venezuela	Expropriation
	Yemen	Expropriation
2006	Belize	Sovereign debt crisis
	Bolivia	Expropriation
	Ecuador	Expropriation
	Mexico	Major episode of domestic political violence
	Russia	Expropriation
	Uzbekistan	Expropriation
2007	Costa Rica	Expropriation
	Georgia	Expropriation
	Kazakhstan	Expropriation
	Mozambique	Sovereign debt crisis
	Turkmenistan	Expropriation
	Ukraine	Expropriation
	Zimbabwe	Expropriation
2008	Ecuador	Expropriation and sovereign debt crisis
	El Salvador	Expropriation
	Gambia	Expropriation
	Guinea	Expropriation
	Iceland	Significant restriction on capital flows
	Kenya	Major episode of domestic political violence
	Latvia	Expropriation
	Tajikistan	Exceptional natural disaster
	Zimbabwe	Deep economic depression

Year	Country	Type of shock
2009	Antigua and Barbuda	Deep economic depression
	Argentina	Expropriation
	Armenia	Deep economic depression
	Belize	Expropriation
	Estonia	Deep economic depression
	Latvia	Deep economic depression
	Libya	Expropriation
	Lithuania	Deep economic depression
	Mongolia	Expropriation
	Nigeria	Major episode of domestic political violence
	Romania	Expropriation
	Sierra Leone	Significant restriction on capital flows
	Ukraine	Deep economic depression and expropriation
2010	Dem. Rep. of Congo	Expropriation
	Haiti	Exceptional natural disaster
	Hungary	Expropriation
	Jamaica	Sovereign debt crisis
	Kyrgyzstan	Expropriation
	Tajikistan	Sovereign debt crisis
	Trinidad and Tobago	Expropriation
	Turkmenistan	Expropriation
	Zimbabwe	Expropriation
2011	Belarus	Expropriation
	Belize	Expropriation
	China	Expropriation
	Ecuador	Significant restriction on capital flows
	Ghana	Expropriation
	Guinea	Expropriation
	Indonesia	Expropriation
	Iraq	Major episode of domestic political violence
	Libya	Major episode of domestic political violence and deep economic depression
	Pakistan	Expropriation
	Papua New Guinea	Expropriation
	Peru	Expropriation
	Saint Kitts and Nevis	Sovereign debt crisis
	Syria	Major episode of domestic political violence
	Turkey	Expropriation
	Uzbekistan	Expropriation
	Yemen	Deep economic depression

Year	Country	Type of shock
2012	Belize	Sovereign debt crisis
	Bolivia	Expropriation
	Bosnia and Herzegovina	Significant restriction on capital flows
	Costa Rica	Expropriation
	Cyprus	Significant restriction on capital flows
	Egypt	Significant restriction on capital flows
	Greece	Sovereign debt crisis
	Kyrgyzstan	Significant restriction on capital flows
	Laos	Expropriation
	Maldives	Expropriation
	Nigeria	Expropriation
	South Sudan	Deep economic depression
	Ukraine	Sovereign debt crisis
2013	Central African Rep.	Deep economic depression
	Cyprus	Sovereign debt crisis
	Guinea	Expropriation
	Indonesia	Expropriation
	Jamaica	Sovereign debt crisis
	Mozambique	Sovereign debt crisis
	Pakistan	Expropriation
	South Sudan	Major episode of domestic political violence and sovereign debt crisis
2014	Bulgaria	Expropriation
	Chad	Sovereign debt crisis
	Egypt	Expropriation
	Hungary	Expropriation
	Kazakhstan	Sovereign debt crisis
	Togo	Expropriation
	Ukraine	Sovereign debt crisis

Sources: Author's classification based on the analysis conducted in Sect. 5.2

References

Barro, R. J., & Jin, T. (2011). On the Size Distribution of Macroeconomic Disasters. *Econometrica, 79*(5).

Beers, D. & de Leon-Manlagnit, P. (2019). The BoC-BoE Sovereign Default Database: What's New in 2019?, *Bank of Canada Staff Working Paper 2019–39*.

Bogart, D., & Richardson, G. (2011). Property Rights and Parliament in Industrializing Britain. *Journal of Law & Economics, 54*(2).

Bruno, M. (1991). High Inflation and the Nominal Anchors of an Open Economy. *Essay in International Finance No.183, Princeton University*.

Cagan, P. (1956). The Monetary Dynamics of Hyperinflation. In M. Friedman (Ed.), *Studies in the Quantity Theory of Money*. Chicago, IL: University of Chicago Press.

Chinn, M. D., & Ito, H. (2006). What Matters for Financial Development? Capital Controls, Institutions, and Interactions. *Journal of Development Economics, 81*(1).

Credendo Group (2014). *Annual Report 2013*.

Dornbusch, R. (1990). General Discussion on 'Extreme Inflation: Dynamics and Stabilization'. R. Dornbusch, F. Sturzenegger, and H. Wolf, *Brookings Papers on Economic Activity*, 2:1990.

Filatochev, I., & Bradshaw, R. (1992). The Soviet Hyperinflation: Its Origins and Impact Throughout the Former Republics. *Soviet Studies, 44*(5).

Fraser Institute (various years). *Economic Freedom of the World*, Vancouver.

Gaillard, N. (2014). Assessing Sovereign Risk: The Case of Rich Countries. *Journal of Financial Economic Policy, 6*(3).

Hajzler, C. & Rosborough, J. (2016). Government Corruption and Foreign Direct Investment Under the Threat of Expropriation. *Bank of Canada Staff Working Paper 2016–13*.

Heritage Foundation (various years). *Index of Economic Freedom*. Washington, DC.

Howell, L. D. (Ed.) (1998). *The Handbook of Country and Political Risk Analysis*. East Syracuse, NY: The PRS Group.

Howell, L. D. (Ed.) (2001). *The Handbook of Country and Political Risk Analysis*. East Syracuse, NY: The PRS Group.

Kaufmann, D., Kraay, A., & Mastruzzi, M. (2010). The Worldwide Governance Indicators: A Summary of Methodology, Data and Analytical Issues. *World Bank Policy Research Working Paper No. 5430*.

McGann, J. G. (2017). 2016 Global Go To Think Tank Index Report. *TTCSP Global Go To Think Tank Index Reports*.

Minor, M. S. (1994). The Demise of Expropriation as an Instrument of LDC Policy, 1980–1992. *Journal of International Business Studies, 25*(1).

Mishkin, F., & Herbertsson, T. T. (2006). *Financial Stability in Iceland*. Reykjavik: Iceland Chamber of Commerce.

North, D. C., & Weingast, B. R. (1989). Constitutions and Commitment: The Evolution of Institutions Governing Public Choice in Seventeenth-Century England. *Journal of Economic History, 49*(4).

Petrovic, P., Bogetic, Z., & Vujosevic, Z. (1999). The Yugoslav Hyperinflation of 1992–1994: Causes, Dynamics, and Money Supply Process. *Journal of Comparative Economics, 27*(2).

Prasad, E. S., & Rajan, R. G. (2008). A Pragmatic Approach to Capital Account Liberalization. *Journal of Economic Perspectives, 22*(3).

SA Ducroire (2006). *Rapport Annuel 2005*.

The PRS Group (2012). *International Country Risk Guide Methodology*. East Syracuse, NY.

The PRS Group (2014). *International Country Risk Guide Methodology*. East Syracuse, NY.

The World Economic Forum (2009). *A Partner in Shaping History: The First 40 Years, 1971–2010*.

World Economic Forum (various years). *The Global Competitiveness Report*. Geneva.

Chapter 6
Concluding Remarks

The main obstacles to international business have evolved considerably over the two centuries, mirroring the transformation of capitalism and its triumph over alternative economic systems.

During the *Pax Britannica*, protectionism was a major risk for importers, exporters, and multinational corporations. For example, Latin America, Russia, and newly industrialized countries (especially Japan and the United States) imposed high tariff rates on European manufactured products in this period (Bairoch 1999, pp. 59, 63). The protectionist risk reached its peak in the 1930s but has waned substantially since then. The main reasons are the progress of multilateralism (until the 2000s), the adoption by emerging countries of export-promoting development strategies, and the spread of "alliance capitalism," which has increased interdependence among nations.

The risk of expropriation risk was, for the most part, confined to years between the 1930s and the 1970s. During this era, many Latin American and African leaders were fascinated by communism and socialism. Once these ideologies lost ground and eventually collapsed, the threat of expropriation declined markedly.

Since the advent of globalization, microeconomic risks have been pervasive impediments to foreign direct and equity investments. Today's MNCs are bound to protect against fraud and copyright infringement as well as social and labor risks; ensuring long-term profitability requires that they also avert boycotts and monitor the reliability of their partners and contractors.

It is noteworthy that the persistence and seriousness of political and macroeconomic risks led to the development of quantitative methods and of indicators designed to *measure* business risks. The high level of political risk in the postwar years motivated researchers and practitioners to establish political stability indices (see Feierabend and Feierabend 1966) and political forecasting systems (Haner 1979). In the 1970s, the growing public debt of LDCs stirred concern among the BIS, the IMF, and major private creditors; this concern engendered the concept of *country risk* and paved the way for creation of country risk ratings (Gaillard 2015).

N. Gaillard, *Country Risk*, https://doi.org/10.1007/978-3-030-45788-4_6

A plethora of political and country risk indicators were introduced during the last two decades of the 20th century. Assessing the most prominent indicators' accuracy reveals that four-fifths of the misratings observed during the globalization era were due to a sovereign debt crisis, a sudden control of capital flows, or an expropriation. These findings suggest that country risk raters are prone to assign excessively high ratings to countries with experience in attracting FDI and in accessing international capital markets, but that are vulnerable to a capital flow reversal or a rapid deterioration of their credit position.

A crucial outcome of the globalization years was the new "geography of risks." The increasing number of high-income countries (e.g., Cyprus, Greece, Iceland) that suffered a severe economic crisis since the late 2000s contrasts with the greater resilience of major emerging economies during this period. Among the latter category, the case of China deserves closer examination.

The Middle Kingdom enjoyed annual GDP growth averaging 10% for more than three decades and transformed itself from a potential El Dorado for Western MNCs into a major host country and the third most capital-exporting nation.[1] This mutation has led to four far-reaching yet essentially incommensurable consequences.

First, the rise of China has contributed to inflate the price of commodities and to depress the price of manufactured goods. This dynamic has enhanced the purchasing power of consumers all around the world and created business opportunities for countries that export agricultural products and raw materials. The main losers have been some industrial firms located in high-income countries.

Second, Chinese state capitalism has challenged liberal capitalism in a much more insidious manner than did communism during the Cold War. As a response to the deindustrialization process that has shaken the European and US economies, neo-mercantilism and protectionism have been praised by many politicians. In this respect, the election of Donald Trump reflects American fears of being superseded by a global rival whose political and geopolitical goals are unclear (Cohen 2014). One can argue that Washington's drift toward weaponizing its trade and monetary policies (and its criminal courts) to confront Beijing and its firms (e.g., Huawei)[2] is a legitimate way to retaliate against a competitor that has not hesitated to provide its domestic companies with exorbitant state support for the purpose of attaining greater market shares abroad.

Third, as a striking illustration of what Luttwak (1990) calls "geo-economics," the new normal of antagonistic trade policies could upset international business relations. For instance, some countries may thus be led to limit investment and financing from either superpower or to establish a "dual business environment" in which US firms, or Chinese firms, are assigned junior status. The prospect of such geo-economic bipolarization would oblige experts to revise thoroughly their ways of assessing country risk.

[1] Data for 2018; see https://unctad.org.

[2] See https://www.justice.gov/opa/gallery/acting-attorney-general-whitaker-announces-national-security-related-criminal-charges.

Finally, tensions between China and the United States may jeopardize the international cooperation that is indispensable to addressing what is surely the world's greatest risk: global warming. Changes in climate have already affected ecosystems on all continents—and absent concerted and major efforts, worse is still to come. Climate risk should be viewed as a matrix of all other risks: it is likely to destabilize entire economies, including developed ones (as illustrated by the fires ravaging Australia), to trigger massive migration flows, and to undermine extant societies.[3] It is therefore time for world policy makers to coordinate their efforts at reducing vulnerability and exposure to climate change. Country risk experts must incorporate climate risk factors into their methodologies.[4] Citizens and business sectors (especially insurance and reinsurance companies) must likewise accept their responsibility to force their respective governments to address, as vigorously as possible, what has become humankind's most imminent and potentially devastating threat.

References

Bairoch, P. (1999). *Mythes et paradoxes de l'histoire économique*. Paris: La Découverte/Poche.

Cohen, B. J. (2014). The China question—Can its rise be accommodated? In E. Helleiner & J. Kirshner (Eds.), *The Great wall of money—Power and politics in China's international monetary relations*. Ithaca and London: Cornell University Press.

Feierabend, I. K., & Feierabend, R. L. (1966). Aggressive behaviors within polities, 1948–1962: A cross-national study. *Journal of Conflict Resolution, 10*(3).

Gaillard, N. (2015). Le concept de risque pays. *Politique Etrangère, 80*(2).

Haner, F. T. (1979). Rating investment risks abroad. *Business Horizons, 22*(2).

Luttwak, E. N. (1990, Summer). From geopolitics to geo-economics: Logic of conflict, grammar of commerce. *The National Interest, 20*.

[3] The United Nations International Organization for Migration estimates that there could be between 25 million and 1 billion environmental migrants by 2050; see https://www.iom.int/oped/managing-climate-driven-migration.

[4] See William J. Harrington, "Investors who want to fast-track sustainable fixed-income investments should inundate credit rating agencies with methodology critiques," *Responsible Investor*, 28 January 2020; available at https://www.responsible-investor.com/articles/investors-who-want-to-fast-track-sustainable-fixed-income-investments-should-inundate-credit-rating-agencies-with-methodology-critiques.

The manufacturer's authorised representative in the EU is Springer Nature Customer Service Centre GmbH, Europaplatz 3, 69115 Heidelberg, Germany. If you have any concerns regarding our products, please contact ProductSafety@springernature.com

Printed and bound by CPI Group (UK) Ltd, Croydon, CR0 4YY
22/09/2026
02221058-0013